Extreme Killing

Third Edition

Extreme Killing

Understanding Serial and Mass Murder

Third Edition

James Alan Fox

Jack Levin

Northeastern University

Los Angeles | London | New Delhi
Singapore | Washington DC

Los Angeles | London | New Delhi
Singapore | Washington DC

FOR INFORMATION:

SAGE Publications, Inc.
2455 Teller Road
Thousand Oaks, California 91320
E-mail: order@sagepub.com

SAGE Publications Ltd.
1 Oliver's Yard
55 City Road
London EC1Y 1SP
United Kingdom

SAGE Publications India Pvt. Ltd.
B 1/I 1 Mohan Cooperative Industrial Area
Mathura Road, New Delhi 110 044
India

SAGE Publications Asia-Pacific Pte. Ltd.
3 Church Street
#10-04 Samsung Hub
Singapore 049483

Printed in the United States of America

Library of Congress Control Number: 2014934498

ISBN 9781483350721

This book is printed on acid-free paper.

Publisher: Jerry Westby
Publishing Associate: MaryAnn Vail
Production Editor: Stephanie Palermini
Copy Editor: Diane DiMura
Typesetter: C&M Digitals (P) Ltd.
Proofreader: Jen Grubba
Indexer: Molly Hall
Cover Designer: Anthony Paular
Marketing Manager: Terra Schultz

14 15 16 17 18 10 9 8 7 6 5 4 3 2 1

Brief Contents

Detailed Contents

Preface

More than 30 years ago, we began researching the phenomenon of multiple homicide for our first book on the topic, *Mass Murder: America's Growing Menace* (Levin & Fox, 1985). Over the decades, we have continued to study both serial and mass murder, gradually modifying and fine-tuning our thinking about the behavior and motivation of multiple-victim killers. Writing the third edition of *Extreme Killing: Understanding Serial and Mass Murder* provided us an opportunity to reassess some of the prevailing notions about these crimes—most notably, the artificial and often problematic distinctions between serial and mass murderers based primarily on the timing, the victim count necessary to qualify as serial murder, the uncritical embrace of sociopathy as an explanation, the epidemic thinking about multiple homicide encouraged by excessive media coverage, the role of assault weapons in mass shootings, and the nexus between mental illness and mass murder.

This edition contains a number of important additions including a new chapter on the role of firearms and the impact of gun control laws; a new section on criminological theories that specifically apply to serial and mass murder; expanded discussions of DNA, copycat killers, school massacres, and mental illness as a causal factor; updated empirical data on patterns and trends in serial murder and massacres; discussions of new cases of multiple homicide both inside and outside of the United States; and updates on cases covered in the previous edition.

We have also maintained or expanded a number of highlights from previous editions of the book. In Chapter 1, we focus on those serial killers—BTK, Zodiac, the Unabomber, and the DC Snipers—who, while on the loose, have communicated with the police and the press. Chapter 3 contains an examination of the "extraordinarily ordinary" veneer with which many serial killers avoid suspicion. In Chapter 5, we discuss the role of self-control and social control, with particular reference to control theory, the distinction between psychopathy and sociopathy, and the impact of shame and humiliation in the etiology of the serial killer. Also in Chapter 5, we discuss elements of normalcy in the mindset and behavior of the serial killer. In particular, we apply the sociological concept of presentation of self in everyday life to examine the serial killer's manipulative character.

In Chapter 9, we offer a section on the link between animal cruelty and human violence, including an examination of animal abuse in the biographies of serial killers, and coverage of the problem of prediction from early warning signs. Chapter 9 also contains a discussion of biological predispositions toward extreme violence, including an introduction to research being conducted by neurocriminologists. Chapter 12 includes a discussion of behavioral profiling and other investigative approaches. Chapter 13 contains a section in which the role of psychiatric medications is examined. Also in this chapter, we offer an expanded discussion of concepts of social learning, including theories of differential association and differential reinforcement, as well as the frustration–aggression hypothesis and general strain theory. Chapter 14 introduces research in which the impact of the unemployment rate on family annihilations is investigated. Chapter 15 examines rampages in the workplace as well as the "going postal" phenomenon. Chapter 16 focuses on mass shootings in schools and colleges, including discussion of the copycat phenomenon and the role of violent entertainment. Chapter 19 contains an extended discussion of the role of mental illness in rampage shootings. In a new Chapter 20, we have expanded our discussion of the role of firearms in mass murder and the effect of gun control policies.

To articulate these and other ideas, the book features many notable cases of serial and mass murder, including the Texas mom who drowned her five children in 2001 in a perverted act of love; the two snipers who terrorized the District of Columbia area in October 2002; the man linked in 2004 to the Green River killings in Washington State; Milwaukee's Jeffrey Dahmer; Danny Rolling, who brutally murdered college students in Gainesville, Florida; Dylan Klebold and Eric Harris, the mass shooters at Columbine High; and the Unabomber. In addition, we draw upon classic cases of yesteryear, such as Theodore Bundy, John Wayne Gacy, and Charles Manson. We also examine the case of Derrick Bird, the cab driver in northern England who shot to death 12 people in June 2010, including his twin brother and his lawyer; the case of Anthony Sowell, who, until his October 2009 arrest, killed and buried 11 women in Cleveland, Ohio; the mass murder perpetrated in February 2010 by Professor Amy Bishop, who decided to get even with her colleagues at the University of Alabama, Huntsville, after her bid for tenure was denied; Major Nidal Hasan, who was convicted of slaughtering 13 members of the Fort Hood community in November 2009; the rampage of Seung-Hui Cho, a student at Virginia Tech who shot to death 32 students and faculty members on campus in April 2007; the case of George Sodini, the despondent and angry resident of suburban Pittsburgh who murdered three women at a local health club in August 2009; the shopping mall rampage of Robert Hawkins who shot to death eight customers and employees in a department store in Omaha, Nebraska, in December 2007; and the case of Kyle Huff, a vengeful young man in Seattle who took the lives of six ravers in March 2006 while attending an after-hours party.

Of course, in the years since the second edition was published, the nation and the world have been shocked by additional acts of cruelty and mayhem resulting in the senseless loss of human life. Such recent cases covered in this edition include the Sandy Hook school shooting; the Aurora cinema massacre; the DC Navy Yard rampage; the Boston Marathon bombings; the mass shooting at a Sikh Indian temple; the massacre of 77 in Oslo, Norway, in July 2011; and the apprehension of the Grim Sleeper in Los Angeles.

For the purpose of adding perspective, we previously presented empirical data on hundreds of serial killers and mass murderers. Throughout this revision, we have updated all the tables and figures that characterize patterns and trends in extreme killing.

Several of our current and former students helped significantly by tracking down facts and data sources used in this book. We are especially grateful to Monica DeLateur, Lyndsay Thompson, and Enzo Yaksic for their hard work in gathering data and reference material for the new edition. We are indebted to Jenna Savage for her skillful editorial assistance. We appreciate the efforts of our editor, Jerry Westby, who provided the right blend of urgent encouragement and gentle patience. In addition, we have benefited greatly from our associations with the Lipman and Brudnick families. Finally, we are indebted to the members of our families—our wives, Sue Ann and Flea, and our children—for their infinite tolerance and understanding. With good humor, they accommodated the many disruptions associated with researching this subject matter and writing this book.

—James Alan Fox and Jack Levin

Boston, Massachusetts

Part I

Multiple Murder

CHAPTER 1

America's Fascination With Multiple Murder

The break of dawn on November 16, 1957, heralded the start of deer hunting season in rural Waushara County, Wisconsin. The men of Plainfield went off with their hunting rifles and knives, but without any clue of what Edward Gein would do that day. Gein was known to the 647 residents of Plainfield as a quiet man who kept to himself and his aging, dilapidated farmhouse. But when the men of the village returned from hunting that evening, they learned the awful truth about their 51-year-old neighbor and the atrocities that he had ritualized within the walls of his farmhouse.

The first in a series of discoveries that would disrupt the usually tranquil town occurred when Frank Worden arrived at his hardware store after hunting all day. Frank's mother, Bernice Worden, who had been minding the store, was missing; so was Frank's truck. But there was a pool of blood on the floor and a trail of blood leading toward the place where the truck had been garaged.

The investigation of Bernice's disappearance and possible homicide led police to the farm of Ed Gein. Because the farm had no electricity, the investigators conducted a slow and ominous search with flashlights, methodically scanning the barn for clues. The sheriff's light suddenly exposed a hanging figure, apparently Mrs. Worden. As Captain Schoephoerster later described in court,

> Mrs. Worden had been completely dressed out like a deer with her head cut off at the shoulders. Gein had slit the skin on the back of her ankles and inserted a wooden rod, 3½ feet long, and about 4 inches in diameter, and sharpened to a point at both ends, through the cut tendons on the back of her ankles. Both hands were tied to her side with binder twine. The center of the rod was attached to a pulley on a block and tackle. The body was pulled up so that the feet were near the ceiling. We noticed that there was just a few drops of watery blood beneath the body on the dirt floor, and not finding the head or intestines, we thought possibly the body had been butchered at another location. (Gollmar, 1981, p. 32)

The brutal murder and dismemberment of Bernice Worden was not the only gruesome act of the reclusive man whom no one really knew. In the months that followed, more of Gein's macabre practices were unveiled. Not only was he suspected in several other deaths, but Gein also admitted to having stolen corpses and body parts from a number of graves. Gein used these limbs and organs to fashion ornaments such as belts of nipples and a hanging human head, as well as decorations for his house, including chairs upholstered in human skin and bedposts crowned with skulls. A shoe box containing nine vulvas was but one piece of Gein's grim collection of female organs. On moonlit evenings, he would prance around his farm wearing a real female mask, a vest of skin complete with female breasts, and women's panties filled with vaginas in an attempt to recreate the form and presence of his dead mother.

The news of Gein's secret passion devastated Plainfield. The townspeople were shocked to learn of the terrible fate of Mrs. Worden and to hear of the discovered remains belonging to 51-year-old barkeeper Mary Hogan, who had disappeared years earlier after being shot by Gein. They were outraged by the sacrilege of their ancestors' graves. They were literally sickened remembering the gifts of "venison" that Gein had presented to them.

THE GEIN LEGACY

Any small town is shocked by a murder in its midst, but the horror of Gein's rituals surpassed anything that the people of Plainfield had ever encountered or even imagined. Outside Wisconsin, however, few people had heard of Edward Gein. As bizarre and offensive as his crimes were, Gein never really made headlines in other parts of the country; what happens in Plainfield is not nearly as important, at least to the national media, as what occurs in a large city like Chicago or Washington, DC. Very few eyebrows are raised at the mention of the name Ed Gein. Hardly a household name or a box office attraction, he might have been immortalized like Charles Manson in the film *Helter Skelter* (1976) had he killed in Los Angeles. Had he lived in a metropolis like New York City, director Spike Lee might have featured Gein in a retrospective docudrama, as he did serial killer David Berkowitz in the film *Summer of Sam* (1999). A killer from Plainfield, Wisconsin—which rings very much like Anywhere, USA—however, probably will never be regarded as important enough to warrant a major movie release called *Autumn of Ed*.

Although the name of Edward Gein is unknown to most moviegoers, he was discovered by Hollywood. His legendary place in the annals of crime has inspired a number of fictional films, both popular and obscure, as well as a low-budget portrayal of the Gein story, simply titled *Ed Gein* (2000).

The promoters of *The Texas Chainsaw Massacre* (1974) claimed that it was based on fact, although a crime of this description cannot be found in reality. One thing is for sure: The film contains numerous elements reminiscent of Gein's patently deviant behavior. For instance, the farmhouse of the Chainsaw family of killers, like Gein's house, is littered with spare body parts and bones. Also similar to Gein, the family has an armchair with real arms.

A little-known film imported from Canada more closely parallels the Gein theme. In *Deranged* (1974), a killer known as the "Butcher of Woodside" slaughters and stuffs his victims. At one point, he parades in the skin of a woman he has just killed, similar to Gein's moonlight escapades. A poster ad for the film depicts a woman hanging from her ankles, just as the body of Bernice Worden was discovered.

Probably because of Anthony Hopkins's memorable portrayal of Hannibal Lecter in 1991's *The Silence of the Lambs*, some may forget the presence of a second despicable character in the film known as Buffalo Bill. Just as Edward Gein collected women's skin in order to recreate his mother, so the serial killer Buffalo Bill trapped and murdered his female victims for the same purpose, to harvest enough human skin to complete his "girl suit."

Perhaps the most noteworthy cinematic production inspired by the Gein case was the classic thriller *Psycho* (1960), the original version of which was directed by Alfred Hitchcock. Operating out of a warped sense of reverence, Norman Bates (played by Anthony Perkins in the original and by Vince Vaughn in the 1998 remake) stuffed and preserved his deceased mother just as Gein had tried using female body parts to symbolize and resurrect his mother. Both conversed with their dead mothers, and both struggled with strict moral constraints that had been enforced by their dominating and sickly mothers. Finally, Norman Bates was implicated in the deaths of two other young women, just as the excavation of undersize bones near Gein's farm suggested his role in the disappearance of two teenage girls.

MULTIPLE MURDER IN POPULAR CULTURE

Hero worship has always been an integral part of popular culture. Over the decades, we have celebrated those members of society who have reached the pinnacle of success in their fields by honoring them in movies, in documentaries, in magazine profiles, and even on trading cards. More recently, we have extended our celebration to what some consider our new antiheroes, those who have distinguished themselves in the worst possible ways by reaching the pinnacle of "success" as murderers.

In 1991, a California trading card company published its first series of mass and serial killer cards, spotlighting such brutal criminals as Edward Gein, Jeffrey Dahmer, Theodore Bundy, and Charles Manson. Selling for $10 per pack (without bubble gum), they were no joke. Several other card makers soon followed suit, hoping to cash in on the celebrity of multiple murderers.

Even comic books have been used as vehicles for celebrating the exploits of vicious killers like Jeffrey Dahmer rather than traditional superheroes. One comic book, *The Unauthorized Biography of a Serial Killer* (Fisher, 1992), goes as far as to portray, in drawings, Dahmer sodomizing one of his victims. By taking on a starring role once held by the likes of Batman and Superman, the killer is unnecessarily glorified. As in Marshall McLuhan's famous adage "the medium is the message," the victims' memory is trivialized by placing them in a comic book format.

In a more respectable context, the coveted cover of *People* magazine has become a spotlight for infamous criminals. It was bad enough that Milwaukee's confessed cannibal Jeffrey Dahmer was on the cover of *People,* an honor usually reserved for Hollywood stars and Washington politicians, but the popular celebrity magazine also chose Dahmer as one of its "100 Most Intriguing People of the 20th Century."

During the 1970s, only one killer was featured on *People*'s cover. By the 1990s, in contrast, the incredibly popular celebrity magazine printed more than two dozen different cover stories about vicious criminals, including Dahmer, David Koresh, Laurie Dann, and Theodore Kaczynski (see Levin, Fox, & Mazaic, 2002).

The public's taste and tolerance for front cover attention afforded multiple murder reached a limit when *Rolling Stone* magazine gave star treatment to one of the men suspected of setting off bombs at the 2013 Boston Marathon that had killed three spectators and seriously injured hundreds of others. The August 2013 issue featured 20-year-old suspected terrorist Dzhokhar Tsarnaev on the front cover in a photograph that had been touched up considerably. With his youthful face and wavy hair, Tsarnaev's image was reminiscent of rock stars that over the years have made it big when gracing the cover of *Rolling Stone*. Whether it was the recency of the bombing, the apparent anti-American sentiment behind the attack, or the photo editing toward glamour that struck a raw nerve, the magazine came under intense criticism for its approach. Numerous newsstands and stores refused to sell the controversial issue. Yet despite a grassroots campaign to mount a boycott, the magazine flew off the shelves wherever available, giving *Rolling Stone* double its usual street sales for the issue.

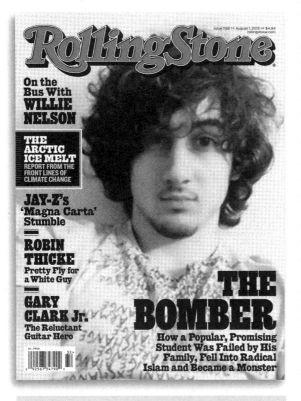

Photo 1.1 Boston Marathon bombing suspect Dzhokhar Tsarnaev appears on the August 1, 2013, cover of *Rolling Stone*. (Associated Press/Wenner Media)

Television has also helped to turn criminals—real ones like Florida's Aileen Wuornos and fictional ones like Showtime's Dexter Morgan—into celebrities. In fact, some observers have characterized serial killing as a chiefly media event (Gibson, 2006) that allows people to obtain close knowledge of the essential characteristics of serial killing and the propensities peculiar to specific offenders (Jenkins, 1994). This is a particularly salient by-product of the media-saturated nature of serial killing, given that it is statistically one of the least common types of crime (Haggerty, 2009). Media, at their worst, have catered to public hunger for gripping topics, financially exploiting gruesome events and turning the horrific into an institution of celebrity culture (Haggerty, 2009). The prevalence of attention to rare but horrifying events such as serial killing is not limited to television media. These stories saturate detective and true crime books and can be seen often in film and police dramas along with collector cards and comic books (Jarvis, 2007; Schmidt, 2005).

Docudramas on television or in the theaters are often biographies of vicious criminals—many of whom are played by leading actors and actresses, such as Mark Harmon as Theodore Bundy, Brian Dennehy as John Wayne Gacy, Jeremy Davies as Charles Manson, Michael Badalucco as David Berkowitz, and Jean Smart as Aileen Wuornos. Actress Charlize Theron also played Wuornos in the 2003 movie titled *Monster,* winning an Academy Award for the performance and, in the process, winning Wuornos some posthumous measure of sympathy.

Having glamorous stars cast in the roles of vicious killers unfortunately infuses these killers with glamour and humanity.

Besides the undeserving focus on the criminal as the "star of the show" in these programs, television docudramas are sanitized by virtue of the restrictions that are placed on network television. Ironically, though, theatrical films such as *The Silence of the Lambs* (1991), *The Red Dragon* (2002), *Along Came a Spider* (2001), *Copycat* (1995), *Natural Born Killers* (1994), *The Cell* (2000), and *The Horsemen* (2009) are able to depict all the horrible details of purely fictional crimes without fear of censorship.

A rare true-crime film that does not glorify serial murder can be found in *Henry—A Portrait of a Serial Killer* (1986), a low-budget motion picture based on serial murderer Henry Lee Lucas and his partner Ottis Toole. Among others of their dastardly misdeeds, Toole and Lucas are strongly suspected of abducting and decapitating 6-year-old Adam Walsh, the son

Photo 1.2 Sometimes multiple murderers are played by celebrities. Actress Charlize Theron won an Oscar for best actress portrayal of serial killer Aileen Wuornos in the 2003 feature film *Monster.* (Mark J. Terrill/Associated Press)

of John Walsh of the long-standing Fox TV program *America's Most Wanted.* In *Henry,* the two killers are shown for what they really were—cruel and inhuman men without any redeeming social value. They weren't portrayed as smart, friendly,

Photo 1.3 Photo of an exhibit of John Wayne Gacy's clown paintings as displayed May 2011 in the Arts Factory in Las Vegas. (Author)

handsome, or charming, and they weren't played by actors most people would recognize as stars. Most important, the film refused to soft-pedal the monstrous acts of this killing team, showing their unmitigated cruelty without compromise.

THE SELLING OF MULTIPLE MURDER

The glorification of multiple killers has created a market for almost anything that they say or do. For example, the art work of John Wayne Gacy became much in demand, but only after he was convicted of killing 33 young men and boys in Des Plaines, Illinois, and especially after his execution by the state of Illinois. His very ordinary paintings of clowns have been displayed in art galleries and have become collector's items. His paintings had special significance because he had been known to dress as a clown to entertain children at neighborhood birthday parties. While he was still alive, Gacy made $100,000 on sales of his paintings through a broker. Similarly, the paintings of deceased mass murderer Richard Speck, who slaughtered eight nurses in Chicago and then died in an Illinois penitentiary, now sell for up to $2,000. Although this kind of price tag may seem relatively slight for original art, his paintings would hardly be worth the canvas they're painted on were it not for his bizarre notoriety.

Along the same lines, a Denver art studio produces and sells serial killer action figures. Similarly, collectors of what has been termed *murderabilia* can purchase a wide variety of clothing items emblazoned with their favorite serial killers or can bid on such items as a lock of Charles Manson's hair or a pair of his sandals at an Internet auction site.

Some individuals are so fascinated with serial murderers that they will purchase any item associated even remotely with a killer's hideous crimes. Bricks taken from Jeffrey Dahmer's apartment building were considered by some as prized souvenirs. Other serial murder fans were willing to bid for the refrigerator in which Dahmer had held his victims' body parts. Several websites auction off souvenirs associated with Dennis Rader, who was captured in 2005 for the BTK killing spree, including dirt taken from his home and sold by the ounce.

After it was discovered that Gary Ridgway was the so-called Green River Killer who had murdered at least 48 prostitutes in the Seattle area, eBay customers were eager to purchase Green River-related merchandise over the Internet. Until it was yanked from the website, customers could bid on a blood-red T-shirt bearing the image of Gary Ridgway and the words "I was good at choking." Or they could purchase a business card from the Green River Task Force and a used mug taken from the truck factory where Ridgway had worked for 30 years. The business card was sold for $29; but the old mug brought only $4.25.

Before his arrest in 1995, 47-year-old serial killer Keith Jesperson was dubbed the "Happy Face Killer" because of the doodle he scribbled on his anonymous confession. The long-haul trucker, who took the lives of at least eight women in five states, sells his artwork online. At two websites, his colored-pencil drawings of various animals in the wild were displayed with their price tags of $25 each. A signed photograph of the killer came free of charge with every purchase (Suo, 2002).

A song written by multiple murderer Charles Manson became a cult classic when recorded by the heavy metal rock group Guns N' Roses on their 1993 album *The Spaghetti Incident*. To publicize their release, lead singer Axl Rose wore a Charles Manson T-shirt on the album cover. Patti Tate, sister of the Hollywood actress Sharon Tate, murdered in 1969 by Manson followers, said in response that the record company "is putting Manson up on a pedestal for young people who don't know who he is to worship like an idol" (Quintanilla, 1994, p. E1). Patti Tate's judgment was confirmed when an iconoclastic young rocker adopted the stage name Marilyn Manson. Charles Manson himself still maintains his own music "career," even from his prison cell. Tapes of his music have been smuggled out from the penitentiary and then distributed on CDs. No small wonder that Manson, even in his 70s, after four decades behind bars, still boasted that he is the most famous person who ever lived (Levin, 2008). Although his sense of importance is absolutely inflated, at least in terms of name recognition, Manson's claim may not be that much of an exaggeration.

Americans have become fascinated with the many "talents" displayed by vicious killers. Apparently, Sacramento serial killer Dorothea Puente was renowned for her culinary skills, so much so that in 2004, author Shane Bugbee published a collection of her favorite recipes in a book titled *Cooking with a Serial Killer*. Drifter Danny Rolling, convicted in the Gainesville student slayings, performed his own musical compositions. He sang love songs to his sweetheart, both in court and, with guitar accompaniment, on the national television program *A Current Affair*. He and his then-fiancée Sondra London (1996) published a book containing his artwork and poetry, which many fans purchased at leading bookstores around the country.

Decades ago, the New York State legislature passed the Son of Sam law, prohibiting murderers like David Berkowitz from profiting off of their crimes. In 1991, however, the U.S. Supreme Court ruled that this law was unconstitutional on First Amendment grounds. This decision by the Court hasn't prevented creative attempts to ensure that killers would not reap financial reward even while being punished for their crimes. For example, in 2010, Senator John Cornyn of Texas filed a bill to prevent the proceeds from the sale of murderabilia to be transmitted to convicted criminals through the U.S. mail.

It is disgraceful enough when private citizens buy and sell killer art and artifacts, but even the federal government has gotten into the sordid business. Compelled by court order, the General Services Administration (GSA) in May 2011 launched an online auction of personal items that belonged to "Unabomber" Theodore Kaczynski, the reclusive misfit who killed three victims and injured 23 others during an 18-year-long campaign of mayhem. Included on the auction block were his driver's license, birth certificate, academic transcripts, and personal checks, which had been recovered from Kaczynski's secluded Montana cabin (the same structure that drew large crowds when it was on display at the Newseum in Washington, DC).

The prized centerpiece to the GSA sell-off, of course, was the original 35,000 word manifesto that Kaczynski negotiated by threat of violence to have published in the *Washington Post*. Both the handwritten and typed versions were available for the highest bidder.

The auction was mandated as part of a $15 million restitution order for Kaczynski's victims and their families. Although the objective was certainly laudable, hawking macabre property to those fringe collectors who wish to own a piece of infamy is a dubious way to raise money.

Rarely do serial killers have the financial means to contribute as restitution to the innocent people they harmed. For this reason, it is the government's place to establish and fund victim compensation programs. It is unfortunate, however, that the celebrity of someone as undeserving as Kaczynski would be advanced in the process.

CRAVING ATTENTION

Not only is the value of multiple murderer artwork and music inflated, but their statements to the press, both spoken and written, also are treated as "words of wisdom." Suddenly, they become instant experts in everything from psychology to criminal justice. The media often solicit their opinions about how victims might protect themselves from murder, what motivates other serial killers, and the role of pornography in the development of a sexual sadist. In fact, Ted Bundy's "expert testimony" on the eve of his execution concerning the dangers of erotic materials became ammunition for ultraconservative groups lobbying for federal antipornography legislation widely called the "Bundy Bill."

Thirty-eight-year-old serial killer Leslie Allen Williams, after his 1992 arrest under suspicion for the slayings of four women, exploited the Detroit-area media to the hilt. Rather than giving an interview to every media outlet that wanted one, Williams took requests. In a contest, the outcome of which he alone would decide, one local television station won an exclusive interview with the serial killer. In addition, one daily paper, the *Detroit News,* was chosen for the "privilege" of printing his 24-page open letter to the public that expounded on the theories and philosophy of Leslie Williams. Anyone who would question whether this was a privilege for the *Detroit News* should consider what it did to boost street sales over its competitor.

The relationship between the media and serial killers has become so intertwined that it has been described as "symbiotic" (Haggerty, 2009). The media seek the attention of their captivated audience by exploiting its interest in scintillating themes. For their part, the murderers look to the media to help them construct their serial killer identities. In fact, reading their own press clippings helps them to complete an identity transformation in the same way that reading the press does for athletes and entertainers.

Donald Harvey, who confessed to killing scores of patients while working as an orderly in Cincinnati-area hospitals, agreed to a taped, face-to-face interview with popular talk show host Oprah Winfrey as part of a show on nurses who kill. During the taped segment, Harvey visibly showed enjoyment in recounting the details of how he killed his victims. He described with glee how he had injected some with poisons and had suffocated others. Realizing that Harvey was having the time of his life talking about murdering patients, producers of the Oprah Winfrey show wisely decided that it would be insensitive—if not unethical—to air the program and canceled it. By doing so, the producers deprived Harvey of a chance for stardom on a national stage. The show's producers correctly recognized the fine but critical line that divides informed analysis from unhealthy glorification.

KILLER COMMUNICATION

Some Americans disparagingly refer to serial killers as animals—of course, only in a figurative sense. Actually, what distinguishes humans from animals is the ability to communicate verbally and in writing, and some serial killers have, in fact, chosen to reach out through such means to contact the police, the press, or the public.

Letter carrier David Berkowitz, initially labeled "The .44 Caliber Killer" for his repeated gun assaults on young couples in parked cars in 1976 and 1977, did more than just tote the mail. During his killing spree, Berkowitz sent a series of letters to brash *New York Post* columnist Jimmy Breslin. Besides his lengthy and sometimes incoherent ramblings, Berkowitz offered the police a bit of assistance, with Breslin as the go-between, in the closing of one of his notes:

P.S. Please inform all the detectives working on the case that I wish them luck. Keep them digging, drive on. Think positive. Here are some clues to help you along. The Duke of Death, The Wicked King Wicker. The 22 Disciples of Hell. John Wheaties, rapist and suffocater of young girls.

At the same time, Berkowitz was displeased about his new-found public image. The killer wrote a letter of complaint to Captain Joe Borelli of the NYPD, hoping to set the record straight:

> I am deeply hurt by the newspaper calling me a woman hater. I am not. But I am a monster. I am a little brat. I am the "Son of Sam."

Unlike Berkowitz, most serial killers elect strategically to remain silent regarding their identity and their activities. Some murderers-at-large, those who are social isolates in personality, resist any impulse to go public out of their own personal awkwardness and discomfort in interpersonal relations. Others recognize that killing "under the radar" is most advantageous for continuing their crime sprees without detection or apprehension—that is, if pleasure and fantasy fulfillment are what motivates them.

Of course, not all repeat killers are driven by sexual sadism or the need to dominate their victims. Certain motivations for murder necessitate that the killer expose and publicize his or her existence, if not identity.

One type of power fulfillment involves not so much dominating innocent victims but spreading fear throughout a community, gripping an entire city or region in an atmosphere of panic and hysteria. In a series of chilling unsolved homicides in Wichita, Kansas, beginning in the mid-1970s, for example, the unidentified killer began writing to the police and the media. His one-way communication intensified the level of fear and apprehension among residents of this previously relaxed Midwestern community.

Early on in his crime spree, the killer phoned a local newspaper reporter and directed him to locate a mechanical engineering textbook on the shelves of the Wichita Public Library. Inside the text, the reporter found a letter in which the writer claimed credit for the recent massacre of a local family and promised more of the same in the future. In his letter, the killer wrote, "The code words for me will be . . . Bind them, Torture them, Kill them." He signed the letter "BTK Strangler," for bind, torture, and kill.

The BTK moniker, originating with the killer himself, was commonly used by newspaper reporters in their articles about his string of seven murders. In January 1978, BTK sent a poem to a reporter at the *Wichita Eagle-Beacon*, in which he wrote about a victim he had slain a year earlier. In February of the same year, BTK wrote a letter to a Wichita television station complaining about the lack of publicity he had received for his murders. "How many do I have to kill," BTK asked, "before I get my name in the paper or some national attention?" (C. Scott, 1978). In addition, the killer compared his crimes with those of Jack the Ripper, Son of Sam, and the Hillside Strangler.

BTK's killing spree apparently ended in 1977. The murders seemed to have stopped, the leads in the case never panned out, and the media no longer heard from the killer. After more than 25 years, however, BTK resurfaced to terrorize the Wichita community again. In 2004, the *Wichita Eagle* marked the 30th anniversary of BTK by speculating what had become of his fate—the man had moved away, was imprisoned for some other crime, or had died, according to various theories. Feeling challenged and wanting everyone to know that none of those hypotheses was true, BTK reopened lines of one-way communication, insisting that he had been around town all along. In a letter addressed to the *Eagle*, the retired serial killer included his usual contrived BTK return address and enclosed a photocopy of a missing driver's license belonging to a woman who had been strangled in 1986 and copies of three snapshots of her body lying in front of her television.

BTK was back—back not to resume his killing spree but only to toy with the police and the press for his enjoyment and fame. He even went so far as to send out a word puzzle, created from a computerized spread-sheet, which contained various hidden clues about his identity and whereabouts. It is arguable that he resurfaced in part because of feeling slighted and

Photo 1.4a Convicted "BTK" killer Dennis Rader. (Sedgwick County, KS, Sherriff's Office)

upstaged by contemporary serial killers such as the DC Snipers, who were publicized all over the Internet and cable television. Of course, these communication outlets were not in existence during BTK's prime crime years.

Unfortunately for him, but fortunately for the residents of Wichita, the BTK Strangler's ego and narcissism were his downfall. The police were able to trace the IP (Internet Protocol) address of the computer he had used to create the puzzle—that being a desktop machine located at Christ Lutheran Church in Wichita. It didn't take the authorities long to identify the source: Dennis Rader, president of the Congregation Council.

Rader mistakenly believed that he and a police lieutenant of the Wichita Police Department shared a special bond. Rader must have been disappointed when he learned that police reassurances that a floppy disk could not be traced back to a specific computer were false (Hansen, 2006).

Even following his capture, Dennis Rader couldn't resist the urge to talk with the cops about his crimes. Having failed in his life's ambition to join the police force, he chatted with the detectives as if he was one of the guys. Rader described his arrest and admission of responsibility to Harvard University psychologist Robert Mendoza:

I saw this whole line of police cars. That's not good. And—they were right on me. Just that quick. I thought maybe it was a traffic stop or something. But as soon as one of 'em's behind me with the red lights and sirens, I knew that was it.

They pulled guns on me. Told me to lay down. And I sprawled out and they grabbed me real quick like in handcuffs and stuck me in a car. "Mr. Rader,

CHAPTER 8

```
M   O   A   S   D   D   O   P   J
C   R   U   I   S   E   X   F   G
P   J   K   W   P   T   H   G   O
R   L   E   O   O   A   G   R   F
O   Z   F   L   T   I   J   Y   O
W   N   A   L   P   L   M   U   R
L   F   N   O   V   S   N   I   I
X   C   T   F   I   V   B   S   T
Q   I   A   M   C   L   D   D   L
W   O   S   R   T   T   B   L   S
T   P   I   N   I   P   U   I   L
Y   H   E   L   M   Q   E   U   F
X   N   S   T   E   A   M   B   X

I       T   I   6       2   D   X
    2S  E   A       20  P   R   F
    5U  L   N       R   3   E   G
    9Q  E   D               6C  H
    W   P   E       S       I   J
        H   R       Z       F   K
Q   E   O   S       T   D   F   L
A   N   N   O       C   X   O   L
G   R   E   N       P   S   S   D
S   T   C   D           H       3L
F   Y   O   T       F   L       K
H   U   A       2   I       2   W
L   I           R       G       X
K           6           H
X               8M      N

R   U   S   E   T   Y   U   I   X
E   I   E   O   P   F   A   S   D
A   N   R   E   M   O   D   E   L
L   S   V   F   G   R   H   J   O
T   U   I   S   K   S   L   P   S
O   R   C   S   T   A   S   L   T
R   A   E   E   E   L   O   E   P
S   N   M   R   Z   E   X   H   E
Q   C   A   D   C   V   B   N   T
W   E   N   D   I   E   K   A   F
E   R       A   G   N   O   R   W
X   N   A   M   Y   D   N   A   H
```

Photo 1.4b Rader taunted police by sending a word puzzle containing hidden clues to his identity. (Author)

do you know why you're going downtown?" And I said, "Oh, I have suspicions, why?'"

At first it was kind of—kind of a cat and mouse game. That they had a suspect. But it, but it, but it did kind of hurt, you know. Like you said, I had the power, you know, I was a law enforcement officer technically and here I am—these law enforcement officers were trying to do my duties. That kind of hurt a little bit.

I know a lot of the police terminology. I know how they do things. So it, yeah, it's kinda a bonding type thing, you know.

I enjoyed it. And once the confession was out and I admitted who I was, then, then the bonding really started. You know, I just really opened up and you know we shared jokes and everything else. It's just like we were buddies. (Secret Confessions, 2005)

For some serial murderers, boasting about their violent exploits is more accurately an act of taunting. Out of sheer arrogance, certain killers tease the police or the public with a "you can't catch me" message. For them, winning the cat-and-mouse game with law enforcement is a powerful fringe benefit to their killing sprees—potentially as fulfilling as the homicides themselves.

California's Zodiac killer, whose first suspected murder—that of Cheri Jo Bates—dates back to 1966, appeared unconcerned about being captured as he sent letter after letter to the newspapers, claiming intellectual superiority over the police. Even his first communiqué, received by the Riverside Police Department in November 1966, long before he had established his elusiveness, tauntingly announced his intentions (Wark, n.d.). His use of capital letters reflected a certain bravado and confidence:

SHE WAS YOUNG AND BEAUTIFUL BUT NOW SHE IS BATTERED AND DEAD. SHE IS NOT THE FIRST AND SHE WILL NOT BE THE LAST I LAY AWAKE NIGHTS THINKING ABOUT MY NEXT VICTIM. MAYBE SHE WILL BE THE BEAUTIFUL BLOND THAT BABYSITS NEAR THE LITTLE STORE AND WALKS DOWN THE DARK ALLEY EACH EVENING ABOUT SEVEN. OR MAYBE SHE WILL BE THE SHAPELY BRUNETT THAT SAID NO WHEN I ASKED HER FOR A DATE IN HIGH SCHOOL. BUT MAYBE IT WILL NOT BE EITHER. BUT I SHALL CUT OFF HER FEMALE PARTS AND DEPOSIT THEM FOR THE WHOLE CITY TO SEE. SO DON'T MAKE IT TO EASY FOR ME. KEEP YOUR SISTERS, DAUGHTERS, AND WIVES OFF THE STREETS AND ALLEYS. MISS BATES WAS STUPID. SHE WENT TO THE SLAUGHTER LIKE A LAMB. SHE DID NOT PUT UP A STRUGGLE. BUT I DID. IT WAS A BALL. I FIRST CUT THE MIDDLE WIRE FROM THE DISTRIBUTOR. THEN I WAITED FOR HER IN THE LIBRARY AND FOLLOWED HER OUT AFTER ABOUT TWO MINUTES. THE BATTERY MUST HAVE BEEN ABOUT DEAD BY THEN. I THEN OFFERED TO HELP. SHE WAS THEN VERY WILLING TO TALK TO ME. I TOLD HER THAT MY CAR WAS DOWN THE STREET AND THAT I WOULD GIVE HER A LIFT HOME. WHEN WE WERE AWAY FROM THE LIBRARY WALKING, I SAID IT WAS ABOUT TIME. SHE ASKED ME, "ABOUT TIME FOR WHAT?" I SAID IT WAS ABOUT TIME FOR HER TO DIE. I GRABBED HER AROUND THE NECK WITH MY HAND OVER HER MOUTH AND MY OTHER HAND WITH A SMALL KNIFE AT HER THROAT. SHE WENT VERY WILLINGLY. HER BREAST FELT WARM AND VERY FIRM UNDER MY HANDS, BUT ONLY ONE THING WAS ON MY MIND. MAKING HER PAY FOR ALL THE BRUSH OFFS THAT SHE HAD GIVEN ME DURING THE YEARS PRIOR. SHE DIED HARD. SHE SQUIRMED AND SHOOK AS I CHOCKED HER, AND HER LIPS TWICHED. SHE LET OUT A SCREAM ONCE AND I KICKED HER IN THE HEAD TO SHUT HER UP. I PLUNGED THE KNIFE INTO HER AND IT BROKE. I THEN FINISHED THE JOB BY CUTTING HER THROAT. I AM NOT SICK. I AM INSANE. BUT THAT WILL NOT STOP THE GAME. THIS LETTER SHOULD BE PUBLISHED FOR ALL TO READ IT. IT JUST MIGHT SAVE THAT GIRL IN THE ALLEY. BUT THAT'S UP TO YOU. IT WILL BE ON YOUR CONSCIENCE. NOT MINE. YES, I DID MAKE

THAT CALL TO YOU ALSO. IT WAS JUST A WARNING. BEWARE . . . I
AM STALKING YOUR GIRLS NOW.

CC. CHIEF OF POLICE

ENTERPRISE

Three years later, the killer's communications, both letters and phone calls, picked up in pace. He also adopted the sign of the Zodiac, as well as its name, as his calling card and monogram for murder. The moniker only intensified the frightfulness of the assailant whom police would never identify.

There are two general classes of multiple murderers based on their motivation— those who find killing a fulfilling end in itself, and those for whom murder is a necessary, but not necessarily desirable, means toward some larger objective, often political or profit based. The former is focused squarely on the act of killing, whereas the latter generally requires communication with third parties to get their compliance.

For the DC Snipers, who gunned down 10 innocent people near the nation's capital during a 3-week period in 2002, communication with the investigative task force, and ideally its leader, Chief Charles Moose of the Montgomery County Police, was necessary to gain their ultimate prize—a ransom of $10 million.

Through notes left at the sites of shootings (one of which was scribbled on a tarot card for added effect), the killers gave instructions for the head of the task force to read at a press conference the phrase, "We have caught the sniper like a duck in a noose," adapted from a children's folktale. The snipers, later identified as John Allen Muhammad and Lee Boyd Malvo, were frustrated in their repeated attempts to reach the man in charge who could authorize the transfer of funds to a stolen debit account. For Muhammad and Malvo, communication was nothing more than negotiation for profit.

Unlike the DC Snipers, Theodore Kaczynski, the central figure in the 2011 GSA auction mentioned earlier, was a prolific communicator and relentless negotiator. Given the moniker "The Unabomber" created by the Federal Bureau of Investigation (FBI) for his series of bombings directed at university-based scientists and airline executives, Kaczynski was focused on advancing his cause, rather than seeking profit, power, or revenge. He wished to send a clear message of impending doom to alert the nation to what he saw as the evils of technology, and he used murder and the threat of further bombings in order to get everyone's attention.

Despite his distorted view, Kaczynski was a brilliant individual, a Harvard-trained PhD in mathematics who landed a coveted teaching position at the University of California. But he also struggled with mental illness throughout his life. As he withdrew deeper and deeper into minimalist ideology and schizophrenia, Kaczynski abandoned his teaching post and moved to a remote spot in Lincoln, Montana, to take up a simple, reclusive existence.

From his tiny, secluded cabin, lacking in the basic comforts of electricity or running water, Kaczynski toiled away making bombs and sending occasional letters to the *New York Times* outlining his outlook and philosophy, excerpts of which were published by the *Times* in the hope that someone would recognize the ideas and phrasing.

More importantly, Kaczynski spent long hours polishing his 35,000-word treatise, "Industrial Society and Its Future," in which he warned of the dangers of human enslavement to technology:

The Industrial Revolution and its consequences have been a disaster for the human race. They have greatly increased the life-expectancy of those of us who live in "advanced" countries, but they have destabilized society, have made life unfulfilling, have subjected human beings to indignities, have led to widespread psychological suffering (in the Third World to physical suffering as well) and have inflicted severe damage on the natural world. The continued development of technology will worsen the situation. It will certainly subject human beings to greater indignities and inflict greater damage on the natural world, it will probably lead to greater social disruption and psychological suffering, and it may lead to increased physical suffering even in "advanced" countries.

Kaczynski sent copies of his work to both the *New York Times* and the *Washington Post,* along with an ultimatum: Either his document is published unedited and in its entirety or more people will die. With advice from the FBI, the *Post* capitulated to the killer's coercive tactics and published the manifesto as an eight-page supplement to its September 19, 1995 edition.

KILLER GROUPIES

Because of their celebrity status, infamous multiple murderers attract a surprising number of extreme sympathizers, so-called "killer groupies." Several convicted serial killers, such as Hillside Stranglers Kenneth Bianchi and Angelo Buono, were pursued and married while serving life sentences for their brutal and sadistic murders of young women on the West Coast. Other multiple murderers have married from death row, giving the traditional vow "til death do us part" an ironic twist. The pattern of behavior is sufficiently common to have been assigned a clinical label: *hybristophilia*, a paraphilia in which someone is sexually aroused or attracted to a person who has committed particularly vicious or gruesome crimes. In its more common form, hybristophiles merely seek to be close to some "bad boy." Occasionally, however, hybristophilia can lead to behaviors far more dangerous than mere adoration and devotion, including participating in murder for the sake of their loved one.

So why would someone in her right mind correspond with, visit, or even fall in love with a man who has raped, tortured, and mutilated innocent victims? Why would hundreds of women attempt to visit Los Angeles Night Stalker Richard Ramirez, who was convicted of stealthily entering more than a dozen homes in the dark of night and killing the occupants? And why would so many women send proposals of marriage to suspected repeat killer Joran Van Der Sloot just days after his incarceration in the country of Peru? Why would a woman like Veronica Crompton be so attracted to Sunset Strip killer Douglas Clark that she would break off her relationship with Hillside Strangler Kenneth Bianchi, but and only

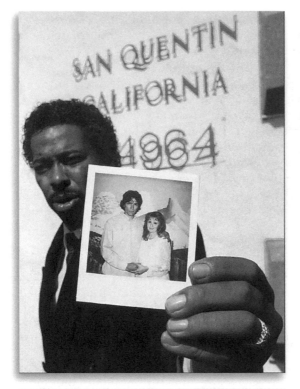

Photo 1.5 The celebrity of killers often attracts adoring fans and groupies, even marriage proposals. A spokesman for San Quentin Prison holds photo of "Night Stalker" Richard Ramirez and his new bride Doreen Lioy, taken during their wedding ceremony inside the prison. (Associated Press/Lacy Atkins)

after she had committed a copy-cat crime in hopes of exonerating her incarcerated boyfriend?

Actually, there are several reasons why serial killers are pursued by adoring women. Some groupies may be attracted to their idol's controlling, manipulative personalities. A Freudian might attempt to trace this attraction to a woman's need to resurrect her relationship with a cruel, domineering father figure. At least a few killer groupies strive to prove that their lover is a victim of injustice. These women's fight for right gives their otherwise unfulfilling lives a strong sense of purpose. Others wish to break through the killer's vicious façade with thoughts such as, "The whole world sees Johnny as a monster. Only I see the kindness in him; he shares that only with me. . . . I feel so special." Still other devotees simply are comfortable in always knowing where their man is at 2 a.m.—even if it's on death row: "He may be behind bars, but at least he's not out in the bars with some other woman."

Dozens of women wrote love letters to Danny Rolling, the serial killer who in 1990 brutally murdered five college students in Gainesville, Florida. One adoring fan wrote to the killer, "I fell in love the first time I saw you. I have even seen you in my dreams. . . . You're a very handsome man" (Blincow, 1999, p. 42). A 29-year-old woman sent Rolling bikini-clad photos of herself and wrote, "I love you with all my heart. . . . I don't care what you've done in the past. . . . I wish I could hold you and comfort you." She addressed her letter, "To my sweet prince" (Blincow, 1999, p. 42). Many other women sent Rolling red roses, locks of their hair, and love poetry. Some sprinkled their letters with perfume and begged the killer to allow them to visit. Of course, Rolling's 2006 execution put an end to the romantic fantasies of many adoring fans.

Underlying all these motivations, however, are the glamour and celebrity status that killer groupies find exciting. One teenager from Milwaukee appeared years ago on a national TV talk show to admit that she would give anything to get an autograph from serial killer Jeffrey Dahmer; it is likely that she also collected the autographs of rock stars or rap artists. The young girl never got her wish fulfilled before Dahmer was murdered by a fellow inmate.

In general, serial killers are more accessible than other celebrities. If a fan wants to get close to rock idol Justin Timberlake or rapper Eminem, she generally doesn't have a chance. But with someone like Night Stalker Richard Ramirez, all she would have to do is write a few gushy love letters and she might even get to meet him and perhaps even marry him. After watching TV coverage of Ramirez's 1985 arrest, Doreen Loiy, a freelance magazine writer, carried on a decade-long courtship with the convicted serial killer. Following her 1996 marriage to the condemned inmate, Doreen Ramirez told CNN, "He's kind, he's funny, he's charming . . . I think he's really a great person. He's my best friend; he's my buddy." Because her husband was on death row, Doreen was not permitted conjugal visitation at any time. Despite the physical limitations, the marriage survived until 2013 when Richard Ramirez suffered a fatal heart attack.

THE IMPACT OF CELEBRATING MURDERERS

Is the glorification of multiple murder—trading cards, art galleries, songfests, and killer groupies—nothing more than harmless media hype? Certainly the families of murder victims don't think so. From their point of view, the sanitized, romanticized, and glamorized image of a killer who is, in actuality, little more than an unrepentant, vicious, sadistic destroyer of human life only adds insult to injury.

The harm extends well beyond the victims and their loved ones. Worshipping a killer whose actions are so hideous that he ought to be soundly condemned debases our entire society. Making monsters into celebrities only teaches our youngsters—especially alienated and marginalized teenagers—a lesson about how to get attention. "Want to be noticed? Want to feel important? Simple. Shoot lots of your classmates. Then, you'll be on the cover of *People* magazine, you'll be interviewed on CNN, and you'll make headlines all over the nation, if not the world!" Columbine High shooters Dylan Klebold and Eric Harris appeared on the cover of *Time* magazine under the headline "The Monsters Next Door." Adult readers may indeed have viewed them as monsters, but how many young teens instead saw them more as celebrities and heroes? From the perspective of a few alienated youngsters, not only did Klebold and Harris get even with the bullies and the jocks, but they are famous for it!

By featuring the vicious acts of villains, therefore, we may be inadvertently providing young people with a dangerous model for gaining national prominence. We may also be giving to the worst among us exactly what they hope to achieve—celebrity status.

SENSITIZE, NOT SANITIZE

Author Lonnie Kidd might have recklessly, albeit unwittingly, put a stamp of approval on murder with his failed attempt at satire. His 1992 book *Becoming a Successful Mass Murderer or Serial Killer: The Complete Handbook* might easily be misunderstood as a murder how-to book by people who are looking for an excuse to kill. In a section titled "To Get Rid of Your Children, Your Spouse's Children, Others' Children," for example, Kidd (1992) suggests,

> You will have no problem finding lots of brat children to kill. They are also easily convinced to go off alone with you. You could easily beat them to death. Kick and stomp their little faces and heads into the ground! Hear them promise to be good little boys and girls; but, you know better! They will continue to be little brats if you do not do away with them. (p. 100)

In a disclaimer, Kidd (1992) argues that his book is "a way of calling attention to very serious phenomenon [sic] in a satirical manner" (p. 1). Notwithstanding the legitimacy of his avowed objective, not all of Kidd's readers would possess the sophistication needed to get the joke. Those who are already predisposed to mayhem and murder might instead find plenty of encouragement in the pages of Kidd's troubling manual.

In the pages to follow, we certainly do not strive to enhance multiple murder celebrity. Rather, we hope to shed light—but not a spotlight—on the motivation and character of these vicious killers. We appreciate the important distinction between analyzing the gory details of a crime and glorifying the image of the criminal. At times, we describe the sickening circumstances of a multiple murder, but always with a purpose—to remind us that these killers are monsters, undeserving of celebration and fanfare.

At the same time, we must be nothing less than candid about what atrocities modern-day serial and mass killers have committed. Leaving out the gruesome details might reduce the reader's discomfort, but it would inadvertently minimize the horror of the murders and maximize sympathy for the perpetrators.

CHAPTER 2

Defining
Multiple Murder

Early in the morning of August 9, 1969, housekeeper Winifred Chapman telephoned the Beverly Hills police to report a ghastly murder at the secluded hillside residence of her employer, Hollywood starlet Sharon Tate, and her husband, film director Roman Polanski. When Chapman had come to clean up the house, she discovered the bodies of five people, including Ms. Tate, who was 8 months pregnant. The word *pig* was scrawled in blood across the front door of the luxurious home.

When the police arrived, they found what one called "a bloody mess." The body of 26-year-old Sharon Tate lay in the living room of the house, a nylon rope tied tightly around her neck as though in preparation for a hanging. She had been stabbed 16 times. Next to Tate on the floor lay the limp body of her close friend, 35-year-old Hollywood hair stylist Jay Sebring. He had been stabbed seven times and shot. A towel partially obscured the rope that had been tied around his neck and then draped over a beam on the ceiling.

Two more bodies were found on the front lawn of the house, some 50 feet apart. Thirty-seven-year-old Wojciech Frykowski, a friend of Roman Polanski, had been shot five times, stabbed 51 times, and bludgeoned 13 times on the back of the head. His girlfriend, 26-year-old coffee heiress Abigail Folger, had been stabbed 28 times. Both Folger and Frykowski apparently had tried to escape but were caught while running away from the house. The fifth body, that of 18-year-old Steve Parent, was found slumped over the wheel of an automobile parked on the narrow road leading to the entry gate of the property. He had been stabbed once and shot four times. Roman Polanski was in London at the time of the slayings.

Though they lacked firm evidence linking him to the slayings, the police quickly arrested and charged 19-year-old caretaker William Garretson, who lived in a small garage-like cottage at the rear of the main house. Subsequent events, however, made it clear that the police had the wrong man. A new development suggested to the police that they were dealing with something, or someone, far more sinister and deadly.

The day after the Tate massacre, the 15-year-old son of wealthy supermarket owners Rosemary and Leno LaBianca walked into his Los Angeles home to

Photo 2.1a   Charles Manson. (Associated Press/Eric Risberg)

find his parents' bloodied bodies. Rosemary LaBianca's body lay in the master bedroom of the house, her hands tied behind her back with an electrical cord and a pillowcase pulled over her face. She had been stabbed 41 times. Leno LaBianca's body was sprawled across the living room carpet, his hands fastened behind him with a leather thong and his face covered with a bloody pillowcase. The killers had left a carving fork protruding from his abdomen and had scratched the word *war* in his skin. He had been stabbed 27 times. Scribbled in blood on a living room wall were the words *Death to Pigs* and on the refrigerator door *Helter Skelter*.

Taken from a Beatles song, Helter Skelter was the name 34-year-old Charles Manson had given to the war between Blacks and Whites that he believed would shortly engulf the nation. He preached to his flock, members of the so-called Manson family, that

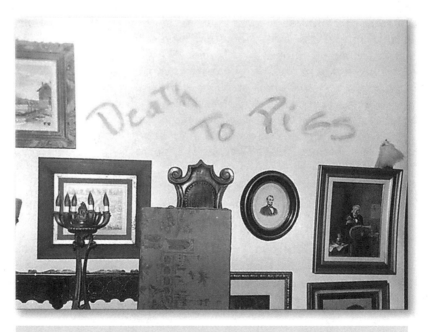

Photo 2.1b   "Death to Pigs" on LaBianca's living room wall. (Author)

they must prepare to move to an isolated desert area to avoid the race war he felt would inevitably result in the victory of Blacks over Whites. Manson also believed, however, that the victorious Blacks would be ineffective in governing the country and would eventually be forced to ask him to rule.

Manson never had a direct hand in the Tate/LaBianca slayings, but he probably orchestrated them through instructions to his obedient followers. He hoped that Blacks would be falsely accused of murdering rich, White folks and that the race war he envisaged would be hastened. Manson and two of the female members of his family, 22-year-old Susan Atkins and 23-year-old Patricia Krenwinkel, were convicted on January 25, 1971, of seven counts of first-degree murder. A third Manson follower, 21-year-old Leslie Van Houten, who participated only in the LaBianca assaults, was convicted of two counts of murder in the first degree.

In the decades since the Tate/LaBianca murders, Charles Manson has remained a counterculture folk hero and a popular culture icon. As described earlier, his image and infamy continue to reap profits in the murderabilia market. For the more serious-minded observers of multiple murder, Manson has been a definitional oddity. Is he a mass murderer? The murders did not take place at the same time or in the same place. Is he a serial killer? The murder spree lasted only a couple of days. Does it really matter how he is defined?

MASS, SERIAL, AND SPREE

Once upon a time, yet not that long ago, all forms of multiple murder were considered mass killing. References to "spree" and "serial" occasionally were used in a descriptive sense (e.g., "he went on a killing spree" or "he murdered his victims in a serial fashion"), but until just three decades ago, neither serial nor spree murder existed as special classifications for homicide.

Serial murder is a relatively new term, even though the crime itself has existed throughout the history of man's inhumanity to man. We may now describe both the Boston Strangler, who terrorized young and elderly women alike in the early 1960s, and Jack the Ripper, who stalked and killed prostitutes in the poor sections of London back in 1888, as serial murderers, yet neither newspapers nor the police ever described these crime sprees as "serial." Rather, the term *mass murderer* seemed to suffice.

In the early 1980s, however, when the FBI launched a large-scale initiative at its training academy in Quantico, Virginia, to document, study, and investigate repeat killers, it established a trichotomy of multiple murder. As shown in Table 2.1, the FBI's Behavioral Sciences Unit (BSU) defined *mass killings* (or massacres) as homicides involving the murder of four or more victims in a single episode, although some researchers (see, for example, Holmes & Holmes, 2001) prefer using a three-victim threshold. Repeat murderers were then classified by the BSU as either serial or spree killers depending on whether or not the offender "cools off" between attacks. Operationally, the spree killer launches a swath of destruction, usually over a period of several days, wherein most of his activity surrounds planning or executing his crimes and evading the police. By contrast, the serial killer, who may continue

Table 2.1   Homicide Classification by Style and Type

Characteristic	Type					
	Single	Double	Triple	Mass	Spree	Serial
Number of victims	1	2	3	4+	2+	3+
Number of events	1	1	1	1	1	3+
Number of locations	1	1	1	1	2+	3+
Cool-off period	NA	NA	NA	NA	No	Yes

Source: Adapted from R. K. Ressler, A. W. Burgess, & J. E. Douglas (1988), *Sexual Homicide: Patterns and Motives* (Lexington, MA: Lexington Books), p. 138.

Note: NA = Not applicable

to kill over a period of months or years, often has long time lapses between homicides, during which he maintains a more or less ordinary life, going to work and spending time with friends and family.

Unfortunately, the classification of multiple homicides into mass, spree, and serial subtypes often has been a red herring, more a meaningless distraction than a helpful distinction. For example, when a sadistic assailant murdered five college students in Gainesville, Florida, over a 3-day time period, for example, too much focus and debate surrounded whether it was a serial killing or a spree murder. "A true serial murderer has a cooling off period between murders," Barbara L. Hart of the University of Texas at Tyler told the *St. Petersburg Times*. "This is more of a spree" (Vick, 1990, p. 6A). When the frightful string of murders stopped, so did the senseless debate over classification. As investigators later learned, moreover, the killer, Danny Rolling, had actually committed a triple murder (which some would describe as "mass") 9 months earlier, revealing a very long cooling-off period for a serial killer. In a sense, therefore, Rolling's crimes could have been considered mass, spree, or serial, depending on the point of reference. This was a case where the distinction added virtually nothing to our understanding of his crimes.

In the decades since the term was coined, serial murder has remained a hot topic for criminologists and journalists alike. At the same time, however, there has been considerable dispute about how it should be defined in practice. Much of the disagreement surrounds its breadth or scope—some practitioners limited the application to the "classic" lust murder, whereas others expanded the range to include profit-motivated slayings, murders by health care practitioners, and repeat murder motivated by hate or terror.

There has even been disagreement about the minimum victim tally to establish a repetition of killing as serial—some defined serial murder as at least four murders separated in time, whereas others preferred a body count of three. Whether three or four was used to distinguish serial killers from more episodic murderers mattered only in estimating the number of such predators who were roaming the highways and back alleys of America. Behaviorally, they are a separate breed from those who kill on one or maybe two occasions and usually in response to situational factors.

But then in 2005, the FBI's renamed Behavioral Analysis Unit forged a discussion of the definition of serial murder—both in terms of victim count and motivational scope—during a 5-day conference that brought together more than 100 law enforcement officials and academics who specialize in homicide research. Despite a lack of consensus, the FBI adopted the broadest possible definition in terms of both motivation and victimization: "Serial murder is the unlawful killing of two or more victims by the same offender(s) in separate events" (Federal Bureau of Investigation, 2008, p. 12).

It is difficult to say for certain why such a broad approach was favored by the FBI's behavioral analysts; it may simply be a matter of resources and funding priorities. Broadening the scope of the problem, even artificially, may help law enforcement secure additional resources for investigating homicides.

Another possible justification for lowering the minimum victim count is that an individual who repeats murder has shown the potential to commit more, even if circumstances, such as apprehension, curtail his criminal career. Nevertheless, we reject this broader definition. Quite apart from the subject of repeat killing, a pair of events usually is not considered a series. The problem with such a general and broad definition is that it loses the important qualitative distinction between someone for whom murder is a significant feature of his lifestyle and someone who happens to have committed murder on a couple of occasions. Without a stricter definition, there is little reason to study serial murder as a separate phenomenon from homicide generally.

But the move to expand the pool of serial murder cases may have been more strategic in terms of politics. Back in the 1980s, the FBI behavioral scientists embraced and promoted the position that thousands of Americans were being murdered each year by serial killers—a position that was without empirical foundation and grossly exaggerated. Some have speculated that the purpose of such outlandish estimates was to demand expanded resources from Congress (see Jenkins, 1994). As many researchers eventually pointed out, the serial murder victim count was in the hundreds annually, rather than the thousands. However, by redefining serial murder as repetitive murder on at least two occasions, the problem—and thus the need for additional funding—would only seem to be magnified, although artificially. Unfortunately, some scholars have been all too willing to play along with this newer criterion, even though it casts doubt on much of the research that has been accomplished to date.

In this book, we strive to minimize the distinctions among the three subforms of multiple homicide, preferring to emphasize similarities in motivation rather than differences based on timing. For the sake of avoiding confusion, however, we shall follow the common practice in both the popular and professional literatures of discussing mass and serial killings as somewhat distinct types. Nevertheless, our focus on motivation rather than timing eliminates the need for the "spree killer" designation—a category sometimes used to identify cases of multiple homicide that do not fit neatly into either the serial or mass murder types.

In his review of the literature on multiple murder, Dowden (2005) concluded that this area of study was deficient in terms of methodological sophistication, typology development, and conceptual creativity. Even though the topic has attracted considerable attention, there is still a long way to go before research on the causes and correlates of multiple homicide achieves sufficient maturity.

A TYPOLOGY OF MULTIPLE MURDER

In criminology, as in most social and behavioral sciences, researchers often struggle to create typologies or taxonomies that help them to understand behavior. When a heterogeneous phenomenon, such as multiple murder, is addressed as a singular concept, it can be difficult to make sense of widely differing patterns of behavior.

There is disagreement about the value of creating typologies. Although many scholars believe that dividing mass killings into homogeneous subclasses helps to conceptualize and explain murderous behavior, some who take a more investigative or crime-solving approach may have less use for these "academic" exercises (see Keppel & Birnes, 2003). Even though the utility of subdividing may be more theoretical than practical, it is important not to lump all multiple-victim killings together as if they all derive from the same underlying factors. This is particularly important given the fact that serial killers possess a great deal of variation among their backgrounds and crimes (Beasley, 2004).

In an early attempt, Ronald M. Holmes and James De Burger (1988) assembled a motivational classification that distinguishes four broad categories of serial killers: visionary (e.g., obeying voices from God), mission oriented (e.g., ridding the world of evil), hedonistic (e.g., killing for pleasure), and power/control oriented (e.g., killing for dominance). The hedonistic type is further subdivided into three subtypes: lust, thrill, and comfort. Although fewer researchers have considered mass (rather than serial) murder types, Holmes and Stephen T. Holmes (2001), drawing from an earlier effort by P. E. Dietz (1986), proposed a five-class categorization, including disciples (e.g., youngsters who follow the dictates of a charismatic leader), family annihilators (e.g., estranged husband who slaughters his wife and children), set-and-run killers (e.g., bomb-setter), pseudocommandos (e.g., military-style assault in a public place), and disgruntled employees (e.g., a fired worker who executes his former coworkers). An empirical test of Holmes and Holmes's typology of serial murderers found that the distinct types were quite difficult to isolate without category overlap (Canter & Wentink, 2004). Specifically, the category of power or control killings was found to be so prevalent, apparent in more than half of the cases, that it frequently eclipsed the other types.

These (and other) typologies of serial and mass murder often have a troubling, but unavoidable, degree of overlap among their categories (e.g., serial killers who at one level seek to exterminate marginal victims yet also enjoy the thrill of conquest, or pseudocommandos who massacre their coworkers). The potential for dual motivation is particularly likely in multiple murders committed by a team or group of offenders. For example, in the Sunset Strip killing spree committed in 1980 by Douglas Clark and Carol Bundy, he was a sexual sadist who killed for power and control, whereas she joined in the murders to remain loyal to her boyfriend–accomplice.

Even more problematic is the apparent extent of overlap between typologies of serial murder and mass killings. A number of serial murder cases better fit a mass killer type, and certain mass killers reflect motives common to serial offenders. For example, Richard Speck, who in 1966 raped and murdered eight Chicago nursing students in their dormitory, may have had robbery as a secondary motive, but his primary objective was, by his own admission, thrill-seeking or hell-raising. Likewise, Theodore Kaczynski, the infamous Unabomber whose fatal mail bombings spanned nearly two decades, was technically a serial killer yet resembles the set-and-run mass killer type.

Incorporating many elements of earlier classification schemes, a unified typology of multiple murder can be constructed using five categories of motivation applicable to *both* serial and mass killing: power, revenge, loyalty, profit, and terror. As shown in Table 2.2, through illustrations of each, the differences in motivations seem to be far more important than the issue of timing.

Power

The overwhelming majority of serial killings, as well as a substantial number of mass killings, express a theme in which power and control are clearly

Table 2.2 Generic Examples of Motivations for Multiple Murder

Motivation	Type of Multiple Murder	
	Serial Murder	**Mass Murder**
Power	Inspired by sadistic fantasies, a man tortures and kills a series of strangers to satisfy his need for control and dominance.	A pseudocommando, dressed in battle fatigues and armed with an assault rifle, turns a shopping mall into a "war zone."
Revenge	Grossly mistreated as a child, a man avenges his past by slaying women who remind him of his mother.	After being fired from his job, a gunman returns to the work site and opens fire on his former boss and coworkers.
Loyalty	A team of killers turns murder into a ritual for proving their dedication and commitment to one another.	A depressed husband/father kills his family and himself to spare them from a miserable existence and bring them to a better life in the hereafter.
Profit	A woman poisons to death a series of husbands in order to collect on their life insurance policies.	A band of armed robbers executes the employees of a store to eliminate all witnesses to their crime.
Terror	A profoundly paranoid man commits a series of bombings to warn the world of impending doom.	A group of antigovernment extremists blows up a commercial airplane to send a political message.

dominant. As indicated earlier, many serial murders can be classified as thrill killings. Although sexually motivated murder is the most common form, a growing number of homicides committed by hospital caretakers have been exposed in recent years. Although not sexual in motivation, these acts of murder are perpetrated for the sake of power and control nevertheless. For example, Donald Harvey, who worked as an orderly in Cincinnati-area hospitals, confessed to killing dozens of patients over a period of years. Although he was termed a *mercy killer*, Harvey actually enjoyed the dominance he achieved by "playing God" with the lives of other people.

The thirst for power and control also inspired many mass murderers, particularly the so-called pseudocommando killers—who often dress in battle fatigues and have a passion for symbols of power, including assault weapons. In 1987, for example, 19-year-old Julian Knight, who was truly obsessed with military might and fashioned himself as a war hero, launched an armed assault on pedestrians in Melbourne, Australia, killing seven and wounding 18.

The motive of power and control encompasses what earlier typologies have termed the "mission-oriented killer" (Holmes & De Burger, 1988), whose crimes are designed to further a cause. Through killing, he claims an attempt to rid the world of filth and evil, such as by killing prostitutes or the homeless. However, most self-proclaimed "reformists" are also motivated—perhaps more so—by thrill seeking and power but try to rationalize their murderous behavior. The Unabomber alleged in his lengthy manifesto that his objective in killing was to save humanity from enslavement by technology. However, his attention-grabbing efforts to publish in the nation's most prominent newspapers, his threatening hoax that shut down the Los Angeles airport, and his obsessive library visits to read about himself in the news suggest a more controlling purpose.

The true visionary killer, as rare as this may be, genuinely believes in his mission. He hears the voice of the devil or God instructing him to kill. Driven by these delusions, the visionary killer tends to be psychotic, confused, and disorganized. Because his killings are impulsive and even frenzied, the visionary is generally incapable of amassing a large victim count. Clearly, the Unabomber does not appear to meet the criteria for this category of multiple killers.

Revenge

Many multiple murders, especially mass killings, are motivated by revenge against either specific individuals, particular categories or groups of individuals, or society at large. Most commonly, the murderer seeks to get even with people he knows—with his estranged wife and all of *her* children or the boss and all of *his* employees.

In discussing family homicide, psychiatrist Shervert Frazier (1975) identified the concept of "murder by proxy," in which victims are chosen because they are identified with a primary target against whom revenge is sought. Thus, a man might slaughter all of his children because he sees them as an extension of his wife, and he seeks to get even with her. In 1987, for example, Ronald Gene Simmons massacred his entire family, including his grandchildren, to avenge rejection by his wife and an older daughter with whom he had had an incestuous relationship.

Frazier's concept of murder by proxy can be generalized to crimes outside the family setting, particularly in the workplace or in schools. In 1986, for example, Patrick Sherrill murdered 14 fellow postal workers in Edmond, Oklahoma, after being reprimanded and threatened with dismissal by his supervisor. He apparently sought to eliminate everyone identified with the boss and the post office. Similarly, during the 1990s, a number of disgruntled students, feeling bullied or socially ostracized by classmates, launched murderous rampages in their schools. For the most part, the students and teachers were targeted at random in an attack against the institution.

These crimes involve specific victims (or proxies) who are chosen for specific reasons. Some revenge multiple killings, however, are motivated by a grudge against an entire category of individuals, typically defined by race or gender, who are viewed as responsible for the killer's difficulties in life (Levin & McDevitt, 2002). In 1989, for example, long-term animosity toward feminists ignited Marc Lepine's murderous rampage at the University of Montreal, which resulted in the violent deaths of 14 female engineering students. The San Francisco "Zebra killings" in 1973 and 1974, in which a group of Black Muslims executed 14 White "blue-eyed devils," illustrates the serial version of the category-specific revenge motive.

A few revenge-motivated multiple murders stem from the killer's paranoid view of society as a whole. He imagines a wide-ranging conspiracy in which large numbers of people, friends and strangers alike, are out to do him harm. William Cruse, for example, suspected that nearly everyone was against him. Unlike Marc Lepine, whose disdain was focused on one group (albeit large), Cruse hated humanity—indeed, all the residents of his community, including the children. In 1987, the 59-year-old retired librarian launched a murderous shooting spree at a Palm Bay, Florida, Winn-Dixie supermarket, killing six and wounding another 12, all total strangers.

In June 2010, Derrick Bird, a cab driver in Northern England who was angry about the size of his inheritance, drove from location to location, searching for victims to shoot. When his rampage ended, he took his own life, but not before killing 12 and injuring 25. Seeking revenge, his first three murder victims were his twin brother, his lawyer, and a fellow cabbie.

Loyalty

Unlike multiple murders for power or revenge, the remaining forms are more instrumental than expressive; that is, in the killer's mind, murder serves as a necessary, even if distasteful, means toward some desired outcome. A few multiple murderers are inspired to kill by a warped sense of love and loyalty—a desire to save their loved ones from misery and hardship. Certain family massacres involve what Frazier (1975) describes as "suicide by proxy."

Typically, a husband or father is despondent over the fate of the family unit and takes not only his own life but also those of his children and sometimes his wife, in order to protect them all from the pain and suffering in their lives.

For example, in May 1990, Hermino Elizalde, described by friends as a devoted father, was concerned that his recent job loss would open the door for his estranged wife to gain custody of their five children. Rather than losing his beloved children, he killed them in their sleep and then took his own life. By killing them all, Elizalde may have reasoned, they would be reunited spiritually in a better life after death.

Some cases of family mass murder appear to involve at least some degree of ambivalence between revenge and loyalty. Such mixed feelings can be seen in the 1991 case of a 39-year-old suicidal father, James Colbert of Concord, New Hampshire, who strangled his wife out of jealousy and then killed his three daughters to protect them from becoming orphans.

Multiple murders committed by cults reflect, at least in part, the desire of loyal disciples to be seen as obedient to their charismatic leader. In an extreme case, more than 80 Branch Davidians died in 1993 in a fiery conflagration at their Waco, Texas, compound. As devoted followers of David Koresh, they were willing to die for their radical religious cause and their beloved leader who had inspired them. Similarly, members of the Manson family, who on their own were hardly the murdering type, were nevertheless prepared to do anything that their "messiah" dictated.

Profit

Some serial and mass murders are committed for profit. Specifically, they are designed to eliminate victims and witnesses to a crime, often a robbery. For example, in 1983, three men crashed the Wah Mee Club in Seattle's Chinatown, robbed each patron, and then methodically executed all 13 victims by shooting them in the head. More unusual, over a 3-year period in the late 1980s, a 64-year-old Sacramento landlady murdered and buried nine elderly tenants so that she could steal their Social Security checks.

The 1989 ritualist cult slayings of 15 people in Matamoros, Mexico, were committed by a band of drug smugglers practicing Palo Mayombe, a form of black magic. Human and animal sacrifice was thought by the group to bring them immunity from bullets and criminal prosecution while they smuggled 2,000 pounds of marijuana per week from Mexico into the United States.

Terror

Some multiple homicides are, in fact, terrorist acts in which the perpetrators hope to send a message through murder. In 1969, the Manson family literally left the message "Death to Pigs" in blood on the walls of the LaBianca home, hoping to precipitate a race war between Blacks and Whites. Also, in 1978, three brothers—Bruce, Norman, and David Johnston—protected their multi-million-dollar crime ring by eliminating several gang members whom they suspected would testify against them to a federal grand jury in Philadelphia. In the process, they also sent a message to the many remaining gang members: "Snitch and the same thing will happen to you." In the Johnston brothers case, there was, of course, an element of profit in their crime ring, but the main objective in the murders was to create terror, that is, to remind everyone—not just gang members—of just how powerful the Johnston brothers were.

It is not always possible to identify unambiguously the motivation for a multiple murder, to determine with certainty whether it was inspired by profit, revenge, or some other objective. In 1982, for example, seven residents of the Chicago area were fatally poisoned when they unknowingly ingested cyanide-laced Tylenol capsules. The killer responsible for placing the poisoned analgesics on the shelves of area drugstores and supermarkets was never apprehended. If the killer's motivation was to exact a measure of revenge against society at large, then the victim selection was, in all likelihood, entirely indiscriminate or random. If, however, the motivation involved collecting insurance money or an inheritance, the killer may have targeted a particular victim for death and then randomly planted other tainted Tylenol packages to conceal the true intention.

THEORIES OF MULTIPLE HOMICIDE

Throughout the book, we have located discussions of various theories and concepts developed by criminologists and other social scientists to explain aspects of multiple homicide. The following theories of violence—strain, social learning, routine activity, and control—have been especially useful for explaining either serial murder, mass murder, or both.

STRAIN THEORY

Social scientists have long argued that criminal behavior frequently results from an individual's experience of dealing with the difficulties of everyday living. In 1938, Robert Merton suggested that American culture emphasizes economic success without also emphasizing the requisite opportunities for attaining it. Members of society are urged to pull themselves up by their bootstraps and do what it takes to become wealthy, but many of them lack access to the structural means for improving their socioeconomic status.

As a result, some Americans "innovate," using Merton's terminology. That is, they continue to strive to be financially successful, but they give up on mainstream society and no longer employ the legitimate system, for example, getting good grades, attending college, working hard in the corporate world, and so on. Instead, they go outside of conventional society and seek to "get ahead" by engaging in criminal behavior such as robbery or embezzlement.

The so-called DC snipers who in October 2002 shot to death 10 residents of the Washington DC area tried both robbery and embezzlement. Coming to regard conventional society as the enemy to be challenged and overcome, they had already committed a series of armed robberies in several states. Then, having taken five lives in the DC area, they had hoped to negotiate with the authorities for $10,000,000 in return for ending their killing spree. But when law enforcement failed to respond, their murderous acts continued, leading finally to their apprehension and conviction. The penalty they received was not unexpected: 42-year-old John Mohammed was executed and Lee Malvo, his 17-year-old partner, received a life sentence.

The profit motive is hardly the one and only basis for frustration and strain. Broadening Merton's conception, Robert Agnew (1992) proposed his general strain theory whereby a range of negative experiences or disappointing events in social relationships at home, school, or work, or in the neighborhood can lead to frustration, anger, depression, anxiety, and ultimately, to criminal behavior. Agnew identified several sources of strain in addition to material success, including the failure to achieve positively valued goals, the loss of social status, and the gap between aspirations and achievements.

Agnew's broad conception of strain is useful for explaining why certain middle and high school students would go on a rampage, taking the lives of many of their schoolmates. Their successes are typically evaluated by them based not on the accumulation of money or excellent grades but on their popularity with peers. American youths who have gone on a shooting spree at their middle and high schools have been both academic successes and failures (Hermann & Finn, 2002; Vossekuil, Reddy, Fein, Borum, & Modzeleski, 2002), but almost all of them had been physically bullied, teased, humiliated, or ignored by their fellow schoolmates on a regular basis (Kimmel & Mahler, 2003; Larkin, 2009; Newman, Fox, & Harding, 2007; Vossekuil et al., 2002). Mark Leary, Robin Kowalski, Laura Smith, and Stephen Phillips (2003) found that chronic rejection of the shooters was present in at least 13 of the 15 school shooting cases they examined (Levin & Madfis, 2009).

Certain individual factors may help to determine which youngsters do and do not react to strain by engaging in violent crime. Some rampage shooters may be psychotic; others share a personality disorder such as sociopathy or antisocial personality disorder in which a strong sense of conscience and empathy are missing. Still others suffer from depression and poor impulse control. At least a few rampage shooters have been traumatized. They come from broken homes, suffer physical or sexual abuse, or have at least one parent with a criminal history (Langman, 2009).

In 1969, Charles Manson was convicted of conspiracy to commit the murders of seven innocent people in Beverly Hills, California, over the period of two consecutive evenings. His victims included actress Sharon Tate and her house guests, on the first night, as well as Leno and Rosemary LaBianca, on the second. Manson was convinced that the murders would be falsely attributed to Black residents of the Los Angeles area, helping to precipitate a war between the races. In his Helter Skelter fantasy, an idea that he borrowed from the Beatles, the army of Black Americans would be victorious and would then ask Manson to assume a position of leadership in the new society.

Manson's childhood was filled with strain. Early in life, he experienced being repeatedly abandoned by his mother, a promiscuous and hard-drinking teenager who gave birth to him at the age of 16 and, 4 years later, was convicted of robbing a service station. While his mother was serving a 5-year sentence, Manson stayed with various relatives. He never knew his biological father (Atchison & Heide, 2011).

By the time his mother was released from prison, Manson was already on a path to a life of crime, repeatedly stealing and skipping school. At the age of 12, he was sent to a Catholic school for delinquents and then to one reform school after another, where he was beaten and raped by fellow inmates and guards alike. By the time he reached his 21st birthday, Manson had graduated from committing petty crimes to driving stolen automobiles across state lines. Even as a child and teenager, he was characterized as an incessant liar who blamed other people for all of his failings and who had an obsession for being at the center of attention. By the time he had begun to form his murderous "family" of youthful followers in the mid-1960s, Manson was an unemployed ex-convict who, from an early age, had been in and out of reform schools, jails, and prisons.

There are serial killers who seem to have normal experiences during the early development of their personalities, but who are still victimized by strain. Later on, especially during adolescence, they experience a *fracture*—that is, a small but profound breakage—in their personality, as a result of some traumatizing episode or series of episodes. In most cases, they are able to conceal this destructive and painful element of their personality, appearing to the world to be normal, healthy, and decent individuals who would never commit a brutal act of violence. As subsequent hurtful incidents accumulate, however, the violent side of their personality becomes more and more explosive (Holmes, Tewksbury, & Holmes, 1999).

To illustrate, criminologist Ronald Holmes draws from his conversation with a serial killer who, as a 9-year-old child, was falsely accused of eating a banana that his father had stored away for his own breakfast. After being punished by standing for 8 hours in a corner, the child finally admitted taking the banana. The lesson he learned remained with him over the next 30 years: namely, that lying is beneficial. Deceit gets you out of trouble; it has practical value (Holmes et al., 1999).

SOCIAL LEARNING THEORY

According to social learning theory, individuals develop a propensity to kill from what they learn during their interaction with other people. Early on, Edward H. Sutherland and Donald R. Cressey (1984) proposed that criminal behavior derives from differential association with a group of intimates—close friends and family members—who reinforce positive attitudes toward and teach the skills associated with criminality. Decades later, Ronald L. Akers (2000) refined and expanded Sutherland and Cressey's original formulation of differential association by recognizing that the impact of interacting with people who commit crimes and hold positive attitudes toward criminality varies depending on the frequency, duration, intensity, and priority of the interaction.

Moreover, social learning is stronger when individuals perceive they are likely to be rewarded rather than punished for their criminal behavior. Akers also argued that close friends and family who are admired and respected often serve as role models for criminality to be imitated and emulated. He recognized as well that well-publicized crimes reported in the mass media might also serve as a source of models for criminal behavior.

It has been suggested that a military background provides an effective learning experience for the development of a potential serial killer, providing an environment in which he is taught to be violent and to kill the enemy. Beginning with boot camp, cadets are verbally and physically abused by their superiors. The cadets eventually come to be desensitized to violence and begin to accept it as an important survival skill. Unfortunately, there has been little research directly testing the impact of military training on serial murder. According to Tammy Castle (2001), moreover, only about 7% of all serial killers have previous military experience.

Of course, the brutalization associated with military training can be learned outside of the armed forces. According to the graduation hypothesis (Arluke, Levin, Luke, & Ascione, 1999; Levin & Arluke, 2009), certain serial killers may learn and rehearse their propensity for torture and murder by brutalizing animals (especially dogs and cats) during childhood and adolescence. Decades later, when their violence-prone tendencies become expressed in the extreme, some employ the same means for destroying human beings that they had used as youngsters to abuse the family pet (Levin & Arluke, 2009).

In addition, those killers who had never rehearsed on animals or spent time in military training may have had role models for violence in their own families or in their peer relations. From an early age, for example, Charles Manson had many role models for violent crime. He moved from one reform school to another, where he interacted with other crime-prone young people, received brutal punishments, and may also have been influenced by his mother who was serving a prison sentence by the time that Manson was barely out of diapers (Atchison & Heide, 2011).

As recognized by Akers, not all of social learning comes from face-to-face relationships. Media images of infamous murderers have also served as role models for mass and serial killers (Levin & Madfis, 2009; Madfis & Levin, 2013). In July 2011, Anders Breivik took the lives of 77 people first by bombing a building in central Oslo, Norway, and then by gunning down dozens of young people at a nearby summer camp of the Labour Party's youth wing. In Breivik's 1,500-page manifesto, he took entire sections verbatim from the writings of Unabomber Theodore Kaczynski, whose own manifesto had led to his ultimate apprehension after 17 years of sending bombs through the mail (Madfis & Levin, 2013).

Similarly, since the April 1999 Columbine massacre, school rampage shooters both in the United States and in countries around the world have referred to this infamous case for their inspiration to kill (Larkin, 2009). For example, in April 2002, 19-year-old Robert Steinhäuser shot to death 13 teachers, two students, and one police officer at the Johann-Gutenberg-Gymnasium in Erfurt, Germany, during final exam week. In his home computer, police later located newspaper articles about Eric Harris and Dylan Klebold, the two students whose massacre at Columbine High School resulted in the death of 12 schoolmates and a teacher (Bondü & Scheithauer, 2010).

In September 2006, 25-year-old Kimveer Gill shot to death one student and injured another 19 at Dawson College in Montreal, Canada. During a police search, police found a letter to his family in which he praised the deadly rampage committed by Harris and Klebold. Gill was known to spend his idle hours visiting a website called VampireFreaks.com, where he listed the Internet-based video game Super Columbine Massacre as one of his favorites and displayed photos of himself carrying a rifle and wearing a black trench coat and combat boots reminiscent of the outfit worn by the Columbine killers (Travers, 2006). Similarly, Sebastian Bosse, who bombed and shot students and staff at his former school in Emsdetten, Germany, on November 20, 2006, praised Harris in his diary (Larkin, 2009).

ROUTINE ACTIVITY THEORY

According to Lawrence Cohen and Marcus Felson's (1979) routine activity theory, everyday situations that offer opportunities for victimization present more important causal factors than social conditions such as poverty and inequality. For a violent crime to occur, Cohen and Felson's theory specifies that appropriate targets must be available, effective guardians must be absent, and the offenders must be motivated to commit the offense.

Serial killers often select their victims based on the presence of routine opportunities in their victims' lifestyles to lure them into vulnerable positions. The frequent choice of serial murderers to attack prostitutes may be based less on any childhood hatred toward women (or the killer's mother, in particular) and more on the ease with which a street walker can be lured into a customer's vehicle where she is totally at the killer's mercy. In addition, potential victims may have minimal contact with friends and family, being stigmatized by their choice of an illegal occupation and living apart from anyone who might provide them with protection. Finally, the police pressure to solve the case of a prostitute slaying tends to be less than the pressure associated with the murder of middle-class women who do not feel they are at risk.

The choice of victims in a mass shooting may be influenced by the elements specified in routine activity theory. Would-be rampage shooters who are interested in maximizing their body count know that classrooms hold large numbers of potential victims. They may be drawn to lecture halls in which dozens, perhaps hundreds, of students are seated. At Northern Illinois University in February 2008, for example, former student Steven Kazmierczak was familiar with the auditorium-style lecture hall in Cole Hall where he had taken classes. The killer entered from the stage of the auditorium while an oceanography class was in progress. Taking aim at the 120 students in attendance, Kazmierczak shot to death five people and injured another 21 before taking his own life.

Routine activity theory may also give clues as to why certain venues are not selected by the killer as an appropriate scene for a mass shooting. In 2011, James Holmes enrolled as a graduate student in neuroscience at the University of Colorado in Aurora, after having had an outstanding undergraduate career at the University of California, Riverside. By the summer of 2012, however, Holmes's academic performance (as well as his mental health) had deteriorated sharply. His score on the department's comprehensive exam was unacceptably low, he had failed an important oral exam, and, in June, he decided to drop out of the graduate program. To a gifted but psychologically compromised student who was used to being at the top of his class, failure in a graduate program may have been viewed by him as totally unacceptable. Most rejected graduate students go away quietly; a few decide to express their anger through the barrel of a gun.

Still, the relatively small classes on the campus of the University of Colorado Anschutz Medical Campus must have seemed far less appealing targets to a rampage shooter than was the crowded theater for a Cinemark Century midnight showing of the film *The Dark Knight Rises*. Wearing a gas mask and the costume of Batman's nemesis, the Joker, Holmes was able to overpower the unsuspecting crowd with tear gas grenades and gunfire.

According to John Lott (2012), aside from the potential of a packed cinema for amassing an enormous body count, Holmes may also have been attracted to this particular venue because he had less to fear from armed customers and law enforcement personnel. The Cinemark Century Theater was the only cinema in the state of Colorado where firearms were explicitly banned. In addition, security guards were not immediately on the premises, as they would have been at some neighboring cinemas. Holmes killed 12 and wounded another 70 before being taken into police custody.

An even larger body count was amassed by Virginia Tech killer, Seung-Hui Cho, a student at Virginia Tech, where in April 2007—just weeks before he was to graduate—he shot to death 32 fellow students and faculty members in a dormitory and a large classroom building on campus. Cho's real enemies may have been all those middle-school classmates who had humiliated him on a daily basis for his flat affect, his shy nature, and his lack of fluency in English. But these students had long ago graduated from the eighth grade and high school. They had scattered beyond the local area, having gone on to various universities or to a variety of jobs in many different cities and towns. There was no realistic chance now to gather a large number of those who years earlier had made his life miserable. In a sense, then, the Virginia Tech students who lost their lives as a result of Cho's rampage were nothing more than surrogates for the real culprits, at least in the killer's mind. Their collective presence and vulnerability in a large classroom made them sitting ducks for Cho's desire to get even with his tormentors.

CONTROL THEORY

An important insight provided by control theory is that commitment or attachment to conventional individuals and institutions immunizes human beings from committing violent offenses. Early on, Sigmund Freud argued that the internalized representative of society's cherished values (called the *superego*) develops during the first few years of life. Before the age of 5 or 6, however, children follow rules and avoid harming others in order to gain material rewards (cookies and candy) and avoid punishment (a spanking or reprimand) as administered by their parents. Through a process of identification, the child later attempts to imitate the parents in order to please them. The child no longer acts in a moral or ethical manner only for the sake of securing external rewards and avoiding external punishments, but in order to feel proud and escape feeling guilty. The presence of a superego assures that an individual will grow up having enough self-control to reduce the likelihood of committing acts of extreme violence, including murder, even if the child feels capable of avoiding punishment by the state.

The process of behaving appropriately in order to maintain relationships continues into adulthood. Travis Hirschi (2009) argued that criminality is often controlled by an individual's commitments and attachments to conventional institutions, beliefs, activities, and groups. Many people refrain from engaging in violent behavior because they fear losing their relationships with significant others—with family, friends, and peers. However, members of society who lack strong social ties may also lack the motivation to become law-abiding citizens. It is the person who has nothing to lose—who lacks attachments to others, doesn't make commitments to conventional behavior, and fails to adopt a belief in the moral appropriateness of the law—who is most likely to commit murderous acts.

Michael R. Gottfredson and Hirschi, in their 2003 book *A General Theory of Crime*, point to the importance of parental love, supervision, and consistent discipline in the formation of self-control. Moreover, as noted by Robert J. Sampson and John H. Laub (2003), the ability of young people to develop connections through stable informal bonds as well as job and career relationships may protect them from committing criminal acts. Regrettably, in recent years some Americans have suffered a sharp decline in close bonds with others in their communities. Those areas that have large numbers of individuals lacking in social bonds—the impoverished, the drug addicted, the unemployed, the drifters and transients—also tend to have high rates of crime, including murder.

Thus, being in the presence of close friends and relatives might immunize a potential killer from committing a murderous act. While Ken Bianchi was living in Rochester, New York, he was surrounded by family members and friends who encouraged and supported him through good and bad times. At the age of 26, however, Bianchi relocated to Southern California in late 1977, where he was pretty much on his own with the exception of a relationship with his older cousin, Angelo Buono, whom he admired and respected. Together, the two men (known as the Hillside Strangler, because authorities thought there was only one killer on the loose), raped, tortured, and strangled to death 10 girls and women in and around the Los Angeles area.

It is arguable that Bianchi would never have killed anyone, if he had not moved to the West Coast, and instead had maintained his close personal (and protective) relationships in Rochester. Not unlike many other serial killers, Bianchi seems to have been a sociopath (aka antisocial personality type) who was able to commit hideous crimes with moral impunity. When an individual lacks the internal controls (superego), it becomes even more important that he reside in a network of significant others who are able to limit his propensity for violence.

Mass murderers also lack sources of social control. In April, 2012, 43-year-old One Goh, a former student at Oikos University in Oakland, California, opened fire on campus, killing seven and injuring another three. A native of South Korea, Goh had relocated to the United States as a child where he and his family took residence in Springfield, Virginia. At the time of the attack, he was living in Oakland, but apart from his family members. Goh's mother had died a year earlier after returning to her home in Seoul, South Korea; one of his brothers remained in Virginia, and his second brother was killed in an automobile accident in 2011. When Goh was expelled from the college a few months before his shooting spree, he could have depended on his family members to help get him through the tough times. Instead, he found himself to be alone in what he saw as a hostile environment.

The killer of 20 first graders and six staff members at Sandy Hook elementary school in Newtown, Connecticut, in December 2012 also lacked sources of social control, owing to serious mental illness and a reclusive lifestyle. Twenty-year-old Adam Lanza would rarely leave his home. Considered a "shut-in" by his neighbors, he spent hour after hour, day after day, playing videogames by himself in the basement of his mother's house. Years earlier, he had almost totally eliminated any contact with his father and his older brother (Kleinfield, Rivera, & Kovaleski, 2013).

APPLYING THE FRAMEWORK

The typology and theories presented in this chapter provide a basic framework for understanding and making sense of seemingly senseless crimes. In the chapters to follow, we shall describe in greater detail each of these motivational patterns and causal factors as they apply both to serial and mass murder. Along the way, we offer a large number of case examples. The goal is not so much to describe grisly and ghastly killings but to see the method and methodical behavior in what seems to be, on the surface, sheer madness.

Part II

Serial Murder

CHAPTER 3

An Anatomy of Serial Murder

Christina Powell's parents had grown increasingly upset about their inability to reach their 17-year-old daughter at school. At first, they assumed that she was probably out partying. After all, this was August 1990, orientation week for freshmen at the University of Florida, and she more than likely was out making new friends and buying things for her new apartment before hitting the books. But after a few more days without a word from Christina, the Powells became frantic. As a last resort, they called the Gainesville Police Department to ask them to meet at their daughter's apartment in the Williamsburg complex. Suspecting that something was wrong, a Gainesville police officer entered the apartment by breaking down the door on the second floor to investigate. He was sickened by what he discovered.

Immediately, he saw the bloodied and ravaged body of Sonja Larson, Christina's 18-year-old roommate. She had suffered multiple stab wounds to her arm and right breast, and a large gash to her leg. From the pattern of blood marks on the sheets, she appeared to have been dragged across the bed so that her legs dangled over the edge in a hideous pose.

Moving cautiously down the stairs to the bottom floor, the officer then encountered the corpse of Christina Powell. Revealing evidence of ritualistic murder, the young victim lay spread-eagled on the living room floor, a bottle of detergent and a towel placed between her legs. The nipples of both her breasts had been removed with surgical skill, leaving almost perfect circles, nearly 3 inches in diameter, where her nipples had been.

As shocking as these murders were, they appeared to be an isolated case. The police expected that they would soon find the culprit, perhaps a disgruntled boyfriend who had been rejected and went berserk. That theory soon dissolved in the face of new and equally chilling events.

Only 2 days after the homicides at Williamsburg, 18-year-old Christa Hoyt, a part-time file clerk for the Alachua County Sheriff's Office, uncharacteristically failed to report for work. A deputy sheriff was dispatched to her apartment on 24th Avenue to check on her. After getting no response at the front door, he walked around to the rear of the apartment and peered through the sliding glass door leading into her bedroom. The deputy was unprepared for what he witnessed.

Photo 3.1a Sonja Larson

Photo 3.1b Christina Powell

Photo 3.1c Christa Hoyt

Photo 3.1d Tracy Paules

Photo 3.1e Manuel Taboada

Photo 3.1 The brutal murder of five college students in Gainesville, Florida, by a serial killer horrified the nation. (Author)

Hoyt's lifeless, decapitated body was slumped over on the waterbed, naked except for her pink-trimmed athletic socks and tennis sneakers. Her nipples had been cut off and her torso sliced open from the chest straight down to the pubic bone. Hoyt's head had been severed neatly at the neck and carefully placed on a bookshelf for all to see. The tranquil expression on her face masked the horror of her last moments of life.

Similarities between the Powell/Larson murders and the Hoyt killing suggested to the police that they probably had a serial killer on the loose in Gainesville. Any hope that these killings were linked only by coincidence evaporated with the discovery of two more victims the very next day.

Gatorwood was a popular off-campus apartment complex that had experienced a series of break-ins over the past year, but no one had gotten hurt. Tracy

Paules and Manny Taboada were not so lucky. Longtime friends from American High School in Miami, they had moved into Gatorwood just prior to the fall semester at the University of Florida. Disturbed by Tracy's absence from class, a friend of hers contacted the maintenance man at Gatorwood, who used a master key to enter the apartment that Tracy and Manny shared.

Because of the recent slayings, the maintenance man was understandably apprehensive about what horror he might find inside. Still, he was stunned when he opened the door. Paules's nude body was displayed in the hallway. A trail of blood leading from her bedroom indicated that she had been stabbed in bed and then dragged into the hallway for effect. Manny Taboada also was dead, although it was clear from the defensive wounds on the inside of his arms and the blood sprayed on the wall behind the headboard that he had put up a frantic struggle.

News of the five murders spread quickly throughout the college community, igniting widespread anxiety, if not hysteria, on the campus. In a massive evacuation, thousands of frightened students left town. All the flights out of Gainesville's community airport were booked solid, and long lines of cars and buses led students away from the campus.

But the traffic into town was just as heavy. Journalists and camera crews from around the country, and as far away as Italy, rushed to Gainesville, transforming the usually peaceful college town into a three-ring circus. Newspapers across the state competed fiercely to be the first to uncover and publish the gruesome details of the case. Even popular national talk show host Phil Donahue did a live telecast from the center of town, despite the efforts of some residents to sabotage the broadcast. Citizens of Gainesville were outraged by the invasion of their privacy and by what they perceived to be an undeserved stigma against their hometown. To the chagrin of University of Florida officials, students nicknamed the school "Murder U."

Given how grotesque and hideous the Gainesville slaughters were, it is not surprising that Americans were repulsed by the gory details. At the same time, however, many found themselves drawn to learning precisely what the killer did to the victims. Others demanded to know how the investigation was being handled. Eventually, everyone wanted to understand what motivated the Gainesville culprit not only to kill, but to kill in such a gruesome, savage way.

PREVALENCE OF SERIAL MURDER

Serial murder involves a string of four or more homicides committed by one or a few perpetrators that spans a period of days, weeks, months, or even years. Although the most publicized and prominent form of serial killing consists of a power-hungry sadist who preys upon strangers to satisfy his sexual fantasies, the motivations for and patterns of serial homicide are quite diverse. Included within our definition of perpetrators of serial homicide are, for example, a nurse who poisons her patients in order to "play God," a disturbed man who kills prostitutes to punish them for their sins, a team of armed robbers who execute store clerks after taking money from their cash registers, and a satanic cult whose members commit a string of human sacrifices as an initiation ritual.

Judging from the increasing number of criminologists who have become attracted to the study of serial murder (not to mention students hoping to pursue a career investigating such crimes), it might seem that the United States is in the throes of an epidemic. The scientific evidence to substantiate or deny the presence of such an upsurge is, however, limited. Indeed, it is not possible to trace, with a high degree of precision, recent or long-term trends in the prevalence and incidence of serial murder in this country (see Egger, 1990; Jenkins, 1994; Kiger, 1990).

Using a variety of sources—newspaper reports, books on the topic, and Internet profiles—we have pieced together a list of 660 serial killers operating in the United States since 1900 in order to develop a sense, albeit imperfect, of the trends and patterns in serial killing. The group represents known perpetrators who are believed to have murdered at least four victims. Some killers work as pairs or teams in their predatory activity; overall, this collection of 660 assailants represents 592 unique individuals or partnerships.

Determining the number of victims killed by these offenders is, unfortunately, next to impossible. Often, the full extent of their murder tolls can only be suspected, and the documented cases for which they are convicted or linked with a high degree of certainty may understate the extent of carnage. On the other hand, some offenders, grandiose in their self-image as killing machines, exaggerate their victim tallies as they boast to the press and even the police about how powerful and superior they are. Using conservative estimates of victim counts, the 592 offenders, as a group, are responsible for at least 3,915 homicides, and almost certainly many more. In fact, using more speculative upper estimates, the offenders may account for nearly twice that figure.

In addition to these known serial killers, a number of unsolved cases across the country—for example, in New Bedford, Massachusetts, where 11 female prostitutes and drug users were murdered in 1988—continue to stump investigators. Furthermore, despite recent advances in technology and communication, law enforcement may still be unaware of the presence of many other serial killers. In what Steven A. Egger (1984) termed *linkage blindness,* investigators are not always able to connect homicides, separated over time and space, to the activities of a single perpetrator, particularly murder sprees that cross jurisdictional boundaries (see Levin & Fox, 1985). The unsolved or open cases and the undetected cases, taken together, would account for hundreds of additional victims.

These data on 592 known killers or killing teams can be used to examine long-term trends in serial homicide, subject to important methodological caveats concerning the completeness of the database. Not only do these data exclude unsolved and undetected cases, as already noted, but it is further possible that some more obscure killing sprees have escaped the attention of those who have chronicled such events. Notwithstanding these cautions, Figure 3.1 displays counts of serial killers, partnerships, and teams each year since the beginning of the 20th century, using the midpoint of a killer's career as a reference point. For example, Theodore Bundy, whose murders spanned the years 1974 to 1978, having a career midpoint of 1976, is counted in the 1970s. Unabomber Theodore Kaczynski, who was at large from 1978 to 1996, had a career midpoint of 1987 and thus is included among killers of the 1980s, even though he operated both before and after this decade.

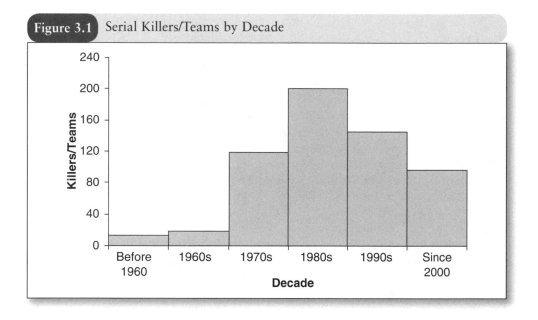

Figure 3.1   Serial Killers/Teams by Decade

There were relatively few known cases during the first half of the 20th century. The pattern emerging during the past few decades is radically different. The number of serial killers and teams grew rapidly from the 1960s into the 1980s. Following the 1980s peak, the number of cases slipped somewhat in the 1990s and then declined even more during the first decade of the 21st century.

Although rapid growth into the 1980s clearly suggests significant shifts in the prevalence of serial murder, these results are vulnerable, at least in part, to alternative explanations related to changes in data accessibility and quality of record keeping. As interest in serial murder increased, so did the likelihood that case histories would be published in some fashion. Additionally, as law enforcement became better equipped to identify linkages between victims slain by the same killer or killers, the detection of serial crimes and criminals became more likely. Notwithstanding these concerns, the trend in serial killings into the 1980s is quite consistent with a more general rise in violent crime, including homicide, as well as in the resident population, strongly suggesting that the surge in serial murder is more than just an artifact of increased reporting and improved detection.

Whatever the actual increase in the prevalence of serial murder in the 1970s and 1980s, it is fairly clear that fear associated with such crimes also grew during that time. Prompted by some exaggerated media reports (e.g., Darrach & Norris, 1984), the American public was scared into believing that there was an epidemic of serial murder in the United States, totaling as many as 5,000 victims annually (for critical discussions, see Fox & Levin, 1985; Jenkins, 1988, 1994).

This grossly distorted estimate was not restricted to the popular press. Many top-notch academic researchers also accepted the 5,000-per-year benchmark, at least initially. Although he has since modified his view (Egger, 1990), in 1984, Egger first placed the annual number of serial murder victims in the 4,000 to

6,000 range. Ronald M. Holmes and James De Burger (1988) also estimated that between 3,500 and 5,000 victims were murdered each year by serial killers.

A close assessment of the reasoning behind the often-cited annual estimate of 3,500 to 5,000 victims exposes a fatal semantic flaw. Each year in the United States, there are approximately 4,000 to 5,000 homicides with unknown motive (i.e., the "unknown circumstance" code from the FBI's *Supplementary Homicide Reports,* an incident-based compilation of homicide victim and offender age, race and sex, weapon, victim–offender relationship, and circumstance). Moreover, serial murder is popularly known as "murder for no apparent motive" or "motiveless" (Ressler, Burgess, D'Agostino, & Douglas, 1984). At some juncture, "unknown motive" was wrongly equated and confused with "no motive," leading to the erroneous inference that serial murder claims 5,000 victims per year (see Fox & Levin, 1985; Jenkins, 1994). Even when the flawed reasoning was uncovered, there remained a tendency to inflate uncritically the extent of the serial murder problem. When asked how many of the 5,000 homicides with unknown motives could be the work of serial killers, Justice Department sources speculated it to be two thirds of the 5,000, or approximately 3,500 (Starr, 1984).

In contrast to the Justice Department's early estimate of thousands of victims annually, our data suggest that during the peak in the 1980s, between 1,190 and 1,760 Americans were slain by serial killers, or about 120 to 180 per year. This significant discrepancy—the FBI's thousands per year as opposed to our hundreds per year—may reflect more than just the difference between estimating and enumerating and cannot be dismissed as the mere result of definitional inconsistency or methodological dissimilarity. More likely, according to Kenna Kiger (1990) and Philip Jenkins (1994), organizational vested interests were at least partially responsible for the gross exaggeration in the "official" estimates of the prevalence of serial murder. That is, congressional approval of expenditures for FBI initiatives related to serial homicide may have depended, at least in part, on establishing a convincing case that the problem had reached alarming proportions.

The 1980s were an unusual era in terms of the serial murder phenomenon. Not only was the term itself coined at the beginning of the decade, and the prevalence of serial killing surely peaked during that time, but both fear and fascination surrounding serial killers were widespread during those years. Even as the attention from the popular media and the academic community remained strong, however, the prevalence of serial homicide appears to have diminished over the past decade or two. To a large extent, this decline parallels a sharp downturn in all forms of murder during the 1990s and is to some extent due to many of the same factors. The growth in prison populations, for example, kept many violent predators, and many potential serial killers, safely behind bars. It may also be that improved law enforcement investigative techniques—the development of DNA profiling and databases as well as interagency communication—thwarted many would-be serial killers before they amassed a large victim count and a prolonged career in killing. Similarly, other advances in technology—including Amber Alerts, sex offender registries, surveillance cameras, GPS tracking of mobile phones and vehicles, and monitoring of social media and chat rooms—have presented law enforcement with additional tools to capture predators (and serial killer wannabes) before they accumulate a significant victim count. It may also be that some cases occurring in recent years have not as yet been identified and solved, causing them to be absent from the database of known perpetrators. Finally, as society has become somewhat jaded, perhaps accustomed to seeing serial murder as a commonplace part of American culture, the more routine cases may not receive the same kind of publicity they would have in an earlier era.

There are other social and cultural changes that may have impacted the behavior of certain offenders or would-be offenders as well as would-be victims. Whereas in an earlier era when sexual predators had few outlets other than kidnapping actual victims, the Internet has provided such individuals a wide variety of options with which potentially to satiate their sadistic desires without resorting to murder. Society may frown on the level of violence in widely available pornography, but it may also serve as a release valve for certain individuals, notwithstanding the largely untestable claims that such material incites violent crime (see Ferguson & Hartley, 2009).

Technology has also provided greater safety for potential victims. Cell phones and their camera functions have added some level of protection from strangers. At the same time, the greater awareness of serial offenders has significantly increased the level of caution about accepting rides or gifts from total strangers. Decades ago, for example, hitchhiking was a common form of transportation. Nowadays, most people avoid hitching a ride unless there is absolutely no alternative.

Whatever the extent of decline during the 1990s and beyond, and whatever the reasons for it, the problem of serial murder remains a difficult and perplexing one for law enforcement and, of course, for the general public that could be victimized by these predators. Even with about 10 serial killers per year captured by the police plus an unknown number of others undetected or on the loose, the fear and suffering provoked by serial murderers is extraordinary, warranting an attempt to understand who these offenders are and why they kill.

EXTRAORDINARILY ORDINARY

The residents and business owners along Imperial Avenue had endured the fetid odor for years. Many assumed the stench emanated from Ray's Sausage Company, a Cleveland institution since 1952, situated just around the corner on East 123rd Street. In an effort to resolve the revolting problem, drain pipes were flushed and a sewer line was replaced as well. But nothing seemed to help very much.

No one in the neighborhood ever imagined that the odor was actually coming from Anthony Sowell's house that abutted Ray's, separated from the sausage producer by a mere 6 feet. No one had reason to consider the possibility that the 50-year-old man who made a living by collecting scrap metal and household junk was a sexual sadist who authorities say had raped, murdered, and buried 11 women over a period of several years—beginning as early as 2006 until his October 2009 arrest, when human remains and the cause of the long-standing stench were discovered.

The story behind the odor that plagued and perplexed the eastside Cleveland community has a familiar ring. John Wayne Gacy, who had buried 29 of his 33 victims in the crawl space of his suburban Chicago home, placated his wife's complaints about the unidentified odor by blaming the problem on sewer gases. Neighbors of Jeffrey Dahmer asked about the strange smell coming from his Milwaukee apartment but seemed satisfied with his explanation that the freezer had malfunctioned, leaving the meat and fish to rot.

The smell of decomposing bodies is supposedly unmistakable, but that presumes one has a point of reference for identifying it. No matter how often stories like these have shocked us, it remains human nature not to imagine the worst when there is a more plausible and less grisly explanation like the fumes of a sausage factory. More important than our proclivity for interpreting suspicious events as benign unless confronted with undeniable evidence to the contrary is the veneer of civility that serial killers like Dahmer and Gacy portray to others. Rather than appearing to be monsters, they are, in many respects, "extraordinarily ordinary."

With each discovery of another serial killer, the level of brutality and gore seems to sink even deeper into the abyss of inhumanity. In the 1970s, we became acquainted with the concept of serial predators in the context of the hideous rapes and murders committed by Theodore Bundy. In the 1980s, we were introduced to new and even more grotesque atrocities—a Philadelphia man who kept sex slaves shackled to a post in his basement and a gruesome twosome who operated a torture chamber at their northern California hideout. The 1990s produced even more chilling abominations, such as the crimes of Milwaukee's Jeffrey Dahmer, who cannibalized at least 17 young men, and the 2-month killing spree perpetrated by Andrew Cunanan, who took the lives of five people, including fashion designer Gianni Versace. Then, early in this century (October 2002), two buddies—John Allen Muhammad and Lee Boyd Malvo—terrified the residents of the Washington, DC, metropolitan area by shooting to death 10 innocent victims, on a random basis, over a period of 3 weeks.

Perhaps because they do not fit the popular stereotype of a crazed lunatic, serial killers who seem like the "boy next door" have become household names. But underneath the trustworthy and smooth veneer often glorified by the media lies the heart of a monster whose supreme passion is stalking his prey.

A PROFILE OF THE TYPICAL SERIAL KILLER

It certainly would be comforting if real-life serial killers acted like those in classic horror movies. If they looked like Jason from the *Friday the 13th* film series, we would be wary whenever they approached. If they were introverted loners like Norman Bates from Alfred Hitchcock's classic 1960 film *Psycho*, they could not charm their victims so easily into their deadly clutches. The frightening truth is that serial killers such as Gary Ridgway, Ted Bundy, and Jeffrey Dahmer are incredibly credible and, therefore, so very dangerous.

The problem is that serial killers just don't look or act like the strangers about whom mothers always warn their children. Even when it is known that a serial killer is on the loose, the precautions that worried citizens take may be inadequate. Many serial killers are clever and inventive. Some will pose as police officers or as stranded motorists in need of assistance. Others will answer classified newspaper ads to get into the homes of unsuspecting victims eager to sell a television set. Still others simply grab victims off the street by force, in broad daylight. If they really want to get someone, they will likely find a way.

This does not mean that all or even most serial killers are handsome and smooth super geniuses. Many people consider Ted Bundy a prototype serial killer in large part because of his attractiveness, charm, and intelligence. Although these qualities are important in understanding his keen ability to lure his victims and elude the police, Bundy is more the extreme.

At the other end of the spectrum are some serial killers who are high school dropouts and some who might even be called ugly by conventional standards. Most, however, are fairly average, at least to the casual observer. But there is one trait that tends to separate serial killers from the norm: They are exceptionally skillful in their presentation of self. Rather than coming across as evil monsters, they are able to project a nice guy image that places them beyond suspicion. This is part of the reason why they are so difficult to detect or apprehend. Baton Rouge serial killer Derrick Todd Lee, for example, stayed on the loose at least in part because he was able to blend in so well. He came across to many as friendly and charming. He cooked barbeque for friends and neighbors and led a Bible study group. Those who grew to know him certainly regarded Lee as more the preacher type than the serial killer type. Along the same lines, Ross Bartels and Ceri Parsons (2009) argue that serial killers may even have something of a Jekyll-and-Hyde personality, consisting of a good side that invites compassion and a darker side that invites terror.

Table 3.1 displays the demographic characteristics of serial killers based on our database of 660 offenders operating in the United States since 1900. Overall, 92.6% of the killers are male and 62.0% are White. Although over half the offenders first started killing before age 30, the average age at mid-career (halfway between first and last kill) was just 33.1. On the whole, the age distribution of serial murderers tends to be older than for murderers in general. It is quite rare for a teenager or young adult to have acquired an insatiable taste for murder. It is equally uncommon for such a youthful offender to have developed the level of skill and cunning needed to carry out a prolonged career of killing without being caught after one or two murders or attempted murders.

The proportion of serial killers who are Black (32.5%) is more than their representation in the population, but considerably below the substantial percentage of Blacks among single-victim killers (just over half). However, the involvement of Black serial killers may be understated proportionately as a consequence of racially disparate linkage blindness (see Jenkins, 1993). Serial murder like murder generally tends to be intraracial (i.e., Whites killing Whites and Blacks killing Blacks); serial killings of Black victims, especially those who are impoverished and marginalized politically, are less likely to be connected, prioritized for investigation, and subsequently solved. Whatever the statistics say about the number of known Black serial killers and whatever speculation there might be about a pool of cases underprioritized by investigators, without a doubt the media tends to overlook Black-on-Black serial killing sprees (Walsh, 2005).

Table 3.1   Characteristics of Serial Killers Active Since 1900 (**N** = 558)

Serial Killer Characteristic	Number	Percentage
Sex		
Male	611	92.6%
Female	49	7.4%
Total	660	100.0%
Race		
White	403	62.0%
Black	211	32.5%
Other	36	5.5%
Total	650	100.0%
Age of onset (Mean = 30.3)		
Under 20	60	10.9%
20–29	237	42.9%
30–39	169	30.6%
40–49	66	12.0%
50 and up	20	3.6%
Total	552	100.0%
Age at mid-career (Mean = 33.1)		
Under 20	23	4.2%
20–29	213	38.6%
30–39	200	36.2%
40–49	76	13.8%
50 and up	40	7.2%
Total	552	100.0%
Age at end career (Mean = 36.0)		
Under 20	18	3.3%
20–29	171	31.0%
30–39	187	33.9%
40–49	109	19.7%
50 and up	67	12.1%
Total	552	100.0%

The disproportionate involvement of males in serial homicide in part reflects, of course, their greater numbers in murder rates generally. However, according to these statistics, the gender ratio among serial killers (92.6% male) is even more pronounced than for murder generally (about 88%), a finding that is consistent with the prevailing view among most researchers that almost all serial killers are men (e.g., Holmes & De Burger, 1988).

Using a broad definition of serial killing, there are pronounced gender differences in victim preference. Male serial killers, frequently sexual predators, tend to target prostitutes, women, or young boys and girls as victims—strangers whom they can stalk, capture, control, and kill to satisfy their sadistic impulses and violent fantasies. Approximately 20% of male killers specifically target prostitutes; women and sometimes men who trade sex for money are extremely accessible to serial predators and, as a result, constitute the most common category of victims. Also, according to Kenna Quinet (2011), the percentage of serial killers who have included prostitutes among their victims has increased in recent years, from about 17% for cases between 1970 and 1989 to as high as 33% since 1990.

Female serial killers, by contrast, generally kill victims with whom they have shared some kind of relationship, often in which the victim is dependent on them. More than 70% target family members or patients of some kind. Gwendolyn Graham and Catherine Wood of Grand Rapids, Michigan, suffocated to death at least six nursing home patients under their care. At the extreme, Marybeth Tinning of Schenectady, New York, killed nine of her own children, not all at once in a murderous fit or rage, but one at a time in a cold, deliberate, and selfish attempt to win attention. More than half of the female serial killers target family members, including a number of so-called black widows, who sequentially marry and then murder several husbands to collect on their inheritances.

One of the very few female serial killers to target strangers was Aileen Wuornos, a Florida prostitute who murdered seven middle-age johns from 1989 through 1990. Erroneously labeled by the press as the "first female serial killer," Wuornos was indeed exceptional only in her victim selection and modus operandi—her style of killing closely resembled that of a male predatory killer. By contrast, female serial offenders usually murder victims they know, either in their personal lives or on the job.

Overall, the victim–offender relationship pattern is one of the most striking dissimilarities between serial murder and criminal homicide generally. Unlike single-victim murder, which commonly arises from some dispute between partners, family members, or friends (less than one quarter of solved murder cases involve strangers), serial murder typically is a stranger-perpetrated crime (see also Riedel, 1993). Among 420 serial killers from 1800 through 2004 studied by Eric W. Hickey (2010), 61% targeted strangers exclusively and another 15% killed at least one stranger among their lists of victims. The unusually large share of stranger-perpetrated crimes in serial homicide may reflect more than just the killer's tendencies for victim selection. A more practical issue related to apprehension may also be involved. Because acquaintance crimes are far easier to solve, those killers who target victims known to them are less likely to remain at large long enough to accumulate a victim count that satisfies the definition of serial murder.

Table 3.2   Estimated Victim Count and Career Length Distribution of Serial Killers

Characteristics of Killing Sprees		Number	Percentage
Victim count per killer/team (Mean = 6.6)			
	Up to 5	245	41.4%
	6–10	261	44.1%
	11–15	56	9.5%
	16–20	14	2.4%
	20+	16	2.7%
	Total	592	100.0%
Career length per killer/team (Mean = 6.8)			
	< 2 yrs	247	41.7%
	2 – 9 yrs	190	32.1%
	10 – 19 yrs	109	18.4%
	20+ yrs	46	7.8%
	Total	592	100.0%
Victim selection (N = 592)			
	Single type	285	48.1%
	Adult males only	68	11.5%
	Adult females only	193	32.6%
	Young males only	6	1.0%
	Young females only	6	1.0%
	Children only	12	2.0%
	Multiple types	307	51.9%
	Some adult males	299	50.5%
	Some adult females	482	81.4%
	Some young males	36	6.1%
	Some young females	66	11.1%
	Some children	53	9.0%

Characteristics of Killing Sprees		Number	Percentage
Weapon use (N = 570)			
	Single weapon type	359	63.0%
	Multiple weapons	211	37.0%
	Firearm	222	38.9%
	Firearm only	137	24.0%
	Knife	176	30.9%
	Knife only	60	10.5%
	Brute force	118	20.7%
	Brute force only	33	5.8%
	Strangulation	220	38.6%
	Strangulation only	129	22.6%

Note: Cases represent lone killers or teams.

Table 3.2 displays estimated victim count and career length distributions for the 592 individual or team serial killers. Nearly 60% of the killers or teams accumulated more than five victims, and about 15% murdered more than 10 victims. Overall, these serial killers or teams murdered an average of 6.6 victims, based on best available estimates. In terms of longevity from first to last homicide, almost 60% stayed at large for at least 2 years, and one quarter remained active for more than a decade. The average career length stood at 6.8 years.

Table 3.2 also displays patterns of victim and weapon selection for the 592 individuals or teams of killers. For age groups, adult victims are those age 17 over, while young adult are ages 10 through 16. Nearly half of the offenders restricted their victim selection to one particular age or gender group, with about one third targeting adult females exclusively. For the perpetrators who varied their targets at least to some extent, adult females were included among their victims in the vast majority of instances. Weapon specialization was somewhat more common than singularity of victim type. Nearly two thirds of the perpetrators or teams killed all their victims in the same way. Overall, when taking into account all weapons used, firearms and strangulation were the most common, with knives not very far behind. It is noteworthy, however, that firearms are far less prevalent in serial murder than in homicide cases generally (where guns are used in over 60% of the cases).

Another well-studied pattern of serial murder is its geographic location (see Rossmo, 1996). In the modern mythology of serial murder, the killer is characterized as a nomad whose compulsion to kill carries him hundreds of thousands

Table 3.3   Patterns of Serial Killing by Location

Geographic Characteristic	Number	Percentage
Location type		
Local	400	67.6%
Regional	54	22.0%
National	130	9.1%
International	8	1.4%
Total	592	100.0%
Region		
East	76	12.8%
Midwest	132	22.4%
South	213	36.0%
West	171	28.9%
Total	592	100.0%
State		
California	87	14.7%
Texas	42	7.1%
Florida	42	7.0%
New York	37	6.2%
Illinois	30	5.1%
Ohio	26	4.4%
Michigan	22	3.7%
Georgia	19	3.3%
Washington	19	3.1%
Rest of U.S.	268	45.4%
Total	592	100.0%

of miles a year as he drifts from state to state and region to region, leaving scores of victims in his wake. This may be true of some well-known and well-traveled killers such as Theodore Bundy, Andrew Cunanan, and Henry Lee Lucas, but not for the majority. John Wayne Gacy, for example, killed all of his 33 young male victims at his home in Des Plaines, Illinois, conveniently burying most of them there as well. Gacy, like Milwaukee's Jeffrey Dahmer, Kansas City's Robert Berdella, and Long Island's Joel Rifkin, operated within driving distance of home. Moreover, most serial killers are not the recluses that movies often portray them to be. They typically have jobs and families, go to church on Sunday, and kill part time—indeed, whenever they have some free time to kill.

In an analysis of German serial murder cases, Harald Dern, Roland Frönd, Ursula Straub, Jens Vick, and Rainer Witt (2004) found that most of the perpetrators lived no further than 10 kilometers from the location of their crimes. Similarly, Brent Snook, Richard M. Cullen, Andreas Mokros, and Stephen Harbort (2005) reported that serial killers in Germany typically dispose of their victims within 8 to 30 kilometers of their homes, although more intelligent offenders are apt to stray further.

According to Hickey's (2010) data, 11% of the killers operating from 1975 through 2004 operated in a specific location (e.g., at their home or workplace), and another 61% confined their murder sprees to the same general location or area (e.g., a city or state). Only 28% traveled wide distances, in a nomadic fashion, to commit their crimes.

Our data on 592 serial killers or teams reflect a similar pattern. As shown in Table 3.3, two thirds (67.6%) localized their killing within a particular city or state. Not surprisingly, the largest states (California, Texas, Florida, and New York) had the greatest extent of serial killer activity. In addition to the localized killers, another 22.0% killed within the same general region of the country, with the Southern region home to 36.0% of the activity. In contrast to the local or regional killing sprees, only slightly more than 1 in 10 serial murderers traveled long distances—region to region, coast to coast, or even outside the United States—in search of their prey. The prevalence of mobile serial killers may be especially attenuated, however, as a result of linkage blindness. That is, law enforcement authorities are less likely to identify connections between homicides that are widely dispersed and cross jurisdictional lines (Egger, 1984, 1990).

Whether road warriors or stay-at-home predators, serial killers develop a certain level of comfort with regard to murder. With cool deliberation, they murder with great ease in order to satisfy a variety of urges and needs at the expense of us all.

CHAPTER 4

*With Deliberation
and Purpose*

Carol DaRonch felt fortunate to have struggled free from the light blue Volkswagen of her abductor, but she had no idea just how lucky she was. Not until almost 5 years after her 1974 kidnapping, when she journeyed from her home in Utah to testify in a Florida court at the sentencing hearing of Theodore Robert Bundy, did she acknowledge the full murderous potential of the man who was suspected of killing dozens of women in four states and who had tried to kill her.

Carol was young, unusually pretty, shy, and very naive. She was a small-town girl, had just graduated from high school, and was working as an operator for Mountain Bell. On a Friday evening, November 8, 1974, Carol drove her Camaro to the Fashion Place Mall in Murray, Utah, to shop for a birthday gift for her cousin. While browsing in Walden's Bookstore, she was approached by a handsome stranger dressed in a sports jacket, green slacks, and patent leather shoes. He identified himself as "Officer Roseland" of the police department. Officer Roseland told Carol that there had been an attempted burglary of a car in the parking lot and that the car might have been hers. After she revealed her plate number, the officer asked Carol to accompany him to check her vehicle.

Carol didn't think immediately of how strange it was that he knew where to find her within the mall. Not only was she generally trusting, but her strong family upbringing in the Mormon faith had taught her to respect and obey authority. So Carol went with the officer to her car to check for any stolen articles. When it was clear that the car was undisturbed, he asked Carol to continue on with him to the police substation at the mall. She hesitated and asked to see the officer's identification. Officer Roseland responded by stealthily flashing his counterfeit gold shield; Carol did not question his identity further. The substation door, which in reality was the rear of a laundromat, was locked, so he then requested her to go with him in his car to the central police station. Carol thought how unlikely his beat-up Volkswagen bug seemed as a police vehicle, but then she recalled TV undercover cops like Starsky and Hutch and the Mod Squad and the offbeat cars that they drove. Coaxed by his commanding manner, she went along for the ride.

Appearances can change quickly. Officer Roseland turned out of the parking lot in the direction opposite that of the police station. When Carol refused his order to fasten her seat belt, his demeanor turned suddenly to rage. This was too unbelievable, even for Carol. When the man pulled over and attempted to handcuff her, she lurched from the car, kicking her abductor. He attacked her with a crowbar, but miraculously she was able to muster enough strength to deflect his swing before it crushed her skull. Finally, she ran, hobbling on one shoe, to the safety of a passing motorist. Mary Walsh, who was out riding with her husband that rainy evening, would later testify in court about the girl they rescued: "I have never seen a human being that frightened in my life. She was trembling and crying and weak, as if she was going to faint" (Michaud & Aynesworth, 1983, p. 95).

Like Carol DaRonch, dozens of other girls trusted and believed the man who would become well-known through a nationally televised trial. A bright student who was respected in Seattle's Republican ranks, Ted Bundy was a likeable and engaging fellow. His many victims were lured into his bloody net by his reassuring tone, which he had polished while working the hotline at Seattle's Crisis Clinic. But while the others were bludgeoned, strangled, sexually molested, and buried, Carol DaRonch survived, most probably the only one to escape the clutches of Bundy until his bungled assault on the Chi Omega Sorority at Florida State University in 1978.

WHEN KILLING IS THRILLING

Serial murder has been labeled "murder for no apparent motive" (see Ressler, Burgess, & Douglas, 1988). Whether it is apparent or not, serial killers generally do not strike without reason or purpose, although their motivations may be difficult for many to fathom. We can comprehend many forms of homicide, such as killings provoked by jealousy or those that are purely committed out of greed, but killing for pleasure or thrill is incomprehensible for most people.

In Chapter 2, we identified five types of motivation for multiple murder, including serial killing. Serial murderers usually kill not for love, profit, terror, or revenge, but instead for the fun of it; approximately two thirds of the murderers in our database of serial killers were motivated by the thrill of power or sexual sadism. Like Danny Rolling, they enjoy the excitement, the sexual satisfaction, and the dominance and power that they achieve over the lives of their victims. Not only do they savor the act of murder itself, but they also rejoice as their victims scream and beg for mercy. Like Leonard Lake and Charles Ng, the buddies who tortured and killed dozens of people in Calaveras County, California, in 1985, some serial killers record on video or audiotape their victims' worst moments of terror for the purpose of later entertainment and celebration. Like Joel Rifkin, the Long Island man who murdered 17 prostitutes in 1993, they often keep souvenirs or trophies—their victims' jewelry, underwear, even body parts—to remind them of the good times they experienced while killing.

Andrei Chikatilo of Russia, serial killer extraordinaire, arguably was more power hungry and control minded than Lake and Ng put together. During a

12-year period of time from 1978 to 1990, Chikatilo killed, dismembered, and occasionally devoured 21 boys, 14 girls, and 18 women in and around Rostov while he worked as an office clerk and part-time teacher. The 54-year-old father of two didn't particularly care about the age or gender of his prey, so long as they were naive and willing to follow him to some secluded area from a bus or rail station, cafe, or other public meeting place. Some of his victims were too young to know better, and others were intellectually challenged or homeless drifters, but many of those whom Chikatilo destroyed were bright youngsters from middle-class families.

What all his victims shared in common was a trusting nature. Any twinge of caution that they may have felt dissolved easily because of the killer's kind and

Photo 4.1 Russian serial killer Andrei Chikatilo, posing for photographers from his prison cell, seemed to fit the common "madman" stereotype. (Associated Press)

assuring manner, what Chikatilo himself termed his "magnetic personality." Once he had them alone, however, his demeanor would change instantly and dramatically. "I was like a crazed wolf," explained the predator. "I just turned into a beast, a wild animal" (Goldberg, 1992, p. 1). Sometimes he tore out and ate their hearts, lips, or tongues; sometimes he cut off their fingers or removed their eyes or genitals—whatever suited his passion at the moment.

Chikatilo's sexual problems were long standing, dating back years before his first murder. Although he did manage to father two children, he was chronically impotent. He found some degree of pleasure and comfort from molesting young boys and girls. This was nothing, however, like the arousal he discovered when he first committed murder, after abducting a 9-year-old girl. He soon learned what pleased him, what atrocities made him feel whole. "When I used my knife," he explained, "it brought psychological relief" (Goldberg, 1992, p. 1).

The thrill-oriented killer hardly ever uses a firearm (Hazelwood & Douglas, 1980). According to Eric W. Hickey's (2010) data, only 18% of male and 8% of female serial killers murder exclusively with a firearm, although others sometimes use a gun as a secondary weapon to intimidate and control their victims. Hickey's figures, moreover, include profit-motivated crimes, in which a firearm frequently is the weapon of choice. In control-motivated cases, by contrast, a gun would only rob the killer of his greatest pleasure: exalting in his victim's suffering and misery. He enjoys the whole experience of murder—of squeezing from his victim's body the last breath of life. Among a sample of 20 serial killers motivated by sexual sadism, only one killed with a gun, compared to six who used a knife and 12 who strangled their victims (Warren, Hazelwood, & Dietz, 1996).

Psychiatrists have focused on the deeper psychological meaning of the firearm in the act of homicide. Freudian psychiatrist David Abrahamsen (1973) suggested that "sexual elements are always involved in the violent act" (p. 11). He illustrated his claim with the case of a serial killer for whom he saw the gunshot as a "symbolic substitute for ejaculation" (p. 11). As intriguing as the gun as a phallic symbol may be, this weapon probably is more instrumental than expressive, preferred by some criminals for its effectiveness rather than for its symbolism. Among serial killers who are sexually inspired, the use of a gun is, in fact, remarkably uncommon. They sometimes sodomize their victims with bottles or vegetables, but hardly ever with the barrel of a gun.

A sexual sadist derives pleasure through inflicting physical or psychological suffering, including humiliation, upon another human being (American Psychiatric Association, 1994). Robert R. Hazelwood, Janet I. Warren, and Park Elliott Dietz (1993) argued that the essence of the sadistic drive lies in the desire to achieve total domination and mastery over another person. From this point of view, the pleasure derived from killing depends, at least in part, on the sadist's role in having caused the victim to suffer. According to a related view (Hazelwood, Dietz, & Warren, 1992), however, the sexual or psychological pleasure that a sadistic killer derives from the act of torturing his victim may be more a result of observing the victim's agony than from the actual infliction of pain. This hypothesis appears to be supported by experimental research in which aggressive sex offenders become sexually aroused when shown simulated scenes of men inflicting pain against women (e.g., Fedora, Reddon, & Morrison, 1992). This begs the question, however, of whether the arousal stems from observing the victim's suffering or from identifying vicariously with the aggressor.

Regardless of whether the critical component is the stimulus (the direct infliction of pain) or the response (the victim's suffering itself), the fundamental objective in the actions of the sadistic serial killer is to achieve complete mastery over his victims. In other words, humiliation, enslavement, and terror are vehicles for attaining total domination over another human being.

A sexual sadist was responsible for a string of brutal slayings in the Baton Rouge, Louisiana, area. The first victim, 41-year-old Gina Wilson Green, was discovered in September 2001, strangled to death in her home on Stratford Avenue near the campus of Louisiana State University (LSU). In January 2002, 21-year-old Geralyn Barr DeSoto was murdered in the bedroom of her mobile home off of Louisiana Route 1 South in Addis. The killer had badly beaten DeSoto at knifepoint and slit her throat. At the end of May 2002, 22-year-old Charlotte Murray Pace, a recent business school graduate of LSU, was stabbed to death in her townhouse. In July 2002, the body of 44-year-old Pam Kinamore was found by a Louisiana surveying crew off Route 10, under the Whiskey Bay Bridge. Her throat had been slashed. Kinamore had been abducted from her Briarwood Place home. Later that month, a stranger forced his way into the home of a Breaux Bridge nurse, Diane Alexander, where he repeatedly beat her. Before he could rape and kill Alexander, however, her son returned home and frightened off the assailant.

An analysis of DNA left at each of the crime scenes indicated that the same person was responsible. News of a serial killer in Baton Rouge, announced during the summer of 2002, caused panic to spread throughout the area. Feeling vulnerable, many women bought pepper spray, signed up for self-defense training, and started to jog in pairs. When months passed without another incident, however, and news of the serial killings receded from the headlines, women in the area began to relax a bit, hoping that the attacks had ended.

Then, in November, just before Thanksgiving, another murder rocked the community. A hunter found the badly beaten body of 23-year-old Trineisha Dene Colomb, along with her abandoned Mazda, in a wooded area on a rural road in the nearby town of Scott, some 30 miles outside Baton Rouge.

Investigators were taken aback when the DNA analysis connected Colomb's killing to the other murders. The earlier victims linked to the killer were White women who resided in the city of Baton Rouge; Colomb was a Black woman who lived nearly an hour away. The killer apparently had broadened his comfort zone well beyond racial and community boundaries. The killer's sixth victim was Carrie Yoder, a 26-year-old graduate student at LSU whose body was found in March 2003, dumped near the Whiskey Bay Bridge, the same vicinity in which Pam Kinamore's remains were discovered.

Recognizing the presence of a serial killer in their midst caused police investigators to go back in their files to an unsolved murder case from 5 years earlier. In April 1998, 28-year-old Randi Mebruer was brutally slain in her home north of Baton Rouge. A neighbor discovered the grisly crime scene after he noticed Mebruer's 3-year-old son playing outside and walked into the house, looking for the child's mother. Although Mebruer's body was never found, the police were able to isolate the killer's DNA among clues found at the crime scene.

Just prior to the discovery that Colomb's murder was linked to the earlier slaying, the FBI had constructed a behavioral profile of the killer. The profile suggested that he was a White male between the ages of 25 and 35, physically strong, awkward around women, in some financial trouble, living with others, seen as harmless by his associates, arrested for minor offenses, and lacking in empathy.

The FBI profilers were right on some characteristics but very much wrong on others. The killer whose DNA was connected to all the crime scenes turned out to be a 34-year-old Black male who lived in the Baton Rouge area with his wife and children; he had a record of minor offenses (property damage, stalking, voyeurism, and family neglect), was deeply in debt, was characterized by some of his associates as a decent guy, was a construction worker who regularly lifted weights, was a charmer with women, and was lacking in empathy. Indeed, when he was forced to leave Diane Alexander without raping and killing her, he had just enough time to stomp hard on her abdomen, inflicting severe pain.

On the evening of March 27, 2003, Derrick Todd Lee was nabbed by police officers outside an Atlanta tire store and arrested for the string of Baton Rouge murders. The police had twice just missed cornering him after receiving tips from the public, first tracking him to a homeless shelter and later to a run-down hotel. They finally found Lee at Green's Tire Shop in the western part of Atlanta.

The serial killer surrendered peacefully, to be extradited back to Louisiana, where he would stand trial for the seven murders.

For some thrill killers, the need for dominance is not necessarily expressed through sexual sadism. A number of murders have been committed by hospital caretakers who seek to "play God"—who exploit their sickly patients to feel the exhilaration of making life-and-death decisions. For example, registered nurse Richard Angelo was arrested in 1987 and later convicted for poisoning a number of patients in a West Islip, Long Island, hospital. Because of a burning desire to be recognized as a hero, he purposely poisoned his patients, then attempted to "save" their lives. Sometimes he succeeded, but not always.

Although not in official caretaker roles, a few serial killers find satisfaction by making healthy human beings into totally dependent pets or sex toys. Milwaukee's Jeffrey Dahmer, for example, expressed his need to control others by attempting literally to lobotomize his victims into submission. He was not interested in inflicting pain and suffering; he sedated his victims before performing surgery on them. His ultimate purpose was not sexual sadism but sexual ownership.

As another expression of their need for power and their quest for attention, thrill-motivated serial killers, as described earlier, often crave the publicity given to their crimes. It is not just the celebrity status that they enjoy; more important to them, they are able to control the lives of thousands of area residents who are held in their grip of terror. These killers do not always specifically turn to homicide as an attention-getting move, but the media hype is a powerful fringe benefit that many of them enjoy. Some might even exaggerate the scope of their crimes to attract television cameras and front-page news coverage.

ON A DEADLY MISSION OF TERROR OR REVENGE

Although most pursue their victims for the thrill, some serial murderers are motivated instead by a strong urge to further a social, political, or religious cause. In effect, they are committing an act of terrorism—using extreme violence as a vehicle for change. For others, the mission is to seek revenge against particular groups or all of humanity through a series of attacks.

In either case, this kind of serial killer is on a mission to rid the world of filth and evil. His moral crusade motivates the killer to target marginal groups, such as prostitutes, gays, or the homeless, who he believes to be destroying the moral fiber of our country. In a profoundly warped sense of good and evil, he views his killing spree as "self-defense."

From 1981 to 1987, for example, at least a half-dozen members of a cult known as the Temple of Love, based in Miami, conspired to kill "White devils" in retaliation for the oppression of Blacks. Their Black-separatist leader, Yahweh Ben Yahweh (the name translated from Hebrew as "God, Son of God") sermonized that all Whites were "demons and serpents." The Temple's "entry fee" required that new members murder a White devil and then produce a severed ear as proof. In the name of racial justice, Temple members savagely murdered eight homeless vagrants, who probably had no idea that they were chosen for slaughter strictly because of the color of their skin.

As a result of severe mental illness, other "mission" killers actually see their victims as "devils." In their delusions, they believe that they must extinguish the lives of their victims for the good of the world. Their inspiration to kill is not religious or political fanaticism, but psychosis. They hear the voice of the devil or God instructing them to kill. Driven by these delusions, they tend to be psychotic, confused, and disorganized.

In 1972 and 1973, for example, Herbert Mullin of Santa Cruz, California, killed 13 people over a span of 4 months in order to avert an earthquake—or at least that's what the voices in his head told him. He had been raised in an oppressively religious home, and his crimes had decidedly religious overtones. Mullin believed that he was obeying God's "commandment" to make human sacrifices for the greater good of humanity.

Mullin's severe psychological problems began in late adolescence, a point in life when schizophrenia characteristically surfaces. He was institutionalized on several occasions, diagnosed as a paranoid schizophrenic. The same voices that told him to kill had previously commanded him to shave his head and to burn his penis with a cigarette—orders that he also dutifully obeyed. While hospitalized, Mullin wrote dozens of letters to strangers, signing them, "A human sacrifice, Herb Mullin."

Few serial killers have motivations that, like Mullin's, arise out of a psychotic illness. Many more mentally ill individuals may repeatedly have thoughts that compel them to commit murder, but most lack the clearheaded state of mind needed to carry out the act. Cleo Green, a 26-year-old from Louisville, Kentucky, had the ambition but not the wherewithal to become a serial killer. During the summer of 1984, he assaulted four elderly women, inflicting multiple stab wounds to their necks and throats. Each attack gave him temporary relief from the "red demon" that inhabited his body and unmercifully tortured his soul. In one case, Green was able to succeed in taking a life, but only after stabbing his victim 200 times and decapitating her. On other occasions, he was simply too out of touch to complete the act of murder (Holmes & De Burger, 1988).

The distinction between fanaticism and severe mental illness is significant but not always obvious. Both are motivated by a righteous mission—to eliminate evil. The fanatic responds in a seemingly logical, though depraved, manner to an actual person (a charismatic leader) or a genuine social problem (for example, racism, homelessness, or prostitution), whereas the psychotic responds to hallucinations, delusions, and imaginary voices.

In 1969, members of the Charles Manson family slaughtered seven wealthy residents of Beverly Hills in two separate incidents and may have been responsible for other murders as well. Their motivation was symbolized by the hideous graffiti, such as "Death to Pigs," that the killers scrawled on walls, using the blood of their victims. A form of domestic terrorism, the murders and their excessive brutality were a critical part of Manson's grand scheme. According to his plan, the savage murders of affluent suburbanites would, at a time of racial unrest, inflame racial tensions and be blamed on radical Blacks. This would help to precipitate an all-out race war, which ultimately would be won by the Blacks. In the meantime, Manson had moved his commune out to the desert, where its members would be sheltered from the impending conflict. Manson reasoned

Photo 4.2 From a cabin in a remote area of Montana, Unabomber Theodore Kaczynski composed the 35,000-word manifesto that was ultimately published, upon threat of violence, in the Washington Post. (Associated Press/Elaine Thompson)

that the victors would be ineffective in leading the new world and would be forced to call on him from his hideout to take over the reins of authority.

Manson's mission sounds as crazy today as it did in 1969, but it was grounded in a certain reality of the times—the flower children, the generation gap, the antiestablishment spirit, the antiwar movement, civil rights demonstrations, and the rise of radical groups such as the Black Panthers and Students for a Democratic Society. Even given this social and political context, Manson's response was absurdly extreme and fanatical, but not psychotic. Like thousands of small-time political rebels around the world who have attempted unsuccessfully to overthrow their governments, Manson responded to social discontent in the streets rather than to imaginary voices in his head.

The bombing offensive committed by the Unabomber, Theodore Kaczynski, represents one of the most deadly examples of domestic terrorism committed by a single individual. Not only was the Harvard-educated mathematician alone when he perpetrated his 18-year killing spree, but he also was, in general, a loner who despised high-tech society and, to communicate his message of destruction, decided to blow it up through the mail. Injuring 23 people and killing three more was as close as he came. The Unabomber had spent his days in an out-of-the-way Montana cabin, constructing mail bombs to be sent to his "enemies" and typing his 35,000-word manifesto, in which he railed against the evils of postmodern, technology-dependent America. In a perverted case of "publish or perish," Kaczynski threatened to continue his campaign of terror unless his manifesto was published in its entirety by one of the nation's leading newspapers. The *Washington Post* complied.

KILLING FOR EXPEDIENCY

In our database of serial murderers operating in the United States since 1900, about 20% have killed for the sake of expediency or profit. In 1992, for example, a series of murder–robberies occurred in mom-and-pop convenience stores throughout the Midwest. After taking the money from the cash register, the robbers would attempt to protect their identities by shooting their victims in the head, leaving no witnesses.

The important distinction between the thrill killer and the profit-motivated killer can be seen in the style of murder. Whereas the thrill killer eliminates his witness in the most brutal manner possible, the profit-oriented serial killer almost always uses a gun. The former enjoys the killing, whereas the latter just feels that it is necessary.

In 1989 and 1990, 35-year-old prostitute Aileen Wuornos perpetrated a 13-month serial-killing spree along Florida's highways. Her motive: greed. Typically, she would be picked up by a stranger, have sex with him, ask for payment, shoot him several times, take his money, and then dump his body. After being found guilty of first-degree murder, Wuornos whispered in the direction of the jurors as they filed out of the courtroom, "I am innocent . . . I was raped." In her view, it was absolutely essential to kill each and every one of her seven victims—men whom she felt had "threatened" her—for her to stay in business. Given the constant danger under which she operated as a highway hooker, Wuornos saw killing a few violent johns as self-defense. Of course, most people would get out of the business rather than shoot seven customers in self-defense, and that's why the jury found her guilty.

Although her premise was reprehensible, Wuornos's way of thinking is not unlike that of a liquor store proprietor in a crime-ridden neighborhood who decides to keep a gun under the counter. Rather than closing the store, he reasons that he might have to shoot some intruders. The key difference between the proprietor and Wuornos is, of course, that selling alcohol is a legitimate business, but selling sex is not.

Aileen Wuornos was not the first female serial killer, as the press often made her out to be. In 1985, Betty Lou Beets was sentenced to death for murdering her fifth husband, a Dallas firefighter, in order to collect on his $100,000 insurance policy. Suspected of foul play in the mysterious deaths of her former spouses, she was charged with murder when the body of her "missing" fourth husband was discovered buried in the backyard.

Although Wuornos is far from alone in the annals of female serial killers, she is distinctive. Unlike other women who killed repeatedly, she targeted perfect strangers rather than family members or acquaintances. Also unusual was the fact that her victims were exclusively middle-age males who were out for a good time.

Even though almost anyone is at some risk of victimization, serial killers tend to prey on the most vulnerable targets—prostitutes, drug users, skid-row alcoholics, homeless vagrants, hitchhikers, runaways, and children, as well as elderly hospital patients. Part of their vulnerability concerns the ease with which these classes of victims can be abducted or overtaken. As a result of physical stature or disability, many children and elders are not able to defend themselves against a sudden attack by a 200-pound killer. Hitchhikers and prostitutes become vulnerable as soon as they step into the killer's car or van; hospital and nursing home patients are vulnerable because of their total dependence on caretakers.

The vulnerability of the elderly is shown dramatically in the case of a 64-year-old Sacramento landlady, Dorothea Montalvo Puente. Her victims, because of their advanced age and relative poverty, had nowhere else to go and no one else to take care of them. And "take care of them" she did. In 1988, Puente was arrested and charged with killing nine of her boarders and then stealing checks sent to them by the government.

Looking more like a grandmother than a grand larcenist, the white-haired, diminutive landlady argued in her defense that her tenants had died of natural causes or of suicide. She admitted having taken the boarders' money after they perished. She also admitted having buried most of their bodies in the yard of her ramshackle Victorian house. But she had nothing to do with their deaths, she insisted.

Puente even had an excuse for failing to report the deaths to the authorities: She was on parole following a 1982 conviction for drugging and robbing two elderly tenants. As a condition of her parole, she was prohibited from taking in any boarders. Informing the police of the deaths would have jeopardized her freedom. After all, she reasoned, she was only protecting herself through her silence.

In 1988, the silence was broken. A social worker became suspicious when she discovered that her client, Alviro Montoya, had been missing for 3 months, yet her Social Security checks were being cashed. Based on this lead, the Sacramento police went to Puente's F Street boardinghouse and were immediately alarmed by a nauseating stench emanating from the backyard. As the police started digging for evidence, Puente skipped town, only to be arrested several days later in a hotel on Los Angeles's skid row.

The prosecution argued that Puente had deliberately poisoned her elderly roomers so that she could cash their Social Security checks and then had buried the bodies to conceal the crime. Over a 3-year period, Puente collected $75,000 from her deadly scam.

Puente's transgressions were more than crimes of opportunity, the prosecution claimed. Puente had aggressively recruited her victims. On parole following her 1982 robbery conviction, she was able to convince a social worker, notwithstanding the restriction otherwise related to her parole, that she was equipped to care for 19 senior citizens living on fixed incomes. As it turned out, many of these elderly men and women instead died on fixed incomes.

Puente counted on the inefficiency of social services agencies, and she was right. The lack of coordination among agencies that dealt with indigent elders enabled her to kill a large number of people without being detected for years.

Puente's first victim was initially thought to have committed suicide by an overdose of codeine; her body was found in Puente's boardinghouse. The body of the second victim, a former boyfriend of Puente, was discovered floating in a wooden box downriver. Seven bodies, in varying stages of decomposition, were found buried in Puente's yard.

Deliberating a record 24 days, the jury returned a conviction on three of the nine counts of murder. Because of the length of time that many of the victims had been buried, physical evidence was sparse. Although traces of a sedative were found in all of the bodies, the cause of death—drug overdose—could be established in only one case. Regardless, the three convictions were sufficient to earn Puente a life sentence.

FOR LOVE AND LOYALTY

Ironically, at least a few serial murders have been committed out of a perverted sense of love or loyalty. The slayings in the Alpine Manor Nursing Home near Grand Rapids, Michigan, involved not one but two female perpetrators. One of them was 26-year-old Catherine May Wood, who would do anything for her new lover, a fellow nurse's aide. Catherine had left her husband, Kenneth, and her 6-year-old daughter to be with Gwendolyn Graham, a 25-year-old lesbian from Tyler, Texas.

One evening in October 1987, Catherine went to Ken to reveal her deep, dark secret. He was just getting used to the idea that his former wife, the mother of his child, was gay. What other bombshell was she going to drop now, he wondered. Was she sick? Had she lost her job? He never imagined that Cathy would confess that she and Gwen had killed several elderly patients in the nursing home where they worked.

Thinking that her story was nothing more than a wild tale, Ken figured that Catherine was stressed out and needed a vacation, so he took her to Las Vegas rather than to the police station. Over the next 14 months, however, it became increasingly difficult for Ken to deny that his former wife was a killer.

Catherine described how she stood at the door as a lookout while her girlfriend, Gwen, forcefully smothered each elderly patient with a washcloth over the victim's nose and mouth. Their victims were chosen because of their frail state—each candidate for death was tested first by holding her nose, to see if she resisted. After their first two victims—Marguerite Chambers and Edith Cook—the partners in killing discussed the idea of spelling out the word *MURDER* with the initials of their victims' given names. Having difficulty finding a *U*—one candidate whose first name was Ursula was too strong to be targeted for a premature grave—they abandoned their perverse anagram.

Graham and Wood killed for fun—for emotional release. They also did it for loyalty and love. According to Catherine, murder would be the special secret she shared with Gwen—a lover's pact to bind them together and seal their relationship forever.

When the news of the murders hit the newspapers, relatives of the victims were incredulous. They would rather have believed that their mothers had died peacefully in their sleep than violently through foul play. Linda Engman, whose 79-year-old mother had, according to the death certificate, died of cardiac arrest, gave a typical response. "There's no evidence," she insisted (Chandler & Mathews, 1988, p. 3A).

Kenneth Wood and the relatives of the slain victims had their own reasons for choosing to deny that wrongdoing had occurred, but so did the killers. On a psychological level, Graham and Wood weren't killing human beings—they were killing "vegetables." They targeted only the weakest of the weak, those who were on the verge of death anyway. In one case, in fact, they even convinced themselves that they were angels of mercy who ended the misery of a woman suffering from gangrene.

Whether they admitted it or not, Graham and Wood's decision to kill the infirm had practical advantages. Not only were their sick and elderly victims easy to overpower, but the normalcy of death in a nursing home setting also would lessen the chance that anyone would become suspicious. Similarly, Dorothea Puente targeted indigent elders over whom she had some control, and she expected to escape the attention of authorities. As we discuss later, the modus operandi of many repeat killers includes deliberate decisions about where, when, and whom to kill in order to evade apprehension.

CHAPTER 5

Murder Without Guilt

The gruesome discovery in June 1985 of the vicious crimes of 39-year-old Leonard Lake and 24-year-old Charles Ng left residents of northern California shaking their heads. For the San Francisco police, the afternoon of June 2 began routinely enough. They were called by the owner of South City Lumber when he observed Ng stealing a vise from the store. Arriving at the scene, the police witnessed the young thief depositing goods in the trunk of his buddy's car. Before they could reach him, Ng ran off, leaving Lake holding the bag. In Lake's trunk, alongside the stolen vise, the police found an illegal .22-caliber automatic pistol equipped with a silencer.

Leonard Lake was arrested and taken to the police station for questioning. During the interrogation, he asked for some water with which to take an "aspirin." Almost immediately, he slumped over, appearing to have suffered a heart attack. Instead, he was suffering the lethal effects of a cyanide pill that he had ingested.

The investigation of the bizarre suicide of their suspect led the San Francisco Police to Leonard Lake's small ranch near Wilseyville, about 150 miles northeast of the Bay Area in Calaveras County. *Calaveras* is Spanish for "skull", but the police found much more than skulls when they arrived at Lake's two-bedroom bungalow, down Blue Mountain Road.

It did not take investigators long to realize that the ranch was not so much a rural retreat as it was a torture chamber. They found hooks and chains, as well as photographs on the walls of women in various poses of submission. Backdrops to the "artwork" indicated that the photos had been taken from inside the ranch itself. The police also found a well-stocked library of homemade snuff films in which real-life murder victims were captured on tape. Viewing the movies on the living room television, the police replayed gut-wrenching scenes of victims being raped, tortured, and murdered by the directors—Leonard Lake and Charles Ng. One chained-up woman had been filmed as she pleaded on behalf of her child, who was being tortured in front of her eyes. Another woman, while tied naked to a chair, was shown being told by Lake, "You'll wash for us, clean for us, fuck for us." Outside the house, the police found the killers' refuse—large garbage bags filled with human bones, somewhere between two and four dozen people's worth.

Unlike most serial killers who prefer certain kinds of victims, Lake and Ng showed no favorites. They killed acquaintances and strangers, men and women, children and adults, and people of all races. They abducted their captives in equally diverse ways. One man was kidnapped from his home when Lake and Ng answered a classified ad for a camcorder he was selling—the same one they later used to produce their torture films. In another instance, they snatched two young lovers who were camping in the woods.

In part, Lake and Ng were motivated by a ghoulish desire for sexual sadism. The torture tapes revealed the vicious rapes that the gruesome twosome perpetrated against their defenseless victims. The murders were also part of a power game—a team sport—in which the two players set loose some of their victims into the woods, only to hunt them down as if they were wild animals. The police found, at the hideout, an inscription bearing the killers' creed: "If you love something, set it free. If it doesn't come back, hunt it down and kill it."

Lake and Ng also were inspired by their survivalist theory that a nuclear war would soon destroy the world. At their ranch, they built a concrete bunker to shelter them from the impending apocalypse, and they planned to stock it with sex slaves who would keep them entertained and later bear the children of the new world.

SELF-CONTROL AND SOCIAL CONTROL

According to the father of psychoanalysis, Sigmund Freud, the internalized representative of society's cherished values, which he called the superego, develops in children only when they come to identify with their parents and decide to imitate their parents' moral behavior. Before the age of 5 or 6, children instead follow rules and avoid harming others in order to gain material rewards (cookies and candy) and avoid punishment (a spanking or reprimand) as administered by adults. If the process of identification is effective, then the child develops a superego. He or she no longer acts in a moral or ethical manner only for the sake of securing external rewards and avoiding external punishments, but in order to feel proud (the ego ideal) and escape feeling guilty (the conscience). The presence of a superego assures that individuals will grow up having enough self-control to refrain from committing acts of extreme violence, including serial murder, even if they feel capable of avoiding punishment by the state.

Control theory recognizes the importance of individuals developing self-restraint. Those who internalize a strong sense of morality and ethical standards—that is, a superego—grow up with a distaste for doing harm to others. But control theory also takes account of the fact that not everyone's moral sense prevents them from committing acts of extreme violence.

Travis Hirschi (1969) argued that criminality is often controlled by an individual's commitments and attachments to conventional institutions, beliefs, activities, and groups. Many people refrain from engaging in violent behavior because they fear losing their relationships with significant others—with friends, family, and peers. But lacking in strong social ties, members of society may also lack the motivation to become law-abiding citizens. Robert J. Sampson and John H. Laub (1993) similarly suggested that the ability of teenagers to bond with other human beings, a job, or an organization tends to protect them from committing criminal acts as they make the transition into adulthood.

An important insight provided by control theory is that commitment or attachment to conventional individuals and their representatives inoculates human beings from committing violent offenses generally.

Regrettably, Americans have suffered an eclipse of community. Geographic areas that draw large numbers of individuals lacking in social bonds—drug addicts, the unemployed, the impoverished, drifters, transients, migrants, and newcomers—also tend to have high rates of social pathology, including suicide and murder.

THE SOCIOPATHIC PERSONALITY

As suggested earlier, murder for profit, jealousy, or revenge, although unjustifiable, makes some sense to most people, at least at some level. By contrast, anyone who kills for fun, pleasure, or power would appear to be irrational, if not insane; after all, it would not seem to make logical sense that taking another person's life could be in any respect entertaining. Contrary to the popular view, however, most serial killers are neither insane in a legal sense nor psychotic in a medical sense. For example, only 1 of 20 sexually sadistic serial killers studied by Janet I. Warren, Robert R. Hazelwood, and Park E. Dietz (1996) was psychotic. These killers know right from wrong, know exactly what they are doing, and can control their desire to kill but choose not to do so. They are more cruel than crazy.

Psychologically, the thrill-motivated, sadistic serial killer tends to be a sociopath, indicating a disorder of character rather than of the mind. He lacks a conscience, has a weak superego, feels no remorse, and cares exclusively for his own pleasures in life. Other people are seen merely as tools to fulfill his own needs and desires, no matter how perverse or reprehensible (see Harrington, 1972; Magid & McKelvey, 1988). The sociopath is bad, not mad; his crimes are sickening, but his mind is far from sick.

The term *sociopathy* is often used interchangeably with psychopathy and antisocial personality disorder. Initially, the word *psychopathy* was widely used by psychiatrists and psychologists to identify the syndrome of character traits involving the impulsive, reckless, and selfish disregard of others. In the 1950s, however, the psychiatric profession recommended the use of the diagnostic term *sociopathy*, in part to distinguish the psychopathic personality from the much more serious psychotic disorders. Then, in the late 1960s, psychiatrists once again proposed a change in terminology, replacing both the sociopathic and psychopathic diagnoses with that of *antisocial personality disorder* (APD). Some experts in psychopathology, however, maintain distinctions among the three diagnostic categories, even offering various subtypes for each (see Samenow, 2004). They view psychopathy as a significantly more serious disorder—essentially "sociopathy on steroids." In the pioneering work of psychologist Robert Hare (1993), psychopathy represents an extreme condition reserved for individuals who, over the course of a lifetime, control others and satisfy their own selfish desires through manipulating, charming, and intimidating. According to Hare, the characteristics of psychopathy include superficial charm, lack of empathy, impulsivity, lack of remorse, and pathological lying.

Leonard Lake, who tortured, raped, and killed dozens with the help of his "playmate" Charles Ng, illustrated in his rationale for murder the mind-set of a classic (albeit unusually honest) sociopath. Preparing to build an elaborate underground bunker in which to imprison young women as sex slaves, Lake sat calmly in front of his camcorder and described in logical, although patently selfish, terms why he felt the need to proceed with what he called "Operation Miranda."

> I am a realist. I am 38 years old, a bit chubby, with not much hair, and I'm losing what I have. I am not particularly attractive to women—or I should say particularly attracting to women. And all the traditional magnets—the money, the position/power—I don't have. And yet I am still very sexually active, and I am still very much attracted to a particular type of woman who almost by definition is totally uninterested in me.
>
> Dirty old man, pervert, I'm attracted to young women, sometimes even as young as 12, although to be fair certainly 18-22 is pretty much an ideal range as far as my interests go. I like very slim women, very pretty of course, petite, small breasted, long hair, if I am allowed. And, such a woman, by virtue of her youth, her attractiveness, her desirability to certainly the majority of mankind, simply has better options. There is no particular reason why such a woman should be interested in me.
>
> But there is more to it than that. It is difficult to explain my personality in 25 words or less, but I am in fact a loner, I enjoy the peace, the quiet, the solitude, I enjoy being by myself. And while all my relationships with women in the past have been sexually successful, socially they have almost always been a failure. I've gone through two divorces, innumerable women, 50-55, I forget exactly the count, I counted recently. I'm afraid the bottom line statement is the simple fact that I'm a sexist slob.
>
> I enjoy using women, and of course women aren't particularly interested in being used. I certainly enjoy sex. I certainly enjoy the dominance of climbing on a woman and using her body. But I'm not particularly interested in the id, the ego, all the things that a man should be interested in to complement a woman's needs. Now I can fake these emotions, and I can fake them very well. In the past, I've been very successful at attracting fairly interesting and attractive women simply because I did fake fairly well an interest in their needs and their requirements. So momentarily I had what I wanted and they thought they had what they wanted. But in the long term I don't want to bother.
>
> What I want is an off-the-shelf sex partner. I want to be able to use a woman whenever and however I want. And when I'm tired or satiated or

bored or not interested, I simply want to put her away, lock her up in a little room to get her out of my sight, out of my life, and thus avoid what heretofore has always been the obligation to entertain or amuse or satisfy a particular woman or girlfriend's whims or emotional whatevers.

Such an arrangement, of course, is not only blatantly sexist, but highly illegal. There's no doubt about it. It violates all of the human rights and blah blah, blah blah blah. To spare posterity my concept of other people's morality, I'm explaining my morality—what I feel, what I want. And as of this moment I am going to try to get it. (First author's transcript of a videotape recovered at a crime scene in 1985)

Although Lake understood concepts of morality and right versus wrong, in true sociopathic style, he placed his needs above the rights of others. It has been estimated that 3% of all males in our society could, like Leonard Lake, be considered sociopathic, or as having the antisocial personality type (American Psychiatric Association, 1994). However, most sociopaths are not violent: They may lie, cheat, or steal, but rape and murder are not necessarily appealing to them. The other critical ingredient to the profile of the serial killer is an overpowering need for control. Most thrill killers, for the sake of sexual gratification, tie up their victims in order to watch them squirm and torture their victims to hear them scream. Others find personal fulfillment and control by taking the life out of their victims—by "mercifully" killing a hospital patient or drugging a normal, vigorous captive into the state of an obedient zombie.

Henry Lee Lucas, who at one time claimed to have murdered 600 people across the country, was devoid of any feelings or concern for his victims. Lucas talked, without emotion, of killing someone just because they were around and he decided that it might be fun. "Killing someone is just like walking outdoors," explained Lucas. "If I wanted a victim, I'd just go get one" (Jeffers, 1991, p. 45).

When an absolute stranger, for whatever reason, struck his fancy, he would stalk his prey until the time and place were right to move in for the kill. Although he boasted of killing several hundred people, he was probably fabricating in many cases. Regardless of the exact body count, Lucas didn't draw the line; he didn't even have a line to draw. Indeed, anyone was fair game.

One of Lucas's earliest victims was his 74-year-old mother, Viola. He stabbed her to death after she struck him with a broom and nagged him incessantly. Murder was payback for years of cruelty and mistreatment when he was a child. In his first year of grade school, Viola would dress Henry as a girl and curl his hair in ringlets. She beat him repeatedly and forced him to watch as she performed sexual acts for money.

Another of his victims was a 14-year-old girl whom he claimed to have loved. Frieda "Becky" Lorraine Powell was Lucas's traveling companion and soul mate, at least until she acted out of place and slapped him across the face. Without hesitation, Lucas stabbed Becky to death, then raped her, cut her body into pieces, and stuffed them into pillowcases. Asked why he would commit such an atrocity against someone he purportedly loved, Lucas said, "It was the only thing I could think of" (Jeffers, 1991, pp. 44–45).

Sociopathic serial killers are likely to have internalized shame and humiliation during childhood that are later transformed into anger and rage (Gilligan, 1997). Psychoanalyst Carl Goldberg (2000) explained the genesis of their malevolent behavior—the deliberate infliction of pain and suffering on another living being—as deriving from the experience of shame, the growth of a negative self-image, the acceptance of the "bad" self, and finally a lack of feeling for others. Ultimately, these stages of pathological development result in the worst kinds of behavior.

For serial killers like Lucas, the pain and suffering they cause are meant to give them great personal pleasure in order to compensate for feelings of humiliation. For other serial killers, the injury and death they cause are means to an end—to silence possible eyewitnesses to their crimes, to retaliate for perceived injustices they have suffered, and so on. For example, between 1977 and 1982, Martha Ann Johnson suffocated each of her four children by rolling her 250-lb. body on top of them while they slept; her motive was to get even with her husband following serious arguments.

THE CULTURE OF SOCIOPATHY

The crimes committed by Lake and Ng as well as other sociopathic serial killers were surely horrific. Still, they reflect, in an obviously extreme form, a disturbing general trend in which more and more people feel unconstrained by both conscience and social norms from offending other human beings. Most of this unscrupulous behavior is relatively innocuous, certainly not at the level of Lake and Ng. More people today are willing to cheat their neighbor, lie in a job interview, or steal souvenirs from their hotel room.

During the 1960s and 1970s, America fought two major wars. For one, there was the war in Vietnam, which claimed thousands of lives and occupied the attention of a whole generation of baby boomers. On the domestic front, moreover, Americans also fought the "War Against Guilt." For years, they were encouraged not to feel guilty—"do your own thing," "love the one you're with"—and be assertive.

Blended with the message of individualism that Americans embraced during the 1960s was a more altruistic theme encouraging social responsibility and equality of opportunity. It was this positive focus that led the baby boom generation to join the civil rights movement and push for women's rights. However, when double-digit inflation and repeated energy crises enveloped the American psyche during the 1970s, altruism quickly dissipated, leaving selfish individualism in its wake. Economic exigency forced Americans of all ages to abandon humanitarian impulses.

We continue to be veterans of the war against guilt. The slogan of the day used to be "I'm OK, you're OK." Now, for many people, it's "I'm OK, you're dead." At a societal level, the decline in moral responsibility has been so profound that some observers have called the United States a "sociopathic society." In his book *Money, Murder and the American Dream: Wilding from Wall Street to Main Street*, sociologist Charles Derber (1992) suggests that the collective conscience of America has been seriously debilitated. He sees a declining sense of morality in everything from business decisions to interpersonal relationships.

Thus, Americans may still know cognitively the right thing to do, but to an increasing extent, they don't feel morally compelled to do it. Behavior is determined more by what is convenient and practical than by what is ethical. Morality has taken a back seat to expediency—leaving nobody to steer a righteous path or even to drive the car.

As an important aspect of this trend, there have been repeated scandals at the uppermost levels of society. Familiar incidents include Chappaquiddick, Watergate, Abscam, Irangate, and Enron. People behind widely publicized scandals include Monica Lewinsky, Martha Stewart, O. J. Simpson, Senator John Edwards, Governor Mark Sanford, Bernard Madoff, David Letterman, and Tiger Woods, to mention but a few. In addition, youngsters are now more inclined than ever to resort to violence over seemingly trivial issues—over a pair of Nikes, a leather jacket, or even a challenging glance—or with no reason at all. At the extreme, beyond white-collar criminals and teenage desperadoes, our culture may have created would-be serial killers at the moral margins of society. Unrestrained by conscience, they are free to satisfy their needs and desires, no matter how perverse or reprehensible.

Of course, it takes much more than motive to become a serial killer. Many people seek thrill in their lives but are able to satisfy it in ways that are legitimate, if not entirely safe, such as skydiving or driving at excessive speeds. Other people may have an inordinate need for power and control, but they also are able to find socially acceptable modes of fulfillment. For example, certain business executives derive a sadistic pleasure by "eating alive" their competition; they wheel and deal not just for the profit but also for the feeling of power and the thrill of conquest. Many individuals have a mission in life, but their mission is pursued not by killing, but by organizing a legitimate endeavor in an effective and legal manner. There are, of course, numerous methods, aside from serial murder, to make money or gain power.

There may be tens of thousands of people whose motivations are such that they could find serial murder to be psychologically rewarding. Most have other outlets; a few may experiment with violence but find it distasteful, repulsive, or even more difficult than they had imagined. Remaining a serial killer at large requires some level of criminal savoir faire. Some potential serial killers lack the ability to avoid detection long enough to accumulate large numbers of victims. They may leave physical evidence at crime scenes, abduct their victims in the presence of eyewitnesses, or select a victim who is resourceful enough to escape.

Even if they successfully avoid detection and find murder enjoyable, some would-be serial killers may simply quit after one or two attacks. Feelings of guilt and remorse may deter them. For any of several reasons, guilt does not seem to control the behavior of those men and women who make a career—or at least a passionate hobby—out of killing. Unencumbered by guilt, they murder with moral impunity.

EMPATHY AND SERIAL KILLERS

In line with the notion that almost all serial killers are sociopathic, many investigators have argued that sadistic serial killers lack empathy—that is, they are incapable of knowing or feeling their victims' pain and suffering. In Hare's (1993) Psychopathic Checklist, for example, the callousness and lack of empathy of the psychopath (or sociopath) are indicated by insensitivity to the feelings of others and by the presence of a cold, contemptuous, and inconsiderate attitude.

In the case of repeat killers for whom murder is a means of eliminating the eyewitnesses to their profit-motivated crimes, this may frequently be true—lack of empathy may indeed be regarded as essential for avoiding apprehension. Profit-motivated serial killers may not enjoy the suffering of their victims, but they still take their victims' lives in order to avoid a prison sentence or the death penalty. In the 1970s, for example, Gary and Thaddeus Lewington committed a series of 10 armed robberies around central Ohio in which they took their victims' wallets and then shot each one in the head. A few years later, the brothers Bruce, David, and Norman Johnston of Chester County, Pennsylvania, gunned down a number of their accomplices to protect themselves from a grand jury investigation of their crime ring in Philadelphia. And in 2002, John Allen Muhammad and Lee Boyd Malvo terrorized the Washington, DC, area in an attempt to extort $10 million from the local authorities.

For sadistic serial killers, however, the presence of empathy—even intensely heightened empathy—may be essential in two ways. First, their crimes require highly tuned powers of cognitive empathy in order to trap their victims (Gabbard, 2003). Indeed, killers who do not understand their victims' feelings would be incapable of conning them effectively. For example, Theodore Bundy understood all too well the sensibilities of the female college students who were taken in by his feigned helplessness. He trapped attractive young women by appearing to be disabled, with his arm wrapped in a sling, and asking them for help. Many complied and died for their troubles.

Second, a well-honed sense of emotional empathy is essential for a sadistic killer's enjoyment of the suffering of his victims. That is, a killer who tortures, sodomizes, rapes, and humiliates must be able to both understand and feel his victims' suffering in order to enjoy it. Without the capacity for empathy, there would be no excitement or sexual arousal. Thus, he experiences his victims' pain, but he feels it as his own pleasure.

In the literature of psychiatry as well as that of criminology, lack of empathy—along with a manipulative and calculating style, an absence of remorse, and impulsiveness—is frequently regarded as a defining characteristic of the psychopathic or antisocial personality disorder (Hare, 1993). An earlier study by Alfred B. Heilbrun (1982), however, came to quite a different conclusion. In interviews with 168 male prisoners in the Georgia correctional system, he observed two kinds of psychopaths—those who had poor impulse control, low IQ, and little empathy (the Henry Lee Lucas type), and those who had better impulse control, high IQ, sadistic objectives, and heightened empathy (the Theodore Bundy type). In fact, the most empathic group of criminals in Heilbrun's study were intelligent psychopaths with a history of violence. He found the greatest empathy in high-IQ prisoners who had committed rape—the violent crime in which sexual sadism seems most likely to play a systematic role.

According to Heilbrun, violent acts inflicting pain and suffering are more intentional than impulsive. In addition, empathic skills promote the arousal and satisfaction of sadistic objectives by enhancing the criminal's awareness of the pain being experienced by his victim. Heilbrun's finding of empathic sadistic psychopaths was all but ignored in the literature until recently, when forensic psychiatrists began to question the commonly held view that antisocial types necessarily lack the ability to feel their victims' pain, noting that in many cases, they instead possess "enormous powers of empathic discernment—albeit for the purposes of self-aggrandizement" (Heilbrun, 1982, p. 557).

In the 1930s, social philosopher George Herbert Mead (1934) identified "role taking" as a basic human quality, whereby an individual is able to adopt the viewpoint of another person. Many serial killers apparently share this ability, even if they use it to enhance the pleasure they derive from inflicting pain and suffering on others. In the research of symbolic interactionists, role-taking ability has been shown to take the form not of a dichotomy (able vs. not able), but of a continuum along which any given individual's degree of empathy can be plotted. Thus, there are some individuals whose empathy is so profound and broad that they commiserate with the plight of starving children on the other side of the world. Many individuals are closer to the middle of the continuum, identifying with the grief of victims in proximity to them but emotionally oblivious to the pain and suffering of most strangers, especially those who are physically removed. At the other end of the continuum, however, there may also be millions of Americans, according to the American Psychiatric Association, who are antisocial personality types and completely lacking in empathy. They may not be serial killers, because they are not sadistic in their aims, but they are nonetheless insensitive to human tragedy.

BORDERLINE PERSONALITY DISORDER

Some criminologists have described Danny Harold Rolling, who brutally slew five college students in Gainesville, Florida, in 1990, as a sociopath. He had a long history of criminal activity prior to the student murders, including theft, robbery, and assaultive behavior. Not only did he butcher five innocent strangers, but he also attempted to kill his own father. Rolling also committed a grisly triple murder of a family that lived only a few blocks from his home in Shreveport, Louisiana. Anyone who got in his way or who could satisfy his sadistic desires—family, neighbors, or strangers—was totally expendable.

The commonly accepted conception of the sociopathic or antisocial serial killer may fit the moral immaturity found in violent offenders like Leonard Lake or Henry Lee Lucas. We question, however, whether sociopathy is present, at least in such an extreme form, in many other serial killers. Many probably do have a conscience—some weaker than others, perhaps—and should not be considered pure sociopaths. Others have empathy, although in a perverted self-serving form.

Nancy L. Ansevics and Harold E. Doweiko (1991) offer an alternative to the antisocial personality (sociopath) diagnosis. According to them, many serial killers appear to suffer from a related character abnormality called *borderline personality disorder* (BPD), which is marked by a pattern of instability in mood, relationships, and self-image. In response to a stressful situation, the borderline type may become "pseudo-psychotic" for a short period of time. The makeup of

BPDs often includes impulsivity, intense anger, and chronic feelings of boredom. They often feel a profound sense of abandonment and rejection, and they may be extremely manipulative with other people. Unlike the antisocial personality, however, the borderline personality type is capable of feeling remorse and empathy when he or she hurts other people (American Psychiatric Association, 1994).

Disorganized killers—those who strike in an impulsive and emotionally charged state but who are not genuinely psychotic—may instead be BPDs. Although confused and angry when killing, they still have the capacity for empathy and compassion. Borderline personality disorder may help to explain impulsive attacks of killers who repeatedly murder in a state of frenzy without making much of an effort to cover their tracks. Because of their confusion and impulsivity, they usually are discovered and apprehended before amassing a large victim count.

Despite the merits of their argument, Ansevics and Doweiko appear to overstate the role of BPD among serial killers. Given the care and planning with which they kill, most serial killers are organized in the way they both approach and leave the crime scene, and they generally do not possess the pattern of unstable mood and impulsivity that characterizes borderline personality disorder.

NORMALCY IN SERIAL MURDER

Usually as an aspect of their presumed sociopathic disorder, serial killers are often characterized as being extremely skillful at impression management. They are seen as unusually capable of looking and acting beyond suspicion, of appearing to be more innocent than a truly innocent person, and of being able to lure their victims with charm and cunning.

For example, Derrick Todd Lee, the 34-year-old man who raped and murdered a number of women in the area of Baton Rouge, stayed on the loose at least in part because he was able to blend in so well socially. To many, he came across as friendly and charming. Regarded as a religious man, he led a Bible study group. Those who got to know him informally regarded him as more a preacher than a killer. Green River Killer Gary Ridgway, who was convicted in 2004 of the deaths of 48 prostitutes in Washington State, brought his young son with him to a crime scene in order to look "fatherly" and give his victim a false sense of security. John Wayne Gacy, who brutally murdered 33 men and boys, was regarded by his suburban Chicago neighbors as a gregarious chap. He often played the part of a clown at children's birthday parties and organized get-togethers for the people on his block. Gacy often lured victims to his home by offering to interview them for a job with his construction company.

Even if serial killers seem to be skillful at presentation of self, they are certainly not alone in their concern for projecting an image that is acceptable to others. Sociologist Erving Goffman (1959) long ago suggested that managing the impression that we wish to convey to others was a normal and healthy human characteristic. In fact, successful individuals in many legitimate occupations seem to have a particular knack for using self-awareness to their personal advantage. This is true, for example, of effective politicians who come across as "one of the guys," of skillful actors who base their entire professional lives on their ability to stage a character, and of sales personnel who are able to convince their clients that they really do have their best interests at heart.

Even in the most mundane areas of everyday life, normal people stage a character. Goffman distinguished between the frontstage, where the performance is given, and the backstage region, where it is rehearsed. In a restaurant, for example, the wait staff stages a scene in the dining area by their cordial and hospitable demeanor with customers. In the kitchen, however, the same waiters complain about their working conditions and swap unflattering stories about their experiences with customers.

The difference between serial killers and other "successful" people may not lie so much in the greater effectiveness of the former at impression management as a means to an end, but in their greater willingness to torture and kill as a result of employing the tactic. When individuals use techniques of self-presentation for benign purposes in everyday life, it escapes our attention. Or, we might characterize our friends and family members in a complimentary way, emphasizing their polite manners, attractive smile, or charming style. When a serial killer is polite and charming in order to lure his victims, however, we instead characterize him as inordinately manipulative and devious.

In a diagnostic sense, is the serial killer who flatters his victims into modeling for his photo shoots any different in his manipulative skills from the sales clerk who wants to convince a shopper to buy the most expensive dress on the rack? Does the serial killer who kisses his wife goodbye as he goes off to troll the streets for prostitutes to rape and murder really differ in his role-playing behavior from the loving family man who brutally mistreats his employees at work but loves his family? It may be a different playing field, but a very similar game.

Unlike classic sociopaths, many serial killers also possess powerful psychological facilitators for overcoming or neutralizing whatever pangs of guilt or conscience that might otherwise plague them. They are able to compartmentalize their attitudes toward people by conceiving of at least two categories of human beings—those whom they care about and treat with decency and those with whom they have no relationship and therefore can victimize with total disregard for their feelings.

Hillside Strangler Kenneth Bianchi, for example, clearly divided the world into two camps—those whom he cared about and everyone else. The group toward whom he had no feelings included the 12 young women whom he brutally tortured and murdered, 10 with his older cousin in Los Angeles and two on his own in Bellingham, Washington. Ken's inner circle consisted of his mother, his wife and son, and his accomplice, cousin Angelo Buono. "The Ken I knew couldn't ever have hurt anybody or killed anybody," recalled Kelli Boyd, his common-law wife and mother of his child. "He wasn't the kind of person who could have killed somebody" (M. Barnes, 1984). Similarly, Sean Vincent Gillis, the Baton Rouge man who confessed in 2004 to murdering eight women, was regarded by his live-in girlfriend as "laid back" and "calm." After living with Gillis for some eight years, 46-year-old Terry Lemoine struggled to think of him as a vicious killer. "He wouldn't squish a bug," she said ("Suspect Claims," 2004, p. 1A).

According to psychiatrist Robert Jay Lifton (1986), the Nazi physicians who performed ghoulish experiments at Auschwitz and other concentration camps compartmentalized their activities, attitudes, and emotions. Lifton suggested that any possible feelings of guilt were minimized through what he calls "doubling:" The camp doctors developed two separate and distinct selves, one for doing the dirty work of experimenting with and exterminating inmates, and the other for living the rest of their lives outside the camp. In this way, no matter how sadistic they were on the job, they were still able to see themselves as gentle husbands, caring fathers, and honorable physicians.

The compartmentalization that allows for killing without guilt is an extension of a phenomenon used by many normal people in their everyday roles. An executive might be a heartless son of a bitch to all his employees at work but be a loving and devoted family man at home. Similarly, many serial killers have jobs and families, do volunteer work, and kill part-time with a great deal of selectivity.

Just as it was with Nazi concentration camp doctors, the process of compartmentalization is especially pronounced in the case of a serial murderer who kills for profit, that is, who robs and then executes in order to silence the eyewitnesses to his crimes. Like a hit man for the mob, he kills for a living yet may otherwise lead an ordinary family life. Even a sexual sadist who may be unmercifully brutal to a hitchhiker or a woman he meets at a bar might not dream of hurting family members, friends, or neighbors.

Serial killer John Wayne Gacy of suburban Chicago, for example, was "not all bad," as those closest to him would attest. Despite his conviction on 33 counts of murder, Lillian Grexa, his former neighbor, wrote to Gacy on death row. "I know they say he killed thirty-three," explains Grexa, "but I only know him as a good neighbor . . . the best I ever had" (personal communication).

It wasn't only Lillian Grexa who was fond of John Gacy. Years before his arrest, Gacy was voted the Jaycee Man of the Year, was a respected member of the local Democratic Party, and was photographed with then-First Lady Rosalynn Carter. He played a clown at children's parties and held theme bashes for the neighbors. On weekends, however, when his wife was away, Gacy had private parties for special guests—young attractive males—parties with beer, drugs, sex, and torture. Then he would literally cover up the truth about his deadly passions by burying 29 of his victims in the crawl space under his house. Four others had to be buried elsewhere for lack of space.

Photo 5.1 Most serial killers don't look like monsters. John Wayne Gacy, once a respected member of the community, was photographed with First Lady Rosalynn Carter at a local fundraiser. (White House Photographer/U.S. Federal Government)

It is difficult, if not impossible, to determine for certain if a particular serial killer successfully separates his friends from the rest of humanity or whether he is just a clever sociopath who successfully plays the role of a loving friend and family member. Although sociopaths lack the capacity for human kindness and compassion, they know the right thing to do. In fact, they are often very skillful at maintaining a caring and sympathetic facade, especially when it is in their self-interest to do so. Could John Wayne Gacy have fooled his wife and his neighbor? Or did they know more about his character than those who have analyzed his criminal behavior?

Returning to the extreme atrocities committed by the Nazi doctors, we can learn about another psychological process—called "dehumanization"—that effectively permits killing without guilt. Not only did the Auschwitz physicians compartmentalize their roles by constructing separate selves, but they also were able to convince themselves that their research subjects, their victims, were less than human. The Jews were seen as a disease or plague that had to be stamped out for the health of the country. Seen in more than metaphorical terms, the inmates were regarded as vermin in semihuman form who had to be exterminated. Likewise, Jewish research subjects were truly viewed as guinea pigs who could be sacrificed for the sake of medical knowledge. Thus, by a process of dehumanization, concentration camp doctors made decisions as to who would live and who would die. In one case, they conducted twin studies in which inmates were forced to experience excruciating pain and suffering, all in the name of scientific inquiry.

Dehumanization permits normal people to engage in atrocities. During the war in Iraq, for example, smiling American soldiers were seen posing in digital photos that showed their illegal mistreatment, perhaps even torture, of Iraqi prisoners. On the other side, anti-American Iraqi terrorists cruelly decapitated an American citizen while being videotaped for worldwide television. In both cases, the enemy was treated as subhuman or demonic, as being outside the rules that apply to the members of civilized society.

In fact, the link between military training and serial murder has been interpreted as a result of learning theory (Hare, 1993). Not only are military recruits trained to engage in combat, they also acquire the psychological frame of mind that enables them to take human life. Many recruits are initially reluctant to kill, but over time, their resistance erodes as they become fully desensitized to the horrors of war. At the same time, armed services personnel come to perceive killing as normal and essential to survival. Part of the indoctrination involves adopting the view that the enemy is evil or subhuman. Of course, there is little empirical evidence to support the effectiveness of this learning process. For example, Tammy Castle (2001), in a study of 25 serial murderers, found very few with military experience.

Combatants during warfare aren't the only ones to kill with the aid of dehumanization. Infamous murderer Charles Manson, in fact, was explicit in his use of dehumanizing language regarding his victims. His followers scrawled "Death to Pigs" in blood on one wall of the opulent home of Leno and Rosemary LaBianca just after slaughtering them.

Through the same process of dehumanization, many serial killers have slaughtered scores of innocent people by viewing them as worthless and expendable, or "less dead," using Steven A. Egger's (2003) term. Prostitutes are seen as mere "sex machines," gays as AIDS carriers, nursing home patients as "vegetables," and homeless alcoholics as nothing more than trash. By regarding their victims as subhuman elements of society, the killers can actually delude themselves into believing that they are doing something positive rather than negative. They are, in their minds, ridding the world of filth and evil.

Dehumanization can occur not only for the purpose of selecting deserving victims but also for the sake of justifying excessive cruelty to those who already have been chosen. For example, Kansas City's Robert Berdella, who tortured and sodomized his male captives, didn't necessarily hold a dehumanized view of his victims until he transformed them into sex toys. At that point, they lost their humanity in his eyes. He could then do anything he wanted to his "blow-up dolls." Similarly, Milwaukee's Jeffrey Dahmer, who confessed to killing 17 young men, actually attempted to lobotomize his captives in an effort to change them into walking zombies with whom he could have sex. Both Berdella and Dahmer could avoid feeling guilty about performing ghastly sexual atrocities on their dehumanized playthings. In Dahmer's case, his ability to degrade his victims was aided by their minority status—most were gay, Black, or Asian.

REHUMANIZING THE VICTIMS

The behavior of a serial killer after his capture provides some insight into his level of conscience. Genuine sociopaths almost never confess after being apprehended. Instead, they continue to maintain their innocence, always hoping beyond hope to get off on a technicality, to be granted a new trial, or to appeal their case to a higher level.

To this day, Lawrence Sigmund Bittaker, who was convicted of five murders in Southern California, maintains that his partner, Roy Norris, actually did all the killing. Confronted with an audiotape of a torture session containing his voice, Bittaker had a ready excuse. "You didn't fall for that act, did you? It was all a script. We were playing around. I'd slap my hand, and she would scream. It was all a fake" (personal communication, 1992).

A few sociopathic serial killers have confessed to their crimes not because they were remorseful, but because they considered it in their best interest to do so. For example, Clifford Olson, suspected of killing 11 children in Vancouver, British Columbia, decided that the police "had the goods on him," so he decided that he might as well turn his defeat into an advantage. Olson confessed to murder and led the police to the bodies of his victims in exchange for a $100,000 "ransom." He had struck a deal by which his wife and son would receive $10,000 in trust for each dead child he helped locate; he "graciously" threw the 11th in for free. Olson was later asked to reveal information about other missing children, not for a fee but for the sake of the worried parents. In true sociopathic style, he responded, "If I gave a shit about the parents, I wouldn't have killed the kid" (Gray, 1982, p. 20).

Thus, when authentic sociopaths confess, it is not out of a need to expiate feelings of guilt, but instead for a self-serving reason. The benefit is not always as tangible as Olson's. For example, serial killer Danny Rolling continued to proclaim his innocence in the Gainesville murder case for years after his indictment, despite compelling physical evidence against him. On February 15, 1994, the opening day of what was to be a closely watched trial lasting months, however, he shocked everyone with his confession. "Your honor, I have been running from first one thing then another all of my life. Whether from problems at home, or with the law or from myself," Rolling told Judge Stan Morris. "But there are some things that you just can't run from, and this is one of them" (Fox & Levin, 1996, p. 161). In a press conference, Rolling's attorney explained that the accused wished to spare the families of his victims the agony of a trial. The prosecuting attorney argued more persuasively that Rolling's confession was more calculated than caring—a last-ditch effort designed to play on the sympathy of the court. Because he was already serving a life sentence for other crimes, Rolling's decision to plead guilty to the murders was viewed as a strategic move to escape the electric chair. However clever the legal maneuver, the jury had no sympathy for Rolling and recommended the death penalty. He was executed by lethal injection on October 25, 2006.

Photo 5.2 In a surprise move, Danny Rolling pled guilty to the murders of five college students in Gainesville, Florida. (Associated Press)

In a similar way, Henry Lee Lucas was able to delay his execution by the state of Texas by promising to help police solve their open murder cases. At one time, he boasted of having killed 600 people. Later, he claimed to have committed only one murder. Ultimately, based on lack of solid evidence, Lucas's death sentence was commuted by the governor of Texas to life without parole. Still a suspect in numerous murders, he died while behind bars, but of natural causes.

Shortly after Jeffrey Dahmer made the cover of *People,* Donald Evans falsely confessed to more than 60 murders around the country, perhaps attempting to become famous in his own right. Clifford Olson boasted from his prison cell about his celebrity, "Henry Lee Lucas was small potatoes. I'm like Hannibal Lecter" (personal communication, 1992).

Unlike true sociopaths, who are incapable of feeling remorse, serial killers who must dehumanize their victims frequently confess after being caught. Joel Rifkin of Long Island, for example, on the day after his capture freely confessed to killing 17 prostitutes and provided all the evidence that could be used against him in a court of law. Although caught red-handed with one victim, he willingly implicated himself in a killing spree that would likely put him behind bars for life.

Cannibalistic serial killer Jeffrey Dahmer similarly confessed to his crimes. After his conviction, when it was no longer self-serving to do so, he apologized both in court and on the national television program *Inside Edition*. His statement to the judge asked for no mercy:

> I just want to say that I hope God has forgiven me. I know society will never be able to forgive me. I know the families of the victims will never be able to forgive me for what I have done. I promise I will pray each day to ask for their forgiveness when the hurt goes away, if ever. I have seen their tears and if I could give my life right now to bring their loved ones back, I would do it. I am so very sorry.

> Your Honor, I know that you are about to sentence me. I ask for no consideration. I know my time in prison will be terrible. But I deserve whatever I get because of what I have done. Thank you, Your Honor, and I am prepared for your sentence, which I know will be the maximum. I ask for no consideration. (Associated Press, 1992)

As long as they are alone with their fantasies and private thoughts, serial killers like Rifkin and Dahmer are able to maintain the myth that their victims deserved to die. After being caught, however, they are forced to confront the disturbing reality that they had killed human beings, not animals or objects. At this point, their victims are rehumanized in their eyes. As a result, these serial killers may be overcome with guilt for all the horrible crimes they committed and freely confess.

Some serial killers, the true sociopaths, are beyond redemption. They failed to develop, early in life, the capacity for empathy and affection. As a result, they lack the internal mechanisms that usually inhibit selfish and hurtful behavior. Unlike psychotics, sociopaths understand the wrongfulness of their assaultive behavior. Unlike normal people, however, they understand it only at an intellectual level; the emotional component is absent. Consequently, sociopathic serial killers cannot be rehabilitated. They missed the boat on developing a conscience when they were young, and the boat never returns.

Other serial killers are driven by strong urges—sexual sadism, dominance, pedophilia—that overpower whatever conscience they possess. Treatment strategies do exist for managing or controlling some of these motivating forces, but they have met with limited success. Although some serial killers potentially could be treated for their behavior, the gravity of their crimes makes rehabilitation a moot issue. Public opinion is clear in this regard: Serial killers should never be released from custody, cured or not.

CHAPTER 6

Partners in Murder

For Lawrence Sigmund Bittaker and Roy L. Norris, Southern California was the perfect place. They would cruise together in Bittaker's customized van, looking at bikini-clad teenage girls at the beaches. The two buddies liked to stop and take pictures of "beach girls," and if the girls objected, the men gave them some marijuana to placate them. Bittaker loved teenaged girls, especially blondes, and California provided him with plenty of targets for his passion.

Bittaker, age 38, and Norris, age 30, had met in 1978 while incarcerated in the California State Prison at San Luis Obispo. Norris earlier had served 4 years at the Atascadero State Hospital as a "mentally disordered sex offender." After his release, he had raped a housewife in her home and was sent to the state prison at San Luis Obispo. Bittaker also had spent most of his adult life behind bars. In 1978, their friendship grew as they schemed and plotted a ghoulish murder spree to be carried out upon their release. If prisons are not schools for crime, then at least they are study halls.

Bittaker had a wish: to kill a girl corresponding to each teenage year, like trophies. Bittaker's silver 1977 GMC van, which they nicknamed "Murder Mac," was selected especially for its sliding door, which would facilitate his method of abduction. From the summer through the fall of 1979, Bittaker, along with Norris, kidnapped, tortured, raped, and murdered girls of ages 13, 15, 16, 16, and 18, mistakenly duplicating the 16-year-old category. More important than the strange pursuit to "score" one per age was the excruciating pain inflicted on each of the victims.

Cindy Schaefer, visiting the West Coast for the summer from her home in Wisconsin, was abducted while walking along the street. Her screams were muffled with a gag and by the van's blasting stereo. Bittaker and Norris took her to a secluded mountain spot they had staked out earlier. There, they each raped her several times. Cindy pleaded with the men, asking that if they planned to kill her, to let her know ahead of time so she could pray first. They assured her they weren't going to kill her then strangled her to death. They threw her body down the mountainside for animals to devour. Her body was never recovered.

Photo 6.1 Many serial killers are sexual sadists. Lawrence Sigmund Bittaker earned the nickname "Pliers" for the way he tortured his victims. (Associated Press/Pool)

As is typical of many serial crimes, the killings became increasingly more brutal. The next victim to be drawn into Murder Mac was 18-year-old Andrea Hall, who had been hitchhiking. First, Bittaker raped her. Then Norris tried to rape her, too, but he was disgusted by the blood from her period. They took photographs of Andrea in her subjugated, frightened state, as they did with all their victims. Bittaker asked her to give him some good reasons why she shouldn't be killed. He didn't like her answers. Andrea Hall was stabbed in the ear with an ice pick then strangled to death with a coat hanger and pliers.

The next two victims were the youngest. Thirteen-year-old Jacqueline Lamp, who went by her middle name Leah, and 15-year-old Jackie Gilliam never expected that their hitchhiking would take them where it did. Bittaker and Norris drove their newest prey to their mountain retreat, where they held them captive for days, repeatedly raping them. To add to the disgrace of having to act like she was enjoying her rape, Norris made Leah pretend she was his cousin to satisfy his longtime incestuous desire for his relative. Jackie was then tortured—her nipples were crushed with vise grips, and her breasts were pierced with an ice pick. Finally, both girls were murdered.

Their last killing was the cruelest. Sixteen-year-old Shirley Lynette Ledford was captured, mutilated, and murdered inside Murder Mac while the radio blasted to drown out her screams. She was tortured and poked, and her nipples were torn off with Bittaker's pliers, all while the pleas of the girl, who was reduced to an animal-like state, were recorded on cassette tape. After death had mercifully come for her, Bittaker and Norris gleefully discarded her torn and bleeding nude body on the front lawn of a suburban home to see what kind of reaction its discovery would get in the newspapers.

INSANITY IN THE RELATIONSHIP

According to our database, about 20% of all serial killers, like Bittaker and Norris, murder in teams of two or more—friends, cousins, brothers, or lovers who go out together, when they feel bored and idle, to play the game of murder. It is also not unusual for one of the killers to play a dominant role, inspiring the partner to go along for the sake of their relationship. Their special chemistry seems to ignite the team's willingness to engage in the most despicable behavior—behavior that they might never have tried alone, before they had met and established a bond of loyalty or love. In a sense, the insanity is located in their relationship rather than in their individual minds or personalities. This is not to say that the partners came to their relationship with solid characters or honorable intentions. It does indicate that the chemistry of their association together provided the necessary catalyst for turning them into serial killers.

In nearly half of the cases, one of the partners—the dominant one—is much older than the other. This apparently was true in the case of the Calaveras County killers, Leonard Lake and Charles Ng. It also was true of the Hillside Stranglers, Ken Bianchi and his older cousin Angelo Buono, who, more than two decades earlier, together tortured and killed 10 women and girls in the Los Angeles area.

PARTNERS FOR PROFIT

More recently, the snipers who terrorized the Washington, DC, area turned out to be a 17-year-old Jamaican and his 42-year-old companion. It was widely believed that the older sniper, John Allen Muhammad, a former U.S. soldier distinguished for his marksmanship, had served as the inspiration for their killing spree. This may be at least part of the reason why the teenager Lee Boyd Malvo received a life sentence, whereas Muhammad was sentenced to death. Unlike most other serial murder teams, the DC Snipers never had sexual sadism on their minds. At least in the planning stage of their attacks, they were motivated to make lots of money quickly.

In the beginning, the DC-area sniper attacks went largely unnoticed. Nobody suspected that they were linked by a common set of killers. On a cold, clear Wednesday evening—October 2, 2002—55-year-old James Martin was gunned down as he walked briskly to his car from a grocery store in Wheaton, Maryland. Nobody suspected at the time that Martin's murder marked the onset of a 3-week shooting spree in and around Washington, DC, that would leave 10 people dead and another three injured. By the time residents became aware of the deadly sniper attacks, 24 hours had passed, and four more victims had been shot to death.

What made the attacks so terrifying was the fact that they occurred at all times of the day and night, in a variety of public places, apparently on a random basis. Whites, Blacks, men, women, and children—anybody and everybody was at risk. One victim was shot at 7 a.m. while cutting the grass in front of a car dealership; another was cut down an hour and a half later as he walked outside a post office. Two victims were killed as they were filling their tank or vacuuming their vehicle at local gas stations. One was simply strolling down a city street at night. Some of the attacks occurred in the Maryland suburbs or in Washington, DC, but others happened in Virginia, as far as 70 miles south of the nation's capital.

The weapon linked to most of the shootings was a civilian version of the M-16 military assault rifle. The killers had constructed an effective gun platform by drilling holes in the rear of their blue 1990 Chevrolet Caprice—one for the muzzle of the rifle and a second for its telescopic sights. They had lowered the rear seats, allowing one of them to lie in the back and take aim at their targets without leaving their car.

Photo 6.2 While the D.C. Snipers rode their blue Chevy Caprice from crime scene to crime scene, the police were busy searching for a white van described incorrectly by eyewitnesses. (Associated Press/Marie P. Marzi)

Initially, the police had searched for an older model Caprice that had been observed near the scene of one of the shootings. They quickly shifted the target of their investigation when a white van or box truck reportedly was spotted near several of the crime scenes. Acting on what turned out to be unreliable eyewitness reports, the police reacted to each sniper attack by cordoning off roadways and stopping any and all white vans in proximity to the shootings.

After 3 weeks and 10 victims, a description of Muhammad and Malvo's car was broadcast to the public. A vigilant truck driver phoned the police after spotting the snipers' car at a rest stop off the side of a Maryland highway. The two killers were found asleep in the car.

Unlike sexually motivated serial killers, who opt to be "up close and personal" in their selection of a weapon, Muhammad and Malvo chose to shoot their victims from a distance with a firearm. For the pair, killing was a means to an end. Their motive was not sexual or sadistic, but was to extort a large amount of money from law enforcement agencies. In a note left for the police at a crime scene near a Ponderosa restaurant in Ashland, Virginia, the snipers explained that they had phoned the tip hotline on four different occasions, hoping to begin negotiations with the sniper task force. Believing the calls to be a hoax, however, the tip line operator repeatedly hung up on the pair. Their handwritten message to the police made very clear their extortion demands:

> For you Mr. Police. "Call me God." Do not release to the Press. We have tried to contact you to start negotiation.... These people took our call for a Hoax or Joke, so your failure to respond has cost you five lives. If stopping the killing is more important than catching us now, then you will accept our demand which are non-negotiable. You will place ten million dollar in Bank of america account...We will have unlimited withdrawl at any atm worldwide. You will activate the bank account, credit card, and pin number. We will contact you at Ponderosa Buffet, Ashland, Virginia,...6:00 am Sunday Morning. You have until 9:00 a.m. Monday morning to complete transaction.

Profit apparently was not the snipers' only motive for murder. Malvo's attorney later argued that Muhammad had "brainwashed" his younger companion into believing that their personal problems were a result of American racism and anti-Muslim, antiimmigrant sentiments. Malvo, a Jamaican citizen, was in the

United States illegally and had a deportation hearing scheduled for November. Muhammad was a member of the Nation of Islam and recently had changed his name from John Williams and had suffered a nasty divorce from his second wife, Mildred. A couple of months prior to their killing spree, Malvo and Muhammad were seen sleeping in bus terminals. A few weeks later, they committed a double shooting while robbing a liquor store in Montgomery, Alabama.

Before their attacks in Virginia, Maryland, and Washington, DC, Muhammad and Malvo were down-and-out, alienated nobodies. During their killing spree, however, they felt powerful and in charge. They felt they were winning their cat-and-mouse game with the police and the FBI. Even before they were identified and in custody, they were celebrities—their murders featured on the cover of *Newsweek* and *U.S. News & World Report*, and their random attacks terrifying the residents of the Washington, DC, area. Schools were closed, youth sporting events were canceled or relocated, motorists pumped gas under tarps, and people were afraid to shop. As Muhammad and Malvo wrote in one of their notes to the police, "I am God."

In December 2003, Lee Boyd Malvo was convicted of capital murder and given a life sentence. John Allen Muhammad was sentenced to death. They were tried separately, but fully understanding their motivation requires an examination of their relationship. Muhammad enjoyed being the boss, having authority, guiding a protégé, and being respected. Malvo enjoyed having a father figure who loved him and praised him for his "kill skill." Their partnership fulfilled some important emotional needs for both killers.

PARTNERSHIPS OF MEN AND WOMEN

In May 1987, women in the Toronto suburb of Scarborough were terrified by the presence of a serial rapist who always seemed to outwit the police. The pattern of his 13 assaults was clear: He would grab a young woman as she came off the bus, then he would throw her to the ground, force her to have anal sex, and let her go. The descriptions of his victims provided the basis for what the police considered to be an accurate composite drawing of the rapist, but the drawing failed to lead to his apprehension.

The rapist was Paul Bernardo. The 23-year-old charming and handsome accountant was one among hundreds of men asked by the police for a sample of their DNA, but it was never tested. In the thinking of law enforcement personnel, the professional, well-educated, and sophisticated Bernardo just didn't fit the profile of a sadistic serial rapist.

In October 1987, Bernardo was having a drink in a hotel bar in Toronto, where he met 17-year-old Karla Homolka from the town of St. Catharines, about 60 miles from Toronto. Homolka was in the city to represent her employer, a chain of pet stores, at a convention. After their initial meeting in Toronto, Bernardo began making frequent trips to visit Homolka at her family's home in St. Catharines.

Bernardo and Homolka were instantly obsessed with one another. Both were "beautiful people" who were unusually interested in kinky sex. She encouraged Bernardo's sadistic desires and eagerly sought to satisfy all of his sexual

Photo 6.3   Hardly loners, a surprising number of serial killers operate as teams. Paul Bernardo and Karla Homolka enjoyed committing rape and murder as part of their passion for one another. (Associated Press/ Frank Gunn; Associated Press/*Toronto Sun*, Greig Reekie)

demands, no matter how demeaning or perverse. He was more than willing to take the leadership role in pushing their deviant sexual pursuits beyond the borders of decency. Not much later, Paul and Karla moved into a rented two-story pink clapboard house in the lakeside area of St. Catharines. There was a deadly chemistry in the happy couple's relationship, and it was growing. Paul wanted Karla's help in raping her pretty younger sister Tammy. Karla complied by plying Tammy with alcohol and drugging her with Halothane, an anesthetic used in preparing animals for surgery. While Paul raped her sister, Karla kept her unconscious by holding a sedative-soaked washcloth over the young girl's face. Then, it was Karla's turn to make sexual advances to her sleeping sister. Bernardo used his new camcorder to videotape the entire sexual assault.

The pair really hadn't intended to kill Tammy, but that was the result. The combination of drugs and alcohol made her throw up, and she choked to death on her own vomit. After unsuccessfully attempting to revive her, Karla and Paul hid the drugs, dressed Tammy, placed her in her bed, and called for an ambulance. Virtually everybody believed the story that the pretty 15-year-old girl had accidentally choked to death.

One evening in June 1991, while cruising the streets of nearby Burlington, Paul and Karla spotted 14-year-old Leslie Mahaffy, a troubled youngster who had stayed out past her parents' curfew and was trying to get back into her home without waking them. With the help of Karla, Paul forced Leslie, at knifepoint, into his car and drove her to his house, where he repeatedly raped and beat her. When not joining in the torture of their young victim, Karla ran the video camera. She stopped recording just before the couple's fatal attack— Leslie Mahaffy died when Paul strangled her with an electrical cord. Paul and Karla then cut the victim's body into pieces, which they encased in a concrete block; they deposited the block in a nearby lake.

Three weeks later, a couple was canoeing on Lake Gibson when they discovered the concrete block containing the remains of Leslie Mahaffy. On the same day, Paul and Karla were married in a lavish ceremony in a historic church in Niagara-on-the-Lake. The festivities included the bride and groom being transported by horse-drawn carriage and a dinner of veal-stuffed pheasant and champagne for 150 guests.

Ten months passed before Paul and Karla struck again. Teenager Kristen French was walking home from school when she encountered the couple standing by their car in a church parking lot. Before she was able to call for help, French was pulled into the backseat of the car and threatened at knifepoint. For 3 days, the pretty young girl was beaten and forced to engage in various sexual acts. Paul and Karla took turns videotaping the torture. Paul then strangled their victim and, along the route to Karla's parents' house, dumped her nude body in a ditch. It was Easter Sunday, and the couple were on their way to a family dinner. Karla's Easter card to her husband was certainly poignant: "To the most wonderful man in the whole wide world."

Notwithstanding the Easter message to her husband, Karla's love for Paul didn't last. During the 9 months after the murder of Kristen French, Paul became increasingly more brutal in his treatment of his spouse, so brutal that Karla was hospitalized for her injuries. It was at that point that Karla began to talk to the police.

On February 17, 1993, Paul Bernardo was arrested and charged with the murders of French and Mahaffy as well as the rapes in Scarborough. Police searched the couple's house in St. Catharines, where they removed some 900 pieces of evidence. They discovered also that the carpet in the second-floor bedroom was stained with the vomit of Kristen French. At the same time, Toronto's medical laboratory finally decided to analyze Bernardo's blood, some 3 years after it had been taken. Test results matched the DNA in Bernardo's blood to semen samples from three crime scenes, showing definitively that Bernardo had raped the three female victims.

Certainly Karla Homolka was extremely convincing as the victim of a battering spouse rather than as a sexual predator. When police questioned Homolka about Bernardo's possible involvement in murder, they offered her a "sweetheart deal" to talk. What the authorities did not realize at the time was that Karla herself (who admitted to performing oral sex on her own unconscious sister and wanting to give her husband her sister's virginity as a Christmas present) was a dangerous sexual sadist who played much more than an ancillary role in the rapes and murders. The deal had already been confirmed by the time police and prosecutors saw videotapes of the murders and heard other evidence about her deep involvement. With the plea bargain set in stone, the courts had no choice but to free Homolka from prison in 2005, at the end of her 12-year sentence. By contrast, Bernardo received a life sentence.

As shown in Table 6.1, the vast majority of serial murder teams consist of two or more males killing in tandem. Except for a few all-female partnerships, female serial murderers, such as Karla Homolka, occasionally do team up with males in deadly crimes, often committed simply for the thrill of it. In some cases, these women participate in the slayings in order to please their murdering mates; in others, they develop their own sense of satisfaction from killing. Regardless, it is often assumed, as was the legal response to the crimes of

Table 6.1   Gender Combinations of Serial Killer Teams

	Serial Killer Cases		Serial Killers	
Killers/Teams	Number	Percent	Number	Percentage
Lone male	507	85.6%	507	76.8%
Lone female	26	4.4%	26	3.9%
Male team	40	6.8%	85	12.9%
Female team	3	0.5%	6	0.9%
Mixed team	16	2.7%	36	5.5%
Total	592	100.0%	660	100.0%

Bernardo and Homolka, that the male was the major culprit, while his female companion was merely an accomplice who deferred to her lover in order to preserve their relationship.

The "Sunset Strip Killer," named for the strip in Los Angeles where many of the victims were picked up, turned out upon arrest to be a pair of killers. Douglas Daniel Clark, a handsome, 32-year-old boiler operator, and his accomplice, Carol Mary Bundy, an obese 37-year-old divorced mother of two (and no relation to Ted), were partners: They lived together, loved together, and killed together. In a patently pornographic murder spree in 1980, they slew and mutilated at least seven people. Some were juveniles and some were adults; some were prostitutes; most were female but one was male; some they killed together, and some they killed independently. Reportedly, Clark was striving to fulfill his fantasy of cutting the throat of a woman during intercourse to feel the contractions of her vagina during death spasms. Bundy initially just wanted to hold onto and please her man, but she, too, learned to enjoy killing.

The usual scenario, described by Carol Bundy, would start with Clark cruising the Strip for prostitutes, preferably blondes, whom he would get to copulate with him orally, often while Bundy watched. The woman's skill at oral sex would determine her fate. If he liked her performance, she was released; if he didn't like it, she was executed. One woman did not please Clark. While the prostitute was still trying to arouse him, he shot her in the head. With the thrill of killing, he then climaxed and ejaculated into the mouth of the dead victim.

Clark nicknamed all of his victims. One victim who had a dental plate was named "Toothless," and her head was kept by Clark. He took the head home and placed it in the freezer, not as a souvenir but as a sex toy. After Bundy painted the head with makeup, Clark would then take it into the shower with him and masturbate into its mouth.

With some of the victims, Bundy would help out by handing Clark the murder weapon, a .25-caliber automatic pistol. The one male victim, however, was killed by her alone. While performing oral–anal sex on her former lover, she took out her gun and shot him in the head twice; she then decapitated him.

To this day, Clark argues that he was victimized by a shoddy legal defense and by a secret plea bargain with the woman whom the prosecution claimed was his accomplice. Carol Bundy was able to convince the court, with her testimony, that Douglas Clark was the main culprit in their killing spree and that, mesmerized by his charm, she merely went along to please her lover. Despite assurances to the jury that the district attorney would go for the death penalty, Carol Bundy received a parolable sentence. She died in prison of natural causes. Douglas Clark lives on California's death row.

Whether he is actually innocent or guilty, Douglas Clark's argument on his own behalf directs attention to the use of a controversial procedure in the prosecution of certain killers, especially serial killers. To secure a conviction, one of the defendants is convinced by the prosecuting attorney to turn state's evidence in return for a lesser sentence. From the prosecution's standpoint, it makes sense to convict at least one defendant on the word of another, rather than to convict no one at all. This may have been the thinking on the part of the prosecution in the case of Paul Bernardo—without the cooperation of Homolka, the major player in this set of heinous crimes might have gone free.

The advantage of plea bargaining with one of the defendants is not always properly weighed against its potential for abuse. How much credibility should the court give to the testimony of an accomplice who is eager to escape the death penalty or a lifetime behind bars? To what extent does a plea bargain with accomplices actually promote lying and perjury? Sociopathic serial killers already are pathological liars, even when they don't have a practical reason to avoid the truth.

In the Sunset Strip Killer case, one defendant, Douglas Clark, was a man; the other, Carol Bundy, was a woman. The prosecutor chose to plea bargain with the female rather than the male defendant, to use Carol Bundy's version of the crimes against Douglas Clark.

There seems to be a consistent willingness for juries, prosecuting attorneys, and citizens generally to side with female defendants who stand accused of committing heinous crimes. At least in some of these cases, long-standing stereotypes of women—according to which they are capable of nothing more than submissively following orders—may become the basis for discriminating against men.

In 1958, 19-year-old Charles Starkweather and 14-year-old Caril Fugate went on an 8-day killing spree across Nebraska and Wyoming that resulted in the slaughter of 10 victims. Jurors heard testimony that implicated both defendants, yet only Starkweather went to the electric chair. His younger partner, Fugate, was released from prison in 1976 following an outpouring of public sentiment on her behalf. According to Starkweather, however, Fugate was as guilty as he was. His position was that if he died in the electric chair, then Caril should be sitting on his lap.

CHAPTER 7

Killing for Company

"Hi, I'm Jeff. I like the way you dance." Jeffrey Dahmer's icebreaker may not have been a clever come-on, but it was effective enough for his purposes. Dahmer, a 31-year-old chocolate-factory worker, spent his spare time trolling gay bars in Milwaukee's decaying Walker's Point, seeking out pretty young men he could make his own. Sometimes he offered money, other times just a drink. But all of his victims got more than they bargained for.

Tracy Edwards was luckier than the rest. He lived to tell what went on inside of Apartment #213, at 924 North 25th Street. Edwards looked much younger than his 32 years, primarily on account of his diminutive frame. Dahmer liked them young—or small, especially with dark skin—and he surely liked Tracy Edwards.

The night of July 22, 1991, was typically warm and humid in the city known for its beer and social tolerance. Edwards was out for the evening with some friends when he met Jeffrey Dahmer, who invited them all over to his place for a few beers. Dahmer suggested that he and Edwards go buy some six-packs and then meet up with the others at his apartment. Wanting to get his new friend alone, Dahmer purposely gave Edwards's companions the wrong address.

Arriving at the second-floor flat in the dilapidated Oxford Apartments, Edwards first noticed the photos of nude males hanging from the living room walls. He was repulsed by a sickening stench and thought about how he could make a graceful yet quick exit. Before Edwards could plan his escape, his host returned from the kitchen with drinks. As Edwards guzzled down his beer, Dahmer kept asking, oddly, "Are you high yet?" ("'The Exorcist' and 'the Devil,'" 1991, p. 1).

Things soon went from strange to worse. Dahmer suddenly pulled out a knife and pressed the blade against Edwards's chest, warning him, "You die if you don't do what I say" ("'The Exorcist' and 'the Devil,'" 1991, p. 1). Dahmer then maneuvered his latest captive into the bedroom to watch his favorite film, *The Exorcist,* on the VCR. As Dahmer was readying the tape, Edwards glanced at the photos on the bedroom walls—photos more outrageous than those he had seen earlier in the living room. These pictures—hanging on the walls of the "dying room"—portrayed nude men whose bodies had been mutilated as though eaten by acid. Edwards also noticed, in a corner of the room, a large barrel that gave off a putrid odor. He was not aware that Dahmer had used the drum to dispose of his earlier guests.

As the soundtrack from *The Exorcist* blared in the background, Dahmer made his move. At knifepoint, he grabbed Edwards from behind and attempted to handcuff him to the bedpost. "I'm going to cut your heart out and eat it," Dahmer warned ("'The Exorcist' and 'the Devil,'" 1991, p. 1). Before Dahmer could secure his victim, Edwards fought back. Trained in the martial arts, he belted Dahmer across the face and kicked him in the groin. As Dahmer struggled to recover, Edwards bolted from the apartment, the handcuffs still dangling from his left wrist.

Flagging down a passing police cruiser, Edwards excitedly told of his escape and convinced Officers Rolf Mueller and Robert Rath to return with him to Dahmer's apartment. Once inside, the police found Polaroid photographs of butchered corpses. They were shocked to realize that the backdrop for the pictures was the very room in which they were standing. Continuing to search the premises, Mueller peered inside the refrigerator and found a human head on the bottom shelf. He also discovered a chilled human heart, which Dahmer later explained he had kept as a leftover, in the event that he wanted a light snack.

The police had more than enough evidence—fingerprints and the fingers to which they belonged—for probable cause to make an arrest. A more thorough search later that evening turned up more sinister evidence of Dahmer's sickening preoccupation with death and destruction, including hearts, heads, skulls, scalps, and other body parts. Inside the drum in the bedroom, the police found the remains of three bodies—all apparently dismembered with an electric saw.

PLACING THE BLAME

The more atrocious a crime, the greater the tendency to point fingers in an effort to place the blame. Involving one of the most hideous acts of serial murder of all time, the Dahmer case triggered extreme accusations and condemnations—some legitimate and some not.

Dahmer's family members were the first to be put on trial in the court of public opinion. Neighbors from his hometown of Bath, Ohio, stepped forward—and onto national television—to recall all their favorite "weird Jeff" stories as well as evidence that his parents were negligent, if not abusive. His mother and father, they charged, should have known about and done something about his excessive drinking and about his fascination with dead things. Dahmer's family life gave "Monday morning psychologists" plenty of material to analyze in the worst possible light. Dahmer felt abandoned by his mother and allegedly was abused by his dad. Even his stepmother was implicated in his abnormal upbringing. The fact that she didn't even meet her stepson until he was 18 years old didn't prevent her from being scapegoated as well.

The accusations weren't limited to Dahmer's family. Dahmer's probation officer, who was entrusted with supervising him following a conviction for sexually molesting a 13-year-old boy, failed to make home visits. Even one visit to Dahmer's den of destruction might have revealed his evil hobby—assuming, that is, that the probation officer lived to file a report.

Many others also were given a share of blame. Public opinion was decidedly critical. Shouldn't the residents of the Oxford Apartments have recognized the fetid odor that filled the hallway outside Dahmer's unit? How could they possibly have believed him when he explained that the meat inside his broken freezer had spoiled in the heat? And why did the police ignore a phone call from one concerned resident, complaining about Dahmer's strange activities?

What about the victims themselves? Shouldn't they have detected the odor of death once they entered Dahmer's apartment? And what about the ones who were lucky enough to survive? Why did four would-be victims who escaped from Dahmer tell only their friends about their bizarre encounter and not go to the authorities? And what about the 14-year-old Laotian boy who fled from Dahmer's captivity, only to be brought back by the police? How could three police officers have been so irresponsible in returning a minor back to Dahmer's custody, despite the fact that the boy was naked, bleeding from the rectum, and intoxicated?

Critics in Milwaukee charged that much of the blame could be placed under the heading of *racism*. Had the victims been middle-class Whites, some critics argued, the police would have been more aggressive and Dahmer would not have gone unnoticed for so long. This argument seems to have some basis in fact. There is a disgraceful tendency for public officials around the country to discount the complaints and grievances of marginal groups, including immigrants, gays, and people of color. To the police officers who negligently returned Dahmer's Laotian captive, the boy would have appeared to be all three.

Notwithstanding the questionable police response, how could so many neighborhood residents have let the bizarre circumstances involving Jeffrey Dahmer continue for so long—indeed, for years—without intervening? In fact, it was quite easy in the context of a variety of social norms, customs, and rules that prescribe "Mind your own business," "Keep your nose out of other people's affairs," and "Somebody else will do something about it anyway."

Even for people inclined to intervene, the very last thing one imagines in smelling a horrible odor from a nearby apartment is that someone is cutting up bodies and eating human organs. When the culprit attributes the stench to a malfunctioning freezer, neighbors naturally accept his plausible explanation. Psychologists may call this denial; if so, it is not a negative form of denial. It would be unfortunate indeed if people were to become so jaded that they automatically imagined only the worst of one another—"There's that smell again; Jeff must be cooking bodies."

Of all the people who might be blamed for the hideous crimes in Milwaukee, the one who is clearly most responsible is Dahmer himself. Although legitimate questions remain surrounding the ineffectual responses of the Milwaukee police as well as Dahmer's probation officer, the killer himself refused to deflect blame and instead assumed total responsibility for the crimes. Speaking in court prior to sentencing, Dahmer testified:

> I take all the blame for what I did. I hurt many people. The judge in my earlier case tried to help me and I refused his help and he got hurt by what I did. I hurt those policemen in the Konerak [Sinthasomphone] matter and shall forever regret causing them to lose their jobs. And I hope and pray

that they can get their jobs back because I know they did their best and I just plain fooled them.

For that I am so sorry. I know I hurt my probation officer, who was really trying to help me. I am so sorry for that and sorry for everyone else that I have hurt. I have hurt my mother and father and step-mother. I loved them all so very much. (Associated Press, 1992)

KILLING FOR COMPANIONSHIP

Notwithstanding his courtroom remorse after the fact, what seems to be Dahmer's motive for killing? Why would an ordinary-looking, even handsome, man—one who doesn't hear voices or see things that aren't there, who holds a steady job and comes from a substantial family background—desire to have sex with dead bodies and to eat their organs? According to British author Brian Masters (1985), Dahmer felt so rejected and was so devoid of satisfying human relationships that he killed for companionship. He was almost a carbon copy of Dennis Andrew Nilsen, the case study for Masters's true-crime classic *Killing for Company* (1985).

From December 1978 to February 1983, Nilsen, a 37-year-old British government worker, killed and mutilated 15 young men in his north London flat. Over the 4-year period, Nilsen developed a routine for murder. Nilsen typically solicited his victims in a nearby pub, then invited them home for a nightcap. In a ritualized manner, he waited for them to pass out from drinking and then strangled them. He then dunked their heads in a pail of water to ensure that they had stopped breathing. Afterward, he scrubbed their bodies in the bathtub, then carried them to his bed for lovemaking.

But sex wasn't Nilsen's only motive. He was lonely and needing companionship, and he realized that dead men don't leave. He dined with his dead friends, watched television with them, and even carried on (one-sided) conversations with them.

Nilsen saved his favorite corpses by temporarily storing them under the floor boards in the living room. The cool temperature under the floor could preserve his partners for only so long, however. Once his silent partners were too decomposed to be either desirable or satisfying, Nilsen got rid of them. He carefully dismembered the bodies, boiled the remains, and either burned them or flushed them down the toilet.

Jeffrey Dahmer, in a similar way, wanted to keep his victims around for a while. He, too, was lonely and forlorn. As a boy, he collected dead animals for companionship. Ever since his youth, Dahmer had trouble making friends and spent much of his time alone with his dead things. He didn't want to be rejected anymore. Like Nilsen, Dahmer as an adult attempted to find lasting friendship with his victims. He sedated them, strangled them to death, and then had sex with their lifeless bodies. Unlike his English counterpart, however, Dahmer also sought, unsuccessfully, to keep some of his captives alive by drugging them into unconsciousness and performing a crude lobotomy. In this way, he hoped that they would permanently become zombie-like sex toys, capable of fulfilling his every desire.

THE FUNCTIONS OF CANNIBALISM

Surgery wasn't Dahmer's only strategy for keeping his victims around. As disgusting as it may seem, Dahmer's practice of eating his victims was as much an expression of love or affection as of hate. What he couldn't keep alive, he ate. To maintain the presence of his lovers, he actually consumed the body parts including the organs. Tracy Edwards, Dahmer's surviving final victim, recognized that his assailant's statement about literally "taking his heart" was more a benevolent sign of affection than a malicious threat. Through what anthropologists have called "affectionate cannibalism," Dahmer's young captives literally became a part of him—and that was his objective.

Reportedly, some primitive cultures practiced affectionate cannibalism by consuming their loved ones as part of the funeral ritual. Other cultures have sublimated this practice by eating cookies bearing the image of the deceased or devouring animals placed upon the grave of the departed loved one.

Thus, cannibalism has both aggressive and affectionate motivations (Sagan, 1981). Both of these motivations, in fact, can be found in the psychological and symbolic meaning of some of the language that we use every day. For example, "grilling someone" indicates a hostile interrogation, and harsh criticism is known as "chewing someone out." On the other hand, a parent will say lovingly to his or her child, "I could just eat you up," and complimentary remarks are known as "buttering someone up."

From a Freudian point of view, separation from a loved one through death gives rise to mixed feelings of sadness and anger. Grieving children confronted with the premature death of a parent, for example, have been known to feel abandoned and to express feelings of hostility toward the deceased. Not understanding illness or death, they blame the parent for "choosing" to leave them. Already suffering from a profound sense of rejection, Dahmer similarly resented the death of his victims, even though he was the one who caused it.

DESIRE FOR TOTAL CONTROL AND OWNERSHIP

The total control of another human being can be seen most clearly in the case of 36-year-old Robert Andrew Berdella, owner of Bob's Bizarre Bazaar in Kansas City, Missouri. Berdella's curio shop was nowhere nearly as bizarre, however, as his three-story home on Charlotte Street, inside of which he murdered six young men between 1984 and 1987. Berdella may have killed a seventh person—and possibly more—had not 22-year-old Christopher Bryson been lucky enough to escape his 3-day captivity. Pretending to be Berdella's obedient sex slave, Bryson waited for his opportunity to make his break for freedom. Jumping from a second-floor window, he ran down the street wearing nothing but a dog collar. The deep ligature marks on the escapee's wrists and ankles and his badly swollen eyes gave the police an ominous preview of what they would find in Berdella's house of horrors.

With Christopher Bryson, Berdella thought he had succeeded in achieving his dream of owning a doll-like sex object that he could play with in whatever way he chose. His plan, which had failed with his earlier captives, involved breaking the will and spirit of strong young men; once they were broken, he expected them to comply with his every desire.

Berdella sedated his victims with animal anesthetics and tranquilizers that he had obtained from a local veterinary supply house. To render his captives unconscious, he placed drugs into their food or gave them potent sedatives in place of vitamins, aspirin, or recreational drugs. Once they had passed out, he restrained them with ropes, gags, and a dog collar around the neck. In the days following a capture, Berdella progressively dehumanized his captives. He deprived them of all sensation—except the sensations that he inflicted. He blinded his victims with chemicals and probed his finger into their eyes, poured drain cleaner down their throats, squirted bathtub caulking into their ears, and restricted their intake of food and water.

Berdella also used various instruments of torture, including an electrical transformer and metal spatulas with which he applied electric shocks to various parts of their bodies. He also beat them on the head with a rubber mallet; stuck them with needles; and pounded their limbs with boards, sticks, and a heavy metal pipe. At the extreme, Berdella sodomized his victims with his arm and a variety of vegetables.

The circumstances surrounding the deaths of Berdella's sex slaves varied in many respects. None of them apparently was killed for the sake of pleasure or excitement. Two of the victims were suffocated with plastic bags when Berdella feared he would be discovered. Others died from medical complications arising from their maltreatment, such as drug overdoses, infection, and head injuries.

To hide evidence of his dark passion, Berdella dismembered each corpse by cutting it at the joints and wrapping the body parts in plastic garbage bags, which he set out for the garbage collector. None of these bodies was ever recovered, although police did find two heads that Berdella had kept, one hidden in a closet and the other buried in the backyard.

Berdella sought total submission of another human being. He confessed to experiencing an exhilarating sense of power by holding his victims captive. He wanted his victims "reduced to the level of, say, a blow-up doll or clay figure you would make as a kid: moving [them] around, having complete control [of them]" (Blakeman, 1989, p. A18).

Berdella's explanation is quite revealing. Like Dahmer and Nilsen, he sought to own someone. Berdella's objective was not so much to inflict pain on his victims as to dominate their total existence. Thus, this type of power is very different from the kind of control sought by purely sexually sadistic killers like Theodore Bundy and Kenneth Bianchi. Typically, serial killers like Bundy and Bianchi celebrate the suffering of their victims. The more their victims scream and beg for mercy, the more stimulated they become. A killer like Bundy would never have sedated his victim before raping her. A killer like Bianchi would never have drugged his victim before strangling her. That would take all the fun out of it. Bundy and Bianchi discarded their victims like refuse, but Berdella hoped to keep his pliant "playmates" forever.

CHAPTER 8

Fantasyland

Randy Kraft was considered by neighbors, friends, and business associates as a decent and intelligent 30-something man whose casual lifestyle seemed to fit the California scene. Homeowner, computer consultant, and college graduate, "Uncle Randy," as he was known to his nieces and nephews, was meticulous in his personal appearance and caring in his demeanor. His short walrus-style mustache and sandy blond hair were always trimmed and neat, and his frequent visits to the beach left him looking tanned and healthy.

Carefully concealed behind a facade of civility and kindness, however, there was another side to Randy Kraft. When he wasn't busy tinkering with his computers or visiting relatives, he was butchering young men. Over a period of at least 12 years, he sodomized and mutilated as many as 67 victims in California, Oregon, and Michigan. Until May 14, 1983, nobody suspected this activity.

It was 1 a.m. on a warm spring night, about 50 miles south of Los Angeles on Interstate 5. Kraft had been drinking heavily. He tried to control his brown 1979 Toyota Celica, but it weaved back and forth across the shoulder of the highway—so much so that Kraft attracted the attention of Orange County highway patrol officers who had been following his Toyota in the right-hand lane for several minutes and finally pulled him over to make sure he wasn't under the influence.

The two officers discovered more than a few bottles of beer. Slumped in the passenger seat was the body of a 200-pound, 25-year-old Marine who had been strangled with a belt. His penis and testicles were exposed through the open fly in his jeans. Fresh ligature marks were deeply embedded into both of his wrists. His shoes had been removed and placed beneath the front seat.

A search of Kraft's car uncovered evidence of much greater carnage. First, even though the dead Marine had not suffered open wounds, the passenger's seat was soaked with blood. Under the driver's side floor mat was an envelope containing 47 color photographs of young men. Some were nude; others were clothed. Some looked unconscious or asleep; many looked dead. In the trunk, investigators found a briefcase that contained a two-column list of 61 printed notations, all in code, which turned out to be a record of Kraft's murder victims.

Kraft never admitted to the killings, and to this day, his family believes him to be innocent. But an Orange County jury didn't see it that way. In a 13-month trial, prosecutors presented convincing physical evidence—fibers from Randy's carpet, stolen property in Randy's home, Randy's sofa shown in one of the photographs—to implicate the defendant.

Prosecutors also showed that Kraft had the opportunity. Between June 1980 and January 1983, he had worked for a California company that required him to make visits to its offices in Oregon and Michigan, at precisely the periods of time when the unsolved murders in these states occurred.

It wasn't only the large number of killings that shocked the members of the jury; it was also the grotesque and brutal quality of the crimes. Kraft was incredibly cruel and vicious, torturing his victims by burning their scrota, nipples, lips, and eyes with an automobile cigarette lighter; slicing deeply into their arms and legs with a knife; jamming sharp instruments into their penises; hacking off their testicles; cramming leaves into their rectums; and stuffing dirt down their bronchial tubes until they gagged to death.

On May 12, 1989, after 11 days of deliberation, the jury found Randy Kraft guilty of committing 16 murders. During the penalty phase of the trial, however, the prosecution brought up the details of 21 more brutal killings to support asking for the death penalty. Sickened by the evidence, the jury gave the prosecution the verdict it had sought.

KEEPING SOUVENIRS

Like a ballplayer who keeps the baseball from his first major league hit, Randy Kraft saved the memory of his crimes in gruesome photographs and maintained an up-to-date scorecard of his exploits. Actually, many serial killers collect memorabilia or souvenirs—diaries, clothing, photos, even body parts—to remind them of their most cherished moments with their victims. In their study of 20 sexually sadistic serial killers, Janet I. Warren, Robert R. Hazelwood, and Park E. Dietz (1996) found that 13 collected trophies and nine recorded their crimes by various means. For example, Danny Rolling, the serial killer who murdered five young college students in Gainesville, Florida, in 1990, removed and kept the nipples of some of his female victims. Joel Rifkin, who confessed to murdering 17 prostitutes in New York in 1993, kept his victims' underwear, shoes, sweaters, cosmetics, and jewelry in his bedroom. Jeffrey Dahmer proudly displayed pictures of his victims on the walls of his apartment. New Jersey serial killer Richard Cottingham collected the clothes and jewelry of his victims in a special room of his home, which he kept locked to keep away his unsuspecting wife and children.

When police searched the apartment of child slayer Wesley Allan Dodd, they found plenty of incriminating evidence. Dodd had maintained a neatly labeled photo album of his victims, including grotesque pictures of one boy hanging by the neck. Dodd had also kept a diary of his crimes, which included an itemized list of his victims and a chart of murder techniques classified by the speed with which they caused death.

Kansas City killer Robert Berdella had a particularly rich collection of souvenirs, including two human skulls, a pouchful of teeth, and more than 200 photographs of his victims, shown in a variety of degrading poses, taken during various stages of captivity and after death. He also chronicled his accomplishments in a detailed log of his tortures. Methodically recording the time and date of each physical attack, each sexual assault, each injection of sedative, and each physiological response of the victim, his hand-scrawled notebooks resembled more a hospital's medical chart than the ravings of a madman.

Even though it was ultimately used as condemning evidence against him, Berdella's prized collection of macabre mementos also served several important purposes for him. First, for a man who had otherwise led an unremarkable life, his treasures made him feel proud. They represented the one and only way in which he had ever distinguished himself. It may have been fiendish, but it was a power trip that few others had ever attempted, let alone achieved.

More important, the souvenirs became tangible reminders of the "good times" Berdella had spent with his playmates. With the aid of his photographs, he could still get pleasure, between captives, from reminiscing, daydreaming, fantasizing, and even masturbating.

NORMAL AND ABNORMAL FANTASIES

Not all fantasy life is pathological. In fact, ordinary, healthy human beings often dream about their hopes and pleasures, even those that are beyond their reach. Some of the fantasies may include deviant and bizarre sexual practices, such as fetishes, pedophilia, bondage, and rape. Some may lust in their hearts and their heads but not in their habits. Because of their strong sense of conscience or concern about their public image, they resist translating desire for sexual violence into action.

Lack of self-control is not the only characteristic separating serial killers from those who don't act on their aggressive fantasies. The serial killer tends to have incredibly rich, detailed, and elaborate fantasies inspiring him to disregard both law and convention. Through murder and mayhem, the serial killer literally chases his dreams. With each successive victim, he attempts to fine-tune the act, striving to make his real-life experiences as perfect as his fantasy.

As the crimes become more vicious with time, the serial killer's mental script becomes more demanding. Not only is the behavior inspired by fantasy, but the fantasy also is nourished and crystallized by the memory of offenses already committed. As a result, the crimes grow increasingly brutal and grotesque as the killer remains caught in a never-ending spiral of image and action.

Because of the important role of thought and fantasy, serial killers often have remarkably vivid and detailed memories of their killings. Using his "torture diary" as a guide, Robert Berdella recounted to authorities the specific events of his crimes dating back several years as though they had just occurred. In a matter-of-fact fashion, Berdella described how his victims were captured and subdued, how they responded to his "experiments," and how they died.

Many other serial killers keep only a mental diary, yet they are no less precise in their recollections. For example, in his lengthy confession, Joel Rifkin amazed the New York State Police by reciting the specifics of each of his 17 prostitute murders. Rifkin confessed in detail, recalling the criteria for choosing his victims, the color of their hair, the clothing they wore, his method of strangling them after performing sex in his truck, and his strategy for disposing of the bodies. With chilling precision, he told how he dismembered some of the murdered women and stored others in his garage. During the entire 8-hour confession, Rifkin was nothing less than calm, cool, and dispassionate. Between lurid revelations of murder and mayhem, he munched on hamburgers and sipped tea.

How could Rifkin have kept straight in his mind so many details of the 17 slayings to which he confessed? How could he remember exactly what he did to whom and when he did it? The answer has less to do with intelligence and memory skills than with motivation. Like a boy who remembers every detail of a major league ballgame he attends but can't seem to recall his assigned vocabulary words, Rifkin easily kept track of what was really important to him. Killing was his passion. These were his most precious memories. Not only could he experience the thrill of killing, but he also could relive them over and over again in his fantasies.

THE IMPACT OF PORNOGRAPHY

When the police search the home of a suspected serial killer, they sometimes uncover not only clothing and jewelry, as in Rifkin's residence, but also extensive libraries of films and tapes that depict acts of rape, torture, and murder. Sometimes the movies are homemade. Leonard Lake and Charles Ng, as we've noted, used a camcorder that they had stolen from one of their victims to record their torture sessions. Paul Bernardo and Karla Homolka videotaped their sexual assaults. In other cases, pornographic materials are commercially produced. John Wayne Gacy, for example, had a prized collection of pornographic videotapes that would be the envy of almost any serial killer.

According to FBI research on sexual homicide, serial killers typically collect hardcore pornography, often containing themes of violence, dominance, and bondage. Among 36 convicted perpetrators of sexual homicide, 81% reportedly had a keen interest in pornographic material, particularly of a violent nature (Ressler et al., 1988). Undoubtedly, the preoccupation with violent pornography plays a role in the fantasy life of a serial killer. Films showing rape and torture may provide examples to enrich his own imagination.

The connection between violent pornography and sexual aggression may possibly be generalizable from experimental research showing that a steady diet of violent pornography causes male subjects to be more aggressive, sexually aroused, and desensitized to the plight of victims of sexual assault (see Malamuth & Donnerstein, 1984). Moreover, Neil M. Malamuth and Edward I. Donnerstein (1984) suggest that the research literature "strongly supports the assertion that the mass media can contribute to a cultural climate that is more accepting of aggression against women" (p. 40).

The critical question, however, is whether pornography operates as a drive mechanism for serial murder—that is, does an interest in violent sexual films and photos cause or merely reflect the serial killer's fascination with murder? The problems of distinguishing cause from effect have long plagued researchers eager to understand the development of violent impulses. Not surprisingly, people who

are, for whatever reason, predisposed to violence will be drawn to violent pornography. This does not necessarily mean that the pornography created their
predisposition toward violence, although it may reinforce or exacerbate it. It may
also tend to desensitize viewers to the pain and suffering of real-life victims of
sexual violence.

In the same way, it is commonplace to learn that serial killers, when captured, are found to possess extensive libraries of violent pornographic materials. This, too, is not surprising, nor does it implicate violent pornography as a
fundamental cause of serial murder. Rather, it reflects a general preoccupation
with sexual violence that pervades every aspect of the killers' leisure time.
When they're not killing, serial murderers can at least fantasize about killing
with the aid of photographs and videos.

In other areas of life, we find a correspondence between what people do for
work or recreation and what they choose to read or watch in their leisure time.
A successful business executive may read the *Wall Street Journal* on a regular
basis, but we would hardly claim that the interest in business resulted from
reading that paper, although it may have encouraged and supported it. Similarly,
an avid hunter may subscribe to *Field and Stream* for entertainment when not
out hunting.

Thirty-nine-year-old Leslie Allen Williams, who confessed to killing four
women and raping several others in suburban Detroit in 1992, diagnosed the
impact of sex in the media. In a detailed 24-page letter to the *Detroit News*
(June 18, 1992) about his crimes, he wrote,

> Females are fortunate in that they are pretty much given one message
> from the very beginning: "NO, NO, NO." . . . Save it for love and mar-
> riage. Meanwhile, males are given messages of "GO, GO, GO." . . . Get it
> when and if you can to be a man. . . . Along with and on top of all that,
> males are subjected to a barrage of stimulators . . . everything from
> advertisers and TV shows, books and tabloids, to entertainers and role-
> models. . . . Everywhere they turn, they are told it is OK to be sexually
> active and aggressive.

Some multiple murderers may pattern their behavior—their modus operandi—
after real or fictional accounts of similar crimes. But the larger problem is, as
Williams suggests, found in our popular culture. Some isolated individuals may
learn how to kill from the media, but countless others might get the general message that it's acceptable.

For decades, social analysts have suggested that media portrayals—particularly
visual images of fictional events aimed at a younger audience—may normalize
the expression of violence. To concerned parents of the 1960s, motion pictures
were responsible for teaching America's children a dangerous lesson—namely, that
the consequences of violence are temporary and trivial. Cinematic characters that
were shot, slashed, or punched in the mouth rarely ever bled. Their injuries or
deaths typically were presented in a sanitized or cleaned-up manner.

If one were to judge only by the body counts, movies of today are no more
violent than their counterparts 25 years ago, but their portrayal of murder and
mayhem no longer leaves anything to the imagination. In fact, the consequences

of violence are now routinely depicted as graphically as possible, without regard for how they may strike impressionable young viewers. Violence is not just central to the plot; it is central to the purpose. The various ways of bringing about a gory death become the main object of the movie.

In one motion picture after another, viewers are treated to disgusting scenes of decapitation and dismemberment. Victims are shown with their brains literally blown apart, their heads missing, their fingers sliced off, and their intestines exposed. Because of the DVD, moreover, children can now replay their favorite gory scenes over and over, never leaving the privacy of their own homes.

Parents who used to be worried about teaching their children that violence has consequences now have a much more difficult problem: how to keep them from becoming totally desensitized to human misery, mayhem, and murder. Even worse, how can parents keep children from lusting for scenes in new movies showing more novel ways of inflicting pain and torture on a victim? The fun once achieved in a "spook house"—anxiously anticipating the next horror to scare you personally—has been replaced by the sadistic kick in seeing someone else tortured. Because of the steady diet of gory films to which they are exposed, children are slowly but surely growing more tolerant of the effects of violence. They are no longer repulsed by stories of extreme brutality, even when they are real.

The change in mass culture involves more than just how graphic a portrayal of violence we will accept or desire. Virtually all forms of media violence—in television and movies, in commercials and rock videos—have become sexualized. Not only does the combination of sex and violence suggest that violence is pleasurable, but it also identifies certain kinds of people—and women in particular—as appropriate victims. In these forms of entertainment, women are depicted as objects. They are dehumanized, cast in the role of sex machines whose only purpose in life—and in death—is to give men pleasure. The dehumanization of certain groups of people—"fast" women, prostitutes, and gays—tells us not only that violence is OK, but also which victims are OK.

So-called slasher films routinely fuse sex with violence to seduce a youthful market. In the 2006 film *Hostel*, two male students travel to an eastern European youth hostel seeking out promiscuous women but instead find unimaginable torture. In the earlier film *The Toolbox Murders* (1978), promiscuous girls are punished for their passions by a moralistic maniac with power tools. One particularly powerful scene shows an attractive young woman who is nailed to the wall after she masturbates in a bubble bath. All the while, a romantic country ballad plays gently in the background. In what some regard as the most offensive slasher film ever produced, *I Spit on Your Grave* (1983, 2010), a young woman is stalked and tormented by four men in a remote wooded area. They gang rape and humiliate her for nearly half an hour in a spirit of fun, festivity, and friendship. For many youth whose first exposure to sex is a rape scene in a movie, the lesson is that violence is sexually arousing.

The possible effects of R-rated pornography have not gone unnoticed. For example, a 1986 task force assembled by U.S. Attorney General Edwin Meese strongly denounced this form of entertainment as being harmful to young Americans. Spearheading the movement to ban pornographic films, Focus on the Family, a Colorado-based nonprofit group, publishes eight magazines and broadcasts six radio programs, one of which is carried by nearly 2,000 radio stations in North America. Its outspoken leader and antiporn activist, Dr. James Dobson, interviewed Ted Bundy just prior to his execution by the state of Florida. According to the condemned man's 11th-hour confession, pornography is responsible for the rise of serial murder during recent years:

> People need to recognize that those of us who have been so much influenced by violence in the media—in particular pornographic violence—aren't some kind of inherent monsters. We are your sons, and we are your husbands. We grew up in regular families.
>
> Pornography can reach out and snatch a kid out of any house today. It snatched me out of my home thirty years ago. And as diligent as my parents were, and they were diligent in protecting their children, as good a Christian home as we had, and we had a wonderful Christian home, there is no protection against the kinds of influences that are loose in society. (Interview with James Dobson, Florida State Prison at Starke, February, 1989)

Ted Bundy's condemnation of pornography as an excuse for his own violent impulses wasn't so much a fabrication as it was a misunderstanding of the role of pornography in our culture. Violent pornography may not directly cause or inspire its consumers to develop into serial murderers, but it unquestionably provides a cultural context in which sexual homicide is encouraged. In this respect, violent pornography hurts all of us. But with regard to serial murder in particular, it is noteworthy that the increased accessibility to violent pornography over the past couple of decades has come at a time when the prevalence of serial murder has declined.

CHAPTER 9

The Making of
a Serial Killer

In June 1987, 40-year-old Arthur Shawcross was granted his freedom—freedom to kill. He had been convicted in 1972 of murdering two young children in upstate New York. His first victim was 10-year-old Jack Blake, whom he kidnapped while Jack was on his way to a friend's house to play. Shawcross confessed to having raped and butchered the boy, and then devouring his genitals. Shawcross's other victim was 8-year-old Karen Ann Hill, whom he raped and murdered. Shawcross served the minimum of a 15- to 25-year sentence before being paroled.

Despite his hideous past, Shawcross blended well into the Rochester community where he settled after his release from custody. It didn't take him long to pick up where he left off, only this time victimizing prostitutes rather than children. The middle-age killer appeared, to the hustlers he targeted, like just another john. Overweight and balding, he hardly seemed threatening to the women he picked up, even after they had been alerted that a serial killer was on the loose and preying on streetwalkers.

By March 1988, the police in Rochester had discovered the partially nude bodies of two prostitutes floating in the Genesee River gorge. One woman had been asphyxiated, the other shot. The police saw no clear-cut pattern to link these homicides, other than the victims' occupation. The homicides drew little attention in part because it is hardly unusual for prostitutes to get killed because of the sleazy clientele with whom they do business.

Six months later, however, the police found the skeletal remains of a third victim in the same area; shortly thereafter, they uncovered a fourth body, also in the river gorge. By this point, if only because of the high frequency of the killings, the police were forced to confront the frightening probability that a serial killer was on the prowl and targeting women of the night.

By Thanksgiving 1988, the 10th body, that of 29-year-old June Stott, was discovered. This case was strikingly different from the other nine, however. Not only was the murder particularly grotesque—the woman's body had been eviscerated from the neck down to her pubic bone—but Stott also was the first victim who was not a prostitute. It is commonplace for serial killers to increase their level of brutality as they get bored with less vicious behavior and as they grow more comfortable with murder. It is also commonplace for them to branch out to more respectable victims as they become convinced that they are smarter than the police and will never be apprehended.

Shawcross was no different in this regard. His sense of invincibility and carelessness ultimately led to his demise. Long after dumping the body of his 12th victim, June Cicero, in Simon Creek, Shawcross returned to mutilate her corpse. Surveying the area by helicopter, the Rochester police spied Shawcross getting into his car, which was parked on a bridge some 15 feet above Cicero's body.

After Shawcross was arrested for suspicion of murder, his mug shot was placed into a photo lineup. Detectives often compile a sheet of photographs, mixing a suspect's picture with those of several others, to approximate an actual station-house lineup for field use. The police showed the photo lineup to local prostitute Joanne Van Nostrand. She immediately picked out Shawcross as the perverted john who needed her to play dead for him to get sexually aroused. As Van Nostrand recalled about her encounter with Shawcross,

> He was real nervous. That made me nervous and I carry a knife to protect myself. . . . So I just let him know point-blank that I had a weapon and that I was nervous that there was a serial killer. The only time he was really abusive to me is when I asked him why was it taking so long—I had been there, like, 40 minutes. That's when he really said, "Well, if you just play dead, bitch, we'll get this over in a few minutes." Little things kept clicking, and the hairs on the back of my neck started standing up and I said [to myself], "This is the guy. I just know this is the guy." (Klein, 1992)

After his arrest, Shawcross began confessing and explained why he had killed 13 women. "I was taking care of business," he stated. Clearly, Shawcross's explanation for his crimes begged this question: Why did he kill these women, and why was he aroused by death and sexual mutilation? Several experts, including New York University psychiatrist Dr. Dorothy Otnow Lewis, who testified on Shawcross's behalf to support his insanity plea, traced the sources of his behavior back to his childhood, particularly to mistreatment at the hands of his sexually provocative mother.

CHILDHOOD SUFFERING

The psychiatric case study of Arthur Shawcross runs true to form. Whenever the background of an infamous serial killer is examined, journalists and behavioral scientists tend to search for clues in the killer's childhood that might explain his seemingly senseless murders. Many writers have emphasized Ted Bundy's concerns over being illegitimate, and biographers of Kenneth Bianchi, the Hillside Strangler of Los Angeles, capitalized on his having been adopted. When it was alleged that Jeffrey Dahmer was abused, Americans felt satisfied that at last they had an answer to his puzzling crimes: "Now we know why he did it—he was abused as a child!"

Ever since Sigmund Freud's psychoanalytic theory revolutionized thinking about childhood development, we have embraced the idea that our first few years largely determine the script by which we play out the rest of our lives. As a result, there is a strong tendency in our culture to blame parents—and particularly mothers—for almost everything that goes amiss later in a child's life, including violent behavior. Thus, when the allegations of sexual abuse in Dahmer's background surfaced in the press, the public uncritically accepted childhood trauma as the true cause of his crime. The *Oprah Winfrey Show* went so far as to air a program on "future Jeffrey Dahmers," featuring mothers who were concerned that their incorrigible youngsters were destined to develop into cold-blooded criminals. Ironically, the host of the show herself had survived a troubled upbringing, involving severe child abuse, yet had become the most successful talk show host in television history rather than a killer—a talker rather than a stalker.

Even the experts have overstated the role of childhood problems as the primary cause of serial killing. According to psychiatrist Dorothy Lewis,

> In the serial killers I've seen, there's almost invariably a history of early and ongoing sexual abuse. The murder victims sometimes represent a symbolic revenge against the abuser, or sometimes the reverse—the killer is identifying with whoever tortured him, and is now the one in power. (Goleman, 1993, p. B6)

Similarly, psychiatrist David Abrahamsen, author of *The Murdering Mind* (1973), speculated that serial killer Ted Bundy may have killed dozens of women as an indirect way to "kill" his mother: "The victim is not really the target; the victim is a substitute, and that is why these crimes seem so random and capricious" (Nordheimer, 1989, p. 1A). Also, psychologist John Watkins, in probing the mind of Hillside Strangler Kenneth Bianchi, explained, "Consumed by pent-up rage at his mother, Bianchi killed the women" (M. Barnes, 1984). Defense psychiatrist Donald Lunde went one step further by suggesting that Bianchi would never satiate his compulsion to kill until he could murder his mother (which he never attempted to do).

This mother-hate theory suggests that serial killers get even for the real or perceived abusive treatment they received at the hands of their parents by displacing their aggression onto surrogate victims who resemble the offending parent, usually the mother, in terms of physical appearance or behavior. By this reasoning, a killer who targets prostitutes is acting out his hostile feeling for a mother he saw as a slut. Alternatively, a killer who preys upon redheaded victims is conjectured to be avenging mistreatment by his redheaded mother.

There may be isolated examples of serial killers who, motivated by mother hatred, seek out victims who ignite angry memories of their childhood. For example, serial killer Henry Lee Lucas included his mother among his many victims; when he was young, she dressed him in girls' clothing and forced him to witness her sexual exploits. In most cases, however, victim selection reflects much more directly issues of opportunity, victim vulnerability, and the character of the killer's sexual fantasies.

Did Arthur Shawcross target prostitutes because he was angry over the sexual provocativeness of his mother, or did he take the easy and safe route? By selecting streetwalkers as victims, he was able to drive to an area of town where he knew they congregated. He could "shop" for one who most closely fit his sexual urges. He could entice her into his car without making a scene. And he was assured that her disappearance would likely not be considered foul play.

What, then, is the role of childhood in understanding the nature or cause of Shawcross's serial killing? The early biographies of most people include an array of both positive and negative events. There is a tendency in our culture, however, to focus selectively on those incidents that are consistent with the outcome that we are trying to explain. Thus, in searching for clues to explain how a serial killer has developed, a psychiatrist who subscribes to the troubled childhood view would tend to emphasize the negative experiences. Some have even used hypnosis to aid in their search for evidence of abuse and trauma that might lie deeply hidden beneath the surface of consciousness.

Dr. Lewis, for example, was hired by defense counsel in the Arthur Shawcross case to reveal Shawcross's motivation and to support a plea of insanity in his trial for the murders of prostitutes. Lewis testified that Shawcross suffered from posttraumatic stress disorder brought on in part by experiences of abuse during his childhood. Lewis based this conclusion on sessions of hypnosis in which she age-regressed Shawcross for early memories of mistreatment. At first, he recalled having a normal upbringing and failed to reveal any abusive experiences. After lengthy and persistent probing under hypnosis, however, Shawcross finally "remembered" being sodomized by his mother with a broomstick and being forced to perform oral sex with her. According to Lewis,

> Most violent men I see would much rather be considered bad or evil than crazy. So they really don't want to talk about the voices they hear or times they have blacked out. And many of them . . . are still intent on protecting their families, even though their families hideously abused them. (Bass, 1991, p. 21)

Did Lewis's discovery of suppressed and painful memories of abuse in Shawcross's background reflect an uncompromising effort to uncover the truth about deeply hidden secrets? Or did Shawcross finally give his examiner exactly what he figured she expected to hear? Either way, Shawcross's mother called her son a liar; given his attempt to save himself through the insanity plea, he certainly had very good reason to fabricate or exaggerate bad childhood experiences. We really can't know for certain, however.

TESTIMONY UNDER HYPNOSIS

The therapeutic uses of hypnosis—from treating compulsive behavior to identifying the sources of emotional conflict—are well documented and widely accepted. The forensic applications of hypnosis are, however, much more controversial. Research on hypnosis indicates that the so-called hypnotic trance is little more than accepting the suggestions of a highly credible source. According to psychologist Theodore X. Barber, author of *Hypnosis: A Scientific Approach* (1969), almost every extraordinary act or recollection that a subject gives under hypnosis can be obtained without hypnosis. All that is needed is a respected and trusted authority figure to make commands—under hypnosis or not—such as "you will lose weight," "you will not smoke," or even "you will remember being abused as a child."

The other important finding uncovered by researchers is that hypnosis increases the level of confidence but not accuracy in recalling events. For example, under hypnosis, witnesses to a crime involving a masked gunman have been asked to remove mentally the criminal's disguise and describe his face. Filling in the details on their own, these hypnotized subjects become convinced about the description they give. It may be a figment of their imagination, perhaps based on stereotypes, but it is one of which they are absolutely sure. In the same way, psychologists studying hypnosis have compared age regression with age progression. After first taking their subjects back several years in life to recall events at that time, they then take them forward into the future and ask them to describe what they are doing. Subjects tend to recollect the future in as much detail and certainty as they recall the past.

The fact that hypnotized subjects can confidently recall, create, or alter their biographies casts doubt on the accuracy of memories. On one hand, it is quite possible that a hypnotized subject will reveal painful yet accurate memories of childhood. On the other hand, subjects can fabricate events in their past if it suits the occasion, the context, or some ulterior motive.

In forensic work, the hypnotist deals with a subject who may have a stake in faking a hypnotic trance and divulging inaccurate information about himself and his past. Someone can be in a trance and still provide false information. The hypnotist can actually create the information through subtle and perhaps not-so-subtle suggestions to the subject. Thus, it is possible for an individual who may indeed have felt intimidated as a child to recall under hypnosis experiences of abuse, particularly if the hypnotist solicits such recollections and the subject has a self-serving interest in providing them.

CHILD ABUSE AND MURDER

The case of serial murderer Kenneth Bianchi provides another revealing example of how hypnosis has been exploited to find support for the child abuse explanation for murderous impulses. In 1977 and 1978, Ken and his cousin Angelo Buono abducted, tortured, raped, and murdered 10 young women, whose bodies they dumped along roadsides in the Los Angeles area.

Kenneth Bianchi's insanity defense was centered on the theory that he suffered from a *multiple personality disorder* (MPD). This psychiatric illness, characterized by the presence of two or more distinct and separate personalities that share the same body, is generally attributed to child abuse. In this view, an abused child escapes from cruel parental treatment by developing a fantasy world of pleasure and kindness. At the same time, the angry and hateful feelings toward the abusive parent are stored in a reservoir that the child suppresses. In later life, the two perspectives—the loving and the hateful—split into their own personalities that compete for control. The angry "person" takes turns with various alter egos for dominance over the same body.

If Bianchi were, in fact, a multiple personality, this could easily explain and reconcile how someone as seemingly nice as Ken could also commit the heinous crimes with which he was charged. Through hypnosis, a second personality surfaced, that of "Steve," a hostile, crude, impatient, and sadistic character who proudly claimed responsibility for the slayings. "Killing a broad doesn't make any difference to me," bragged Steve (M. Barnes, 1984). Everything now made sense to the psychiatrists.

Court-appointed experts on multiple personalities found ample support within Ken's extensive medical history for holding his adoptive mother, Frances Piccione, responsible. For example, Dr. A. W. Sullivan of the DePaul Clinic in Rochester, where Ken was seen at the age of 11, suggested that Frances played a major role in her son's childhood problems: "She has dominated the boy and indulged him in terms of her own needs. Her anxious, protective, clinging control has made him ambivalent but he represses the hostile aggression and is increasingly dependent upon her" (Dr. Sullivan's notes in Bianchi's medical file, unpublished).

Medical records from Ken's childhood characterized Frances as a neurotic and ineffective parent. To account for the emergence of Ken's vicious personality, however, court-appointed psychiatric experts needed to find specific evidence of severe child abuse per se.

Bianchi was advised by his hypnotist that his medical history failed to include the kind of documentation of child abuse that would be needed to support his defense based on multiple personality disorder. Hypnotized once more, Bianchi then recalled a dream about a woman putting his hands over a kitchen stove fire while he was young. Finally, the psychiatrists had the evidence of abuse that was lacking!

When later asked about her son's dream, Frances was candid. She admitted having used the stove as a threat, but not with the intent to inflict pain or injury:

> When Ken was eight years old, I caught him stealing. He had taken some pieces of coral from a greenhouse we had just visited. We had a small kitchen, six or seven feet wide, with a doorway at one end and the stove at the other. Ken was standing at the door with his father. "See this fire," I said. "If I catch you stealing once more, I'll hold your hand over this stove." (personal interview, 1992)

Although harsh and threatening discipline of this sort can be interpreted as abuse, it is usually not considered to be at the level needed to create a dissociative personality state such as MPD. Had Frances done anything more than threaten, surely the many doctors whom Ken had seen for his medical problems would have reported burns or scars on his hand. Had she been a *severely abusive mother*, as some labeled her, there would have been many more stories of brutal treatment. At the very worst, Bianchi, through hypnotic age regression, may have interpreted his mother's threatened punishment as if it had really been inflicted upon him.

A number of psychiatrists hold that the roots of "homicidal proneness" reside not only in maternal brutality but also in sexual seduction, which can be played out in anything from incest between mother and child to inappropriate or excessive conversation about sexual matters. The victim of maternal seduction grows up overly anxious about his sexuality. Fueled by this anxiety, the hostility toward mother generalizes later in life to sexual violence against women.

Court-appointed psychiatrists also attempted to weave a picture of Bianchi's mother as a wantonly seductive woman. A physician at the DePaul Clinic, where Ken was seen for chronic bed wetting, had years earlier scrawled some cryptic—barely legible—observations about Frances that became part of Ken's medical file. An unexplained reference to "sex magazines" was later interpreted by court-appointed psychiatrists to mean that she "showed him sex magazines." It could just as easily have meant that she had punished him for reading them, but this interpretation would not have fit the psychiatrists' point of view and so was never seriously considered.

Having failed to prove insanity and having been found guilty of murder, Ken Bianchi no longer has a self-serving motive for implicating his mother. Ken later confessed:

> There has never been child abuse in my family. I greatly exaggerated certain childhood incidents after they could not find an origin for the alleged multiple personality. I was told that multiples usually begin with child abuse. I lied. My lies were not supposed to have been released. Originally, they were mentioned in confidence. I am not proud of what I did. (personal interview, 1992)

INORDINATE NEED FOR POWER

Whether or not Bianchi's criminal behavior could be traced to parental abuse and seduction, childhood trauma does, in general, play an important role in explaining the development of murderous impulses. Children who are abused, neglected, or abandoned tend to grow into needy adults with difficulty bonding with others, a so-called *attachment disorder* (American Psychiatric Association, 1994). Lacking control over their own lives as children, many remain insecure as they mature, continuing to possess an intense need for control over their environment. From an early age, they are unable to trust others, and instead they learn to manipulate people in order to fulfill their needs.

This overpowering need for control can be fulfilled, however, in many different ways—some bad and others good. For example, some victims of abuse become abusive parents themselves, whereas others are driven toward careers devoted to helping victims of abuse. Additionally, some former abuse victims who have excessive needs for power and control are able to satisfy their needs in unscrupulous but nonviolent ways.

For example, some college professors—one hopes there are only a few—achieve a thrill when flunking students; they gain pleasure by hurting their students' chances for successful educations and careers, and they enjoy it all the more when the students beg for another chance or a make-up exam. Similarly, some business tycoons savor the experience of firing employees or destroying the career of a competitor. They profit from the experience not just financially but also in the sense of power they derive as they rule over the fate of others.

Thus, there are important similarities indeed between the ruthless tycoon and the ruthless serial killer. Had Kenneth Bianchi grown up to be a ruthless business executive—unkind but successful—rather than an infamous killer, his biographers would have pointed to the same childhood issues as critical turning points that ultimately strengthened his determination to succeed. Had Theodore Bundy been able to accomplish his goal of becoming an attorney, he might have done his "killing" in the courtroom to satisfy his need for power.

More than a few serial killers—from David Berkowitz to Joel Rifkin—were raised by adoptive parents. Moreover, based on an analysis of more than 450 serial killers, Michael A. Surrette and Michael G. Aamodt (2010) reported that as many as 8% were adopted, a figure that is almost three times higher than the prevalence of adoption drawn from the 2000 Census. The apparent overrepresentation of adoption in the biographies of serial killers has been exploited by those who are looking for simple explanations for heinous crimes, without a full analysis made of the mechanisms behind or value of the link between adoption and criminal behavior.

The first possible triggering mechanism surrounds the effects of rejection by birth parents. As a consequence of such rejection, some adopted children may develop feelings of abandonment and intense anger that stay with them throughout life. For example, New York's Son of Sam killer, David Berkowitz, who shot and killed six strangers while they sat in parked cars, may have been reacting in part to feelings of rejection. After returning from military service in the Korean War, Berkowitz learned of his adoption and was able years later to locate his biological mother and sister in Long Beach, Long Island. He was shocked, however, when he discovered that they wanted nothing to do with him. Shortly thereafter, his killing spree began.

In addition, some adopted children may be deprived of warmth and affection during the first few months of life, either because of a delay in locating a suitable placement or because the adoptive parents hesitate in making a full emotional commitment until the legal process is finalized. As a result, some of these children may fail to bond emotionally and, therefore, never develop a capacity for love and empathy.

Added to these environmental contributors, certain biological deficiencies related to criminality, such as low IQ and learning disabilities, may be more prevalent among the population of adopted children because of traits common to their biological parents. To whatever extent that criminal propensities are genetically linked, the higher proportions of prostitutes, drug users, and incarcerated women among mothers who give up their children for adoption will translate into a higher involvement of adoptees in criminal behavior. In addition, the poor prenatal care of many of the groups from which adopted children are drawn can similarly predispose these children to the same biological deficiencies that correlate with criminal behavior.

ANIMAL CRUELTY AND VIOLENCE AGAINST HUMANS

For decades, criminologists and psychiatrists have sought to generate a set of warning signs in childhood to predict who would grow up to become a prolific serial killer. From the beginning, investigators focused on animal cruelty as symptomatic of later violence proneness, in general, and serial murder, in particular (Levin & Fox, 1991; Macdonald, 1963).

It makes sense that so much attention would be focused on animal abuse as a precursor of extreme forms of violence, including serial murder. Most criminologists accept the notion that the best indicator of future violence is previous violence; presumably, the early victims can be animals while the future targets are human.

Yet not all research investigating the predictive value of animal abuse has confirmed its connection with human violence, let alone serial murder (see Lea, 2007). In 1963, John Macdonald proposed that assaulting small animals was one of three precursors—along with fire setting and enuresis—of extreme cruelty toward humans. In a controlled study of "Macdonald's triad" in personal histories, however, Macdonald himself failed to confirm the hypothesis that violent psychiatric patients would be significantly more likely than nonviolent psychiatric patients to have abused animals.

By contrast, the overall conclusion of more recent research supports the presence of a link between animal abuse and human violence. Stephen R. Kellert and Alan R. Felthous (1985) uncovered significantly more animal cruelty in the childhoods of "aggressive criminals" than in the childhoods of "non-aggressive criminals" or "non-criminals." In their study of serial killers, Jeremy Wright and Christopher Hensley (2003) found that 75 killers, or 21% of their sample, had a known history of childhood animal cruelty. Robert K. Ressler, Ann W. Burgess, R. B. D'Agostino, and John E. Douglas (1988) similarly reported that a large number of the 36 convicted sexual murderers they studied—many of them serial killers—admitted having engaged in animal cruelty. More than half of these sexual killers had perpetrated animal abuse as either children or adolescents. Arnold Arluke, Jack Levin, Carter Luke, and Frank Ascione (1999), using official reports of animal cruelty and criminal records, determined in a comparative study of 153 animal abusers and 153 of their nonabusive neighbors that the abusers were much more likely to be engaged in antisocial behavior generally—in perpetrating interpersonal violence, but also in committing property offenses, drug offenses, and public disorder offenses.

More recently, Levin and Arluke (2009) examined true-crime books and websites detailing the offenses and backgrounds of 52 serial killers. Of these, 44 killers (or 85%) had reportedly tortured their victims. That is, in addition to causing the death of a human being, they had intentionally inflicted pain and suffering in an up-close and personal manner. Some videotaped the tortures; others audiotaped their victims as they screamed and begged for mercy. Many collected trophies from their victims—their jewelry, underwear, photos, or body parts—to help them later reminisce about their most cherished moments when victims were kept in the throes of unspeakable misery before their lives ended.

Among the 44 sadistic repeat killers in Levin and Arluke's (2009) sample, 32 (or 73%) had apparently also injured or killed animals. Almost all had engaged in animal cruelty during childhood or adolescence before they began committing serial murder. Twenty-four of the 44 sadistic killers (or 55%) also tortured the animals they had abused, by strangling, engaging in bestiality, decapitating while alive, beating, suffocating, stabbing, burning, skinning alive, hanging, or holding them under water. Twenty-one (88%) of the 24 killers who tortured animals had specifically targeted dogs and cats. Many individuals who grow up to be healthy and nonviolent abused animals as children, but very few of them practiced animal cruelty by torturing dogs and cats.

It may not be a coincidence that the ways in which the killers mistreated animals were strikingly similar to the methods the killers employed to end the lives of their human victims. At least 18 of the 24 (75%) killers who tortured animals in Levin and Arluke's (2009) sample used the same tortures on animals as they did on humans. For example, as a child, Robert Berdella decapitated a duck; he later beheaded one of his many male victims; Richard Chase drank both animal and human blood; Carroll Edward Cole strangled puppies and people; John Norman Collins strangled a cat and later on strangled six women; Adolfo de Jesus Constanzo first ritually sacrificed animals as a child and then ritually sacrificed humans as an adult; and Arthur Shawcross practiced bestiality growing up and later raped two of his female victims.

Even the relatively few serial killers who had not tortured their human victims but abused animals seemed to employ the same means for killing both their animal and human victims. For example, Jeffrey Dahmer, at the age of 10, collected and dissected roadkill in the same way that his classmates collected baseball cards. He later dismembered his human victims, keeping their body parts in his refrigerator. As a child, Lee Boyd Malvo used a slingshot and marbles to kill stray cats. As one of the DC Snipers, he shot his human victims with a long-distance rifle.

Many serial killers apparently learn the malicious behavior as a child with animals and then apply what they have learned in subsequently attacking their human victims. At the same time, serial killers may graduate in a number of different ways, not only from animal cruelty. They might, for example, escalate their violence from sexual assault to murder. Or, they might begin by targeting playmates or younger children. Animal abuse may turn out to be an important, but hardly exclusive, pivotal point for certain children who later become repeat killers.

CHALLENGES OF PREDICTING SERIAL MURDER

If any or all of these linkages between violent crime and childhood indicators are true, then is it fair to say that children who were adopted or abused, or those who tortured animals, are destined to kill? As a society, should we not intervene in the lives of these "children at risk" before it is too late?

The methodological problems in predicting violence are well known. For a category of violence as rare as serial murder, the consequent dilemma of false-positive prediction is overwhelming. Simply put, there are millions of adopted or abused Americans, many of whom may suffer from some form of insecurity as a result, but the vast majority of them will never kill anyone, let alone commit serial murder.

To illustrate further the absurdity of attempting to predict such rare characteristics as murder proneness, consider the link between gender and serial murder. Most serial killers are men, but most men are not serial killers—not even close. The same reasoning prevents us from identifying future serial murderers on the basis of such childhood factors as abuse, seduction, or even cruelty to animals that often are found in the backgrounds of serial killers.

Looking retrospectively at the childhoods of serial killers, it comes as little surprise that many were long fascinated with death and dying. Some of them, as children, enjoyed torturing animals and experienced a thrill in determining the fate of small, defenseless creatures. But even if each and every killer had abused animals during childhood, the false-positive factor would still prevent making predictive statements from earlier acts of animal cruelty. This is because so many ordinary, nonviolent individuals engage in animal abuse during childhood but never go on to commit violence against humans (Flynn, 1999; Kellert & Felthous, 1985; Goodney Lea, 2007; Miller & Knutson, 1997; Offord, Boyle, & Racine, 1991).

Therefore, although practicing on animals may be an instructive training ground for many sadistic serial killers, such childhood experimentation hardly guarantees that a youngster will graduate to human subjects. That is, many children maintain a vigorous fascination with dead animals; some even enjoy dissecting frogs in high school biology class. Some eventually do graduate into expressing violence against human beings. Such children, however, are far more likely to grow up to become surgeons, pathologists, nurses, or even morticians than they are to become serial killers. At the same time, the significance of extreme and persistent forms of animal cruelty as an indicator of an emotionally troubled child who is in need of treatment, and someone who is at risk for transitioning to violence directed at humans, should not be discounted. Because serious forms of animal abuse are common among sadistic serial killers, yet rare in the general population, the connection may serve as a red flag in a small number of children (Levin & Arluke, 2009).

Caution regarding the vital difference between explanation and prediction applies equally to today's sensitivity to child abuse. The so-called "cycle of violence" hypothesis rests on the finding that many abusive parents were themselves abused as children. Basing their therapy on this linkage, many well-meaning therapists help child abuse victims deal more effectively with anger and frustration in the hope that they themselves will not become abusive parents.

This strategy may indeed be a good thing, but for the wrong reason. It is appropriate to be concerned about the emotional well-being and quality of life of those who have been victimized by their parents, but to target them and thus stigmatize them for the hideous acts that they may commit sometime in the future, whether child abuse or serial murder, is to victimize them once again. The problem is deeper than just stigma. By labeling them as the abusers of tomorrow, we may actually create the very outcome that we are trying to prevent.

BIOLOGICAL PREDISPOSITION

There exists a long tradition in the study of criminal behavior of viewing the offender as identifiably different from noncriminals in ways related to biology, constitution, heredity, and intelligence. As early as the 18th century, scientific researchers were applying the techniques of physiognomy (the study of facial features) and phrenology (the study of bumps on the skull) in search of clues to criminal behavior.

The apparent breakthrough to uncovering the secrets of criminal conduct, however, came in 1876 when an Italian physician, Cesare Lombroso, published his famous study of Italian prisoners, *The Criminal Man*. Lombroso suggested that criminals were a throwback to an earlier, more primitive evolutionary stage of human development, a notion influenced heavily by Charles Darwin's theory. Lombroso, through his detailed empirical study of his subjects, noted that criminals showed outward signs of their differentness, known as stigmata, such as long arms, sloping foreheads, and protruding jaws. Their brains resembled those of "inferior animals."

Though largely discredited, Lombroso's insights and hypotheses generated what later came to be known as the science of criminology. Much of the subsequent research on criminal behavior, however, focused not on biological causes but on environmental factors located in the family, economy, and society. Searching for variables associated with violent crime, researchers studied such factors as family and neighborhood disorganization, child abuse, poverty and income inequality, educational deficits, and racism.

There may have been practical reasons for early criminologists looking to reduce violent behavior to concentrate on the role played by the social environment—namely, that the environment was amenable to both investigation and human intervention. By contrast, biological factors that might have been responsible for criminal behavior were regarded as fixed characteristics beyond the grasp of researchers and also not susceptible to change. Why study something that you cannot modify?

Recently, criminologists have broadened their research perspective by turning their attention again to biological bases for criminal behavior, especially the perpetrator's brain. Again, the reason may be essentially practical. The recent development of powerful imaging technologies has made it possible to view detailed pictures of the human brain and to trace activities along its neural pathways. For the first time, we are able to investigate the structure and functions of the brain in relation to criminal violence.

The work of neurocriminologist Adrian Raine (Nichols, 2009) is an excellent example of this new approach. Using magnetic resonance imaging, he scanned the brains of 21 sociopaths, comparing their results with those of a control group of "normal" temporary workers. Raine's findings revealed that the volume of gray matter in the prefrontal cortex of the sociopaths was significantly lower than in the brains of his normal subjects. The prefrontal

Photo 9.1 After John Wayne Gacy's execution, his brain was dissected in an unsuccessful attempt to find an organic explanation for murderous behavior. (Associated Press/M. Spencer Green)

cortex is responsible for reasoning and decision making, relating to the ability to distinguish right from wrong, determine future consequences of behavior, and suppress socially inappropriate urges. Raine also found that sociopathic children may be literally "cold blooded." That is, they have significantly lower heart rates, reflecting much less fear and anxiety when they are stressed. Unlike the rest of the population, sociopaths simply do not fear being caught and punished when they do illegal things.

In a related study, Raine and his colleagues compared the neural activity in the prefrontal cortex of 41 murderers and 41 control subjects. Using positron emission tomography scans, the researchers found that murderers had significantly less neural activity in the prefrontal cortex than their control group counterparts. In addition, killers who plead not guilty by reason of insanity lack feelings of morality because of impairments in the neural mechanisms responsible for moral judgments.

Raine's findings suggest the value to criminologists of including variations in brain structure and function when they attempt to explain the extreme violence committed by sociopaths. At the same time, the biological approach does not preclude examining the environment for causal factors in the etiology of murderous behavior. Indeed, there is also evidence that elements of the brain change in response to changes in the environment.

Some neurologists and a growing number of psychiatrists suggest that many serial killers have incurred severe injury to the limbic region of the brain resulting from profound or repeated head trauma, generally during childhood. Psychiatrist Dorothy Lewis and neurologist Jonathan Pincus, for example, examined 15 murderers on Florida's death row and found that all showed signs of neurological irregularities (see Lewis, Pincus, Feldman, Jackson, & Bard, 1986). In addition, psychologist Joel Norris (1988) reported excessive spinal fluid found in the brain scan of serial killer Henry Lee Lucas. Norris argued that this abnormality reflected the possible damage caused by an earlier blow or a series of blows to Lucas's head.

It is incontrovertible that severe head trauma and resulting injury to the brain can have potentially dire effects on behavior, such as inducing violent outbursts, learning disabilities, and epilepsy. It is noteworthy and suggestive that serial killer Henry Lee Lucas reportedly was beaten by his mother with pieces of lumber and broom handles, and that later, he claimed to have experienced frequent dizzy spells and blackouts.

Bobby Joe Long of Florida, who was convicted in 1986 and in 1994 of a total of nine counts of first-degree murder, also appears to have received several severe head injuries. At the age of 5, Long was knocked unconscious when he fell off a swing. A year later, he suffered a serious concussion when he fell off his bicycle and crashed into a parked car headfirst. Several months later, Long fell from a horse onto his head.

The psychiatric evidence linking serial murder to a variety of childhood problems, such as child abuse, is frequently disputed because of the questionable reliability of the source of data—the killer himself. How can we rely on information from a known liar who has a reason to lie? In contrast, biological, physiological, and neurological approaches do not suffer the same reliability problems. It is harder to con an electroencephalogram (EEG), for example, although the significance of the results may be as unclear as a killer's recollections of his childhood.

At the same time, it is critical that we place in some perspective the many case studies that have been used in an attempt to link extreme violence to neurological impairment. Absent from the case study approach is any indication of the prevalence of individuals who did not act violently despite a history of trauma. Indeed, if head trauma were as strong a contributor to serial murder as some would suggest, then we would have many times more serial killers than we actually do.

It is also important to recognize that neurological impairment must occur in combination with a host of environmental conditions to place an individual at risk for extreme acts of brutality. Dorothy Lewis cautions, for example, that "the neuropsychiatric problems alone don't make you violent. Probably the environmental factors in and of themselves don't make you a violent person. But when you put them together, you create a very dangerous character" (Klein, 1992). Similarly, former FBI special agent Robert Ressler asserts that no single childhood problem indicates future criminality. According to Ressler, "there are a whole pot of conditions that have to be met" for violence to be predictable (Meddis, 1987, p. 5A). Head trauma and abuse, therefore, may be important risk factors, but they are neither necessary nor sufficient to make someone a serial killer. Rather, they are part of a very long list of circumstances—including adoption, shyness, disfigurement, speech impediments, learning and physical disabilities, abandonment, death of a parent, and academic and athletic inadequacies—that may make a child feel frustrated and rejected enough to predispose, but not predestine, him or her toward extreme violence.

Thus, we must approach with caution and skepticism any attempt to use neurological assessments in a predictive way. The distinction between explanation and prediction is once again crucial. Let us say that some abnormality—be it neurological, genetic, or environmental—is found more often among serial killers than in the general population. This does not mean that we could or should screen children for violence proneness using physiological, psychological, or neurological examinations.

Joel Norris (1988) suggested that by the end of the 1990s, "most forms of episodic aggression—including serial murder—could be prevented through an organized program of testing and diagnosis and intervention" (p. 244). In retrospect, it is obvious that Norris was essentially wrong. It is questionable that we will soon understand the causes of human behavior well enough to allow predictions to be made with reasonable accuracy. Most of our explanations are incomplete at best, involving a long list of possible contributors. They simply do not permit us to identify in advance who will and who will not turn out to be a serial killer.

This didn't stop Norris from trying. He published a list of biological warning signs that he suggested could be used as part of a pattern to identify future serial killers. Norris's list included a variety of physical features—some general and others quite specific—such as earlobes that adhere to the head, fine and unruly hair, abnormal teeth, a curved pinky finger, and a third toe that is equal in length to or longer than the second toe. Although many of the items reported by Norris may indeed be symptomatic of genetic damage, the connection between genetic abnormality and extreme criminality is tenuous. Even though researchers have found some association between biological makeup and violent behavior, the linkage is not nearly strong enough to permit prudent predictions. Furthermore, even if an individual is predisposed toward violence, whether for biological or environmental reasons, there is no guarantee that this propensity will ever be translated into assaultive behavior.

BLAMING THE FAMILY

There is a final concern surrounding the overemphasis on environmental or biological determinism—the notion that familial, developmental, or genetic abnormalities are always responsible for the propensity to kill. For example, Special Agent John Douglas of the FBI, an authority on serial murder, has claimed, "There are common denominators that you find with *each and every one* of these people. They come from generally broken homes. They are the product of some kind of abuse" (Klein, 1992; emphasis added).

For the serial killer who strives to deflect blame for his actions, the child abuse syndrome, the posttraumatic stress disorder syndrome, and an irregular EEG form the perfect excuse. "I'm not to blame," he insists. "I couldn't help myself. I'm a victim, too."

Unfortunately, clever and cunning serial killers who might exploit these syndromes to their own advantage frequently receive a sympathetic ear. As a sociopath, the serial killer is a convincing and accomplished liar. As a professional trained to be supportive and empathic, his psychiatrist may be easily conned. The case histories of such malingerers as Kenneth Bianchi and Arthur Shawcross, both serial killers who apparently fooled mental health professionals with fabricated tales of childhood trauma, remind us to be skeptical about the self-serving testimony of accused killers eager to escape legal responsibility for their crimes.

If the etiology of their murderous behavior involved only neurological impairment or failure to bond during early childhood, serial killers would, in all likelihood, start murdering people early in life—say, at the age of 12, 19, or 24. Instead, many serial killers do not begin taking lives until they are in their 30s or 40s. Some wait even longer in the life cycle. Not only have they experienced pain and suffering as children, but they also continue to suffer as adults.

Danny Rolling waited until he was 36 years old to kill. Then he murdered three people in his hometown of Shreveport, Louisiana, and five more in Gainesville, Florida. Not only had Rolling been the victim of an abusive father, but his adjustment and personal problems also continued through adolescence into early adulthood. A brief marriage ended in divorce, his adult relationship with his parents continued to be severely strained, and he couldn't manage to hold a job. Instead, he drifted first from job to job, next from state to state, then from prison to prison, and finally from murder to murder.

CHAPTER 10

Nonsexual Control

Until his murder conviction on January 31, 2000, Harold Shipman was widely regarded as a dedicated and competent family doctor. The gray-bearded and bespectacled father of four had practiced medicine in a middle-income suburb of Manchester, England, from 1992 until his arrest in 1998. He was given a life sentence for poisoning to death 15 of his patients, most of them elderly women who lived alone. An official investigation later, however, concluded that Shipman, over a period of 23 years, had actually murdered at least 215 people, making him the most prolific serial killer in English history.

Shipman's strategy for killing was to pay house calls on his patients, either in response to their complaints of an ailment or simply to conduct a routine checkup. While pretending to administer a beneficial medication, the "good doctor" would instead give his patients a deadly injection of heroin, which he had stockpiled over many years either by prescribing it erroneously or by stealing it from his cancer patients.

Shipman always had a credible explanation for the unexpected deaths of his patients, convincingly arguing to their families that an autopsy would be utterly unnecessary. Moreover, many of his victims were cremated, destroying any possible evidence of the doctor's misdeeds.

"Doctor Death," as he was dubbed by the British press, was no mercy killer. Instead, he seemed motivated by an intense desire to control the fate of his victims—that is, to decide who would live and who would die. He apparently gained perverted pleasure from playing God. One patient told investigators that Shipman once suggested to her that he got a "buzz" in the presence of death. Yet his downfall came when he decided to kill for the money rather than the thrill.

Shipman was apprehended when he was caught forging the will of his final victim, Kathleen Grundy, a wealthy 81-year-old former mayor of Hyde. Grundy had died in her home only hours after the doctor had paid her a house call on the pretext of needing to take a sample of her blood. The police became suspicious when, on the same day that Grundy died, a crudely typed version of her last will and testament turned up in a solicitor's office, naming Shipman as the beneficiary, ignoring her devoted daughter and two grandsons, and expressing her wish to be cremated. Incriminating traces of heroin later were discovered in Mrs. Grundy's exhumed body, leading to the arrest of Dr. Shipman.

On the final day of January, 2000, Shipman's fate was sealed. The jury convicted him on 15 counts of murder and one count of forgery. The trial judge sentenced Shipman immediately, summing up the doctor's abuse of his position:

> You have finally been brought to justice by the verdict of this jury. I have no doubt whatsoever that these are true verdicts. The time has now come for me to pass sentence upon you for these wicked, wicked crimes.
>
> Each of your victims was your patient. You murdered each and every one of your victims by a calculated and cold-blooded perversion of your medical skills, for your own evil and wicked purposes.
>
> You took advantage of, and grossly abused, their trust. You were, after all, each victim's doctor. I have little doubt that each of your victims smiled and thanked you as she submitted to your deadly ministrations. (Ottley, n.d.)

Judge Forbes ordered Shipman to serve 15 concurrent life sentences for the murders and 4 years for the forgery count. Shipman would end up serving only a fraction of his term. Not quite 4 years later, on January 13, 2004, prison officials found the body of Harold Shipman, age 56, in his prison cell, hanging from a noose he had fashioned out of bed sheets.

POWER OVER PATIENTS

Like serial killers who stalk their victims on the street, Shipman killed to satisfy his cravings for power and control. Unlike the stalkers who must seek out the opportunity to kill, however, Shipman had the opportunity right where he worked. The old and infirm are vulnerable to the misdeeds of so-called "Angels of Death"—caretakers like Harold Shipman, working in clinics, hospitals, and nursing homes, who may have a particularly warped sense of mercy.

In December 2003, 43-year-old Charles Cullen confessed to authorities that he had murdered as many as 40 patients during his 16 years working as a nurse at 10 hospitals in New Jersey and Pennsylvania. By his account, Cullen overdosed patients to spare them the pain and humiliation of being "coded." He insisted that his actions were merciful, to bring a speedy end to his patients' suffering and avoid having them dehumanized by extraordinary medical procedures.

After his arrest and conviction, Cullen also wanted to minimize his own suffering and humiliation by seeking to avoid any confrontation with the families of his victims. However, the judge required the defendant to remain in court to hear their victim impact statements, and then sentenced the former nurse to life imprisonment.

Most sexually motivated serial killers are men, but it is not surprising that many Angels of Death, unlike Harold Shipman and Charles Cullen, are women. Traditionally, women have dominated the helping professions, including nursing. In addition, their need for power does not usually involve sexual sadism. Instead, female serial killers derive satisfaction from playing God—those who are health practitioners hold life and death in their grasp. Whereas a woman might have difficulty subduing a healthy victim, she would have little trouble at all overpowering a defenseless patient who already is near death. Finally, men kill violently with brute force, but women choose less aggressive means, such as medicines, poisons, or even suffocation.

Between December 1995 and February 1996, seven patients at the Veterans Administration Hospital in Northampton, Massachusetts, became gravely ill when they were injected with epinephrine, a stimulant that can cause the heart to race out of control. Four of the patients suffered fatal heart attacks; the other three recovered. All of the cardiac arrests occurred in the intensive care ward, on the 4 p.m. to midnight shift.

The culprit turned out to be a 30-year-old nurse, Kristin Gilbert, who had a thirst for being at the center of attention and who injected each of her victims to trigger a medical emergency. Using her medical role to provide access, Gilbert had stolen vials of epinephrine

Photo 10.1 Not all serial killers are sexually motivated. Nurse Kristin Gilbert poisoned her patients in a Veterans Administration hospital to get attention and feel important. (Associated Press/Stephen Petegorsky)

from the hospital storage room. She was the first medical practitioner to arrive on the scene at every one of the deaths, and she resigned from the hospital staff at about the same time that the spate of suspicious deaths ended.

As part of her motivation for murder, Gilbert sought the attention of her boyfriend, a security guard at the hospital. According to protocol, the guard would be called whenever a medical emergency code was sounded. Making the most of the opportunity, Gilbert reportedly would hike up her skirt, exposing her thighs and garter belt, and then climb on top of the gurney to show off both her nursing skill and her physical attributes.

During the 4-month period when she was killing, Kristin Gilbert dropped clues as to her sinister behavior that became clear only after the fact. For example, one of Nurse Gilbert's patients was alone in the intensive care unit on an evening when she was on duty but wanted to leave by 9 p.m. Gilbert's boss reminded her that she still had a patient to supervise, to which the nurse replied, "Well, what if he dies by 9:00? Can I go?" (Richardson, 2000, p. 7). All too conveniently for her, the patient expired before the clock struck 9:00 p.m.

Hospital homicides are particularly difficult to detect and solve. Death among elderly patients is not uncommon, so suspicions rarely are aroused.

Furthermore, should a curiously large volume of deaths occur within a short time span on a particular shift, hospital administrators feel like they are in a quandary. Not only are they reluctant to bring scandal and perhaps lawsuits onto their own facility without sufficient proof, but in addition, most of the potentially incriminating evidence against a suspected employee is buried.

FEMALE SERIAL KILLERS

One of the most striking contrasts between male and female serial killers—aside from the grossly uneven prevalence of male killers—involves the relationships, or lack thereof, between the killer and the victims. Overwhelmingly, male serial killers prey upon strangers, whom they select on the basis of some sexual fantasy involving capture and control. Female serial killers, by contrast—with the notable exception of Aileen Wuornos—almost always kill victims with whom they have shared some kind of relationship, most often in which the victim is dependent on them. Nurse's aides Gwendolyn Graham and Catherine Wood of Grand Rapids, Michigan, disposed of nursing home patients under their care. At the extreme, Marybeth Tinning of Schenectady, New York, killed several of her own children, not all at once in a murderous fit of rage, but one at a time in a cold, deliberate, and selfish attempt to win attention.

Tragedy first struck the Tinning household in 1972. Joe and Marybeth Tinning's third child, Jennifer, was born with hemorrhagic meningitis and died in the hospital after barely a week-long struggle for life. Following Jennifer's death, Marybeth was, most understandably, surrounded with friends and family who showered her with sympathy and compassion. The steady stream of support did much more than comfort Marybeth; she craved the attention, almost to the point of emotional addiction.

Just as the attention began to die down, tragedy again struck the Tinnings as it did once more after that. Less than 3 weeks following Jennifer's death, 2-year-old Joey died, and then within 6 more weeks, 4-year-old Barbara died as well. Doctors attributed both deaths to Reye's syndrome.

Bad luck, it is said, comes in threes, and so it seemed for Marybeth and Joseph Tinning in the winter of 1972. The same adage suggests that the streak of bad luck ends there, and, sure enough, life went back to normal in the Tinning home . . . for almost two years.

Left childless after burying three children, Marybeth and her husband Joe tried to rebuild their family, but the couple's fourth child, born late in 1973, died just 3 weeks later. Marybeth rushed baby Timothy to the emergency room after he stopped breathing, but the doctors were unable to resuscitate the boy. The cause of death was listed as sudden infant death syndrome (SIDS), also known as crib death.

A dreadful pattern was developing. Marybeth would give birth to yet another child—her fifth, her sixth, and more—and soon thereafter the baby would die, with the cause of death usually given as SIDS. Marybeth began theorizing—almost bragging—about a genetic defect that she was passing on to each of her babies. As her sixth, seventh, and eighth children died, however, sympathy for Marybeth turned into suspicion. During one of her later pregnancies, a former coworker of Marybeth's quietly remarked to a mutual friend, "Marybeth's pregnant and she's going to kill another baby!" (Egginton, 1990, p. 247).

Following the death of the eighth child, Jonathan, in March 1980, the Tinning household remained childless for 5 years—an unusual span of empty nest syndrome for Marybeth. Understandably, she was overjoyed with the birth of her ninth child, Tami Lynne, in August of 1985, and as Tami Lynne's first Christmas approached, all seemed well indeed. The baby girl was growing beautifully and, more important, was full of health.

But Tami Lynne's first Christmas was never to be. Early in the morning of December 20, Marybeth went to check on her baby and found her lying on her stomach, motionless and breathless. Despite efforts to restore her breathing, Tami Lynne was pronounced dead. She too seemed to have fallen victim to SIDS, the same affliction apparently to blame in the deaths of her siblings.

Marybeth responded routinely following yet another loss. She called all her friends and relatives to announce the newest reduction in the Tinning family, expecting the usual round of pity and attention. Her death announcements had become as emotionally arousing for her as the birth announcements; both made her the center of attention, something she craved. As one relative would later say about Marybeth, "Every funeral was a party for her, with hardly a tear shed" (Egginton, 1990, p. 248).

Marybeth's sister-in-law, unable to turn her head once again, called the police with her suspicions. Out of concern for possible foul play, Tami Lynne was autopsied carefully and thoroughly. With improved methods for distinguishing SIDS from induced asphyxiation, it was determined that the baby had not died of natural causes but instead had been suffocated. Despite the fact that implicating evidence from earlier deaths had long since been buried, there was enough direct and circumstantial evidence to charge and convict Marybeth of murder.

Following Marybeth's conviction, the poor mother became the evil mother. In retrospect, there was a connection between the repeated occurrence of sudden death and Marybeth's peculiar enjoyment of the attention and sympathy that she received after each of her babies died. So addicted was she to her role as grieving mother that she learned to create the tragedies on her own.

MUNCHAUSEN SYNDROME BY PROXY

Marybeth Tinning's bizarre pattern of behavior has been termed Munchausen syndrome by proxy. In this syndrome, one person, typically a child, is used or even sacrificed by another (most often the mother) as a means of getting attention. The attention seeker causes symptoms in the victim and then seeks medical attention for the victim and sympathy for herself. The notion of proxy distinguishes it from the classic Munchausen syndrome, in which a patient feigns illness or self-inflicts injury in order to be pampered and to get attention. The proxy form has been seen, for example, in child abuse cases in which mothers induce illness in their children by poison or other means in order to place themselves in the role of concerned, distraught protector and of attracting attention from friends, family, and medical staff. For many of these mothers, both being around a hospital and conferring with medical staff make them feel important.

According to Dr. Herbert Schreier, chief of psychiatry at the Children's Hospital Medical Center in Oakland, California, Munchausen syndrome by proxy has a more sadistic motivation than simple attention seeking (see Schreier & Libow, 1993). Herbert A. Schreier notes that women with this psychiatric disorder typically felt, during childhood, a profound sense of neglect and low self-esteem. As a result, they later aspire to get even with their parents, but they choose doctors as parental surrogates. Their own children are little more than pawns to be manipulated in their sadistic game. They induce illnesses in their youngsters and then parade them before confused and bewildered medical specialists who try unsuccessfully to diagnose the mysterious symptoms. Not only do the Munchausen mothers attempt to outwit the doctors, but, more important, they also try to humiliate and embarrass them for the sake of vengeance—that is, to get even for the humiliation they had suffered as children. Schreier reports that these mothers often display a "sadistic glee at moments of crisis" (Burne, 1993, p. 17).

Munchausen syndrome by proxy, although often seen in emotionally needy mothers, also is implicated in some Angel of Death cases. Typically, a medical professional—for example, a nurse or nurse's aide—creates a life-and-death emergency so that he or she can step forward in a seemingly valiant attempt to save the patient. Successful or not, the Angel of Death can expect to be showered with praise and adulation for the heroic effort.

For example, 24-year-old nurse Beverly Allitt was convicted in Nottingham, England, on 13 counts of murder, attempted murder, and assault on children, many of them infants. Nurse Allitt's symptoms started appearing early in her life, when she inflicted injuries on herself. Between 1987 and 1991, she sought treatment dozens of times at Grantham Hospital's emergency ward for minor and apparently self-inflicted injuries to her hands, legs, back, and head. It wasn't until a large number of young hospital patients under her care died or suddenly became critical, however, that her activities were scrutinized. Autopsies on the children revealed that Nurse Allitt had been murdering the patients by suffocation or with injections of insulin or potassium.

When later examined by a court-appointed psychiatrist, Dr. James Higgins, Nurse Allitt confessed that she had been upset over not having been admitted to a nursing course and over having been chosen last for her nursing assignment. Allitt's scheme provided the validation that was otherwise missing in her life. By stealthily killing a child, she could outsmart the brilliant doctors and play God. As she told the psychiatrist, "I had to prove I was better than what people thought" (Pendlebury, 1993, p. 9).

In an extraordinary case, licensed vocational nurse Genene Jones earned the nickname "Death Nurse" for her seeming affinity for death. In March 1982, Jones left her job at a San Antonio, Texas, hospital under a black cloud of suspicion. From May to December 1981, 10 children in the intensive care unit had died suddenly and inexplicably, all while Nurse Jones was in attendance. An internal hospital inquiry was inconclusive: "The association of Nurse Jones with the deaths of ten children could be coincidental. However, negligence or wrongdoing cannot be excluded" (Elkind, 1983, p. 109).

Despite the mysterious deaths on Nurse Jones's shift, she was given a positive letter of recommendation from the hospital (Elkind, 1989, p. 108):

To Whom It May Concern:

Due to the recommendation of a recent pediatric Intensive Care Site Team Visit, the Pedi ICU Unit is being converted to an all RN Staff composition at Medical Center Hospital.

Ms. Genene Jones, LVN, has been employed in the Pedi ICU since 1978. This move in no way reflects on her performance in the unit. She has gained valuable knowledge and experience in pediatric intensive care nursing. During the time of employment this employee has been loyal, dependable, and trustworthy.

Ms. Genene Jones, LVN, has been an asset to the Bexar County Hospital District, and I would recommend continued employment.

Shortly after leaving the hospital, Nurse Jones took a position at a small pediatric clinic in nearby Kerrville, Texas. One of her first patients in the clinic was 15-month-old Chelsea Ann McClellan, whose mother had brought her in for an examination because of the sniffles. While the doctor discussed Chelsea's medical history with her mother, Nurse Jones took care of the baby in an examining room. Moments later, Nurse Jones screamed out that the child had stopped breathing. She quickly took charge. She performed heroically in the ambulance on the way to the local hospital, so much so that little Chelsea pulled through. The McClellans were relieved, and they told everyone they knew about the wonderful new nurse in town—a real life-saver.

But lightning struck twice, and the second time the damage was devastating. A few weeks later, Petti McClellan was back at the clinic with Chelsea for a follow-up examination. Nurse Jones administered the girl an injection after which she suddenly stopped breathing, turned pink, and went into a seizure. Once again, Nurse Jones went along on the ambulance ride to the hospital, but this time Chelsea was dead on arrival.

Hardly suspecting foul play, the McClellans placed an ad in the local newspaper, thanking everyone—especially Nurse Jones—for all that they had done. The *Kerrville Daily Times* contained the following open letter (Elkind, 1989, pp. 154–155):

To All Our Friends in Kerrville:

Often we live our lives without a tendency to acknowledge those friends around us. Then something will happen which causes us to become aware of others. Such was the case in the loss of our little Angel, Chelsea Ann McClellan. The response from the people of Kerrville, many of whom we only knew in passing, was both heartwarming and most helpful in our grief. The many beautiful flowers, cards and letters we received made us realize the city of Kerrville has a heart.

A special thanks to Dr. Kathryn Holland and Genene Jones for extending Chelsea's stay longer by their caring in such a sensitive way. A care which extended beyond loss and helped us more than anyone could ever know.

Sincerely,

Reid & Petti McClellan

Chelsea's life-and-death emergency was just the first of many that occurred in children treated in the small clinic in which Nurse Jones was employed. In fact, during the 6-week period in which Jones had worked for the town's new pediatrician, six children had stopped breathing and were rushed to the hospital for resuscitation. Nurse Jones reportedly was euphoric when she was able to administer CPR to help save their lives.

A pattern was emerging so clearly surrounding Nurse Jones that officials at the local hospital launched an investigation. The critical question surrounded a missing bottle of Anectine, a powerful muscle relaxant that could debilitate a person's normal breathing response. Subsequent examination of Chelsea McClellan's body uncovered traces of Anectine, which had caused her respiratory system to stop. Apparently, Nurse Jones craved the fast pace and high drama of life-and-death situations; however, she wasn't always successful in responding to the medical crises that she engineered. She was convicted of murder in 1984.

Sociopathic serial killers and Angels of Death share much in common—more than just the fact that they have taken many innocent lives. Both types of killers are sadists: They both inflict death, with or without suffering, for the sake of personal gratification. As noted earlier, this gratification can consist of sexual pleasure, as in the crimes of Rochester serial killer Arthur Shawcross or Russian cannibal killer Andrei Chikatilo, or of psychological empowerment, as in the medical atrocities of Nurse Allitt or Marybeth Tinning.

When men manipulate and fabricate for the purpose of luring their victims and covering their tracks, they are called sociopathic killers. When women exploit their role as caretakers, when they are cunning and deceitful for the very same reason, they are labeled as victims of Munchausen syndrome by proxy. At the basis of both forms of serial murder, however, are an excessive need to overcome deep-rooted feelings of powerlessness and inferiority, a desire to control others, and a craving for attention.

CHAPTER 11

Killing Cults

ighting back nausea, Mexican police performed their unenviable task of digging for bodies. On April 12, 1989, they unearthed a mass grave on an isolated ranch some 20 miles west of Matamoros, Mexico, just south of the Texas border. Among the 15 corpses buried in the makeshift grave was the body of Mark Kilroy, a blond, 21-year-old University of Texas student who, a month earlier, had been literally grabbed off the street while he and three of his college buddies celebrated spring break.

Amid the stench of decaying human flesh, authorities uncovered the bizarre signs of ritualistic sacrifice. Several large cauldrons were filled with the remains of animals—a rooster, a turtle, a goat's head and feet—floating in a murky broth of human blood and boiled body parts. In a dilapidated shack nearby, searchers found a bloodstained altar surrounded by dozens of cigars, chili peppers, boxes of candles, and bottles of cheap Mexican tequila. Understating the horror, Cameron County Sheriff Alex Perez described the grisly scene as "a human slaughterhouse" (Williams, 1989).

Within 24 hours, police had arrested four young men and sought several others, all members of a major drug ring, who allegedly were involved in the killings. In an unusual turn of events, the four suspects appeared before reporters at a crowded news conference and confessed to murder without the slightest hint of remorse. They laughed as they described their group's crimes, including the abduction of Mark Kilroy. Kilroy had been slashed to death with a machete when he attempted to flee his captors some 12 hours after he had been kidnapped.

"We killed them for protection," claimed 22-year-old suspect Elio Hernandez Rivera of Matamoros (Sedeno, 1989). Rivera gave police their first clue concerning the motive for what appeared to be random, senseless murders.

Rivera's idea of protection was physical and spiritual. His band of drug smugglers practiced *Palo Mayombe*. This black-magic derivative of *Santeria* ("the way of the saints"), a Caribbean voodoo belief, was blended with both Satanism and *Bruja*, a form of witchcraft practiced by 16th-century Aztecs. Human and animal sacrifice was thought by the drug-smuggling group to bring them immunity from bullets and criminal prosecution while they illegally transported 2,000 pounds of marijuana per week from Mexico into the United States.

The choice of victims may not have been as random as first believed. According to one member of the cult, Mark Kilroy was abducted because he resembled the group's spiritual leader. By removing his brain after death, they could feed off Kilroy's intelligence.

The police identified the ringleader of the drug smuggling cult as Adolfo de Jesus Constanzo, a 26-year-old native of Cuba. His loyal followers called their charismatic leader "El Padrino"—the Godfather. Because of his spellbinding influence over his devotees, Constanzo allegedly was able to convince them that their drug activities could never be touched by the law as long as they obeyed his commands, among them to kill for survival.

The followers of Constanzo were hardly the crazed lunatics that many people associate with ritualistic slaughter and human sacrifice. Most of the cult members grew up in relatively affluent families and did not have histories of violence. Believed to be the high priestess or witch of the operation, 24-year-old Sara Maria Aldrete Villareal was tall, thin, and attractive. An honor student at Texas Southmost College, Aldrete was listed in the college's *Who's Who* directory. According to one of her professors, Tony Zavaleta, Sara "was the perfect student. If I had a roomful of students like her, I'd be happy" ("Police Hunt," 1989, p. A21). Professors and fellow students never saw her darker side. "Sara was a model, respectful student. Little did we know that she was apparently leading a double life" (Fox & Levin, 1989, p. 50).

KILLING FOR A CAUSE

How could apparently normal, intelligent people buy into a philosophy promising that human sacrifice would miraculously protect them from harm? As illogical and immoral as this belief may seem, many people could be made to accept it—even to the point of killing for survival—given the right set of circumstances. Abnormal situations can make normal people do "crazy" things, especially if they perceive a strong self-serving purpose in doing so, such as profit, power, or protection.

In a sense, Constanzo was the Hitler of his cult. Adolf Hitler, as a charismatic leader, had transformed ordinary German citizens into brutal killers through constant marches, all-day group singing of the National Socialist Party's anthem, and required cheering. Hitler capitalized on the promise of turning around Germany's terrible economy to help convince his followers of the urgency of his grand plan. Constanzo similarly capitalized on a powerful economic incentive, as well as group pressure, to foster obedience to his commands. As Hitler did with his marches and chants, Constanzo involved his followers in elaborate and mysterious rituals—animal sacrifices and demonic incantations—to instill in his flock selfless devotion to the cause.

Constanzo's final command was to perform a death ritual—this time, his own death. Several of his followers obediently shot Constanzo to death as police authorities closed in on them in Mexico City. Apparently, the practice of Palo Mayombe couldn't really protect Constanzo from bullets, nor could it immunize Aldrete and other cult members from prosecution for murder.

The Matamoros incident was widely publicized in the United States and was regarded by many as an isolated tragedy that could never happen there. Skeptics suggested that belief in the power of human sacrifice depended on ancient superstitions that surely would be rejected by civilized Americans. Besides, law enforcement authorities in the United States would have the operations of any dangerous cult under surveillance long before it could engage in multiple homicide.

Such ideas may have been no more than wishful thinking. On April 17, 1989, barely 5 days after the Matamoros slaughter was discovered, a cult killing did indeed happen north of the border—far north, in a sleepy Ohio town. The five members of the Dennis Avery family of Kirtland were sacrificed by a man who considered himself a prophet of God.

With the assistance of his loyal followers, 39-year-old Jeffrey Don Lundgren was determined to do God's work, or so he professed. Having broken away from a branch of Mormonism, the Reorganized Church of Jesus Christ of Latter-Day Saints, Lundgren was convinced that God sent messages to him directly—a virtual fax from the Creator. It was his sacred duty to carry out God's will, no matter how distasteful or violent. God's commandments transcended human laws.

The armies of Satan would come, Lundgren had preached. He and his followers would have to live off the land until Christ returned. There would be no electricity or shelter. They would have to protect the temple by whatever means possible. There would be much bloodshed. That was his vision.

In joining Lundgren's army, the Averys had given all of their worldly possessions—worth more than $20,000—to the divine cause. In exchange for their donation, Lundgren had moved them to Kirtland and promised to pay the rent on a small home for Dennis, his wife, and their three children. Even though Dennis had enlisted his entire family in Lundgren's prophecy, he remained somewhat skeptical of the cult leader's legitimacy and at times challenged his divine authority.

Less than an hour after Dennis Avery handed over his donation to the cause, Lundgren was in Kirtland buying weapons and supplies to prepare the members of his cult for Armageddon. At Veith Sports Supply, Jeffrey purchased a .45-caliber semiautomatic pistol. Then, he drove over to Pistol Pete's sporting goods, where he bought a second .45-caliber semiautomatic and a .243-caliber Ruger rifle. A week later, Lundgren went into town again and purchased a Ruger .44-caliber Magnum handgun. He also bought tents, camouflage clothing, canned food, camping supplies, and hundreds of rounds of ammunition.

Early in April, in one of many visions witnessed only by Lundgren, he was told that the enemy had already infiltrated his flock and must be eliminated. The prophet wasted little time carrying out the commandment. On the evening of April 17, he led the unsuspecting members of the Avery family, one by one, into the New England-style red barn behind his farmhouse and to their deaths. Lundgren and five of his men had already dug a deep pit in the barn's dirt floor. Now, each victim—Dennis, his wife Cheryl, and their three young daughters—was walked from the farmhouse to the barn, where their hands and legs were bound with duct tape. Then,

Lundgren repeatedly pumped his victims with hollow-point slugs from his .45 semi-automatic and kicked their lifeless bodies into the pit.

The murder of the Avery family may not have been shrouded in the intricate ritualism and symbolism of cult killings such as the Matamoros slayings. Like other instances of cult murder as well as the Nazi exterminations, however, Lundgren's massacre grew out of and reinforced the strong group bond that his members shared. Also, as in these other atrocities, Lundgren depended a great deal on maintaining obedience to authority by convincing his followers that he was all-powerful, that he had the ability to lead them down the path of righteousness and to conquer all of their enemies.

Judgment Day came early for Jeffrey Lundgren—not at St. Peter's pearly gates, but in a crowded Ohio courtroom. On September 21, 1990, he was sentenced to die in the electric chair. After hearing the judge's decision, Lundgren told his attorneys that his death sentence was predetermined, that everything was going according to God's plan for him. Of course, Lundgren knew he would ultimately appeal to a *much* higher court.

THE APPEAL OF DANGEROUS CULTS

Joining a cult like Lundgren's fulfills a lonely and frustrated person's need to feel good about self and to be valued by others. Typically, the would-be cultist is a failure in everyday life who feels unappreciated by family and unaccepted by peers.

But even valedictorians and prom queens, doctors and lawyers, have been known to join cults. Even when successful by conventional standards, the recruit may resent the feeling that there are strings attached: To be loved and appreciated at home, in school, or on the job, one must compete successfully and behave in a respectful manner. In contrast, as Tufts University psychologist David Elkind has pointed out, the great appeal of cults is that when people join, "they are assured that support is not contingent on achievement" (Fox & Levin, 1989, p. 50). Instead, the cultists, in order to be accepted, need only follow orders dutifully.

The cult welcomes the recruit into the "family" and provides a strong, charismatic father figure who structures everyday life and goals. In turn, cults seek out those who are prime targets for mind control, cleverly screening those who are miserable—from an adolescent suffering an identity crisis to a mature adult suffering a midlife crisis.

Slowly, recruits may be initiated into cult activities, urged to reject traditional values, and praised for seeing "the truth." Participation in ritual further reinforces the bond between the newcomers and the cult. They may be instructed to decorate their bodies with symbols to show their loyalty or to drink the blood of sacrificial animals for strength. They may even be asked to steal clothing of humans to be used in rituals. As their ties to the cult grow deeper and deeper, they may finally be directed to participate in human sacrifice. As renowned psychologist Dr. Joyce Brothers once suggested, "When Papa says this is something you should do because the whole family will be safe, you do it" ("Desire for a Family," 1989, p. 7A).

SUICIDE OR HOMICIDE?

Because of the tremendous potency of cult leadership, there is a fine line between homicide and suicide. Out of loyalty to their spiritual mentor and to one another, cultists are especially vulnerable to commandments for self-destruction. Not only will cult members starve to death if instructed to do so, but they also have been known to take poison, as hundreds did in Jonestown, Guyana, in November 1978.

More recently, Armageddon came for followers of a self-styled messiah, 33-year-old David Koresh. On April 19, 1993, the world watched on television as more than 80 members of Koresh's Branch Davidian cult, including 24 children, perished in flames at their compound near Waco, Texas. For weeks, they knew that doomsday was near; they just didn't know how, when, or by whom their lives would be taken. In any event, they were prepared to follow Koresh, the "son of God," to eternal salvation.

The prelude to the final conflagration started on the morning of February 28, 1993. More than 100 agents from the U.S. Bureau of Alcohol, Tobacco and Firearms (ATF) raided the remote compound on the basis of a tip that Koresh was stockpiling illegal weapons in preparation for an apocalyptic showdown with federal officials. A 45-minute gun battle between the ATF agents and those inside the compound left as many as 10 people dead, including four federal officers.

Over the next 51 days, cult members and federal agents competed for leverage in a bizarre standoff. While Attorney General Janet Reno went on television to defend her directives, David Koresh bargained for radio airtime to expound on his religious philosophy. As the weeks dragged on, more and more details emerged to explain the intense stranglehold that Koresh exercised over his followers.

Born in 1959 as Vernon Howell, David Koresh grew up troubled. He was raised by a single mother, suffered from learning disabilities, and experienced problems in school, eventually dropping out of high school. Notwithstanding his many disadvantages, Koresh had one outstanding strength: He was able to recite passages of the Bible at length and to invoke biblical references to argue persuasively whatever position he held. Later, he was able to hold his followers spellbound with powerful lectures from the Bible, often lasting many hours.

It took more than his charisma and religious acumen, however, to attract and hold devoted followers. Koresh skillfully manipulated their minds through ritual and punishment. He insisted that his Branch Davidians awaken before dawn and march in military fashion before they were permitted to eat or drink. He taught that all the women belonged to him, including girls as young as 12. He insisted that they have sex only with him and no one else, not even their spouses. Because he desired his women lean, Koresh placed them on meager diets of popcorn and fruit. He also forced them to wear both their hair and their skirts long to conform to his image of womanhood. Koresh eventually "married" 19 of his followers and fathered at least 10 children.

Koresh believed in strict discipline for all the youngsters in the compound. They were restricted from speaking—to be seen but not heard—and they were harshly punished for disobeying. Koresh often beat the children, some as young as 8 months of age, until they were bruised and bloody.

Koresh was fanatical about controlling disrespectful children as well as disobedient adults. As if his rituals and regimes weren't enough to maintain order, Koresh carried a Glock 9mm pistol for good measure.

Isolation from "infidels" of the outside world was a critical element in Koresh's ability to establish total control. The Branch Davidian compound was situated on a remote prairie, miles from the city of Waco. The more isolated the residents became from their homes and families, the more focused on Koresh they became. He redefined their world, resocialized them, and replaced their belief systems with his own. In this way, Koresh came to own them.

The FBI tried to force out the Branch Davidians by isolating them and harassing them. They cut off utility services to the compound, controlled all lines of communication to the outside, and irritated the cult members with noxious stimuli around the clock, including loud noise and bright lights. Ironically, the strategies implemented by federal authorities actually served to intensify the bond between Koresh and his followers in the compound and may have made them more intransigent. They were more than ready and willing to follow their messiah anywhere, even to their death.

The Waco cult included not only disenchanted youth in the throes of their identity crisis but also mature adults who were alienated from the mainstream of society and conventional religion. In today's world, millions of Americans feel powerless to determine their own fate. Instead, they feel manipulated by big business, big government, and the media and controlled by such ubiquitous threats as nuclear war, global warming, earthquakes, and AIDS.

Even successful and intelligent individuals have joined the ranks of murderous cults. In March 1995, the members of a doomsday cult known as *Aum Shinrikyo* (Supreme Truth) killed 12 people and injured another 5,500 in a sarin nerve gas attack in the Tokyo subway system. The cultists left packets of frozen sarin on the trains, timing their assault so that the nerve gas thawed just in time to poison the rush-hour commuters.

Orchestrated by its 41-year-old charismatic leader, Shoko Asahara, the subway massacre was part of a vastly broader plot intended to overthrow the Japanese government, establish a kingdom ruled by Asahara, and then ultimately to precipitate a worldwide nuclear disaster that only he and his disciples would survive. Along the way, the cultists had committed murder and kidnappings, smuggled firearms, and produced the Nazi-era nerve gas. This deadly subway attack was designed to divert the attention of the police from an imminent raid on the cult's headquarters in the village of Kamikuishiki near the foot of Mt. Fuji. By the time they perpetrated the subway assault, the cultists were already under suspicion in a wave of violent acts including the murder of a local lawyer and his family, the kidnapping and murder of a notary public, the explosion of a letter bomb in city hall, and the shooting of the police chief. Their ultimate objective was world annihilation.

Many talented and wealthy people were attracted to the cause of Supreme Truth, including physicians and scientists who sincerely believed that Asahara possessed supernatural powers. In total, Aum Shinrikyo had more than 9,000 members, including 500 who lived in urban centers around Japan; many of them donated their entire life savings and personal property to the cult. They were attracted by Asahara's Hindu and yogic teachings, his powerful presence, and his promise to develop their supernatural talents.

SATANISM AND SERIAL MURDER

Cults can be organized around any theme. Some experts have suggested that satanic cult activity, in particular, is expanding in the United States and that countless unsolved murders are actually the doing of the Devil's disciples. These same experts have also claimed that even certain murders that authorities had attributed to a serial killer acting alone may, in fact, be the work of a satanic cult.

David Berkowitz, the infamous Son of Sam, confessed to killing six innocent people and wounding seven others as they sat in cars parked on the streets of New York City during 1976 and 1977. It was widely believed that Berkowitz killed in response to demonic messages relayed through the howling of dogs. Although many attempted to pass off the satanic elements as a product of Berkowitz's diseased mind, investigative reporter Maury Terry, author of *The Ultimate Evil* (1989), contended instead that the Son of Sam shootings, as well as many other murders around the country, including the Manson family murders, were accomplished by an expansive network of satanic cults. Terry was convinced, through Berkowitz's sworn depositions and personal correspondence, of the existence of a conspiracy, one bound together by devil worship (Terry, 1989). According to Terry's conspiracy theory, Berkowitz killed only two of the victims but served as a scout while his fellow cultists murdered the others.

To help understand Berkowitz's role in the murders, Terry looked for hidden messages in the Son of Sam letters sent to *New York Daily News* columnist Jimmy Breslin. Consistent with what he saw as a common ploy used by Satanists to encode their messages, Terry assumed that Berkowitz would have spelled words backward and would have used a system of word games. Terry (1989) wrote, for example,

> I looked at the first phrase, "keep em digging." Why, I wondered, would the ever-careful Son of Sam, so language-conscious throughout the letter, slip into "em" instead of "them" Maybe it wasn't a slip: "em" backwards spelled "me." The word preceding it, "keep," then became "peek"—as in "look for" or "see." The last word, "digging," couldn't be reversed, but using the crossword or word association approach, it did become "home." In the United Kingdom, as the dictionaries pointed out, a "digging" is a home (often shortened to "digs"). The first phrase now read: LOOK FOR ME HOME.
>
> The next expression, "drive on," offered two possibilities. Reversing the word "on" resulted in "no."—the abbreviation for "north." If "drive" was left as it was, the phrase became: DRIVE NORTH. However, using word association, a "drive" was also a street, an avenue, a roadway or broadway. So the phrase could have said: NORTH AVENUE (street, roadway, etc.). (p. 144)

In a televised interview on *Inside Edition,* Berkowitz concurred with the cult theory, self-servingly deflecting responsibility and appealing to a higher cause— the coming of Satan. According to Berkowitz,

> In the Bible it talks about this person who is going to come one day in the future called The Beast. . . . In order to allow him to appear, his

workers . . . those of us who dedicated our lives to his service, we had to create an atmosphere that would be conducive to his coming upon the world scene. . . . Our goal was to create havoc, lawlessness, create fear, to bring chaos to the city. We did succeed, tragically, in bringing the City of New York to its knees. (quoted in Polner, 1993, p. 6)

More recently, Terry proposed, based on the word of a "reliable" informant, that the 1990 Gainesville, Florida, student murders may have involved much more than just the passions of a single sexual sadist. Terry hinted that the five killings were part of a larger scheme conceived by a satanic network, a scheme involving a number of student slayings on various campuses around the state of Florida. However interesting Terry's hypothesis may be, it was never substantiated by law enforcement authorities or by Danny Rolling, the confessed killer.

Larry Kahaner, author of *Cults That Kill* (1988), has spent years studying the movement and practices of cults. He, like many experts, has seen a disturbing trend in satanic cult activity. Said Kahaner, "Crimes involving Satanism, and murder in particular, are increasing" (quoted in Fox & Levin, 1989, p. 50).

The principles embodied in Satanism turn the teachings of the Judeo-Christian ethic inside out. Rather than "love thine enemy," Satanism preaches kindness only to fellow devil worshipers. Rather than advocating to "turn the other cheek," Satanism preaches vengeance and getting even. Rather than self-denial, Satanism preaches self-indulgence.

According to these principles, individuals who feel powerless and resentful may embrace some countercultural worldview, frequently satanic, even if they do not join an organized cult. Their actions then may be patterned, influenced, or justified by the directives of some external force, be it material, such as a cult leader, or a philosophy, such as writings concerning the occult.

For those who are hate filled and distrustful of others, Satanism, in particular, offers identification with an omnipotent though mythical figure from whom they can draw their own personal sense of supremacy and power. Kahaner (1988) has suggested that followers of Satan can derive an exhilarating sense of strength from performing certain rituals, such as wearing special robes, chanting, and sacrificing animals or even humans.

Some Satanists come together with like-minded cultists in Black Masses to worship and perform their rituals collectively. Others observe their faith more privately without joining an organized group. They chant incantations; burn religious candles; and draw satanic symbols, such as inverted pentagrams and the number 666, in solitude.

Serial murderers have a particularly acute need for power, one that is far greater than that of the normal population. The principles of Satanism, when taken to their extreme, can provide these individuals with a convenient justification for satisfying their need for dominance through murder. According to Steve Daniels, a Wisconsin Department of Corrections official who has studied the connection between Satanism and serial murder, "Satanic precepts seem to foster an 'if it feels good, do it' attitude. The twisted mind of the serial killer could certainly interpret this as a license to kill" (quoted in Fox & Levin, 1989, p. 51).

During the summer of 1985, Night Stalker Richard Ramirez wreaked havoc on the Los Angeles area by entering homes at random and brutally attacking their occupants while they slept. Before fleeing his victims' homes,

Ramirez offered his tribute to the "Great Satan." He inscribed satanic messages on the walls and even drew satanic pentagrams on the bodies of some of his victims.

Ramirez's murder spree actually began a year before the Los Angeles murder panic of 1985. In June 1984, a 79-year-old woman was viciously murdered in her Glassell Park suburban home. Her throat was slashed and she was stabbed to death. Accustomed to responding to such homicides in the Los Angeles area, the police regarded the crime as a routine case.

Then, on March 17, 1985, a 30-year-old woman was dragged from her car in Monterey Park and shot to death by someone who appeared to be a total stranger. On the same day, a 43-year-old woman was killed and her roommate wounded in their Rosemead condominium. The survivor remembered the intruder for his long face, curly dark hair, protruding eyes, and discolored teeth.

What nobody suspected at the time was that Richard Ramirez had committed all three attacks. By the end of August 1985, his death toll had climbed to 13. In addition, the 25-year-old drifter from Texas had injured or raped a number of other victims.

The absence of a discernible pattern in his modus operandi and choice of victims confused police investigators. Ramirez raped, sodomized, stabbed, slashed, shot, and bludgeoned. His victims were young and old; married and single; men, women, and children; and from all races.

On August 25, the Night Stalker escaped in a stolen car after shooting a 29-year-old man in the head and raping his fiancée. Three days later, the police recovered the stolen vehicle, complete with a set of fingerprints, which they traced to Richard Ramirez. They immediately issued an all-points bulletin and gave the suspect's mug shot to the media. Ramirez's photo was publicized widely, appearing on the front page of every major newspaper in southern California as well as on all local television newscasts. At a press conference, the serial killer's name was announced for the first time.

The next day was the last day of freedom for the Night Stalker. It seemed as if every citizen in East Los Angeles recognized his face. After showing himself in public, Ramirez was vigorously chased on foot by angry residents who were eager to put him in the hospital, or maybe in his grave. The police arrived just in time to save his life. The apparently fearless and diabolical Night Stalker, who, for many months, had terrified the people of southern California, had been turned overnight into a cowering and frightened victim. As an officer took his handcuffs from his belt, the serial killer raised his hands over his head and begged, "Save me. Please. Thank God you're here. It's me. I'm the one you want. Save me before they kill me" (Linedecker, 1991, p. 158).

After being arrested for the string of murders, Ramirez claimed satanic inspiration. His palm bore the tattooed image of a pentagram, the five-point star enclosed within a circle that is linked to devil worship. In court, Ramirez loudly proclaimed his allegiance to Satan and blamed his murder spree on the satanic lyrics in the record "Highway to Hell" by the heavy metal band AC/DC.

Even when a seemingly normal person commits atrocious acts, friends and neighbors often search for extraordinary circumstances that might have driven that person to behave in such an uncharacteristic way. The specter of satanic worship is frequently invoked to try to explain otherwise inexplicable behavior. Ramirez hardly could be described as the "boy next door."

The residents of the sleepy town of West Memphis, Arkansas, were at a loss to understand the arrest of three local teenagers on suspicion of savagely murdering three 8-year-old boys who had been out for a bike ride. It wasn't just the act of multiple murder that shocked the townsfolk, but the grotesque nature of the crimes. The three slain youngsters had been found hog-tied with shoelaces, and with their skulls fractured. One victim's genitals had been entirely carved out, and another had suffered stab wounds to his penis. Two of the boys had been drowned, and the boy whose genitals had been excised bled to death. According to the medical examiner, all three victims appeared to have been raped. The latter boy had been raped and sexually mutilated while still alive (S. Barnes, 1994).

On June 9, 1993, days after the arrest of the three suspects, the Memphis newspaper, *The Commercial Appeal,* published portions of a 27-page statement from one of the arrested teenagers, in which he described bizarre, cultlike rituals including animal sacrifice that he and his friends had performed. "We go out and kill dogs and stuff," said 17-year-old Jessie Lloyd Misskelley Jr., "and then we carry girls there [to the woods] . . . and we have an orgee [sic]" (Lambert, 1994, p. 43). According to Misskelley, in order to be accepted by his buddies, each of the cultists had to barbecue a freshly slain dog and then eat its back leg. Rumors spread through West Memphis that one of the three suspects was a devil worshiper who frequently dressed in black and was known to carry a cat's skull.

News references to cult activity and satanic symbolism gave the incredulous public a focal point for speculation. Perhaps the murders involved the activities of a satanic cult in their midst. Maybe that could account for the gruesome and macabre nature of the crimes.

All three youthful defendants were originally convicted; one was sentenced to death by lethal injection. Much of the case against the defendants, however, was based on the unreliable testimony of witnesses who later changed their stories, may have been motivated to collect reward money, or were determined to be lying.

Despite the concern over witness credibility, the Arkansas Supreme Court upheld the guilty verdicts. Based on DNA evidence, however, a plea bargain was later struck, maintaining the credibility of the case against the three defendants but also allowing them to go free. It is doubtful we will ever know the full extent to which Satanism influenced the West Memphis slayings. Were the three young defendants innocent victims of a hysterical community, whose residents were all too eager to blame someone—perhaps anyone—for a hideous crime? Were the defendants local teenagers whose youthful experiments with the mysteries of the occult got out of hand? Or were they truly on the road to becoming committed disciples of Satan who would be willing to kill in their hero's name?

Satanism may have been a critical motivating factor in cult murders like the Matamoros slayings or for serial killers like Ramirez. We should be careful, however, not to exaggerate the influence of Satanism on multiple murder. Satan is only one of many external forces that killers have been known to use to excuse their murderous behavior. Members of the Manson family blamed LSD, and Ted Bundy blamed pornography. For some killers, devil worship may be merely a convenient excuse and incidental to their tendency to be violent. For many, murderous impulses likely existed long before they found Satan. We should therefore be more than a bit skeptical when killers invoke the often-used line, "The devil made me do it."

CHAPTER 12

So Many Victims

Twenty-seven-year-old Kendall Francois lived with his parents and his younger sister on a quiet, tree-lined street in Poughkeepsie, New York. His ramshackle green house was located near downtown on Fulton Avenue, just a stone's throw from the ivy-draped halls of Vassar College, and it was two blocks from a sleazy area of Main Street where prostitutes regularly plied their trade.

On September 1, 1998, Poughkeepsie police got a frantic phone call from a woman who claimed she had just been attacked by Francois while they were seated in his car. The police arrested the 6-foot, 4-inch, 300-pound, out-of-work school custodian. They soon became aware that he might have committed much more than a single assault. Based on statements he made while being interrogated, and after police discovered that he had recently served 15 days for assaulting a prostitute, Francois was charged with eight brutal murders committed over a 2-year period beginning in 1996. All of the victims had been reported missing, all but one had been arrested for prostitution, most were drug users, and none was a college student.

Indeed, the residents of Poughkeepsie, an economically depressed center of manufacturing with a population of some 40,000, had been on edge because of the string of missing women. Francois's arrest brought relief not only to the victims' families and friends but also to residents of the Poughkeepsie community generally. The fact that the missing women were drug users and hookers kept the city's residents from experiencing collective hysteria. The Vassar campus was no exception. Students and faculty members there were relieved when the killer was apprehended, but his killing spree had never held the campus in the grip of terror. Francois hadn't gone after college students, only prostitutes.

Not unlike other prolific serial killers, Francois had murdered his eight victims in one place and then disposed of their bodies in another place. After strangling his victims in his car, he carried each of their bodies to his home on Fulton Street, where he hid them in various sections of the house. The stench eventually was noticed by neighbors. It became so putrid by the time of his arrest that the police who searched the premises were forced to wear masks and jumpsuits. Still, family members who shared the house with Francois were genuinely surprised when they later learned of the murders. They simply did not suspect that the odor was that of decomposing bodies. To admit this to themselves, they would first have had to acknowledge that a murderer was living among them.

On August 7, 2000, Judge Thomas Dolan of County Court sentenced Francois to eight consecutive life terms without parole eligibility, but his punishment had a medical aspect as well. It was revealed that the killer had tested HIV-positive; he may have contracted HIV from one of the women he had murdered. Disappointed that the killer had not received a death sentence, the daughter of one victim called the news "poetic justice."

VULNERABLE VICTIMS PREFERRED

As Kendall Francois knew all too well, prostitutes are especially vulnerable to sexual predators because of the accessibility required by their trade, and this vulnerability explains their extremely high rate of victimization by serial killers and their extremely large body counts. A sexual sadist can cruise a red-light district, shopping around for the woman who best conforms to his deadly sexual fantasies. When he finds her, she willingly complies with his wishes, until it is too late.

Because of these risk factors, prostitute slayings have occurred in cities across the country—in Rochester, New York; in Seattle, Washington; in New Bedford, Massachusetts; in San Diego, California; in Detroit, Michigan; and in dozens of other locales. Even when it is widely known that a killer is prowling the streets, far too many prostitutes place profit over protection, hoping or assuming that they can avoid death. Some see no other life for themselves, particularly if they have expensive drug habits to support.

The ease with which prostitutes can be targeted explains why their slayings have resulted in some of the largest body counts amassed by serial killers. On October 9, 2002, Robert Lee Yates Jr., was sentenced to death by lethal injection for murdering 24-year-old Melinda Mercer and 35-year-old La Fontaine Ellis in Tacoma, Washington. The 50-year-old former Army helicopter pilot and father of five became the 11th resident of Washington State Penitentiary's death row in Walla Walla, the same prison where he had once worked as a guard. Two years earlier, Yates had confessed to committing 13 more murders since 1975, most of them in Spokane County. All but one of his victims were women who had ties to prostitution, illicit drugs, or both.

In an earlier negotiation with authorities, Yates had avoided the death penalty in a plea agreement designed to provide a degree of closure not only to law enforcement but also to the families of the victims. In one case, for example, Yates drew a map that led the police to unearth a body that he had buried in a shallow grave in the yard of his Spokane home.

In April 2000, Yates was arrested for the August 1997 slaying of 16-year-old runaway Jennifer Joseph. In May, the prosecution filed seven additional counts of murder and one count of attempted murder and robbery for a 1998 attack on 32-year-old Christine Smith, who survived a gunshot wound to the head. Yates was linked to these other killings by DNA and other physical evidence. In July, he was charged in Pierce County with two additional counts of murder.

Yates was known to have cruised Spokane's red-light district in his white 1977 Corvette. Joseph was last seen in August 1977 in what witnesses described as a light-colored Corvette driven by a White man. Later, over a period of several months, the police pulled over Yates's sports car on several occasions along the strip where prostitutes worked and in an area where a body had been found. At a stop in November 1998, he had a known prostitute in the passenger's seat of his car.

At first, Yates was only one of hundreds of potential suspects. After a tense conversation in the police precinct, he refused to give the police a blood sample for DNA analysis. Then, the police tracked down his Corvette, which he had sold in May 1998. As it happened, the car yielded substantial physical evidence implicating Yates. Carpet fibers from the car were matched with fibers found on Jennifer Joseph's shoes as well as with a towel left near her remains. In addition, a button made of mother-of-pearl was matched to one missing from Joseph's jacket. Blood was found on the seat and seat belt of Yates's Corvette. In the end, DNA proved to be the conclusive evidence linking Yates to at least 12 of the slayings.

Yates was a prolific serial killer, to be sure, but even his body count pales by comparison with that amassed by Gary Ridgway. On November 5, 2003, in a tense King County, Washington, courtroom, 52-year-old Ridgway pled guilty to 48 counts of murder. The longtime truck painter confessed to being the notorious Green River Killer, a man who seemed to kill with impunity, taking the lives of dozens of prostitutes while staying on the loose for two decades. Forensic evidence linked Ridgway to seven of the killings, for which he assumed responsibility.

Most of Ridgway's victims were slain in the early 1980s. Between January and July of 1982, the strangled bodies of four women, ages 16 to 27, were recovered from areas in or around Seattle's Green River. On July 15, two boys riding their bicycles across the Meeker Street bridge in Kent spotted the body of a fully clothed girl floating in a stream. She was later identified by the police as a 16-year-old middle school dropout and runaway. She had been strangled to death.

The bodies of three more women were dragged from the Green River on August 15, 1982. The remains of still another woman were recovered in the woods of nearby Maple Valley on May 8, 1983. All four of these victims had been asphyxiated.

The victim list attributable to the Green River Killer continued to grow, causing local police investigators to focus more and more attention and resources on these unsolved prostitute slayings. A task force was convened, the FBI offered its assistance, and a national telethon was aired to encourage the public to phone in tips. FBI profilers suggested that the killer was likely a White man in his 30s or 40s who had unresolved issues with the women in his life and had spent a good deal of time in the woods.

Police investigators had questioned Ridgway in 1987. At that time, they were able to secure a sample of his saliva by having the suspect chew on a piece of gauze. This evidence was preserved for almost 15 years, until DNA technology became more effective and reliable. It was Ridgway's DNA taken from that saliva sample that finally connected him, years later, to seven of the Green River murders and sealed his fate.

Photo 12.1 Serial killers frequently victimize marginal groups. Police searched hard for the remains of prostitutes slain by Green River Killer Gary Ridgway. (Associated Press/ Elaine Thompson)

Using only evidence linking the defendant with the deaths of seven prostitutes, the state of Washington easily could have secured the death penalty for Ridgway, but instead prosecutors asked for a sentence of life imprisonment. The plea bargain that spared Ridgway's life was designed to ease the suffering of the victims' loved ones. In return for a life sentence, the killer agreed to cooperate with police authorities in helping them to locate the bodies of his victims, reveal the identity of his victims, and close their cold cases.

The Green River Killer also explained his motivation for victimizing prostitutes. Not only did it serve him physically and psychologically, but his plan also was designed specifically to avoid capture (*State of Washington v. Gary Leon Ridgway*, 2003):

I picked prostitutes as my victims because I hate most prostitutes and did not want to pay them for sex. I also picked prostitutes as victims because they were easy to pick up without being noticed. I knew they would not be reported missing. I picked prostitutes because I thought I could kill as many of them as I wanted without getting caught.

Another part of my plan was where I put the bodies of these women. Most of the time I took the women's jewelry and their clothes to get rid of any evidence and make them harder to identify. I placed most of the bodies in groups which I call "clusters." I did this because I wanted to keep track of all the women I killed. I liked to drive by the "clusters" around the county and think about the women I placed there. I usually used a landmark to remember a "cluster" and the women I placed there. Sometimes I killed and dumped a woman, intending to start a new "cluster," and never returned because I thought I might get caught putting more women there.

The plea bargain with the Green River Killer raises a question that was troubling to those who believe that consistency is required in the administration of justice. If the state of Washington refuses to execute someone who admits to killing 48 human beings, how can it ever again administer the death penalty?

The vulnerability of prostitutes derives in part from their willingness to get into automobiles with total strangers and the lack of response from the larger community.

The vulnerability of one additional class of victims—young boys and girls—stems both from their naïveté and their small size. For decades, pedophiles—adults who desire sexual relations with children—have capitalized on the ease with which many children can be deceived by a contrived story or ruse. Even the most street-wise child will not necessarily think twice about going with someone impersonating a police officer. Other children can be grabbed easily so that their attempts to flee are futile.

By the time he was 27 years old, Wesley Allan Dodd had logged years of experience in molesting and raping young boys. Dodd started out, as a teenager, by exposing himself in public. As he grew into adulthood, that simply wasn't enough to gratify him. His sexual desire for young boys continued to escalate. "[Exposing myself] wasn't fun anymore," recalled Dodd. "I needed more physical contact. I started tricking kids into touching me. Then that wasn't fun anymore so I started molesting kids" (McCleod, 1993).

At first, Dodd's passion was purely sexual; he never felt compelled to murder any of his victims. Because many of his young victims reported him, Dodd had had numerous brushes with the law, and he had served 4 months of a 10-year sentence in an Idaho prison. Upon his release from custody, he was determined to stay out of the joint. He had no intention to go straight, however, only to avoid apprehension.

"In Seattle, June 13, 1987, I tried to kidnap a boy," said Dodd. "My intentions, at this point, were to kidnap him, rape him, and kill him so that he couldn't report me" (McCleod, 1993). He realized at that point that murder would be a necessary evil to enable him to continue his career of rape and molestation. However, the boy he accosted in Seattle screamed his way to freedom, sending Dodd back to prison for another short stay.

Dodd had to prepare himself mentally—to "psych himself up"—to cross the line into homicide. "I wasn't sure that I could kill, so in my mind I had to fantasize about it. To be able to kill, I had to make that thought exciting," Dodd explained. "And in a matter of just a couple of weeks . . . I was ready to kill" (Griffiths, 1993).

After his release, Dodd was prepared to try again to abduct and molest young boys, and this time he was determined not to fail. His first murder occurred during the Labor Day weekend of 1989. Dodd accosted 11-year-old Cole Neer and his 10-year-old brother Billy as they rode their bikes through a park in Vancouver, Washington. Dodd stabbed both children to death after molesting the older boy. A month later, he abducted 4-year-old Lee Iseli from a playground, molested him, and then hanged him by a rope in a bedroom closet. Dodd clearly had developed a taste for murder; he was totally hooked. In his own words, "I became obsessed with [killing]. That's all I thought about 24 hours a day. I was dreaming about it at night, constantly all day at work, all I thought about was killing kids" (McCleod, 1993).

Fortunately, Dodd had neither the skill nor the luck of more prolific serial killers. Two weeks after the Iseli murder, Dodd was again on the prowl. He attempted to abduct a boy from a movie theater bathroom, but his victim started screaming frantically. Dodd managed to wrestle the boy into his car. The vehicle was in poor mechanical shape, however, and not equipped for a quick getaway. Unable to accelerate, Dodd was captured only two blocks from the theater. On January 15, 1993, following months of intense publicity surrounding his unusual choice of mode of execution, Dodd was hanged at the state penitentiary in Walla Walla, in eastern Washington State.

The vulnerability of certain groups of victims rests not so much in their naïveté, accessibility, or small stature but in the sense that serial killers can prey upon them with relative impunity. As one example, when extinguishing the lives of elderly nursing home residents, a caretaker can capitalize on the normalcy of death in such an environment; moreover, a thrill killer, when trolling for prostitutes along a red-light strip, can be reasonably assured that the disappearances of his victims, because of their typically transient lifestyle, will not immediately be deemed foul play. Society devalues women and men who sell their bodies. The capture of their killer, therefore, often takes low priority; and the killer knows this. Some serial killers, moreover, select other marginal groups—among them minorities, immigrants, and homosexuals—in the expectation that the public and police responses will be muted. If nothing else, serial murderers are opportunists, and they seek out conditions that will allow them to kill repeatedly without detection or apprehension.

CATCHING THE SERIAL KILLER

There is a long-standing myth, which consistently runs through popular television shows and mystery novels, that serial killers, at least at some level, wish to get caught. According to this view, serial killers—even the most sociopathic—actually *do* have a conscience strong enough to affect their behavior; they subconsciously leave clues to their crimes so that they will be punished for their sins. This notion dates back years, at least to the 1946 case of William Heirens, the so-called "lipstick killer," who scrawled a message for the Chicago police on the apartment wall of one of his victims, "For heavens sake catch me before I kill more I cannot control myself" (Scott, n.d., 1).

Unlike Heirens, most serial killers do everything they can to avoid getting caught. They are clever and careful: When it comes to murder, they are brilliantly resourceful. They methodically stalk their victims for the best opportunity to strike so as not to be seen, and they cleverly dump the bodies far away from the crime scene so as not to leave any clues. The cool and calculating manners in which many sociopaths cover their tracks arise out of the fearlessness that typifies this personality type. They respond unemotionally and without panic to the prospect of capture, undeterred by the risk of apprehension.

A self-selection process operates to separate the cool-headed men from the hot-tempered boys. If killers like Andrew Cunanan and Jeffrey Dahmer weren't so adept at killing and covering their trail, they never would have remained on the streets long enough to qualify as serial killers.

Murders committed by serial killers—at least the methodical ones—typically are difficult to solve because of lack of motive and useful evidence. Unlike the usual homicide, which involves an offender and victim who know one another, sexually motivated serial murders are almost exclusively committed by strangers. Thus, the usual police strategy of identifying suspects—boyfriends, neighbors, or coworkers—by examining their possible motives, be they jealousy, revenge, or greed, generally helps very little. With no such clear-cut motive, there are no immediate suspects.

After his 1995 arrest in the state of Oregon, Keith Jesperson, the notorious Happy Face Killer, explained the elaborate planning that permitted him to stay on the loose while he murdered at least eight women in a number of states. Jesperson's advice, in his own words, to aspiring serial killers was to put time and distance between them and their victims:

> Meet a victim one place, dump her someplace else—in another town, another county, another state—somewhere no one is looking for the missing. But you don't have to take it 20 miles away to dump it. You can put a body in the dumpster next door if you feel comfortable that no one can pin it on you. That's why it's best to take strangers, victims who can't be linked to you. (Kamb, 2003, p. A1)

In Gainesville, Florida, in August of 1990, a large task force investigating the murders of five college students had a wealth of crime-scene evidence for the lab to analyze, including pubic hairs and semen. For months, the task force operated on a "pubes and tubes" strategy, collecting hair and blood samples from hundreds of "donors"—just about anyone who could have had a connection to the crime. When seeking a stranger who had no prior relationship to the victims, however, this hunt for the killer was like searching for a needle in a haystack. The high-profile character of the Gainesville murders, furthermore, made for a huge haystack of "suspects;" in addition, well-intentioned citizens from around the country phoned in the names of unscrupulous or sleazy people they thought might be involved.

The Gainesville investigation team was fortunate to have plenty of clues—perhaps more than they needed. Other serial murder investigations have very little evidence of a tangible nature to go on. The more successful serial killers transport their victims from the scene of the murder to a remote dump site or makeshift grave. The police may never locate the body and thus never determine that a homicide has occurred. Even if the bodies of the victims do eventually turn up at a dump site, most of the potentially revealing forensic evidence remains at the scene of the slaying, perhaps in the killer's house or car. Without a suspect, the police do not know these locations. Moreover, any trace evidence, such as semen within the vagina and skin beneath the fingernails, left on the discarded body tends to erode as the corpse is exposed to rain, wind, heat, or snow as well as insects and animals.

In 1988, for example, the police in New Bedford, Massachusetts—some 50 miles south of Boston—were stymied by a profound lack of physical evidence in their hunt for a killer of at least nine prostitutes and drug users. The unidentified predator had abducted his victims from the sleazy Weld Square area of town and discarded their remains along highways in southeastern Massachusetts. By the time the decomposed bodies were discovered, the police had trouble putting names to the skeletal remains, much less to the killer.

To the present day, the New Bedford case remains unsolved. Some people have speculated that the killer recently may have taken up where he left off years earlier. In 2004, the murdered remains of three prostitutes from Worcester, Massachusetts, were discovered in a couple of desolate areas around the Boston metropolitan area. Any police efforts to link these killings with the New Bedford slayings some 16 years earlier would be extremely difficult.

Given the extreme vulnerability of prostitutes, it should come as no surprise that serial killers often target them. Many of their murders go unsolved for long periods of time—months, years, even decades. A few are never solved. In fact, it would not be unexpected to find two or three serial killers independently targeting prostitutes in the same geographical region at about the same time.

Serial killers don't always travel great distances to remote mountainsides and densely wooded areas to dispose of evidence. John Wayne Gacy buried his victims in the crawl space under his suburban home. Jeffrey Dahmer tried to dissolve his dead companions in a barrel of acid that he kept in his Milwaukee apartment. In Detroit and neighboring Highland Park, Michigan, Benjamin Atkins, 29, a homeless drug addict, confessed to killing 11 women in 1991 and 1992; he had dumped their bodies in vacant and abandoned buildings. In one particularly chilling discovery, the police found three corpses in the shower stalls of three different rooms of the boarded-up Monterey Motel.

BEHAVIORAL PROFILING

Common forensic approaches to tracking serial killers range from traditional fingerprinting to cutting-edge DNA analysis (genetic fingerprinting). A relatively new strategy for serial murder investigations is to exploit the crime scene in the search for psychological or behavioral clues. Psychological profiling has been used occasionally over the years by forensic psychiatrists, but since the early 1980s, it has been enhanced by behavioral scientists at the FBI. Through behavioral assessment of crime scene photos, autopsy records, and police incident reports, FBI profilers compose a "portrait" that speculates on the killer's age, race, sex, marital status, employment status, sexual maturity, possible criminal record, relationship to the victim, and likelihood of committing future crimes.

At the core of its strategy, derived from its study of 36 killers (25 serial and 11 nonserial), the FBI profiling team distinguishes between organized and disorganized killers, the former being methodical or careful, and the latter being haphazard or frenzied (Ressler, Burgess, et al., 1985). The organized and disorganized types are distinguished by clusters of personal and social characteristics. The organized killer typically is intelligent, is socially and sexually competent, is of high birth order (one of the oldest children in the family), is a skilled worker, lives with a partner, is mobile, drives a late-model car, and follows his crime in the media. The disorganized killer, on the other hand, generally is unintelligent, is socially and sexually inadequate, is of low birth order, is an unskilled worker, lives alone, is not mobile, drives an old car or does not own one, and has minimal interest in the news reports of his crimes (see Ressler, Burgess, & Douglas, 1988).

According to FBI analysts, the personality of a killer is reflected in his behavior at a crime scene. Organized and disorganized types tend to differ in terms of the manner in which they operate before, during, and after their crimes. Specifically, the organized killer uses restraints on his victims, hides or transports the body, removes weapons from the scene, sexually molests the victims prior to death, and is methodical in his style of killing. In sharp contrast, the disorganized killer tends not to use restraints, leaves the body in full view, leaves a weapon at the scene, sexually molests the victim after death, and is spontaneous in his manner of killing. The task of profiling therefore involves drawing inferences from the crime scene to the behavioral characteristics of the killer.

Psychological profiles may be perfectly on target in television programs and films, such as *Criminal Minds* and *The Silence of the Lambs*, but they are only rough indicators in real life, even when constructed by the most skillful profilers at the FBI Academy in Quantico, Virginia. The profiles are intended to be tools to narrow the range of suspects rather than to point precisely to a particular suspect. Even in meeting this limited objective, the profiles are not always successful. In Baton Rouge, Louisiana, months after the police had linked several murders to a serial killer, the task force released details of an FBI profile of the unknown assailant. The profile described the killer as a strong man, 25 to 35 years of age, who was awkward in interacting with attractive women. The task force also speculated that the killer was White or Hispanic because of the racial pattern in his victim selection. Derrick Todd Lee, a muscular 34-year-old, eventually was arrested for the crimes. Friends and neighbors described him as "disarmingly charming" and "easy to get along with." Also contrary to the FBI profile, Lee was Black.

The FBI's Unabomber profile, which guided the investigation of a series of bombings during the 1980s and 1990s, suggested that the perpetrator was in his mid-30s or early 40s, was a blue-collar worker possibly with some college education, and had resided in or around Chicago and later San Francisco. When Theodore Kaczynski was captured, he was in his 50s; he held a doctorate degree and lived as a hermit in Montana.

In 2007, Malcolm Gladwell, staff writer for the *New Yorker,* published a critique of the history and practice of criminal profiling in which the usefulness of the investigative strategy was questioned. He described a 1984 skull session involving several renowned profilers who collaboratively pieced together a behavioral portrait of the then-unidentified BTK strangler. The composite, as described by Gladwell, contained a variety of generalizations and contradictions:

> Look for an American male with a possible connection to the military. His I.Q. will be above 105. He will like to masturbate, and will be aloof and selfish in bed. He will drive a decent car. He will be a "now" person. He won't be comfortable with women. But he may have women friends. He will be a lone wolf. But he will be able to function in social settings. He won't be unmemorable. But he will be unknowable. He will be either never married, divorced, or married, and if he was or is married his wife will be younger or older. He may or may not live in a rental, and might be lower class, upper lower class, lower middle class or middle class. And he will be crazy like a fox, as opposed to being mental. (Gladwell, 2007)

Profiling is more an imprecise craft than an exact science. Behavioral inferences from crime scene evidence cannot be made with substantial reliability. An FBI study revealed a 74% agreement rate in classifying crime scenes as organized or disorganized (see Ressler et al., 1988). While this may seem impressive on the surface, it actually is deficient in view of the base rate of organized killers in the sample. Of 64 crime scenes classified in the FBI reliability study, 31 were organized and 21 disorganized, while 9 were mixed and 3 indeterminable. Thus, the 74% agreement rate is not much better than that for a strategy of classifying all scenes as "organized." More to the point, the profiles have a very low rate of success in leading to the identity of a killer. Although psychological profiles work wonderfully in fiction, they are much less than a panacea in real life. Profiles are designed not to solve cases but simply to provide an additional set of clues in cases found by local police to be difficult to solve. Moreover, one should not expect a high success rate; only the most difficult cases ever reach the attention of the FBI unit.

It is critical, therefore, that we maintain some perspective on the investigative value of psychological profiles. Simply put, a psychological profile cannot identify a suspect for investigation nor can it eliminate a suspect who doesn't fit the mold. Rather, a profile can assist in assigning subjective probabilities to suspects whose names surface through more usual investigative strategies (e.g., interviews of witnesses, canvassing of neighborhoods, and tip phone lines).

VICAP

One of the problems confronting the investigators in the 1988 New Bedford, Massachusetts, case was that the task force was not launched until months after the murders had begun. It was not until the fourth victim's body was found that the police determined that a serial killer was on the loose. Similarly, the three bodies of women from the Worcester, Massachusetts, area discovered in 2004 may have been deposited months, even years, earlier.

This time delay is not unusual. Before trying to solve a case, or even during investigations, police are not always certain that a serial killer is operating in their area. Serial killers do not always leave unmistakable and unique signatures at their crime scenes. Although some killers "specialize," others are far more versatile. A particular murderer may target a redhead on one occasion and a blonde on another—whomever is available. He may also vary his style or mode of killing, using a knife on one occasion and a club on another. His varying modus operandi may reflect not so much an attempt to confuse the police as a desire to experiment with different kinds of victims and different styles of killing. As a result, the police may not recognize multiple homicides as the work of the same perpetrator.

Moreover, some serial killings, even if consistent in modus operandi, cross jurisdictional boundaries. A killer might abduct a woman in Wyoming and duplicate the crime with another victim two states away, a problem characterized as linkage blindness (Egger, 1984).

To aid in the detection of serial murder cases that involve multiple jurisdictions, the FBI has designed and implemented a computerized database for linking unsolved and bizarre homicides. The Violent Criminal Apprehension Program (VICAP) is designed to flag similarities in unsolved homicides around the country that otherwise might not be connected in the minds of investigative teams (Douglas & Munn, 1992; Howlett, Haufland, & Ressler, 1986).

Although it is an excellent concept in theory, VICAP has encountered numerous practical limitations in constructing a national clearinghouse of unsolved murder cases. First, the questionnaires that local police use to provide information for VICAP are long and complicated. Consequently, cooperation from local law enforcement agencies in reporting cases has been less than satisfactory. VICAP cannot link cases that are not reported to it. Furthermore, even with full participation by police agencies around the country, recognizing a pattern to unsolved murders in different states is not as easy as some people might believe, regardless of how powerful the computer used or how sophisticated the software.

Despite the problems encountered by the VICAP initiative, computers clearly are indispensable tools in managing homicide investigations. Large-scale investigative task forces rely heavily on them for information storage and retrieval. In a case that drags on for weeks or months, particularly when there are multiple victims and multiple crime scenes, the volume of information is nearly unmanageable without the use of technology. This is especially true in high-profile cases in which the public is encouraged (often with promise of reward) to call in information to a tip line.

The annals of law enforcement reveal many instances in which a large-scale investigation failed because certain key pieces of information were difficult to access, lost, or not relayed to the appropriate detectives. In recent years, software for indexing investigative data (including witness statements, tips, and field reports) has allowed detectives to query a database to link, for example, forensic analysis of tire tracks with a witness's statement about observing a truck leaving the scene of a crime.

Of course, a computer does only what police ordinarily do—tracking down leads and comparing information—but at lightning-fast speed. Recent advances in information database matching and artificial intelligence have assisted law enforcement in drawing critical clues from seemingly disparate and incomplete sources. For example, the Coplink program, designed by an Arizona-based software firm, searches and matches arrest records, emergency calls to 911, motor vehicle registration files, and other existing databases to help police track down information in a timely fashion. Coplink was installed late in the Washington, DC, sniper investigation—in fact, on the very day that the police closed in on the two suspects while they slept in their blue Chevrolet Caprice in a rest stop off Route 95. In response to investigators' request for a list of all vehicles stopped within a travel distance of 1 hour from any of the shooting sites, Coplink flagged the fact that the same blue Caprice was stopped by police at multiple post-shooting roadblocks.

DNA

DNA (deoxyribonucleic acid), the genetic basis for all inherited traits, has unquestionably been the single greatest advance for law enforcement for identifying serial killers and for prosecutors in convicting them at trial. Except for identical twins, each person has a unique blueprint or genetic code, which can be identified from samples of human cells contained in various forms of biological material.

The forensic applications of DNA testing extend back only a few decades. In the 1980s, DNA extracted from semen and blood recovered at crime scenes was first employed to match with blood samples secured from suspects, especially in rape cases. At that early stage of development, ample and relatively fresh crime scene samples were required to extract a so-called DNA fingerprint. However, more recent advances in testing methods have allowed analysts to extract DNA not only from fluids such as blood, semen, saliva, and sweat, but also from skin, bone, and follicles of hair, even in trace amounts.

The probative value of a DNA match is absolutely unparalleled, especially in the opinions of jurors who give great weight to its scientific authority. There is a big difference, of course, between matching DNA evidence to a known suspect, and trying to locate and apprehend an unidentified killer based on DNA from a crime scene.

In searching for a serial killer from DNA recovered at one or more crime scenes, investigators attempt to find a match in computerized DNA databanks of known individuals, usually persons previously convicted of violent crimes. This approach, of course, is only as good as the comprehensiveness of the databank itself. Launched in 1990, the FBI has maintained a computerized DNA database, known as CODIS (Combined DNA Index System). All 50 states submit genetic data to the national DNA index system, which as of 2013 had topped over 10 million offender profiles. State laws differ with respect to their rules governing when a subject's DNA can be archived. DNA profiles of convicted murderers and sex offenders are generally retained and computerized, although some states have expanded their guidelines to include other violent felons, nonviolent criminals, or even their entire prison populations. There has also been a push toward broadening routine DNA testing to include all persons arrested, although privacy concerns have been raised with regard to retaining DNA records on persons not yet convicted of a crime.

In many serial murder investigations, especially for offenders who have remained at large for years, DNA evidence recovered from crime scenes will find no matches in computerized DNA records of prior offenders. Tracking a series of murders of young women near Louisiana State University between 2001 and 2003, for example, the Baton Rouge police attempted a controversial alternative approach by mounting a DNA dragnet. Over 1,000 potential suspects were asked "voluntarily" to permit a swab to be taken from their inner cheek for the purpose of DNA analysis. As it happened, a genetic match was made to one of the volunteers, Derrick Todd Lee, a 34-year-old man who also bore some similarity to a police composite sketch. Lee was ultimately convicted and sentenced to death.

Another recent advance in genetic testing has allowed investigators to identify potential suspects based on the analysis of familial DNA, capitalizing on the similarity in genetic markers of blood relatives. It was the means by which a very cold serial murder case was finally cracked by the Los Angeles authorities.

The so-called "Grim Sleeper" serial murder case was named for the 1988 to 2002 hiatus in the assailant's killing spree. But then in 2010, after years of investigative dead ends, the arrest of 57-year-old Lonnie David Franklin Jr. closed the book on at least 11 unsolved murders that had occurred since 1985. The big break in the case came when investigators expanded their DNA search to

California's prison population. Finding a possible familial DNA link to Franklin's son, the police began following and watching the elder Franklin. Retrieving his DNA from an partially eaten piece of pizza discarded in a restaurant, the police were then able to make a full match to DNA from one of the unsolved homicides.

Familial DNA also provided the key to resolving a half-century long debate over the identity of the Boston Strangler, who terrorized the region by murdering at least 13 women between 1962 and 1964. The confessed killer, Albert DeSalvo Jr., was never actually charged with the crimes and was murdered while incarcerated for burglary. For decades, there was significant doubt in many circles about whether DeSalvo had committed any of the murders at all. Many argued that DeSalvo's confession revealed many inconsistencies and that he may just have claimed responsibility for murders committed by a fellow inmate as an attention-getting move.

Even with the advent of DNA testing, the Boston Police Department's cold case squad had only a small quantity of biological evidence recovered and saved from one of the murders, the Strangler's last victim, 19-year-old Mary Sullivan, but nothing that would compel a court-ordered exhumation of DeSalvo's remains. Aware of the latest familial DNA approach, the police surreptitiously tailed male descendants of DeSalvo. Saliva from a water bottle discarded by DeSalvo's nephew revealed a Y-chromosome match to the Sullivan crime scene evidence. A subsequent analysis of DeSalvo's exhumed body then confirmed that he indeed was the infamous Boston Strangler.

LUCKY BREAKS

Although forensic investigation, psychological profiling, VICAP, and DNA all play integral roles in trying to apprehend serial killers, there is no substitute for old-fashioned detective work and a healthy dose of luck. In some cases, the police do get lucky because the killer slips up. He may begin to feel, after a while, that he is invincible and that the police cannot match his skill or cunning. He becomes complacent, lazy, and sloppy, and he starts to cut corners and take chances, which leads to his ultimate demise.

In June 1993, the police in Mineola, Long Island, indeed got lucky. After stopping a motorist in the middle of the night because of a missing license plate, state troopers discovered a woman's body in the back of his gray pickup truck. The driver, 34-year-old Joel Rifkin, was on route to dump the body of his 17th victim.

In another case, Colin Ireland of London, England, thought he had all the bases covered, but ultimately he failed to work out every important detail. Over the course of several months in 1993, the 39-year-old Briton stalked and killed members of London's gay community without leaving a single useful clue. All of his five victims were gay men who engaged in sadomasochistic sex; Ireland capitalized on this fetish, binding and gagging his victims at will. Once secured in this manner, they were completely at his mercy.

Ireland was methodical. Before each murder, he emptied his pockets so that nothing would fall out and implicate him. After each, he spent hours wiping away the evidence, even destroying the clothes he wore at the scene of the crime.

Despite his preparation and planning, however, Ireland made a fatal blunder: A security camera captured his presence as he walked behind his fifth and last victim at a subway station, just prior to the murder. Seeing his photo printed in a newspaper, Ireland panicked and came forward to confess.

The police have used a variety of behavioral, investigative, and scientific techniques designed to help identify and capture serial killers. On occasion, however, authorities have lucked out through inadvertent means. On December 12, 1983, Sheriff Pat Thomas of Sarpy County, Nebraska, was interviewed by the press concerning the murder and mutilation of two local boys, 13-year-old Danny Joe Eberle and 12-year-old Chris Walden. Talking with reporters about the murder investigation, Thomas referred to the unidentified killer as "sick, spineless, a coward," and as not having the guts to pick on someone his own size.

Little did Sheriff Thomas realize that the killer was closely following the progress of the investigation in the newspaper. Insulted by the sheriff's remark, 19-year-old John Joubert decided to prove that "he didn't just pick up little boys" (United Press International, 1984). He reacted by selecting an adult—a preschool teacher—as his next victim. Unlike the two murdered children, she was able to break away from her assailant, and she had the presence of mind to memorize the license number of his car. After her escape, she called the police. Joubert was apprehended and later convicted. As luck would have it, Joubert's vanity got the better of him.

Serial killers sometimes are apprehended after being linked to crimes or violations having little apparent connection to their killings. The discovery of human remains from dozens of victims at the Calaveras County, California, retreat of killer Leonard Lake occurred only after his partner, Charles Ng, was caught shoplifting from a hardware store. Serial killer Theodore Bundy was captured after being stopped in Florida on a traffic violation, and New York's Son of Sam killer, David Berkowitz, was identified after the task force investigating his murders followed up on a parking ticket issued to his car near one of his shooting sites. In these and other cases, the police appear to have capitalized on some degree of luck, but they benefited only because of their attention to detail: Luck does indeed favor the well prepared. Bundy's arrest resulted from a police officer doing his job correctly and being alert. Similarly, the lucky ticket associated with Berkowitz's vehicle would not have surfaced had detectives not decided to track down all tickets issued near each of the Son of Sam homicides. As in many areas of life, people make their own luck.

Part III

Massacres

CHAPTER 13

For Love, Money, or Revenge

During the early morning hours of March 26, 1990, New York's Happy Land Social Club was swinging, packed from wall to wall with Spanish-speaking immigrants who, after escaping political or economic repression, had settled in the Bronx. It was 3 a.m., but drinking, music, merriment, and laughter filled the small club—so much so that no one paid much attention to the two people quarreling loudly in a corner.

Thirty-six-year-old Julio Gonzalez, a Cuban refugee who came to the United States in 1980 on the Mariel boatlift, was furious with his girlfriend, Lydia, who worked at Happy Land. The coat-check girl and part-time bartender wanted nothing more to do with her old boyfriend; their 7-year relationship was over, and she told him so in no uncertain terms.

But Julio wouldn't accept the rejection. If he couldn't have Lydia, nobody would. Gonzalez wasted little time in making his move. He ran from Happy Land to an all-night service station, where he bought a dollar's worth of gasoline. He then rushed back to the social club to set it ablaze.

The 92 unsuspecting people inside the building were still having a good time when the unemployed Cuban refugee returned to get even. Without warning, flames began to envelop the small building, and smoke billowed through the crowded rooms. Panic-stricken customers tried in vain to exit through the narrow front door, but most of them were overcome by smoke or trampled to death. Eighty-seven innocent people perished. Ironically, Julio's girlfriend, the inspiration for this vengeful act, was one of only five survivors.

After confessing to the mass murder, Julio Gonzalez tried to explain his motivation. "I got angry," he said. "The devil got into me and I set the place on fire" (Lagnado, 1990, p. 5).

RELATIVE OBSCURITY

Julio Gonzalez killed 87 innocent victims, yet, curiously, he would hardly make most people's list of notorious mass murderers. Part of the reason for Gonzalez's obscurity probably stems from the fact that he and his victims were impoverished Hispanics, many new to the country. Crimes committed against members of minority groups generally do not receive the same level of attention or interest as those affecting White, middle-class Americans. The lack of publicity given nationally to the Happy Land murders also derives from Gonzalez's use of fire as opposed to firearms. In the minds of many Americans, arson is not associated with mass murder in the way that guns are.

Much more important than these factors in explaining the lesser attention given to the Happy Land case is that it was a mass killing or massacre, rather than a serial murder. Had Gonzalez killed 87 people over a period of several years, rather than all at once, he likely would have been as notorious as Theodore Bundy or Jeffrey Dahmer. It's not just the body count that counts; it's the style of killing.

In striking contrast to the expanding scholarly interest in serial homicide, mass killings—the slaughter of several victims during a single act or a short-lived crime spree—have received relatively little consideration (Liwerant, 2007), although there are exceptions (see Dietz, 1986; Duwe, 2000, 2007; Fox & Levin, 1998; Holmes & Holmes, 2001; Levin & Fox, 1985; Leyton, 1986). A number of factors seem to be responsible for this uneven attention to one form of multiple murder over another.

First, unlike serial killings, massacres do not pose much of a challenge to law enforcement authorities. Whereas serial killers are often difficult to identify and apprehend (see Egger, 1984), a person who massacres typically is found at the crime scene—slain by his own hand, shot by police, or alive and ready to surrender. Frequently, the perpetrator welcomes his arrest or suicide, having achieved his mission through murder. In some exceptional cases, however, an execution-style mass killing is designed to cover up some other criminal activity. For example, seven people were murdered in a suburban Chicago restaurant in 1993, with robbery as the motive.

Second, in contrast to serial murders, massacres do not tend to generate the same level of public fear and anxiety. Until a serial killer is caught, he may be on the loose for weeks, months, or years. Citizens are terrified; they want to protect themselves from becoming the next victim. Each newly discovered murder reenergizes the community's state of alarm. However, a massacre, though catastrophic, is a single event. By the time the public is informed, the episode is over. There may be widespread horror, but there is little anxiety.

A third factor responsible for the relative lack of attention to massacres involves the limited availability of primary data. Many mass killers do not survive their crimes. Although they may leave diaries or notes to help us understand their motivation, questions concerning motive and state of mind often remain in doubt. The typical serial killer may twist the truth when and if interviewed, but he nevertheless yields significantly more information than we have on those who massacre.

Finally, perhaps the most prominent reason for the relative neglect of mass murder as a form of multiple homicide is that it cannot compete with the sensational character of serial murder. The public, the press, and researchers alike appear to be drawn to the sexual and sadistic proclivities of such predators as Theodore Bundy and Jeffrey Dahmer (see Dietz, 1996). As further evidence that sensationalism plays a critical role in the level of interest, serial murders that do not contain sex and sadism (e.g., slayings in hospitals and nursing homes, or serial killing for profit) are all but ignored by some researchers (see, for example, Holmes & De Burger, 1988).

A PROFILE OF MASS KILLERS

Calendar year 2012 offered a rich variety of hot topics for media coverage and public debate. The political campaign season featured an unprecedented number of presidential hopefuls and televised candidate debates, while the year's hurricane season resulted in wide-ranging destruction, primarily from Superstorm Sandy. In addition, the debate over universal health care culminated in the most highly anticipated U.S. Supreme Court ruling in decades.

Nothing, however, surpassed the amount and intensity of interest, at least from a news perspective, than the scourge of mass murder, specifically a movie theater rampage in Aurora, Colorado, in July and then a public school massacre in Newtown, Connecticut, in mid-December. As one measure of media attention, the Associated Press's year-end poll of news editors placed mass shootings as the leading news story of 2012 (Associated Press, 2012).

The carnage in Newtown, Aurora, and elsewhere has compelled many observers to examine the possible reasons behind the rise in mass murder. *New York Times* columnist David Brooks noted the number of schizophrenics going untreated (Brooks, 2012). Former President Bill Clinton and other gun control advocates have pointed to the expiration of the 1994 Federal Assault Weapons Ban as the culprit, while gun-rights proponents have argued that the body counts would be lower were more Americans armed and ready to overtake an active shooter. The moral panic and sense of urgency surrounding mass murder were fueled by various claims that mass murder, and mass shootings in particular, were reaching epidemic proportions. For example, the Mother Jones news organization, having assembled a database of public mass shootings from 1982 through 2012, reported a recent surge in incidents and fatalities, including a spike and record number of casualties in the year 2012 (Follman, Pan, & Aronson, 2013). Mother Jones did not include all mass shootings in their analysis, but instead attempted to delineate those that were senseless, random, or at least public in nature. Mother Jones settled on several criteria for inclusion in its mass shootings database, specifically

- the shooter took the lives of at least four people,
- the killings were carried out by a lone shooter,
- the shootings happened during a single incident and in a public place, and
- the murders were not related to armed robbery or gang activity.

By virtue of these selection rules, mass shootings involving family members were excluded, even though they too can involve large body counts. Other massive shootings were ignored because of their relation to gang activity or some criminal enterprise.

Not only was Mother Jones's decision to disqualify cases based on certain criteria that are hard to defend, the criteria themselves were not necessarily applied consistently (see Fox, 2013). The Columbine mass murder and the Westside Middle School massacre, for example, were included despite the fact that both were carried out by pairs of armed assailants. In response to criticism concerning the definitional concerns, Mother Jones emphasized two main themes: the need to focus more narrowly on "senseless" public shootings and the importance of investigating mass shootings beyond just the incident counts (Follman et al., 2013). Obviously, public shootings are worthy of discussion, but then so are mass killings in families or those that are designed to further some criminal enterprise. Widening the net by including mass shootings in all forms can only add to our understanding of extreme killing.

Mass murder consists of the slaughter of four or more victims by one or a few assailants within a single event, lasting anywhere from a few minutes to as long as several hours (Levin & Fox, 1985). The most publicized type of mass murder involves the indiscriminate shooting of strangers in a public place by a lone gunman, but other kinds of mass killing actually are more common. Included within this definition are, for example, a disgruntled employee who kills his boss and coworkers after being fired, an estranged husband/father who massacres his entire family and then kills himself, a band of armed robbers that slaughters a roomful of witnesses to the crime, and a racist hatemonger who sprays a schoolyard of immigrant children with gunfire. Thus, the motivations for mass murder can range from revenge to hatred and from loyalty to greed, and the victims can be selected individually, as members of a particular category or group, or on a random basis.

Unlike the case with serial slayings, for which there are no official data sources for assessing prevalence or patterns, massacres can be studied to some extent from police statistics routinely collected by local law enforcement agencies and transmitted to the FBI for publication and analysis. As part of the FBI's Uniform Crime Reporting program, police departments are asked to supply detailed information about homicide incidents, victims, and perpetrators for the Supplementary Homicide Reports (SHR).

Although these data are hardly flawless, the FBI's SHR provide some ability to examine the characteristics and circumstances of massacres and to compare them with homicide patterns generally. Compiled in incident-based form, these data offer detailed information on location; victim and offender age, race, and sex; victim–offender relationship; weapon use; and circumstances for virtually all homicides known to police for the years 1976 through 2011. The SHR covers approximately 92% of the murders committed nationwide, with a few states missing for certain years. The state of Florida is of particular concern given its size and frequency with which it is missing from the FBI files. Fortunately, homicide data for Florida, including mass murderers, were available directly from the Florida Department of Law Enforcement.

Using these data, we can assess the validity of the widely held view that victims of massacres usually are strangers to their killer, who selects them on a random basis after he "goes berserk." At the same time, it is possible to determine whether massacres differ enough from single-victim homicide that they ought to be regarded as a distinct and separate phenomenon deserving their own theoretical framework.

For this analysis, we removed manslaughters by negligence and justifiable homicides from the data set. Homicides involving arson or suspected arson, an event in which the specific intent of the perpetrator may be to destroy property rather than lives, also were removed from the data analysis. A few cases remained in the data set in which fire was used as a weapon, but the primary target involved people, not property.

Finally, the September 11, 2001, terrorist attack resulting in the deaths of thousands of Americans at New York's World Trade Center, the Pentagon, and a rural area just outside of Pittsburgh was excluded from the data set, consistent with the FBI's determination to treat it separately from its criminal homicide statistics. In the 2001 edition of *Crime in the United States*, the FBI explained its decision:

> The statistics of September 11 are not a part of the traditional *Crime in the United States* publication because they are different from the day-to-day crimes committed in this country. Additionally, combining these statistics with our regular crime report would create many difficulties in defining and analyzing crime as we know it. . . . The murder count of September 11 is so high that combining it with the traditional crime statistics will have an outlier effect that skews all types of measurements in the Program's analysis. (p. 10)

By contrast, the 1995 Oklahoma City bombing was retained in FBI homicide statistics, and therefore our own. The only significant impact of including the deaths of 168 people at the Alfred P. Murrah Federal Building in Oklahoma City was to inflate the total victim count from mass murder for that year because of one unique event; statistics pertaining to mass murder incidents, perpetrators, and even victim characteristics were not affected.

For this analysis, *mass murder* is defined operationally as a criminal homicide claiming four or more victims (not including the perpetrator in the event of a mass murder/suicide). These homicides are then compared with criminal homicides generally, only a tiny fraction of which are multiple killings. To avoid distortion caused by multiple counting, incident-, offender-, and victim-based files are alternately used to examine characteristics along these dimensions (see Fox, 2004, for a discussion of data structure).

The data set used here, spanning the years 1976 through 2011, includes 927 massacres involving 4,330 victims and 1,301 offenders. With considerable fluctuation but no noticeable trend over this time span, as is displayed in Figure 13.1, about 25 incidents of mass murder occur per year in the United States, claiming approximately 125 victims annually. Most incidents, of course, are not as widely publicized as the horrific slaughters of 20 children and six teachers at the Sandy Hook Elementary School in Newtown or 32 students and faculty at Virginia Tech in 2007. Still, the massacre phenomenon is perhaps not quite as rare as many would believe, although it hardly comes close to reaching epidemic levels. Moreover, despite the concerns of many Americans and the somewhat selective analysis by Mother Jones, neither mass murders generally nor mass shootings in particular are moving on an upward trajectory (see Figure 13.2).

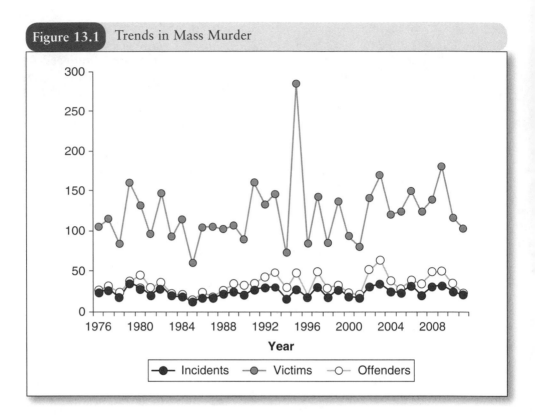

Figure 13.1 Trends in Mass Murder

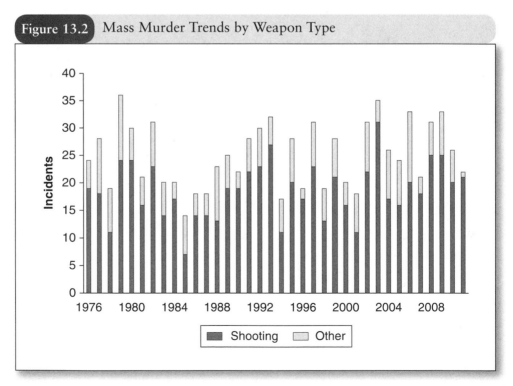

Figure 13.2 Mass Murder Trends by Weapon Type

It is hard to trace exactly when mass murder became an all-too-common feature of American life. Some criminologists have claimed that the mid-1960s was the onset of an age of mass murder (Levin & Fox, 1985). Through an analysis of news accounts and the FBI's Supplementary Homicide Reports, Duwe (2004, 2007) confirmed this observation, but also showed that there had been earlier waves of mass killings, particularly during the 1920s and 1930s.

Tables 13.1 through 13.3 display incident, offender, and victim characteristics for these mass killings and, for comparison purposes, similar statistics for murder generally. The contrasting patterns between the two groups of cases emphasize the ways in which mass murder is a unique form of homicide.

As noted above, the incidence of mass murder, despite yearly fluctuations, has not shown any tendency to increase or decrease since the mid-1970s. Particularly noteworthy, as shown in Table 13.1, is that mass murders have not declined in number since the mid-1990s, even while murder generally has dropped significantly over the same period of years. As also shown in the table, mass murders do not tend to cluster in large cities as much as does homicide in general (43.9% vs. 57.5%). Instead, massacres frequently occur in suburban or rural areas (45.1%), with a higher proportion than for homicide overall (30.7%). Some differences in setting are those associated with region. The South (and the Deep South in particular) is known for its high rates of murder (41.0% of homicides), but this does not hold quite so much for mass murder (38.7%). In comparison with single-victim murder, which is highly concentrated in urban areas populated by poor Blacks and in the Deep South, where arguments often are settled through gunfire (see, for example, Doerner, 1975), mass murder more or less reflects population distribution.

Table 13.1 also displays incident characteristics—weapon use, victim–offender relationship, and circumstance—by type of homicide. Not surprisingly, firearms are the weapon of choice in mass murder incidents (77.8%), even more than in homicide overall (67.4%). Clearly, a handgun or rifle is the most effective means of mass destruction. By contrast, it is difficult to kill large numbers of people simultaneously with physical force or even a knife or blunt object. Furthermore, although an explosive device potentially can cause the deaths of large numbers of people (as in the 1995 bombing of the Oklahoma City federal building), its unpredictability would be unacceptable for most mass killers, who target their victims selectively. In addition, far fewer Americans are proficient in the use of explosives as compared with guns.

The findings regarding victim–offender relationship (for the cases in which it has been determined) are perhaps as counterintuitive as the weapon-use results were obvious. Contrary to popular belief, mass murderers infrequently attack strangers who just happen to be in the wrong place at the wrong time. In fact, 38.2% of these crimes are committed against family members, compared to 29.2% for murder overall. Indeed, it is well known that murder often involves family members, but this is especially pronounced among massacres.

The differences in circumstance (when they are known) underlying these crimes are quite dramatic. About half of all homicides occur during an argument

Table 13.1   Comparison of Mass Murder and General Homicide Characteristics, 1976–2011

Characteristic of Incident	Mass Murders	All Homicides
Incident Count	917	657,751
Time Period		
1976–1984	25.7%	26.8%
1985–1993	23.9%	28.9%
1994–2002	23.8%	23.6%
2003–2011	26.6%	20.7%
Total	100.0%	100.0%
Region		
Northeast	17.2%	16.9%
Midwest	22.1%	19.1%
South	38.7%	41.0%
West	22.0%	23.0%
Total	100.0%	100.0%
Urbanness		
Large city	43.9%	57.5%
Small city	11.0%	11.8%
Suburban	29.9%	21.0%
Rural	15.2%	9.7%
Total	100.0%	100.0%
Weapon		
Firearm	77.8%	67.4%
Knife	10.5%	17.2%
Other	11.7%	15.4%
Total	100.0%	100.0%
Relationship		
Family	38.2%	29.2%
Friend/Acquaintance	38.3%	49.3%
Stranger	23.5%	21.5%
Total	100.0%	100.0%
Circumstances		
Felony	30.1%	23.6%
Argument	24.5%	50.6%
Other	45.4%	25.8%
Total	100.0%	100.0%

between the victim and offender, but it is relatively rare for a heated dispute to escalate into mass murder (24.5%). As it happens, massacres of strangers often are committed to facilitate other felonies—for example, armed robberies. The largest category of mass murder circumstance is unspecified (45.4% "other circumstances"), primarily because of limitations in the Supplementary Homicide Report data. These crimes involve a wide array of motivations, including revenge and hate, as will be discussed later.

Some of the most notable and important differences between homicide types emerge in the offender data presented in Table 13.2. Compared to murderers generally, mass murderers are more likely to be male (94.1% vs. 88.4%), are far more likely to be White (59.3% vs. 46.6%), and are somewhat older (43.0% vs. 38.0% are over 30 years old). Typically, the single-victim offender is a young male, slightly more often Black than White, whereas the massacrer is typically a middle-age White male. This profile

Table 13.2 Comparison of Offenders 1976–2011

Characteristic of Offender	Mass Murders	All Homicides
Offender Count	1,176	648,244
Offender Age		
10–19	14.1%	21.1%
20–29	42.9%	40.9%
30–39	23.0%	20.0%
40–49	15.3%	10.1%
50+	4.7%	7.9%
Total	100.0%	100.0%
Offender Race		
White	59.3%	46.6%
Black	36.5%	51.4%
Other	4.2%	2.0%
Total	100.0%	100.0%
Offender Sex		
Male	94.1%	88.4%
Female	5.9%	11.6%
Total	100.0%	100.0%

Note: Percentages exclude cases with unidentified offenders.

comes into sharpest focus for those mass killers who are motivated by something other than robbery or similar felony: The average age of perpetrators of felony-related mass murder is 26.9 but the average age rises to 31.3 for those offenders in other mass murder circumstances, including grudges of various kinds. Finally, according to Matt Delisi and Aaron M. Scherer (2006), multiple murderers are no more likely than those who have killed just one victim to have a prior criminal record.

The victim characteristics contained in Table 13.3 are, of course, largely a function of the offender characteristics discussed above, indicating that mass killers generally do not select their victims on a random basis. For example, the victims of mass murder usually are White (68.5% compared with 50.5% for all homicides) simply because the perpetrators to whom they are related or with whom they associate are White. Similarly, the youthfulness of victims (34.6% are under age 20 for mass murders compared with 16.2% for all killings) and

Table 13.3   Comparison of Victims 1976–2011

Characteristic of Victim	Mass Murders	All Homicides
Victim Count	4,212	689,319
Victim Age		
Under 10	17.6%	4.1%
10-19	17.0%	12.1%
20-29	23.1%	33.7%
30-39	16.4%	22.3%
40-49	12.5%	13.1%
50+	13.4%	14.7%
Total	100.0%	100.0%
Victim Race		
White	68.5%	50.5%
Black	27.1%	47.3%
Other	4.3%	2.2%
Total	99.9%	100.0%
Victim Sex		
Male	56.6%	76.7%
Female	43.4%	23.3%
Total	100.0%	100.0%

greater representation of females (43.4%) among the victims of mass murder, as compared to all homicides (23.3%), stem from the fact that a typical mass killing involves the breadwinner of the household who annihilates the entire family—his wife and his children.

SELECTIVE AND METHODICAL

Most people, when asked to imagine a mass murderer, think of killers who suddenly go berserk or run amok (see Westermeyer, 1982). They may recall James Huberty, the unemployed security guard who strolled into a McDonald's restaurant in 1984 and fatally gunned down 21 random victims, most of whom were children. Those old enough to remember may think of Charles Whitman, the former Marine who opened fire from atop a tower on the University of Texas campus in 1966, killing 14 people and wounding 31 others, or Howard Unruh, a World War II hero who wandered down a street in Camden, New Jersey, in 1949, killing 13 people in 13 minutes.

Most observers do seem to believe that mass killers suddenly snap. After all, many phrases in the English language describe this kind of rampage, including "running amok," "going berserk," "going off the deep end," "going ballistic," "going bonkers," "flipping out," and "flipping one's lid." It is highly unlikely, however, that an employee who gets fired by his boss and snaps would happen to have two AK-47s and 1,200 rounds of ammunition in the trunk of his car for just such an occasion. More likely, he would have made arrangements long beforehand to commit mass murder.

In actuality, sudden, seemingly episodic and random incidents of violence are as unusual as they are extreme. Most mass killers are quite deliberate, not spontaneous. They do not just suddenly explode. To the contrary, mass killers typically plan their assaults for days, weeks, or months (see, for example, Walkup & Rubin, 2013). These preparations include where, when, and who to kill, as well as with what weapons they will strike. These assailants are deliberate, determined to kill, with little regard for what obstacles are placed in their path.

For example, Dylan Klebold and Eric Harris, the two adolescents responsible for the 1999 Columbine High School massacre, purposely chose Hitler's birthday for their attack (out of admiration for the dictator's power), and spent long hours in the woods fine-tuning their marksmanship skills. They even conceived a grand follow-up plan should they survive the school shooting: to hijack an airplane and fly it into the skyline of New York City (and this was two years before the September 11, 2001, acts of terrorism).

The level of detailed planning may help to explain the calm demeanor exhibited by mass murderers, even in the midst of chaos. Witnesses to a mass shooting often report, for example, that the gunman appeared relaxed, even smiling, while killing or injuring dozens of innocent victims (see Aitken, Oosthuizen, Emsley, & Seedat, 2008). Mass murderers have been known to develop and follow a mental script, one that is rehearsed over and over again, to the point where they become comfortable with the mission.

A majority of mass killers target victims who are specially chosen, not because they are in the wrong place at the wrong time. The indiscriminate slaughter of strangers by a crazed killer is the exception to the rule. Instead, mass murderers typically slaughter people they know—family members, neighbors, and coworkers—based on a clear-cut and calculated motivation. In a study of 30 mass killers, for example, Anthony G. Hempel, J. Reid Meloy, and Thomas C. Richards (1999) reported that half of the rampages were precipitated by problems at work and nearly one quarter involved discordant personal relationships.

Many massacres are actually suicidal rampages. Before taking his own life, however, the killer intends to get even with everyone he holds responsible for his miseries and failures. In an analysis of massacres from 1976 and 1996 drawn from the SHR, Duwe (2000) found that 21% of all mass murderers committed suicide and another 3% were gunned down by the police (possibly suicides by cop). Our follow-up search of cases from 1997 to 2002 found that 21.4% of mass killers took their own lives and 1.4% were fatally shot by police, consistent with Duwe's earlier findings. This prevalence of suicide following mass murder is substantially higher than the figure for murderers generally, estimates of which generally range in the single digits in terms of percentage of homicides leading to suicide (see Eliason, 2009; Stack, 1997). Lankford examined life or death outcomes of 185 rampage-style mass shootings between 1965 and 2010, finding that 48% of the perpetrators either committed suicide or were killed by the police at the scene. The fact that this percentage is somewhat higher likely surrounds a specific weapon (i.e., a gun is certainly more easily turned on oneself than a knife or bomb) and public location of this particular subset of mass murder.

WHEN LOVE KILLS

Twenty-eight-year-old Lawrence John DeLisle of Lincoln Park, Michigan, was undoubtedly a family man, but in a family plagued by misfortune and tragedy. Drowning was a DeLisle family tradition and so was suicide.

Larry was named after his deceased uncle, who had drowned in 1957 while swimming with Larry's father-to-be, Richard, in Wampler's Lake. Years later, in February 1988, Richard DeLisle, then 48 years old, was so depressed that he drove his brown 1977 Ford station wagon into the woods, where he shot himself with a .38-caliber pistol.

The younger Larry was painfully aware of his uncle's tragic drowning and his father's suicide. He never knew the uncle for whom he was named, and he hardly knew his own father, for that matter. Almost from birth, he was raised by his grandparents. His mother left when he was a year old, and from then on, his father had very little to do with him. The only "gift" he ever got from his dad was the Ford station wagon in which Richard DeLisle had taken his own life.

It is said that blood is thicker than water. On August 3, 1989, Larry must have felt especially close to his father when he drove his Ford through two wooden posts at the end of Eureka Road in Wyandotte, Michigan; the car sank to the bottom of the Detroit River.

It was a particularly hot and humid Thursday evening, even for August. To escape the heat, Larry took his wife, Suzanne, and their four kids—8-year-old Brian, 4-year-old Melissa, 21-month-old Kadie, and 9-month-old Emily—out for a drive and some shopping. Larry also wanted to escape, at least for a short time, the burdens of his financial problems. He owed $18,000 in charge accounts, medical bills, and loans. Things were so bad for him that he couldn't make the payments on his life insurance policy and was forced to move his family into his brother's home, where they lived rent free. He also had to sell his new Aerostar wagon and instead drive his father's suicide-mobile.

Notwithstanding his financial problems, or perhaps because of them, Larry was a hard worker, frequently putting in more than 50 hours a week on the job. He often came home late from work, tired and depressed, yet his face would light up in a big smile when his wife and kids greeted him at the front door. As a service manager for a tire store, he earned a $33,000 annual salary, but he spent every penny that he made, and much more, trying to make his family happy. Whenever he wasn't working, Larry was with Suzanne and the children. He loved to take them on day trips, visiting the zoo in Toledo or in Detroit, or simply going out for ice cream together. He loved his family so much that he couldn't bear to see them suffer the hardships and embarrassment of debt or of having to freeload off his brother.

On this sultry summer evening, the family was together for the last time, but in Larry's mind, it would be forever. He stopped at a drugstore and waited in the hot car with the screaming baby while his wife took the other kids inside to buy a treat. At the checkout counter, Suzanne rummaged through her pocketbook for enough loose change to pay for a few cookies. Meanwhile, Larry turned the car around on Eureka Road so that it pointed in the direction of the river.

As soon as his family returned to the car and the kids were safely strapped into their seats in the back, Larry put his foot down on the accelerator. He was tired, hot, annoyed with his screaming baby, and generally fed up with his life. He wanted some peace and quiet, and, as he later told police, he thought to himself, "I just want it to be over. There has got to be an afterlife that's better than this hellhole" (Lawrence John DeLisle's interview with Detective Sergeant Daniel Galeski, August 10, 1989). He contemplated the idea of mercifully putting his wife, his children, and himself out of their misery.

Without thinking twice, Larry DeLisle pushed as hard as he could on the gas pedal, held both hands firmly on the wheel, and aimed the wagon down Eureka Road, straight toward the river. "I can't get my foot off, I can't get my foot off!" he screamed, pretending that he had no control. Suzanne, realizing that they were doomed, tried to grab the wheel. She then reached over to shift the car into neutral and turn off the ignition, but she was too late. Racing at 45 miles per hour, the car plunged through the wooden barricade and into the river. Because of the river's strong current, the car flipped onto its roof before settling on the bottom.

Submerged in 30 feet of water, Larry responded instinctively to save his life. Asked why he changed his mind about committing suicide, he later explained, "Your pilot mechanism says, 'You can't breathe. You are sucking water. Float, fucker!'" (DeLisle's interview with Galeski, August 10, 1989).

Larry and Suzanne both managed to extricate themselves through open windows in the front seat. According to a witness, Larry surfaced just a few moments after the car hit the water: "He was just sitting, treading water." Meanwhile, Suzanne was screaming, "My babies! Get my babies!" (Swickard, 1990). The younger DeLisles were not so fortunate, however. All four children drowned, strapped securely in their seats.

At his trial, Larry blamed the episode on mechanical failure—a frozen accelerator pedal—and leg cramps. The jury was not persuaded and convicted him on four counts of murder and one count of attempted murder. Prior to sentencing, Larry DeLisle made a last-ditch effort to convince the judge of his innocence. "My children were the greatest gifts my wife and I have ever shared," he maintained. "I could never hurt them, never. I loved them with every fiber of my being; they were my life" (DeLisle interview with Galeski, August 10, 1989).

Despite Larry's sorrowful denial of responsibility, Judge Colombo gave him the maximum sentence—life without the possibility of parole. Detective Sergeant Daniel Galeski reflected on Larry's motivation for killing his four children and attempting to take his own life and that of his wife: "He thought they'd all be together in the afterlife. It just didn't work out that way" (Swickard, 1990).

Detective Galeski pinpointed one of the motivations underlying many family massacres: More than a few mass killers feel so desperate and unhappy that they see death as the only salvation. To them, mass murder can be an act of love. Life on earth is so horrible, they reason, that their loved ones will be better off dead. In what psychiatrist Shervert Frazier (1975) calls "suicide by proxy," the killer sees his loved ones as extensions of himself. He feels personal responsibility for the well-being of his wife and children, and he sees no other way out of his and their predicament. He may be depressed or despondent, but he is not necessarily deranged.

Larry DeLisle may have planned to end his own life so that he could rejoin his family, at least in a spiritual sense. When it came right down to it, however, his instinct to survive overpowered his desire to commit murder–suicide.

Most who attempt to commit suicide by proxy are, like 37-year-old Hermino Elizalde of Chicago, better on the follow-through. By May 1990, Elizalde—described by friends as a devoted father—had become hopelessly despondent over his recent firing from his job as a welder's helper. In addition, he was deeply concerned that his estranged wife might take custody of his four daughters and one son; she had accused him of mistreating them. Rather than lose his beloved children, he decided to keep them together, at least spiritually. According to police, Elizalde had told friends that he would rather kill his children than let them go.

The devoted father purchased a gallon of gasoline from a filling station some three blocks from his apartment. After returning home, he doused his sleeping children with gasoline and set them afire, one at a time. When he was sure they were dead, he set himself on fire. By killing them all, he thought he had ensured that they would be reunited in a better life after death.

When love becomes a component in the mass killer's motivation, outsiders—neighbors, friends and extended kin—are typically incredulous when learning that a seemingly loving and normal husband/father has slaughtered his wife and children before committing suicide. In July 2000, residents of the seaside suburban community of Barry, outside of Cardiff in South Wales, were shocked to discover a gruesome family annihilation in their midst. Forty-nine-year-old Robert Mochrie, often described as a "devoted family man," had hanged himself after bludgeoning to death his wife and four children as they slept in their middle-class, single-family home.

Mochrie had a 10-year history of severe depression and had seen a psychiatrist on a number of occasions. He and his wife of 23 years were no longer intimate, and one of their children was autistic. On top of everything else that went wrong, he had recently experienced a number of failed business ventures which left him in deep debt, unable to pay his bills, and faced with bankruptcy. Being a "loving father and good husband," Mochrie made sure that his family members died in their sleep with a blow to the head, minimizing their pain and suffering. He then covered each body with a blanket, as though trying to protect his wife and children from the elements.

SWEET REVENGE

A twisted sense of love and responsibility clearly cannot explain many cases of mass murder. Why would a 31-year-old former postal worker, Thomas McIlvane, go on a rampage in Royal Oak, Michigan, killing four supervisors before shooting himself in the head? And what would provoke a 28-year-old graduate student, Gang Lu, to execute five others at the University of Iowa before taking his own life? And why would 35-year-old Colin Ferguson open fire on a crowded Long Island train, killing six commuters? The common denominator in these three cases is the killer's desire to execute his enemies, real or imagined, for the sake of sweet revenge.

Although each case has its unique aspects, by far the most frequent motivation for mass murder is revenge—the desire to get even for perceived mistreatment by family members, a company, or a whole category of people. In all forms of revenge-motivated mass murder, the perpetrator's objective is to punish all those whom he holds responsible, directly or indirectly, for his failures and disappointments.

On August 20, 1986, the morning after being reprimanded for poor job performance, 44-year-old Patrick Henry Sherrill "gave notice" in a most unconventional way. Arriving at the Edmond, Oklahoma, post office at 6:45 a.m., the part-time letter carrier was dressed in his blue postal uniform and was lugging his leather mailbag over his shoulder. The pouch was full, but not with letters. It contained an arsenal of weapons and ammunition with which Sherrill intended to even the score.

Sherrill's first victim was a supervisor who had threatened his job. After killing him, Sherrill opened fire on his coworkers as they sorted the day's mail. Stunned postal workers dove for cover behind bags of mail and sorting cases as the gunman maneuvered his way through the building in search of additional victims. There was little to protect those trapped inside—little except their prayers as they listened, from their hiding places in broom closets and under tables, for approaching gunfire.

The barrage of bullets finally ended—in the nick of time for some, but too late for others—when Sherrill fired a fatal shot to his own head. By then, he had already killed 14 people and wounded another seven.

Like many other mass killings, Sherrill's assault was more selective than random. He made sure ahead of time that the one coworker whom he liked would not be at work during his rampage. He deliberately started shooting long before the post office opened for business so that he killed only "the enemy;" no innocent customers would be injured. Sherrill's motive, in effect, was to kill the post office.

Revenge was also on the mind of a disgruntled English cab driver. Derrick Bird's 3-hour rampage in June 2010, through serene and picturesque towns in the Lake District of Northern England was, in certain respects, reminiscent of other shooting sprees on both sides of the Atlantic. Bird blamed all of his miseries—economic and personal—on his lawyer and brother as well as fellow cab drivers and his customers. These were the victims with whom he decided to get even through the barrel of a gun.

What differs from most other mass shootings is that Bird opened fire in 30 different locations rather than in one or two, taking the lives not only of individuals close to him but also total strangers. In a figurative and literal sense, Bird was driven not only to earn his livelihood in a taxi but also to cause death to those he blamed for all of his problems. Each victim was apparently shot point blank in the face, suggesting that Bird felt absolutely no guilt. Instead, he regarded his victims as villains who had conspired against him and deserved to die. Rather than take them from behind, he felt no reluctance at all about facing his victims head on, leaving them with no doubt as to who pulled the trigger. Viewing their reaction in death may have added to Bird's satisfaction.

It was Bird's choice of victims that may give us clues as to his mental state. As described later, most mass killers suffer chronic depression and a heightened inability to cope with frustration, even if their friends and relatives are unaware of their psychopathological state. They externalize responsibility for their problems in life, blaming everybody but themselves for their personal miseries.

If they were healthier psychologically, they might only change their philosophy of life or their short-term objectives to be more realistic and then be able and willing to live with the results. If they were to blame themselves, they might commit suicide, but never want to harm anybody else. The more random the massacre, however, the more likely it is that the killer is not only depressed but also delusional. He may hear voices, be paranoid in a clinical sense, and suffer from a profound thought disorder which leaves him convinced of a conspiracy against him involving not only particular individuals but humankind. As a result, he seeks sweet revenge against coworkers and family members, but also total strangers. If the killers live to go to court, they might plead not guilty by reason of insanity (NGI). In the case of Sylvia Seegrist, who was a paranoid schizophrenic, an NGI defense resulted in her being committed to a hospital for the criminally insane where she continues to reside.

There are millions of depressed people who wouldn't dream of killing anyone. They may have close friends or relatives who can be counted on for support and encouragement, people who will get them through the hard times. By contrast, most mass murderers are socially isolated. They may have relocated for the sake of a job, be reclusive in their own community, or have a personality that makes asking for help all but impossible. Their relatives and neighbors may therefore see them as "quiet" or "aloof," or as "loners," but not as potential mass murderers.

On top of everything else that goes wrong in their lives, most mass killers who are depressed and psychologically alone suffer one or more catastrophic losses before they open fire on their victims. From the killer's perspective, it is the final straw—the one that "breaks the camel's back." For some, the catalyst is economic. They have recently been fired at work, do not get the raise or promotion they feel they deserve or have lost large amounts of money in a failed investment. For others, the triggering event is the loss of a relationship—a nasty separation or divorce or a child custody battle. For still others, there are multiple catastrophic episodes. For example, at the same time they suffer job loss, they also discover that their partner is having an affair or they lose a loved one to a terminal illness.

Fueled by publicity, the so-called copycat effect may also have helped to determine the character of Bird's quest for revenge. Michael Ryan's 1987 rampage in Hungerford—often referred to as having left an indelible mark on the entire nation—was similarly carried out in several different locations. Like Bird, Ryan used a rifle. And also like Bird who shot to death his twin brother, Ryan killed strangers as well as a family member—his own mother.

A final element in the development of Bird's killing spree deserves to be emphasized. He had access to and training in the use of high-powered weapons— shotguns and rifles. The effectiveness of firearms as a weapon of mass destruction can be seen clearly in cases where the assailant uses a less lethal approach.

Of course, there is no way ever to reduce the number of mass killings to zero. No matter how much help we are willing to give to our troubled friends and neighbors, no matter how effective our psychiatric services, no matter how humane our firing practices, no matter how difficult it is to obtain a weapon of mass destruction, there will always be exceptional cases that result in multiple homicide.

PROFITING FROM MASS MURDER

Mass murder also can be motivated not by a passion like love or hate, but purely by greed. This form of mass killing is more expedient than expressive. The profit-motivated killer may or may not know his victims, and he doesn't necessarily bear a grudge against them. He commits the murders to eliminate witnesses to a crime, usually robbery.

Profit was the primary motivation involved in the massacre on January 8, 1993, at Brown's Chicken & Pasta restaurant in Palatine, Illinois. Anxious phone calls to the local police reported that several of the employees at Brown's, in the normally quiet Chicago suburb, had inexplicably failed to return home after closing time. Just before midnight, a patrol car was dispatched to Brown's, where two officers shined their flashlights into the darkened building and rattled the windows. The officers failed to locate any irregularities. Shortly afterward, Emmanuel Castro, the father of a 16-year-old boy who worked at the fast-food restaurant, officially notified the police that his son was missing. A police patrol returned to Brown's at 2:30 a.m. This time, the officers entered the building through an unlocked side door. They found seven murder victims—the two owners of the restaurant and five workers—all of whom had died of gunshots from a .38-caliber firearm. One of the owners also had her neck slashed. The safe, containing $1,200 in cash, had been cleaned out.

Police investigators worked with few good leads. At first, suspecting that the massacre had been motivated by revenge, they questioned a 23-year-old man who had been fired recently from Brown's restaurant. After his 2-day interroga-tion and subsequent release, however, investigators began to consider the mass murder as possibly motivated by the desire to get rich rather than to get even. By Monday, just 3 days after the massacre, Cook County State's Attorney Jack O'Malley considered it a likely case of armed robbery. He told the press that the police had no suspects, that "there is a murderer or murderers on the loose," and that "businesses ought to take extra precautions" (Lev & McRoberts, 1993).

A year after the murders, Palatine Police Chief Jerry Bratcher, frustrated over the failure of his task force to crack the case, reflected, "We had seven people murdered. All of them were shot execution-style. Our assumption is it was a robbery that went bad" (Silverman, 1994). It took nearly a decade—until May 2002—for the police to trace a DNA sample recovered from a partly eaten chicken; the finding led to the arrest of Juan Luna, age 28, and James E. Degorski, age 29, for the Palatine massacre.

Because most mass killings are inspired by revenge, it is easy to overlook other motivations, even the most obvious. Like the Palatine case, the August 1991 massacre of nine Buddhist monks in Maricopa County, Arizona, initially was thought to be motivated by hate, as it involved a desecration of the group's temple. As additional evidence surfaced, however, it became increasingly clear that the nine victims were murdered to cover up a robbery of $2,650 in cash plus cameras, stereos, and other items. According to Alessandro "Alex" Garcia, age 16 at the time of the murders, he and his 17-year-old accomplice, Johnathan Andrew Doody, ransacked the temple to rob it of its contents. The two teens then ordered the victims to lie on the floor in a circular pattern, like the spokes of a wheel. Doody said to Garcia, "No witnesses," and they shot the victims execution style.

Profit-motivated mass killings, like robbery–murder generally, typically are committed by young men, often minorities. Revenge-motivated mass killings, by contrast, most often are committed by older, often middle-age, White men who have had enough years of disappointment at home or on the job to evoke extreme desires for vengeance.

The overabundance of men among mass killers, even more than among mur-derers generally, may stem in part from the fact that men are more likely to suffer the kind of catastrophic losses in self-esteem and social support associated with mass murder. Following a separation or divorce, it is generally the husband/ father who is ousted from the family home and, therefore, is the one who is left alone. Job loss also affects men and women differently. Despite advances in the status of women in America, males more than females continue to define themselves in terms of their occupational role (what they do defines who they are) and therefore tend to suffer more psychologically from unemployment. Finally, men do not tend to maintain close relationships away from the family and the workplace; thus, they are less likely to have the benefits of support and encouragement when they lose a relationship or a job.

EXPLAINING MASS MURDER

In the 1960s, researchers purported to demonstrate that inmates in institutions for the criminally insane were significantly more likely to possess the "XYY syndrome," that is, men given to violence were endowed with an extra Y or male sex chromosome (Shah, 1976; Taylor, 1984). Some medical researchers of the day proposed that the XYY genetic disorder predisposed its 100,000 victims to criminality. Others suggested that punishment would do little, if anything, to discourage those bearing the genetic abnormality from committing violent acts. It was, after all, a matter of genetic destiny.

The XYY anomaly later became a standard explanation for extreme forms of violence, after it was erroneously reported that mass murderer Richard Speck was an XYY. In 1966, Speck had committed what was then called "the crime of the century" when he murdered eight nurses in their Chicago apartment. In newspaper articles and even some scientific accounts, Speck's XYY constitution was reportedly apparent in such phenotypical characteristics as facial acne, height, long extremities, mild mental retardation, and a history of mental illness. He was falsely labeled *supermale*—the prototypical XYY man, an identity that, to this day, is occasionally repeated as fact in high school science classes around the country. As an ironic postscript to the false reports of Speck's supermale biology, video footage taken many years later during his incarceration showed him with large, hormone-induced breasts and dressed in women's panties.

Very few violent criminals actually possess an extra Y chromosome. Furthermore, men who do, in fact, have this genetic abnormality may be treated more harshly and even be institutionalized more often, simply because of their abnormally awkward and substantial physical features (Gross & Wilson, 1974). Thus, the disproportionate presence of XYYs in institutions for the criminally insane may be more a function of the way they look rather than the way they act. Yet the stigma and myth of XYY persist.

This is not to say that chromosomes are unimportant in explaining differences in homicidal proneness. Clearly, males have a far greater propensity for committing senseless and extreme acts of violence than do women. This finding seems to hold almost universally, across virtually all cultures and time periods. Thus, it is more accurately the normal Y chromosome (the 46th or male chromosome), not the extra Y (the 47th or supermale chromosome), that might make the vital difference.

Present-day researchers continue to look to biology or chemistry in order to explain and predict homicidal behavior. With regard to mass murder, various psychiatric drugs, widely prescribed to treat depression and attention deficit disorder, have been suspected of altering brain chemistry in such a way as to trigger extreme violence. Joseph Wesbecker, on the morning of September 14,

1989, went on a 20-minute rampage at the Standard Gravure printing plant in Louisville, Kentucky, where he had worked as a pressman. Opening fire with an AK-47, Wesbecker shot to death eight of his coworkers and then took his own life. Some people tried to blame Wesbecker's deadly outburst on his long-standing struggle with depression. Others instead placed the blame on the antidepressant Prozac that he was taking to fight his illness.

In addition to Wesbecker, there is a long list of high-profile killers who were being treated with psychiatric medications just prior to the time they committed a senseless murder. On May 21, 1998, Kip Kinkel, a 15-year-old boy from Springfield, Oregon, who was given prescriptions for both Ritalin and Prozac, killed his parents and then went on a shooting spree through his high school. On April 20, 1999, 18-year-old Eric Harris of Littleton, Colorado, who was treated with the antidepressant Luvox, teamed up with his friend Dylan Klebold to launch a rampage at Columbine High School, killing 12 students and a teacher. On February 14, 2008, Steven Kazmierczak, who had been prescribed Prozac, Xanax, and Ambien, shot to death five students at Northern Illinois University.

The case against psychiatric medications would be stronger if it weren't for the fact that killers who were being treated at the time they committed murder typically had all of the warning signs associated with such crimes. In almost every case, there was a good reason why a psychiatrist had prescribed a psychotropic drug: The killer had been profoundly depressed, disappointed, and discouraged about the future. Moreover, the actions of killers who commit a rampage are typically neither episodic nor spontaneous. Wesbecker, for example, had planned his assault for months, including accumulating an arsenal of weaponry; yet he had taken Prozac for only a few weeks before the massacre. The drug may at most have reduced his inhibitions, but it hardly inspired him to kill.

Biological or chemical factors may be useful for explaining spontaneous or impulsive acts of extreme violence, but mass killings are typically planned and methodical rather than episodic. Massacres occurring at home, work, or school typically involve a complex set of contributors, including those located in the social environment of the perpetrator.

The social environment can be toxic when it involves the violent behavior and supporting attitudes of significant others. In fact, we learn to be violent not only from being directly rewarded and punished; we learn it through the role models we imitate. Clearly, other people may serve as models of learning in many other areas of life—for example, in acquiring language, using facial expressions, and dressing for various occasions. We should probably not be surprised, therefore, that imitation also occurs in learning violent behavior—even multiple homicide.

Early on, Albert Bandura (1977) suggested that the mass media generally, but television in particular, provide a powerful source of models for aggressive conduct. Findings obtained in a large number of studies over several decades on the effects of televised influences on behavior support this argument: They show that our popular culture—television, motion pictures, iPods, video games, and the Internet—can serve as a tutor in teaching violent styles of behavior (Murray, 2008). We really shouldn't be surprised, considering the enormous amount of time that children tune in to popular culture. The typical youngster spends, on average, more than 38 hours weekly—almost 5½ hours on a daily basis—watching TV, playing video games, listening to music, and surfing the Internet. Nearly three quarters of the children in the United States live in a home that possesses at least three TV sets.

The impact of popular culture frequently goes unchallenged. Many parents fail to impose any restrictions on their children's viewing behavior. In fact, some 53% of all parents permit a set in their youngster's bedroom; 58% leave a set on while the family has dinner; and only 5% watch TV with their older children.

Research by David Phillips (1983) suggests strongly that media images can teach even the most violent acts. He examined the homicide rate in America immediately following televised heavyweight prizefights and found a brief but sharp increase in homicides, an overall increase of 13%. This effect seemed to peak on the third day after the prizefights, especially following heavily publicized events. The biggest third-day peak occurred after the fights that received the greatest publicity.

As discussed in Chapter 2, models for murder can also be located in the groups to which an individual belongs. Edwin H. Sutherland and Donald R. Cressey's (1984) differential association theory contends that criminal behavior is learned during adolescence from an individual's most intimate social relations—his peers, family, and friends. Criminal skills are acquired in such groups. In addition, the individual learns from observing group members that violations of the law—from shoplifting and taking illicit drugs to armed robbery and murder—yield favorable consequences. To the extent that one becomes associated with individuals who regard criminal behavior in a positive light, that person is also excluded from associating with individuals who reject the criminal lifestyle. Just as one learns a host of important values, the individual adopts the criminal attitudes and behavior of intimate associates.

Also as introduced in Chapter 2, Ronald L. Akers (2000) includes—in his updated version of social learning theory—differential association along with whether behavior is rewarded or punished to explain the genesis of criminality. In his differential reinforcement theory, Akers suggests that the acceptance of violence doesn't come merely from associating with a particular group of intimates, but from associating with a group whose members reinforce violent behavior and punish law-abiding behavior. According to Akers, violence is learned in several different ways from group members, such as observing the deviant behavior of others and imitating it, being rewarded by group members for engaging in deviant behavior, and learning attitudes from group members that support and stimulate deviant behavior. Researchers have found, therefore, that many of the students who opened fire on their schoolmates belonged to a delinquent peer group whose members encouraged and supported their rampage (Levin & Madfis, 2009).

Representing another aspect of the environment, social scientists have long argued that strain in the form of life's disappointments, pressures, and problems may result in antisocial behavior. According to American cultural values learned from an early age, all members of society are expected to strive to achieve economic success. Yet there is far less emphasis in American society on providing the structural opportunities for achieving that success. This disparity invites what Robert K. Merton (1957) refers to as "innovation:" An individual accepts the cultural emphasis on the success goal but rejects the socially acceptable means for its attainment.

In some cases, an individual will substitute illegitimate (often illegal) but more effective methods of securing wealth and power. For middle-class deviants, the pressure to innovate might take the form of unethical business practices and white-collar crime. But for members of society lacking in education and economic resources, innovation more frequently becomes street crime, including gang membership, drug dealing, property offenses, and violence.

Because it focuses on opportunities for material success, Merton's theory may help to explain mass murder for the sake of profit, such as a robbery in which several customers and employees are killed. For most other types of mass killings, however, a more general perspective on the role of strain is required.

Early on, social psychologists proposed that frustration and aggression are inextricably connected (Dollard, Doob, Miller, Mowrer, & Sears, 1939). In what came to be known as the "frustration-aggression hypothesis," they argued that frustration always causes some form of aggression, and that aggression is always preceded by frustration. Thus, anything that interferes with movement toward a goal—whether something as minor as waiting for a long red light to change or as major as failing to earn enough money to feed one's family—will inevitably lead to the expression of aggression, including murder.

Clearly, we now know that the relationship between frustration and aggression is far from inevitable. For a variety of reasons, many people deal with the frustrations of daily life without harming or killing others. Indeed, people are more likely to wait patiently for a slow light to change or find a faster route home than to get out of their car and shoot at another driver. They are more likely to change jobs or seek training for higher paying work than to stab their boss or a family member. Frustration doesn't always lead to aggression. More likely, people learn to develop effective coping skills in responding to the frustrations of everyday life.

Just as clearly, not every aggressive action is preceded by frustration. Countless examples of violence occur in the absence of any especially frustrating circumstances. A soldier may engage in combat essentially because he doesn't want to let his buddies down or out of a sense of patriotism; a child may shoot her classmate after seeing a violent program on television; a hit man for the mob may eliminate the leader of a rival family because he was paid to do so.

Though the original frustration–aggression hypothesis may have been overstated, it is not without some validity. The propensity for violent behavior does increase when people are prevented from reaching an important goal they expect to attain. At the extreme, a few individuals have murdered their spouse and children as a result of a nasty divorce or custody battle. Others have killed their boss after being fired from a job. Some students have been so frustrated with their relations with peers that they have gunned down their classmates.

In 1960, Stuart Palmer determined that convicted murderers had suffered a number of important frustrations throughout childhood in comparison to the "control group," their nearest-in-age brothers who had never been convicted of committing a homicide. Specifically, the convicted murderers were more likely to have been dissatisfied with their prestige or status, to have suffered physical defects, to have done poorly in school, and to have had fewer friends. In sum, they had led frustrating and problematic lives.

More recently, as noted in Chapter 2, Robert Agnew's (1992) general strain theory broadened the concept of strain beyond the impact of frustrating events to include a range of negative experiences in social relationships in the neighborhood or at home, school, or work. In Agnew's view, strain consists of a wide range of difficulties, including anger, frustration, disappointment, depression, and fear, that originate in destructive social relationships and can lead to violent crime. Agnew identifies four important sources of strain: (a) the presence of negative stimuli (e.g., child abuse, peer rejection, school failure, and physical punishment), (b) the removal of positive stimuli (e.g., death of a loved one, parents' divorce, and residential mobility), (c) perception of inequity (e.g., peers who make more money or get better grades because they have "connections"), and (d) failure to achieve desired goals (e.g., missing out on success because of a lack of educational opportunities).

Aside from its broader perspective, an advantage of Agnew's general strain theory over the frustration–aggression hypothesis is its emphasis on more than just absolute levels of deprivation. In focusing on the gap between expectations and achievements and between the successes of individuals and their peers, Agnew recognizes the influence of what sociologists have called *relative deprivation*. Moreover, chronic strain may play a major role in encouraging mass killings at school, at work, or in the family. When life's disappointments become intolerable, an individual may seek vengeance, restoration of control, or infamy through the barrel of a gun.

CONTRIBUTING FACTORS

In studying mass murderers for more than 30 years, we have identified five factors that exist in virtually all cases. Some factors precipitate violence, whereas others do more to facilitate the extent of carnage.

First, perpetrators typically have a long history of frustration and failure and a diminished ability to cope with life's problems. They are chronically depressed and disappointed.

Second, mass killers externalize blame, frequently complaining that others didn't give them a chance. Sometimes they argue that their ethnic or racial group or gender isn't getting the breaks that others are. If they had blamed only themselves, they might have committed suicide. But because they externalize responsibility, they seek revenge against spouses, coworkers, classmates, or all of humankind.

Third, these killers generally lack emotional support from friends or family. Some have relocated for the sake of a job; others have a personality style that precludes seeking help from others. You've read the "he always seemed to be something of a loner" quote? It has grounding in reality.

Fourth, they usually suffer a precipitating event that they view as catastrophic. This is most often some sort of major disappointment: a profound financial loss or the breakup of an important relationship. In massacres at colleges and universities, it's often about getting a grade the shooter feels he didn't deserve. In high school, it's more likely about suffering a humiliating episode in the hallway. At work, the triggering episode is mostly the loss of a job. In the family, it's about a nasty separation or divorce or a child custody battle.

Fifth, the killers need access to a weapon powerful enough to satisfy their need for revenge. As we discussed earlier in this chapter, the weapon of choice is usually a firearm. Bombs and fire are capable of yielding a large body count when the massacre is indiscriminate. By contrast, guns are vastly more effective weapons of mass destruction when the killers' approach is selective—that is, when they seek to destroy only those victims they believe are implicated in the conspiracy to make their lives miserable.

The following chapters describe and analyze mass murder of various forms and venues: family annihilations; workplace massacres; school rampages; and mass shootings in public places such as restaurants, shopping malls, and city streets. Over and over again, these five factors are implicated as contributors to episodes of extreme killing.

CHAPTER 14

Family Annihilation

Christmas Day, 1987, was wet and cold for rural Pope County, Arkansas. It had rained off and on for most of the week, and the Arkansas River was unusually high. Forty-seven-year-old Ronald Gene Simmons spent the holiday alone, puttering around his rundown four-bedroom mobile home, anchored at the top of a hill 7 miles north of the tiny town of Dover. His 13 acres of land were situated well off the beaten path in a densely wooded area, cut off from the view of any neighbors. An imposing cinderblock wall, 50 feet long and 4 feet high, insulated the house from the main road. The wall served as a symbolic barrier in case the "No Trespassing" signs and long muddy driveway failed to discourage visitors.

Inside the Simmons home, the phone, heat, and toilet had not worked for months. Scores of plastic bottles filled with water, used in place of plumbing, were scattered along the baseboards of the kitchen. Dirty pots and pans remained on the stove. Rubbish and old toys littered the living room.

In sharp contrast to the disarray, the house was meticulously decorated for Christmas. Ornaments of red, green, and white construction paper were taped to the mantel of the fireplace, on which a tiny crèche was displayed. Crepe paper stringers hung from the doorways. Capped with a five-pointed star, the family tree was encircled by silvery strands of tinsel and adorned with multicolored bulbs. Brightly wrapped Christmas gifts were neatly arranged under the tree. It was Christmas Day, but the presents remained unopened. The names on the gifts belonged to the dead.

Gene Simmons's macabre celebration actually had begun several days before Christmas, on December 22. Waking early, he helped his wife, Becky, get their younger children ready for school. When the children were dressed and ready to go, he escorted them down the hill to the bus stop.

After the bus pulled away, Simmons trudged back up the driveway toward the house. He quietly opened the sliding door to the living room, then sneaked into the kitchen, where Becky was making another pot of coffee. He crept up behind his wife and, without hesitating, twice slammed a crowbar into her skull, knocking her unconscious.

Simmons then entered his wife's bedroom, where their 3-year-old grand-daughter, Barbara, lay fast asleep. He wrapped a yellow-and-white-striped fish stringer five times around her neck and pulled with all his might.

Ronald Gene Jr, a 26-year-old, slumbered peacefully in the adjoining bed-room. Simmons quietly entered the room and hovered over the bed, pausing a moment to contemplate his next victim before the kill. Without awakening him, Simmons raised the crowbar and brought it down forcefully against the back of his son's head. He then shot him five times with a .22-caliber revolver.

Simmons had one more murder on his morning agenda—that of his wife. He returned to the kitchen, where Becky's motionless body lay sprawled on the floor. He bent over and put two slugs in her face.

Simmons hurried to clean up before the other children returned home from school. He dragged the bodies of his wife, son, and granddaughter some 40 yards behind the house to a large dirt pit, then lowered them into the grave. But he didn't cover it . . . not yet. There was more work to be done.

In the afternoon, Simmons greeted his children—Loretta, age 17; Eddy, age 14; Marianne, age 11; and Rebecca, age 8—as they got off the school bus. School was out for vacation, and their dad had promised them a "special holiday gift."

After driving them home, Simmons instructed the children to wait out-side for their turn to receive the surprise. The youngest, Rebecca, was first. Innocently, she trailed her father into his bedroom, where he handed her a package. As she began to tear open the paper, Simmons grabbed her from behind and viciously strangled her with a fishing line until her small body went limp. He then carried Rebecca to the bathtub and held her underwater to ensure that she was dead. The other three children met the same fate. He then hauled their lifeless bodies to the "family plot" behind the house and laid them alongside their mother.

The next 3 days at the Simmons residence were uneventful. Simmons stayed at home, talking to no one and thinking only of murder. He patiently waited to implement the second phase of his plan of attack.

On December 26, other members of the Simmons clan, unaware of the massacre of their loved ones, came from out of town for their annual holiday visit. The first to arrive at the family home were Simmons's 23-year-old son, William; William's wife, Renata, age 21; and their 20-month-old infant, William Jr. No sooner had they entered the house than William and his wife were shot several times in the head. Once he was certain that William and Renata were dead, Gene strangled his tiny grandson, wrapping a cord tightly around his small neck. Just to be sure, Simmons then submerged William Jr. in a tub of water, as he had done with his own children days earlier.

Later that afternoon, Gene Simmons's eldest daughter Sheila, age 24, arrived with her husband, Dennis McNulty, age 33, and children—Sylvia, age 6, and Michael, 21 months of age. Sheila removed her overcoat and walked into the living room to enjoy the Christmas tree and holiday decorations. Turning around, she spotted her younger brother's lifeless body lying in a pool of blood on the floor of the dining room. Just as she yelled out, her father rushed into the room and shot her at close range, six shots to the head.

Upon hearing the sound of gunshots, Dennis dropped the suitcases and raced into the house, only to become the next victim. Attempting to disarm his father-in-law, he struggled heroically but in vain. After a few moments, Gene managed to place his .22-caliber gun to Dennis's temple and squeezed the trigger, blowing his brains out with a single bullet.

Sylvia fled to a bedroom to hide, and little Michael, sensing that Mommy and Daddy were hurt, screamed and cried. The children's terror was short-lived; within minutes, they were both strangled to death.

For Gene Simmons, the third phase came on Monday morning, December 28. Simmons drove his son's brown Toyota Corolla 17 miles south on Highway 7 from his Dover retreat toward the town of Russellville. He had several scores to settle.

Simmons's first stop was the law offices of Peel, Eddy, and Gibbons in downtown Russellville. Attractive and shapely 24-year-old Kathy Kendrick was returning to her reception desk as Simmons barged in. Kendrick was not at all pleased to see Simmons. Months earlier, at her previous job, she was forced to tell him off when his unwanted sexual advances became too uncomfortable. It got so bad that she notified her supervisor that she was being harassed.

Simmons never hesitated or spoke a word; he just stood in front of Kendrick's desk, pulled a gun from his pocket, and aimed. "He just kept shooting and kept shooting," recalled legal secretary Brenda Jones. "There was blood coming out of Kathy's head. It was real dark, red blood, not like you'd expect to get from a cut. It was coming out of the back of her head. She was breathing. She had trouble breathing, but she was breathing"

Photo 14.1 Convicted mass-murderer R. Gene Simmons glares into a Clarksville, Arkansas, courtroom during a break in his 1989 trial. Simmons, who was executed in 1990, killed 16 people including 14 family members during the 1987 holiday season. (Associated Press/ Danny Johnston)

(Penman, 1988). Kendrick did not survive for long, however. She died a few minutes after being rushed to the emergency room of a local hospital.

Simmons then drove 20 blocks west on Main Street to his next destination, Taylor Oil Company. He was looking for his former employer, 38-year-old Rusty Taylor, and found him working in the office.

Taylor was surprised by Simmons's visit; but before he could ask him why he was there, Simmons pumped him with two bullets to the chest. The gunman then tried to escape through the loading dock but encountered 34-year-old J. D. (Jim) Chaffin, a part-time employee of Taylor Oil, who inadvertently blocked Simmons's path. Simmons shot Chaffin in the right eye, and the bullet passed through his brain, killing him instantly.

It was the first day on the job for 35-year-old Juli Money, a bookkeeper at Taylor Oil. Hearing gunfire, she eased open the door to her office and saw Chaffin lying on the floor, bleeding from the head. Money also saw Simmons as he stepped over the body. She vividly recalled the "horrid grin" on his face.

"He just had a look in his eye like a mad dog," said Money. "And when he looked at Jim on the floor and Jim was bleeding profusely, he showed no emotion or anything. He just turned around and pointed at me and shot" (Penman, 1988). Fortunately for Money, the bullet sailed through her hair, missing her forehead by a fraction of an inch.

Then Simmons raced 3 miles across town to the Sinclair Mini-Mart, a convenience store on the east side of Russellville. Only a few weeks earlier, after complaining that he was being underpaid and overworked, he had quit his job there as a part-time cashier.

Simmons walked into the mini-mart and immediately blocked the door so that no one could enter or leave. He drew his revolver from under his jacket and aimed it at his former boss, 38-year-old David Salyer. Seeing the gun, Salyer shouted, "If this is a robbery, take what you want!" Money was the last thing on Gene Simmons's mind, however. He shot at Salyer but missed.

Simmons then fired at the cashier, 46-year-old Roberta Woolery. She screamed, and he shot her again. Wounded in the cheek, Woolery collapsed behind the counter. With Simmons's attention diverted, Salyer tried a counter-attack. Shielding himself with a chair, Salyer made a desperate charge at the gunman but was wounded in the process.

Simmons jumped in his car and sped around the corner to Woodline Motor Freight. He walked through a side door and across the office, looking for Joyce Butts, age 35, the former supervisor who had scolded him a year earlier about his romantic advances toward Kathy Kendrick.

With the same single-minded purpose he had displayed all day, Simmons ignored other employees and headed straight to Butts's desk. He pulled his gun from his jacket and shot her in the heart and head.

Simmons then turned into a nearby computer room, where he found Vicky Jackson, a woman he had befriended while he worked at Woodline as an accounts receivable clerk. Jackson pleaded, "Gene, please don't shoot me. Gene, please don't shoot me" (Bowers, 1988). He grabbed her and put a gun to her head, but he assured her, "Don't worry, I'm not going to hurt you . . . I just came to kill Joyce." He then laid his gun on a nearby desk and asked his hostage to call the police.

Although the police had been called from every shooting site, Simmons had managed to stay one step ahead of them. Now he was ready to surrender, and he waited for the police to arrive. "I've done what I wanted to do and now it's all over," Simmons explained. "I've gotten everybody who hurt me" (Simmons, 1988).

The Russellville murder spree lasted 45 minutes. When it was over, Kathy Kendrick and Jim Chaffin were dead, and Rusty Taylor, Roberta Woolery, David Salyer, and Joyce Butts were wounded but would survive. To this day, Butts lives with a .22-caliber slug at the base of her skull. She also lives with vivid memories of a tragedy that continues to haunt her.

Suspecting further foul play, the police hurried to the Simmons home to conduct an "emergency search." There they discovered the gruesome scene of carnage. The 14 bodies found in and around the Simmons home, added to the murders in Russellville, brought the death toll to 16, making this the largest family massacre and one of the largest mass murders in U.S. history.

We know that a large number of people were killed, but do we know why? What are the conditions that might provoke a person like Gene Simmons to commit the heinous crime of mass murder, especially against the very people whom he presumably loved and needed? Why would a family man massacre his wife of more than 20 years, his children, and his grandchildren, and then go on a killing spree through the town of Russellville? After all, he had no record of violence; had an unblemished military career of 21 years; was not known around town as a troublemaker; and raised studious, well-behaved children. At 5 feet 10 inches tall, slightly overweight, and sporting a gray goatee and balding head, Simmons looked innocuous. Did he suddenly go berserk?

Ronald Gene Simmons is the prototypical mass killer. He methodically targeted particular victims, people he knew very well from work and family. His crimes were highly selective, well planned, and purposeful. Like most other mass murderers, he didn't "just snap."

Typically, the road to mass murder is long, lonely, and rocky; it takes more than an overnight journey for the killer to reach the end. It takes years to come to that point where the perpetrator sees mass murder as the only way out.

A PROFILE OF THE FAMILY ANNIHILATOR

The mass slayer often suffers a long history of frustration and failure, through childhood and on into his adult life. He has tremendous difficulty both at home and at work in achieving happiness and success. Over time, repeated frustration can erode a person's ability to cope, so much so that even modest disappointments seem catastrophic.

The lifelong accumulation of upheaval and defeat places the killer on the edge so that the occurrence of a triggering event becomes overwhelming. In most massacres, the precipitating incident is either a separation from a loved one, the loss of a job, or the prospect of either. A separation can leave the killer feeling alone, lost, and abandoned. The loss of a job, on the other hand, causes him to feel hopeless and profoundly inadequate because he cannot fulfill his role as the breadwinner in the family.

As a child and young adult, Gene Simmons led a rather unremarkable life. He wasn't easy to get along with and tended to bully his classmates, but not to the point where it was considered a serious behavior problem. Following high school, Simmons spent an undistinguished 5-year tour of duty in the navy. After a failed attempt to make it in civilian life, he enlisted in the air force, where he served for another 16 years. This time he hit it big, achieving the rank of master sergeant and being decorated with five medals for meritorious service, including the Bronze Star.

Simmons retired from the military in 1979, and things went downhill fast. From that point on, frustration was a central and recurrent theme in his life. He drifted through a string of menial, low-paying jobs. He worked for about 90 days as a records clerk, a year as a waivers clerk, 4 months in a pickle factory, and more than a year as a part-time grocery clerk. Things were getting worse—not better—all the time.

Lacking any authority on the job, Simmons tried to impose military structure on his family life. In his way of thinking, he was the general; his wife and children, the foot soldiers. As a civilian, he was forced to accept low-status jobs—indeed, positions traditionally reserved for women. At home, however, he was the man in charge. There, the woman did woman's work, children did the dirty work, and the man of the house called the shots. For example, the children were forced to dig a deep hole for the outhouse and to haul off heavy buckets of dirt. As it turned out, they even dug their own grave.

Not only did Simmons treat his family as subordinates, but he also imposed a foxhole mentality on them. Friends of the family agreed that he was a strict patriarch who allowed family members little outside contact. He censored his wife's mail, and he didn't allow her to use the telephone or to drive the family car. On the rare occasion when a Simmons child was allowed to be with friends, it was almost always at the Simmons home so that Gene could keep an eye on things.

Many Americans suffer the kinds of disappointments experienced by Simmons, yet they don't kill. But mass murderers are also intensely isolated, physically or psychologically, from sources of emotional support. In short, they are loners. Clearly, Simmons was the instigator. He cut off his family from outside contacts, but in the end, he was even more isolated than they. Feeling like the commander in chief in the family, he simply could not share the burden of decision making or his problems with his underlings.

Although physically surrounded by family members, Simmons was very much alone. He often retreated from his wife and children, and he often went to his room to hide. This was the place where he relaxed and was the place where he slept . . . alone.

As Christmas 1987 approached, Gene Simmons's life was far from merry. He had reached the bottom of the barrel as far as employment was concerned and had decided to quit his job as a part-time clerk at the Sinclair Mini-Mart. Another sore spot was Simmons's lack of success in attracting Kathy Kendrick. His renewed advances toward her had once again been angrily rejected. At first, he sent her cards, flowers, and small gifts. When that failed to get a response, he tried waiting on her front doorstep, which only made her angrier.

Simmons's obsession with Kendrick was in part a consequence of his sexual rejection at home. His wife, Becky, had refused to sleep with him for the past 6 years, ever since she had learned of his incestuous relationship with their 17-year-old daughter, Sheila, which had spawned a granddaughter, Sylvia.

In the spring of 1987, just 6 months before the massacre, Gene Simmons made a futile attempt to patch things up at home. He convened a family meeting to explain his sexual indiscretions to his wife, Becky, and to his daughter, Sheila, and her husband, Dennis. Gene asked for reconciliation. Not believing his sincerity, they mockingly applauded his speech and laughed in his face.

Simmons's performance at the family meeting was a total flop. His efforts to beg for forgiveness were unequivocally rebuffed. It was painfully clear to him that he would never regain the love and respect of his family.

Simmons's family life seemed to be crumbling around him—he was losing control. Although the younger kids still obeyed, they now did so without a shred of respect for their father. The children had grown rude and insulting toward him. To a military man like Simmons, this verbal abuse was sheer insubordination. But insubordination is nothing compared to desertion. Simmons was aware that his wife was on the verge of leaving him and taking the kids with her. When it comes to motivation for mass murder, family man Gene Simmons had it all: frustration, isolation, rejection, plenty of scapegoats, and a means to kill. He had all the factors needed to precipitate a bloodbath. On every front, he was a failure: He was losing his family; his wife, his daughter Sheila, and Kathy Kendrick had rejected him sexually; and he couldn't even keep a part-time menial job. These domestic and work difficulties became too much for Simmons to tolerate. In effect, they were enough to trigger his crime, to serve as the proverbial straw that broke his back.

Simmons had long been frustrated in his pursuit of power, lacked emotional support for his problems, and suffered profound rejection. At this point, he made a conscious and deliberate decision to destroy the lives of many innocent people. He chose murder as his way to get even with unfair bosses, unwilling lovers, and unfaithful kin. Blaming others for all of his unhappiness, he thought they should pay with their lives.

IMPACT OF UNEMPLOYMENT

In January 2009, Ervin Lupoe, a medical technician and resident of Wilmington, California, sent a letter to a local television station's website complaining that both he and his wife had been fired unfairly from their jobs at Kaiser Permanente Medical Center in Los Angeles. According to Lupoe's letter, two days before being terminated, an administrator told the couple: "You should not even have bothered to come to work today. You should have blown your brains out."

Lupoe added that he had given up hope when the medical center failed to offer him any assistance, even though they were aware that he and his wife had no sources of income and were supporting five children under the age of 8. Finally, Lupoe wrote that he planned to kill his children, his wife, and their children as "an escape for the whole family." After gunning down all the members of his family, Lupoe wrote a suicide note in which he explained that he had not wanted to leave their children with a stranger and then took his own life.

In an analysis of FBI homicide data covering the years 1976 through 2007, James A. Fox (2009) found that changes in the unemployment rate correlated fairly strongly with the incidence of multiple family murder. As a follow-up, Jack Levin (2010) compared the number of family murders involving at least 3 victims during the first 4 months of 2009 when the unemployment rate stood at 8.9% against the first 4 months of 2008 when the jobless rate was a modest 4.9%. There were as many as 12 family annihilations in the first few months of 2009 when unemployment had spiked, but only seven in the same months of 2008 when unemployment was relatively low. In terms of the overall victim count, there was a total of 56 killed in the 2009 months, compared with just 29 a year earlier.

Characteristics of family annihilations also changed over the same months studied. In 2008, fathers only slightly outnumbered sons as killers, and few took their own lives after committing multiple murder. The precipitants consisted, first, of a breakdown in the relationship between the killer and his family, and second, of the loss of a job, money, or both. In the majority of incidents, revenge motivated the family massacre. Most of the weapons consisted of guns, knives, or blunt objects.

In contrast to the first quarter of 2008, most of the killers in 2009 were fathers who took their own lives after shooting to death their wives and children. At least half had lost their jobs or were deeply in debt; some had suffered a nasty separation or divorce. Some sought to get even with their spouse; but others had altruistic motivation, believing that their loved ones would be better off dead.

The relationship between unemployment rate and murder generally is rather weak at best. Many criminologists are convinced that bad economic conditions do not produce an increase in the murder rate.

Mass murder in the family is quite different, in many important respects, from the run-of-the-mill homicide. Family annihilations are more likely to be committed by White middle-age husbands/fathers, not inner-city teenagers and young adults; these crimes are disproportionately located not in the Deep South but in cities and towns where large numbers of drifters, transients, and other strangers relocate so that their support systems are absent.

Catastrophic losses such as being fired, losing lots of money in the stock market, and going through a nasty divorce serve as triggers for family annihilations. As the economy softens and the unemployment rate rises, there are simply more opportunities for catastrophic losses to precipitate a massacre. When job loss or indebtedness is involved, the motivation may become a deadly version of altruism. The husband/father is said to have been a devoted husband and dedicated father. He feels personally responsible as the breadwinner for the well-being of his family members. Depressed and frustrated, he becomes hopeless, believing that his wife and children would be better off dead. If religious, he might be convinced that they will all reunite in a better life in the hereafter. He might want to spare his family members the stigma associated with his suicide. And, he might believe that death is preferable to having his children grow up without their parents.

MURDERING MOMS

In family massacres, the killer often feels some ambivalence about the victims. More than just revenge, Simmons wanted to maintain control of his family's destiny. He preferred to commit murder rather than to be rejected or abandoned by his loved ones. For him, their death was better than their desertion, because he alone determined when, where, and how the separation would occur.

For other family annihilators, however, the motive may involve compassion more than anger. The victims, particularly children, are not viewed by the murderer as being in any way responsible for the circumstances necessitating the crime.

Twenty-five-year-old Khoua Her was absolutely convinced that her six children were doomed to live lives of misery and abuse, and only she could spare them the pain and suffering of their mortal existence in this world. On the afternoon of September 3, 1998, the children were playing outside their two-story apartment at the McDonough Homes housing project north of downtown St. Paul, Minnesota. One by one, the children were called inside, where they were choked to death. Their distraught mother caught each of them from behind and tightened strips of black fabric around their necks until their young bodies went limp. Then, having accomplished her objective, she attempted to hang herself with a telephone extension cord tied to a light fixture on the second floor of the townhouse. Instead, the cord broke free, causing Her to tumble down a flight of stairs. Unable to get up, she phoned 911, telling the dispatcher that she had killed her children and attempted suicide.

Her had suffered profoundly throughout her own childhood, and she simply would not have her beloved children follow in her footsteps. As an infant in Laos, she was separated from her mother; at the age of 12, she was beaten and ejected from her house by her stepmother. Soon thereafter, as a refugee in the Ban Vinai camp in Thailand, she was forced to marry Tou Hang, who had twice tried to rape her. Despite the fact that Her was pregnant, Hang's family insisted that she carry 50-pound containers of water for long distances every day. After she and her family finally were able to leave the refugee camp and resettle in St. Paul, her mother-in-law beat her with a stick and spit on her. She worked 7 days a week while her husband remained at home. He engaged in several extramarital affairs, frequently beat her, and threatened to kill her. During the spring of 1997, after phoning the police to intervene on 17 different occasions, Her separated from her husband. Alone with the children, she then suffered financial difficulties that apparently left her feeling hopeless. When she discovered that her 8-year-old daughter had been sexually assaulted by Hang's closest friends, it was clear to her that her children were better off dead than alive.

Her would not stand idly by to see her own life experiences played out again by her six helpless children. They were impoverished, miserable, and abused, and circumstances promised only to get worse. According to her lawyer, Her had no regrets about taking the lives of her children. "She's not thinking that she did a bad thing," he remarked. "She's thinking that she did a loving thing for her children" (Leslie & Brown, 1999).

Based on a plea agreement, Ramsey County District Judge Charles Flinn sentenced the Laotian refugee to 50 years in the Shakopee prison, leaving open the possibility that, with time off for good behavior, she could be released early at the age of 57. In court, she explained: "I have a new life—prison, but I know my kids are safe. I did it for love" (Leslie & Brown, 1999).

Khoua Her is not the only mother who has murdered her children out of a perverted sense of love. For months, Andrea Yates had entertained thoughts of killing her five children, ages 6 months and 7 years. On the morning of June 20, 2001, she followed through by drowning each of them in the family's bathtub. The 36-year-old former nurse waited until her husband, Rusty, had left their Spanish-style single-family house on Beachcomber Avenue in

Houston for his job at NASA. Then, she filled the tub within 3 inches of the top and called her children, one at a time, into the bathroom. Each youngster struggled to stay alive as their mother dragged them into the tub and held their heads underwater, but none succeeded.

Yates then immediately phoned 911, explaining to the dispatcher only that she needed a police officer. When the police arrived on the scene, they found five small bodies covered with a sheet and sprawled across their parents' bed; the lifeless body of the oldest child had been left in the tub, floating face down in the water. Yates had been a devoted mother who homeschooled her children, read Bible stories to them, handcrafted their Valentine's cards, and constructed costumes for each of them from grocery bags. On trips to the grocery store, she insisted that each of her four boys hold on to a corner of her shopping cart, while her infant daughter rode in the basket.

Photo 14.2   Some family annihilators, such as Texas mom Andrea Yates, kill their children as a perverted act of love. (Associated Press/Steve Ueckert)

But Yates was also deeply distraught. She had attempted suicide on a couple of occasions and had been hospitalized repeatedly for mental illness. Some experts suggested that Yates suffered from postpartum psychosis, a hormonally based illness that afflicts a small number of women for a period of time following childbirth. Only a regimen of antidepressants and an antipsychotic medication had temporarily lifted Yates out of her state of confusion and despair, but she stopped taking these drugs. Two days before drowning her children, Yates visited a psychiatrist, but he did not continue her on an antipsychotic medication. When police detectives asked Yates why she had killed her children, she replied that she was a bad mother—her children were not developing normally, and she deserved to be punished.

The court agreed, rejecting Andrea Yates's insanity defense and sentencing her to life in prison. Jurors apparently reasoned that somebody had to pay for the slayings of five innocent children. Yates suffered from depression, and she might even have been psychotic, but her methodical attack suggested rationality. She knew the difference between right and wrong; she must have appreciated the criminality of her murderous behavior. She was therefore guilty of murdering her children.

Yates's relatives tried to direct some of the blame onto her husband. Appearing on television, they accused Rusty of ignoring Andrea's illness and placing too much of the child-rearing burden on her ill-prepared shoulders. Rusty, in turn, threatened to sue the physicians who had seen his wife as a patient, arguing that it was their inept treatment that had allowed her psychological condition to deteriorate into violence.

In November 2005, the Texas court of appeals overturned Yates's conviction. During her trial, a prosecution expert witness had testified in error that Yates had been inspired to kill her children by an episode of the television program *Law & Order*. It was determined later that no such episode ever aired. In 2006, following a retrial on the same charges, Yates was found not guilty by reason of insanity.

THE DEFIANT SON

Overwhelmingly, family annihilators tend to be parents like Simmons, Her, and Yates, who see mass murder as a solution to their personal problems. There have been at least a few cases, however, in which a child—typically a teenage boy—wipes out his entire family in an ultimate act of defiance.

Harry De La Roche Jr. was the eldest of three sons and thereby earned the right to carry his father's name. But with that right came a responsibility, which to Harry Jr. became a burden. The elder expected a lot from his son: He wanted him to be handsome, bright, and athletic—that is, a success. Unfortunately, Harry Jr. was not handsome, bright, or athletic, and he was also rather unpopular at school. Officer Michael O'Donovan noted, for example, that Harry Jr.'s high school yearbook contained only about eight inscriptions from his graduating classmates, most of which were nasty, such as "You're the stupidest kid I met" (Roesch, 1979, p. 64). Although Harry Jr. had little going for him in the eyes of his peers, he did find one area in which he could compete and earn the pride of his father: With practice, he became an excellent marksman. Harry Sr. taught all of his sons how to use guns, and he was proud of how good a shot his eldest had become.

Because of Harry Jr.'s expertise with firearms, it seemed natural to all—all except Harry Jr.—that military college would be perfect for him. He had never done that well in his studies and his vision was rather poor; thus, he was rejected from the major military schools, including West Point, Annapolis, and the Air Force Academy. He did manage, however, better results in his application to two other schools: He was accepted by The Citadel in Charleston, South Carolina, and placed on the waiting list at local Ramapo College.

Being rejected from the academies of the armed forces was another major failure of Harry Jr. in the eyes of his father. He was, however, pleased about The Citadel; a military career for his son was his dream.

Harry Jr. felt differently: "As I considered The Citadel I wasn't sure that I wanted to go since it wouldn't be exactly the same as attending the academies I'd chosen" (quoted in Roesch, 1979, p. 53). Unlike government-supported academies where there is no tuition and cadets receive a salary to defray costs of uniforms and books, The Citadel is a state-supported institution that attempts to mimic West Point. The most important difference between these schools is that all graduates of West Point receive a regular army commission and enter the army at the rank of second lieutenant, whereas graduates of The Citadel receive only a reserve commission. Graduates of The Citadel who complete the ROTC program may apply for a regular army commission if they graduate with distinguished accomplishments, but this was an unlikely prospect given Harry's mediocre scholastic skills.

Harry Jr. also would have preferred to stay near home in more familiar surroundings rather than go to South Carolina. Again complying with his father's onerous demands, however, Harry Jr. went off to The Citadel. Even up to the day he left for college, he expressed his ambivalence about what lay ahead.

As it turned out, Harry Jr.'s reservations proved to be correct. At The Citadel, he was miserable. The school, noted for its *knob system* for freshmen, employed an extremely strict code of discipline. Like West Point, it strongly emphasized a military regimen. The freshman year at The Citadel seemed at that time much like a year-long fraternity hazing.

The obvious purpose of the knob system is to teach submission to military authority and to separate the men from the boys. An additional consequence of this type of initiation may be to enhance the bond of the freshmen to the institution. Social psychologists call this process *cognitive dissonance*. Some freshman knobs may drop out of The Citadel, deciding that it just is not for them, but those who survive the first year have learned to justify their harsh treatment by evaluating the school more favorably. Essentially, after going through all that they had to, upperclassmen will find it difficult to see the school as not worth it. Harry De La Roche Jr. soon proved not to be a survivor of his freshman year.

As in high school, Harry was unpopular and was even ostracized. He had an inauspicious start at The Citadel. Harry's commanding officer (CO) was embarrassed when he mistakenly marked Harry present at formation when Harry actually had forgotten to appear. Of course, the CO took his embarrassment out on Harry, and the other cadets followed suit. As the weeks passed, Harry's peers forgot the particular incident but never reversed their opinion of him. As Harry continued to suffer from scorn, letters from his father urged him on, telling him, "No matter how tough they make it, you know you can take it" (quoted in Roesch, 1979, p. 85).

As Thanksgiving of 1976 approached, he could stand no more, and he left The Citadel for what he hoped was the last time, telling the school that his mother was sick with cancer. Military school was more than he could take: He was fed up with living the way his father wanted him to, and he was tired of being pushed, yet he couldn't bring himself to tell his father about not wanting to return to school. His father had always told him that "quitters were failures."

On November 28, Harry Jr. returned home late, around 3 a.m., after visiting some of his former high school friends. He took a pistol, one of several in the house, and went to his parents' room where they were asleep. He paced the room for some time deciding what to do: Should he stand up to his father or simply release himself from the bondage? He held the gun to his father's head for 15 minutes. Finally, he fired. His mother stirred at the explosion and he shot her. He then shot his father again. Next, he proceeded to his brothers' room. His 15-year-old brother, Ronald, lay there motionless, his eyes wide open. Harry shot and killed him. The other brother—Eric, age 12—made a rush for Harry. Harry shot him twice in the face and once in the chest, but he was still alive and struggling to get up. Harry bludgeoned him to death with the revolver and stuffed his body in a metal cabinet in the attic.

Harry Jr.'s entire life had revolved around guns. They provided his uppermost achievement as well as his greatest tragedy. For Harry, the gun represented an instrument, a means not only to kill his persecutor but also to measure his own self-worth.

Harry's family annihilation ensured that he would never again bear the intolerable burden of his father's expectations or suffer the regimentation of military school. Instead, he would spend his adult years in a much more oppressive environment—a New Jersey state penitentiary.

Harry Jr. received four life sentences to be served concurrently. Based on the New Jersey statute in force at the time of his murders, he became eligible for parole in 2002. However, having failed on several bids for release, he remains incarcerated.

CHAPTER 15

Firing Back

Paul Calden said he'd be back, and he was true to his word. On January 27, 1993, 8 months after being fired from his job at Fireman's Fund Insurance in Tampa, Florida, the 33-year-old former claims manager returned to get even. This time, he'd be the one to do the firing.

Just before noontime, Calden returned to the Island Center office complex, where he once worked. He was dressed in a dark blue business suit and disguised himself by wearing glasses and greasing back his salt-and-pepper hair. Calden walked through the double glass doors into the ground-floor corporate cafeteria in search of his former supervisors—those whom he held responsible for his extended joblessness.

Most of the Fireman's Fund employees in the cafeteria were too busy munching on Tuesday's blue plate special of chicken noodle soup and taco salad to notice that Calden, known to them as a troublemaker, had returned. One man recognized him, however, and thought to himself, "I wonder what he's doing here. Maybe he got a job with somebody else in the building" (Duryea, 1993). Without uttering a word to anyone, Calden strolled to the service counter, ordered lunch, and then sat by himself near the cashier.

After finishing his meal, Calden went outside onto the patio adjacent to the cafeteria, where he made small talk with Denise Gonzalez, a temp worker at Fireman's, about his planned trip to Alaska. All the while, he contemplated another plan and waited.

For more than an hour, Calden paced back and forth between the lunchroom and the patio, drinking a Diet Coke and impatiently watching for his victims to arrive. Constantly scanning the room, Calden finally saw his former supervisors arrive and sit down together at a table near the back wall. As a ploy, he walked over to a trash can next to the managers' table, as though to discard his empty soda can. He then removed a 9mm semiautomatic handgun from a paper bag under his suit jacket. Taking aim, Calden announced, "This is what you get for firing me," then deliberately started shooting (Zucco, 1993).

Calden's first victim was 46-year-old Ronald J. Ciarlone, a controller at Fireman's. Calden placed the barrel of the gun against the back of Ciarlone's head and squeezed the trigger, killing him instantly. Moving around the table,

Calden fired 10 more rounds within a 30-second period. He murdered 43-year-old operations manager Frank Ditullio with six bullets in the head, chest, and thigh, and 46-year-old Donald Jerner, a vice president at Fireman's, with a shot to the head. Two others—human resources manager Sheila Cascade, age 52, and senior underwriter Marie MacMillan, age 56—were shot but survived their wounds.

According to Diane Reed, a company employee who was seated a few tables away, Calden "stood right above them and shot them all in the head—except missing one woman. He killed only those he wanted to kill" (American Broadcasting Company, 1993).

As the shots rang out, chaos erupted all around the lunchroom. A 12-foot plate glass window was shattered by gunfire. Food was strewn over the gray, bloodstained carpet as terrified employees scurried for cover. Some ducked behind overturned tables; others found refuge in the kitchen. Women ran right out of their shoes.

Only Calden remained calm. Amid the mass hysteria and confusion, he deposited his gun at the cash register, with four bullets remaining in the clip, and quietly left through the front door. He had successfully accomplished all but the last stage of his deadly mission.

Calden drove his red Dodge Shadow, rented just for the occasion, 15 miles west along the Courtney Campbell Parkway across Tampa Bay to Clearwater. Standing at the 13th hole of the disc golf course at Cliff Stephens Park, Paul Calden pulled out a Ruger .357 revolver and shot himself in the head.

"Nobody knows why he picked that hole," said C. R. Wiley Jr., a golf pro at the course who knew Calden. "Obviously, he laid himself to rest where he felt most at peace" (Pittman, 1993).

PROFILE OF THE WORKPLACE AVENGER

What kind of person contemplates solving his employment troubles through mass murder? What is the profile of the worker who decides to take out his frustrations on the boss—if not on the whole company?

Like Paul Calden, the vengeful worker typically is a middle-age White man who faces termination (or has been terminated) in a worsening economy. He sees little opportunity for finding another job and suspects that all the breaks are going to younger competitors—or even to Blacks, women, and immigrants. Having grown up in an era of opportunity and prosperity, he feels entitled to a well-paying, meaningful job. Rudely awakened from the American Dream, he resents that his "birthright" has been snatched from him and looks for someone to blame.

Rarely will a younger worker respond so desperately to a termination. For him, it's the loss of a job, not a career—merely a temporary setback along the road to the success that he expects ultimately to achieve. A 20-year-old may respond to his firing by saying, "Take this job and shove it." He'll then just walk down the street and get another "McJob."

By contrast, a 40-year-old feels shoved out by his employer. At this juncture, the middle-age man expects to be at the top of his career, not hitting rock bottom. He is more likely than his younger counterpart to have dependents who count on him for financial support. In fact, his entire self-concept may be defined by his ability to fulfill the role of breadwinner. This set of self-expectations is a result not just of his stage in the life cycle but also of the ideas with which he was socialized.

Like other kinds of multiple killers, the overwhelming majority of vengeful, murderous employees are men. Men brought up in the 1950s and 1960s traditionally were raised in a culture in which the man brings home the bacon and his wife cooks it. Despite changing gender roles, men—much more than women—still tend to judge their self-worth by what they do. If they aren't doing anything, then what good are they?

Furthermore, men tend to regard violence as a means for establishing or maintaining control, whereas women generally see it as a breakdown of control. Thus, men who suffer psychologically because of the loss of a job are more likely to respond violently in order to show them who's boss. For many of them, youthful enthusiasm has been shattered and replaced by anxiety concerning their financial well-being and a growing sense of resentment. More and more of them do not see fulfilling employment alternatives on the horizon, only the grim prospect of impoverished retirement. Even those who normally are immune from economic exigencies—college-educated men in their late 40s and early 50s—have become financially at risk. For this generation, the midlife crisis would call for a trip to a career counselor rather than a psychiatrist.

These demographic changes are exacerbated by the effects of a postindustrial economy in which desirable middle-income jobs, particularly in manufacturing, are becoming increasingly scarce. For a variety of reasons—including foreign competition, the subprime mortgage crisis, economic recession, and computerization of the workplace—the job market for middle-age men has been worsening. Millions of workers are being displaced by plant closings or relocations and by corporate downsizing. Those workers who are displaced are now finding it more difficult to secure comparable employment, that is, new full-time jobs at similar wages.

While the overwhelming majority of workplace avengers are men, women are not insulated entirely from the factors contributing to this kind of rampage. The same types of frustrations and disappointments over the loss of a job can be just as severe for a female worker depending on her commitment to her career.

Amy Bishop, a 45-year-old assistant professor of biological sciences, was upset over being denied tenure at the University of Alabama, Huntsville. On February 12, 2010, she showed up at a Friday afternoon faculty meeting armed with a 9-mm handgun. After sitting quietly for a short period of time, she reportedly rose from her chair and immediately started shooting at her stunned colleagues—human targets who may have been implicated, at least in her mind, in her failed tenure bid. She appeared to act with cool and considered deliberation, seeing the final affront as a one-way ticket to nowhere and choosing to execute those accountable for what she regarded as an intolerable and unfair outcome. When the faculty meeting ended, three faculty members lay dead, and three others were wounded.

Photo 15.1 This Feb. 13, 2010, file booking photo provided by the Huntsville, Ala., Police Department shows college professor Amy Bishop, sentenced to life in prison for capital murder in the Feb. 12, 2010, shooting deaths of three faculty members at the University of Alabama in Huntsville. (Associated Press/Bob Gathany)

It would be inappropriate for us to challenge the fairness of Bishop's tenure review. Her case may very well have been handled carefully, respectfully, and consistent with due process. And, of course, no matter whether or how seriously the process was flawed, that would not justify mass murder.

Bishop, a Harvard-trained neurobiologist, had achieved a more-than-respectable record of grants and scholarly publications, including several papers in leading peer-reviewed journals within her field. In recent years, she had distinguished herself as one of the inventors of InQ, an incubator for human cell growth. Her teaching, though not stellar, was more than acceptable, at least based on available student evaluations.

Professor Bishop was also known on the campus as an outspoken critic of the university's administration. Months before the shooting, she had learned of her failed tenure application. She subsequently appealed the decision but did not prevail. According to several people around the campus quoted in news reports, Bishop was quite bitter and vocal about her plight, as the end of her employment at the university approached.

Unlike many Americans who may interpret employment-related failures as an indication of their own inadequacies, workplace avengers typically externalize blame. Their failures and disappointments, they believe, reflect nothing more than mistreatment by others who, perhaps undeservedly, hold unbridled power over their fate. Might Professor Bishop, as a noted scholar with an Ivy League pedigree, have questioned the legitimacy of the tenure process or those who were in a position to judge her record of achievement?

With reports of Bishop's quirky demeanor and social awkwardness, it would be all too easy to dismiss this violent episode as just some nut who couldn't handle the pressure of publish or perish. Indeed, that seemed to be the prevailing view of the hundreds who posted online comments in the days following the shooting. But to define this tragedy as just a case of psychopathology would discourage a closer look at contributing forces.

Exacerbating the problem, of course, is that with the prevailing economic climate, in which academic budgets are shrinking and tenure lines evaporating, tenure denial—for good reason or bad—can indeed be catastrophic. For highly trained scholars of tenure-track misfortune, the alternative opportunities can be rather slim. As Cary Nelson, president of the American Association of University Professors, told the *Huntsville Times*, "The most likely result of being denied tenure in this nonexistent job market is that you will not be able to continue teaching. . . . You probably can't get another job."

THE IMPACT OF FRUSTRATION

In the context of these demographic and economic changes, increasing numbers of workers are becoming frustrated in their career goals. As indicated earlier, frustration tends to increase aggressive behavior. In the work setting, there are actually two kinds of job frustration that engender enough resentment to be translated into extreme violence.

First, some vengeful workers have endured long-term, cumulative frustration—repeated failures in their careers, resulting in a diminished ability to cope with life's disappointments. Although it is likely that they have contributed to their own demise, they feel that they have been treated unfairly by all of their bosses and coworkers. From their distorted point of view, they never get the right job, the deserved promotion, or a decent raise. Their firing at a crucial time in their lives becomes the final straw.

For example, Paul Calden's employment problems at Fireman's were nothing new for him. Despite doing well in school, finishing college, and showing considerable promise, he never really made it. Instead, he moved from job to job, causing trouble wherever he worked. Just prior to his employment at Fireman's, Calden had been with Allstate Insurance, where he threatened his supervisor by deliberately displaying the butt of a gun inside his briefcase. This manager was so frightened by Calden that he offered him a severance package that he couldn't refuse.

In contrast to Calden's unstable work history, the second type of vengeful employee comes to feel invulnerable to job loss because of long-term employment with the same company. Such employees feel as though they have tenure. From their perspective, they have given their best years to the boss, have unselfishly dedicated their careers to the firm, have helped build the business . . . and what do they get in return? Fired!

Forty-seven-year-old Joseph Wesbecker was proud of his decades of dedicated service to Standard Gravure of Louisville, Kentucky. The plump and balding man had a reputation as a top-notch pressman, one of the best the company had, who put in so many hours of overtime that he earned the nickname "overtime hog." After all that he had done for the plant, Wesbecker couldn't believe that he was being treated with so little respect. Even worse, he felt that management was destroying him, so he would have to get them first.

Wesbecker had tried a nonviolent solution to his grievances. In 1987, he lodged a complaint against Standard Gravure with the Jefferson County Human Relations Commission, claiming that the company had harassed him. At the threat of being fired, he claimed, the company had forced him to operate one of the noisy and difficult high-speed presses. Managers knew very well that he couldn't psychologically tolerate the extraordinary stresses of this assignment, but they made him do it anyway. In settlement, Standard Gravure agreed to put Wesbecker on long-term disability, then to rehire him if and when he recovered enough to go back to work.

Although Wesbecker appeared to be satisfied, in reality he was even more perturbed and bitter than ever. He reasoned as follows: They were responsible for ending his career; they were to blame for his problems. They knew that he was a manic-depressive who couldn't take stress. But they turned the stress level up so they'd have an excuse to fire him.

Bad luck was nothing new to Joseph Wesbecker. On the contrary, it had plagued him throughout his life, beginning with the death of his father when he was only a year old and of his grandfather 3 years later. While growing up, Wesbecker was moved from house to house and, for an 8-month period, was placed in an orphanage. He was a terrible student who finally dropped out of school in the ninth grade. As an adult, he seemed to slide deeper and deeper into a black hole of depression and paranoia. After two divorces, he had lost close connections with family members, coworkers, and friends. Only his job had remained as a constant source of self-esteem. For years, he had worked overtime on a regular basis for extra income and had invested his money in the stock market. Now, even his job was gone, and he was idle and felt alone.

In Wesbecker's mind, his supervisors had been patently unfair. He was depressed, moody, irritable, and angry, experiencing severe bouts of tremors and insomnia. He was so confused that he couldn't even remember his own address. Compulsively, he devoured ice cream by the gallon, a dozen Diet Pepsis daily, and box after box of cookies. To counteract his moodiness, a psychiatrist had prescribed both lithium and an antidepressant. But medication wasn't enough to prevent Wesbecker from wanting to kill the bosses he hated so much.

His emotions fueled by his depression, Wesbecker had murder on his mind. He went as far as to make threats, but for the most part, they weren't taken seriously. He had confided to his ex-wife prior to their divorce that he felt like taking a gun to work and killing "a bunch of people." He had shown one coworker a gun and had indicated that he intended to use it. He had also told an old friend from Standard Gravure about his bizarre plan to blow up the company with plastic explosives: He intended to place the explosives on a large remote-control model airplane, fly the airplane close to the building, and then detonate the explosives. He had considered hiring a hit man to murder three company officials, but he refused to pay the $30,000 fee. Why should he depend on a professional to do his dirty work? Wesbecker would get even on his own.

On the evening of September 13, 1989, Wesbecker cleaned his firearms. The next morning, he awakened early; spread his keys, wallet, and insurance papers on a kitchen table; and set out $1,720 in cash and his last will and testament where his ex-wife would be sure to find them. He then loaded his AK-47, slipped on a tan zippered jacket, grabbed a canvas bag crammed with guns and bullets and made an unscheduled visit to work. He had a job to do. Wesbecker's rampage at Standard Gravure lasted no more than 20 minutes.

He parked his Chevy in the lot and, holding his assault rifle to his hip, took the elevator to the third floor. First, without saying a word to anyone, he shot his way through the business office and the bindery, and then he moved down the stairs to a basement tunnel, where he opened fire on more coworkers. Walking toward the reel room, Wesbecker encountered John Tingle, a friend of many years. Rather than take his friend's life, he urged him to "get back, get away, I don't want to hurt you" (Adams, 1989). His next victim was Richard Barger, a coworker who came down the stairs as Wesbecker moved through the hall. Wesbecker shot Barger five times and then, stepping over the body, took the stairs to the first-floor pressroom, where he opened fire again. As he pumped at least 40 rounds into his victims, Wesbecker laughed out loud. He then pulled out a 9mm semi-automatic pistol and shot himself in the head.

Photo 15.2 Workplace avenger Michael McDermott, who slaughtered seven coworkers, claimed he was shooting at Nazi soldiers. The jury rejected his insanity plea and convicted him of murder. (Associated Press/Victoria Orocho)

Job termination is not the only kind of financial exigency that has been blamed on an employer. On December 26, 2000, 42-year-old Michael McDermott killed seven of his coworkers at Edgewater Technology in Wakefield, Massachusetts, after learning that his wages were to be garnished by the IRS through an arrangement with the company. Blaming his dire financial position on certain offices of the company, McDermott selectively targeted fellow employees only in the payroll and human resources departments. In the process, he ignored a number of coworkers whom he simply did not blame for his poor financial position. Moreover, McDermott's rampage was anything but spontaneous. A day earlier, he had left a cache of weapons and ammunition under his desk so as to be fully prepared for his murderous onslaught. In court, McDermott tried to convince the jury that he was a victim of severe mental illness—that he had been convinced that he was killing not coworkers but Adolf Hitler and six of Hitler's henchmen. There was no explanation, however, for why the imagined Nazis would have worked only in certain departments at Edgewater. The jury, not believing the defendant's story, convicted McDermott on seven counts of first-degree murder, which earned him a life sentence without parole eligibility, the most severe punishment available in the Commonwealth of Massachusetts.

MIXED MOTIVES

Occasionally, workplace murder has mixed motivations, when the profit motive becomes fused with a need for revenge. Thirty-eight-year-old John Taylor was more than just furious. Not only had Wendy's fired him without cause (in his mind), but it then filled his position with Jean Auguste, someone not nearly as qualified as he. The short and stocky former manager became obsessed with getting even with the man who had replaced him, with seeking revenge against the fast-food restaurant where he had worked, and with showing what could happen to the restaurant with someone besides himself in charge.

The date was May 24, 2000. It was 10:30 p.m., just before closing time, when Taylor and his accomplice, 32-year-old Craig Godineaux, entered the fast-food eatery on Main Street in the Queens borough of New York City. Waiting for the last customer to leave, they sat eating as workers cleaned up for the day. Then, the two men walked down to the manager's office in the basement, where Taylor immediately pulled a semiautomatic pistol on Auguste, threatening to shoot him if he didn't hand over the $2,400 in the company safe. Setting aside the money, Taylor forced Auguste to use the intercom to call down the other six workers.

Taylor ordered all of the employees to get on the floor. He instructed his 6-foot, 4-inch, 245-pound accomplice to tie their hands behind their backs, place duct tape over their mouths, and put plastic bags over their heads. Taylor first shot Auguste and then 22-year-old counter girl Anita Smith, both in the back of the head. Handing Godineaux his gun, Taylor then ordered his partner to "finish them." Wearing a puppy-dog sweater and sucking his thumb, Godineaux—who was later described as a "bumbling, child-like giant" because of his large physical stature and his small IQ—immediately complied, killing Ramon Nazario, age 44; Jeremy Mele, age 18; and Ali Ibadat, age 40. He also critically wounded JaQuinone Johnson and Patrick Castro, both 18 years old. Taylor and Godineaux then fled the restaurant, only to be caught days later.

At 12:50 a.m., Castro was able to free himself of his restraints and phone 911 for help. He then dragged Johnson up to the first floor, where the two survivors waited for the police to arrive.

As another expression of mixed motives, a November 2009 shooting at a military post reflected both revenge against coworkers and terrorism. In this case, a U.S. Army psychiatrist opened fire at Fort Hood, located just outside of Killeen, Texas. The shooter killed 13 and injured another 30 before being shot, although not fatally, by emergency personnel who had responded to the incident.

The mass killer turned out to be Major Nidal Malik Hasan, 39, a Muslim American who gunned down his colleagues after suffering a string of negative evaluations for his substandard performance. In addition, Hasan apparently felt harassed by soldiers because of his Muslim faith. And, given his standoffish nature, he was not likely to seek support from others.

The killer's mind-set had not always been so negative. Hasan had enlisted more than two decades earlier, hoping to pursue his education and to express his loyalty as a proud U.S. citizen. This was long before the war in Iraq, the 9/11 terrorist attacks, or even the Gulf War from 1990 to 1991. At this juncture, however, he dreaded going to war against Islam, as he reportedly viewed it. Despite attempts to gain a discharge from the army, Hasan was facing deployment overseas. It was one thing to counsel returning soldiers in the United States, but quite another to support the war from the front lines.

It is no coincidence that Hasan's mass murder occurred just outside his workplace, the Soldier Readiness Center, where soldiers receive routine medical treatment immediately before being deployed to war zones. His murderous rampage was probably an act of terrorism, as indicated by Hasan's Muslim affiliation, his Middle Eastern-style clothing, and reports of his having shouted out "Allahu Akbar," an expression of praise to God. He had also communicated by e-mail with Anwar al-Awlaki, a former U.S. resident and al-Qaeda operative, who subsequently declared Hasan "a hero" for shooting down 13 people. Notwithstanding this endorsement, the FBI found no evidence that Hasan was aided or encouraged by any others, but acted on his own volition.

Hasan's rampage was also a classic case of workplace homicide, even though a military base would seem to be an unusual location. Such a crime would seem more likely to occur inside an office building or a factory. Despite its unique function, Fort Hood is indeed a workplace, the U.S. Army an employer, and Hasan a disgruntled worker attempting to avenge perceived unfair treatment on the job. His rampage was selective, not indiscriminate. He chose the location—his workplace—and then apparently singled out certain coworkers for death.

In the aftermath of the Fort Hood massacre, the U.S. Defense Department indeed classified the incident as an act of workplace violence, not terrorism. The administration's decision in this matter came under intense criticism by certain members of Congress, the press, and especially victims who were denied various government benefits that would be available were the deaths and injuries been classified as war related. Whether the Defense Department's position was more political, as some critics charged, it is clear that Hasan's motivation and mind-set contained elements of both extremist terrorism and workplace vengeance.

Hasan was court martialed and tried in a military court on multiple counts of murder and attempted murder. Representing himself at trial, Hasan admitted to the shootings, indicating that he had "switched sides" and was waging "jihad" against the United States. The August 2013 trial was surprisingly brief, in large part because Hasan chose to call no witnesses on his behalf and declined to cross-examine those testifying for the prosecution. He was convicted on all counts and sentenced to death.

WORKPLACE MURDER BY PROXY

Many of those shot by Taylor and Godineaux at Wendy's and by Joseph Wesbecker at Standard Gravure actually had very little to do with the killers' employment problems. If Wesbecker was so methodical and selective, even bypassing an old friend, then why were so many innocent coworkers targeted?

In a domestic murder by proxy described earlier, a man might slaughter all of his children because he sees them as an extension of his wife, against whom his anger is actually directed. In Wesbecker's case, similarly, his boss may have been out of town on the day of the shooting, but there were still plenty of his employees around. Seeing other workers as an extension of management, Wesbecker murdered them as revenge against Standard Gravure. In a sense, Wesbecker was trying to kill the company in the same way that an estranged husband/father may kill the family.

One of the most diffuse cases of murder by proxy occurred on December 7, 1987, aboard PSA Flight 1771 en route from San Francisco to Los Angeles. When the BAe 146 four-engine jetliner took a sudden nosedive into the mountains north of San Luis Obispo, 43 passengers and crew members lost their lives. The death toll included 35-year-old David Burke, who, a few weeks earlier, had been fired from his job as a ticket agent for the airline.

During his 15 years with USAir, which owned PSA, Burke had a spotty employment record. Though he was suspected of a variety of indiscretions both on and off the job, it wasn't until a security camera captured him stealing $68 in beverage receipts that he was terminated.

On the day of the airline disaster, Burke boarded the plane for Los Angeles with the clear intention of getting even with his former boss, who regularly took that flight, as well as with the company as a whole. Burke, recognized by airport security as a "familiar airline employee," was able to smuggle his Smith & Wesson .44 Magnum without being checked. He also carried a note in his pocket addressed to his former supervisor: "Hi Ray. I think it's sort of ironical that we ended up like this. I asked for some leniency for my family, remember? Well, I got none. And you'll get none" (Malnic, 1987, p. 28).

Shortly after takeoff, the pilot radioed to the control tower that there was gunfire in the cabin. Moments later, a flight attendant rushed into the cockpit and reported, "We have a problem here." Burke then barged through the door and confirmed it. "I am the problem," he announced. Following a brief scuffle in the cockpit, the plane accelerated wildly and plunged 22,000 feet to the ground below (Malnic, 1987).

ROMANTIC OBSESSION

Employment troubles frequently combine with other significant difficulties—family, romance, or health problems—to produce the level of despair and anger required to drive someone to kill. Thirty-nine-year-old Richard Farley, for example, was so obsessed with a coworker, 25-year-old Laura Black, that he would do almost anything to get her.

For almost 4 years, Farley, a pudgy software engineer with Electromagnetic Systems Labs Inc. (ESL) in Sunnyvale, California, pestered, threatened, intimidated, and stalked the target of his desires. He found her smile irresistible; but the slim, brown-eyed young woman, herself an electrical engineer in the same firm, never returned his affection. She only wanted her pursuer to leave her alone so that she could get on with her life. Instead, Richard sent hundreds of letters, called her at work, bought her gifts, observed her daily activities from a convenience store across from her apartment, joined clubs to which she also belonged, followed her on the campus where she was taking courses, and threatened to do her harm if she didn't go out with him.

Laura Black held her ground as long as possible without resorting to legal or official recourse. Then, in 1986, she charged her stalker with sexual harassment on the job, and he was fired by ESL from his $36,000-a-year position. Not only was it now harder to keep an eye on his loved one, but Richard also was running out of money. Before finding a comparable job in another company, he lost his house, car, and computer, and he owed $20,000 in taxes. Farley moved from the affluent suburbs into a dilapidated single-story cottage in a low-rent district near downtown San Jose.

Despite these financial setbacks, Farley's fixation on Black continued in full force. When the frightened young woman discovered that her obsessed fan had somehow gotten hold of the key to her apartment, she felt that she had no choice but to file suit against him. In February, a temporary restraining order was issued by the Santa Clara County Superior Court. Farley was forbidden to come within 300 yards of Black and was ordered not to threaten, follow, or phone her. The hearing to make the restraining order permanent was then scheduled for the morning of February 17. What Richard Farley did on the afternoon of February 16 made the court hearing an unnecessary footnote to his one-sided love affair.

Farley loaded up several firearms—two shotguns, an assault rifle, and four handguns—as well as 1,100 rounds of ammunition and drove his motor home to ESL. He parked in a lot adjacent to the building in which Laura Black's second-floor office was located.

After sitting for a while to consider what he was about to do, Farley climbed out of the motor home with his arsenal of weapons and walked toward Laura's building. He was about to get even by committing suicide in front of his precious Laura and making her feel guilty. He would get revenge against the company that protected Black and fired him.

In both economic and human terms, the damage Farley actually did was much greater than anyone might have anticipated. First, he fired his 12-gauge repeating shotgun at a man who just happened to be coming out of the building. He then blasted his way through the glass security door, dropping another man whose desk stood between the gunman and the stairs. A third victim was felled as he stood helplessly in the stairwell, attempting to get to the first floor.

Upon reaching the second floor, Farley aimed his shotgun at anything that moved. Horrified workers scattered in all directions, trying to avoid the gunman's bullets. Four more employees—two men and two women—failed to get out of the way in time and were killed in the corridor.

Meanwhile, Black was in her office and heard the commotion outside. Hearing the gunman approach, she slammed shut the door to her office and locked it. Farley raised his shotgun and fired through the door, hitting his beloved in the shoulder and causing her lung to collapse. He then moved on.

After a 5-hour standoff, Richard Farley gave himself up to the police—but only after he had negotiated for a turkey sandwich and a Diet Pepsi. In all, Farley had killed five people and injured another four at the Sunnyvale plant where he had once worked.

EXTERNALIZING RESPONSIBILITY

Most disgruntled employees and former employees don't take out their anger on the company. Some may blame themselves, become depressed, and consider suicide as their only option. Others may take out their frustrations on their family or loved ones. But for the one who typically externalizes blame, responsibility is unacceptable.

"It's not my fault," he reasons. "The boss doesn't give me good assignments, my supervisor doesn't appreciate my work, and the guy at the next desk keeps taking credit for my accomplishments." When cited for poor work performance, he lashes out at those he holds accountable for his failures.

Valery I. Fabrikant was a brilliant engineer and researcher who had come to Canada as a refugee in 1979. His heavy Russian accent was a challenge to his students at Concordia University in Montreal, but not enough to prevent his advancement in the academy. After he had spent years as a researcher, the university promoted Fabrikant to the rank of associate professor in 1990.

But all was not well with the 51-year-old educator. He became increasingly embroiled in a series of heated exchanges with Concordia's professors and administrators. In the fall of 1991, Fabrikant's department recommended that he be fired, but a faculty review committee reversed the original ruling, at least for the time being. Fabrikant was not appeased.

In the spring, he sent e-mail messages to hundreds of faculty members at universities throughout Canada and the United States, accusing Concordia engineering professors of engaging in fraud. He suggested that his department wanted to get rid of him before he was able to expose their criminal behavior.

The following excerpt from Fabrikant's August 20, 1992, e-mail message to the "world" clearly expressed his view of academic injustice:

> I raise question of "scientific prostitution." The main difference between scientific prostitution and "honorary authorship" is that in the first case a completely bogus scientist, not capable of doing any research, hires somebody from developing countries or USSR by using governmental grant. This someone does research in which the parasite supervisor is included as co-author. The more publications this parasite accumulates, the greater grant he gets, the more people he can hire, the more publications he gets, etc. (Kailhla, 1992, p. 53)

In the same e-mail message, Fabrikant proceeded to name names—the identity of the two "parasites" in his department who had taken credit for work that was not theirs. But he did much more than just send e-mail. He filed a civil suit, claiming that his two colleagues had forced him to list them as the coauthors of his journal articles even though they had not contributed at all to his research. He also alleged that it was routine among the professors in his department to claim responsibility for research that they had not done. In Fabrikant's view, all of the tenured faculty and the dean were corrupt, deceitful, and unjust, and they were to blame for his academic problems.

On a muggy August afternoon in 1992, Fabrikant walked into Henry Hall on Concordia's campus in downtown Montreal, wearing a dark suit, a white shirt, and sunglasses. He carried three pistols: a semiautomatic MEB, a snub-nose Smith & Wesson .38-caliber, and a semiautomatic Bersa with an eight-round clip.

Fabrikant took escalators to the ninth floor, where his own office had been located, and wandered slowly down a short corridor looking for his former colleagues. His first victim was Associate Professor Michael Hogden. Entering Hogden's office, Fabrikant fired three bullets from his Smith & Wesson point blank into the skull of the 53-year-old biochemist. He then turned back into the hallway and walked to an adjoining office, where he calmly pumped two slugs, one from each of his semiautomatics, into Aaron Saber, a 46-year-old professor of mechanical engineering. As his second victim fell to the floor, mortally wounded, the gunman moved to the door, shooting Elizabeth Horwood, a 66-year-old secretary in the department.

Fabrikant then moved purposefully past frightened students running for cover or ducking out of the way. He had no reason to hurt them. Down the hall, he entered the office of 48-year-old Phoivos Ziogas, chairman of the Electrical and Computer Engineering Department, and shot him in the abdomen. His final victim was Professor Matthew Douglass, 65, whom he blasted twice in the head. When the police finally subdued Fabrikant and took him into custody, the body count was four professors killed and one secretary wounded. Ironically, he failed to include the two "parasites" among his victims because they were not around during the shooting.

Although, as we have indicated, employment-related rampages typically involve middle-age White men, minorities also can be so filled with enough rage and blame that they target their work sites for the sake of revenge. Not surprisingly, the perceived mistreatment can easily involve racial themes. On February 9, 1996, 2 years after being fired from his job at the Fort Lauderdale Parks Department for drug use and making threats against coworkers, 41-year-old Clifton McCree, an African American, returned with a gun, with which he killed five people and injured another. McCree then turned the gun on himself, leaving a suicide note explaining his grievance:

> None of this would have happened. All the hope, effort, and opportunity at employment only prove to be futile after [being] terminated by the city of Ft. Lauderdale. I felt I was treated very unfairly by the city after 17 years. The malicious and racist nature of how my situation was "set up" and handled. The economic lynching without regard or recourse was something very evil. Since I couldn't continue to support my family, life became nothing. I no longer wanted to live in this kind of world. I also wanted to punish some of the cowardly, racist devils that helped bring this about, along with the system. I'm glad I did it. It became war. There should have been a more humane system. But NO.... (Winfield, 1996)

SOCIAL ISOLATION

Even disgruntled employees who hold their bosses and colleagues responsible for their misfortunes may not resort to mass murder, especially if they enjoy strong support systems—such as family and friends—to help get them through the tough times. Those who do become violent tend to be loners. They may live by themselves, have recently separated or divorced, or have moved thousands of miles from home. Socially isolated, they regard work as the only meaningful part of their lives. When they lose their job, they lose everything.

By all accounts, Paul Calden had little going for him besides his job at Fireman's Fund Insurance. He was single, lived alone in a large apartment complex, and seldom had much to do with anyone else. One neighbor recalled, "I've never seen him with another human being, man or woman" (Associated Press, 1993). Instead, Calden spent his spare time watching television reruns of *Star Trek*, playing disc golf, and polishing his cherished white Acura Integra.

Joseph Wesbecker, while on long-term disability from Standard Gravure in Louisville, was similarly cut off from those who may have been able to ease his pain. He was twice divorced and had very tenuous relations with his two sons. Furthermore, while out on disability, he was separated from the few friends that he had at work. For Wesbecker, being out on disability was a triple threat: loss of income, loss of self-esteem, and loss of companionship.

Fabrikant was cut off from his sources of encouragement and support by both land and sea. Coming to North America for the sake of a job, he left behind in Russia those who might have been able to help him through his professional disappointments.

SCREENING OUT PROBLEM WORKERS

On the basis of the profile that has emerged—a middle-age, isolated man who blames others, particularly his boss, for his failures—can we screen prospective, current, and former employees for violence proneness and act preventively before they take matters—and guns—into their own hands? This is precisely the approach that many companies are taking to try to deal with the growing problem of workplace murder.

Undoubtedly, many companies could do a better job of screening applicants. It is questionable, however, whether any prediction strategy, no matter how thorough, will pay off. For several reasons, prediction is far more complex than simply following a checklist of warning signs.

In terms of preemployment screening, it may not be feasible or even possible for reasons of privacy to conduct as complete a background investigation as would be needed to weed out undesirable recruits. In Calden's case, for example, his previous employer would have been reluctant to give him a bad reference for fear of being sued. "I had mixed feelings about it," admitted John Dufel, Calden's former supervisor at Allstate. "I was thrilled that he left on good terms, and I was scared to death I was handing him off to someone else who might have to deal with Paul Calden down the road ... just like I'm sure that the people who gave us Paul Calden probably thought the same thing" (American Broadcasting Company, 1993).

Except for verifying dates of employment, many companies, therefore, in effect follow the rule "If you can't say something nice, say nothing at all." In addition, the Americans with Disabilities Act may even restrict screening on the basis of clinical depression, unless it is clear that the job recruit is prone to being violent. Thus, if a person like Wesbecker, with a history of depression, decided to seek a new job, his disability could not legally be used to reject him.

Even with a current employee who has been on the job for some time, it is often difficult to determine with any degree of certainty whether his abrasive disposition is truly a reason for alarm. To his colleagues at Concordia, Professor Fabrikant was a tremendous nuisance, to say the least, and his barrage of e-mail messages was an embarrassment to the university. But nothing that he said or did could clearly have foreshadowed his violent rampage.

As discussed earlier, profiles designed to predict rare events—such as workplace mass murder—tend to overpredict and produce a large percentage of false positives. Regardless of the specific profile characteristics, many more employees likely will fit the profile than will, in fact, seek revenge at work. The problem is a matter of seeking needles in haystacks. There is a very large haystack of people who fit the profile—angry, frustrated employees who never smile and are always ready to blame others for their shortcomings and make threatening statements—but very few needles who will commit mass murder.

Moreover, an effort to identify the problem worker may actually create a self-fulfilling prophecy whereby a combative employee becomes enraged when singled out in a negative way. If urged or even forced to seek counseling, he'll respond angrily to the suggestion that something is wrong with him. "I don't need counseling. You're the one who needs counseling. Actually, all you have to do is to start treating me fairly and everything will be just fine."

In the aftermath of a violent incident, of course, survivors tend to question why certain warning signs were ignored. Employees at Fireman's Fund were stunned but not surprised by Paul Calden's vengeful rampage. During his 2-year stint at Fireman's, Calden had a bad reputation for being a belligerent hothead. He constantly challenged his supervisors' authority, at one point nearly coming to blows because of a reprimand. He threatened to sue the company for denying him a raise that he felt he deserved. He shouted obscenities at a female coworker who had taken his favorite parking place. He even filed a harassment complaint because a fellow employee displayed a bumper sticker that offended him—not because it insulted his race or religion, but because it poked fun at the mascot of his alma mater, the University of Florida. But these warning signs came into focus only with hindsight, and hindsight is 20/20. Prediction is quite another matter altogether.

GOING POSTAL

On October 9, 1991, Joseph Harris, a 35-year-old postal worker in Ridgewood, New Jersey, armed himself with an Uzi assault rifle; a .22-caliber machine gun; and a variety of knives, swords, and explosives. His first stop was the home of his former supervisor, Carol Ott, where he slashed her to death and fatally shot her fiancé. Next on his list of wrongdoers was the post office itself. Arriving at 2 a.m., he shot and killed two mail handlers who had just come to work for the night shift. After a 4½-hour standoff with the SWAT team,

Harris finally surrendered. He had gotten the revenge that he sought, and it was time to give up.

Following his arrest, the police searched Harris's residence, a cramped attic room that he rented in nearby Paterson. In addition to a variety of explosives, the police found a two-page suicide note that detailed the embittered man's plan. Harris described his grudge against the post office and specifically referred to his hero, 44-year-old letter carrier Patrick Henry Sherrill. Harris intended to do the right thing, just like Sherrill had done in August 1986 when he killed 14 employees at the Edmond, Oklahoma, post office in an act of revenge against the supervisor who had threatened to fire him.

Actually, Sherrill's 1986 massacre marked the early stage of a string of vengeful postal workers "going postal"; that is, letter carriers who, in order to get revenge, opened fire on their supervisors and coworkers at post offices around the country. Between 1983 and 1993, 11 separate murderous incidents occurred in postal facilities, claiming a total of 34 lives. For a period of time, it appeared as though violence was fast becoming as much a tradition at the post office as Bermuda shorts and special delivery.

Notwithstanding the bloodstained image of the Postal Service, then-Postmaster General Marvin Runyon, speaking at a 1993 conference on workplace violence, offered a most surprising revelation. According to Runyon, the U.S. Postal Service actually had a lower rate of workplace homicide than the national average.

A closer examination exposes the fatal error in Runyon's reasoning. It is quite true that postal clerks were rarely held up for the contents of the cash drawer or even for the latest and hottest stamp issue—"Your Elvis stamps or your life, buster!" It is also quite true that letter carriers were hardly ever murdered by an assailant attempting to make away with a satchel of Christmas cards: They suffered dog bites sometimes, but gunshots rarely.

But focusing just on disgruntled employees who attempted to get even with their supervisors, the U.S. Postal Service clearly had far more than its share of violent episodes. Most striking, on "Black Thursday"—May 6, 1993—disgruntled postal workers in both Michigan and California went on deadly rampages, giving the American Postal Workers Union yet another opportunity to take aim at management.

According to union president Moe Biller, the fundamental problem was the "quasi-military structure and culture" of the Postal Service. Even Postmaster General Runyon seemed to agree, vowing to change the "authoritarian management style." Postal workers around the country protested bitterly about capricious managers who treated them like children. Some letter carriers complained that their bathroom breaks were being monitored by managers wishing to make certain that time wasn't being wasted. Other workers allegedly were suspended or sent home for minor rule infractions such as whistling on the job. Still other postal employees reported being spied on by supervisors with an overaggressive concern for productivity.

Added to this was the daily stress associated with getting the mail delivered on time, through "snow, rain, heat, or gloom of night" ... even hail of bullets. As further aggravation, postal workers got very little respect from the American public, which blamed them whenever the mail was late or damaged. Postal workers often were stereotyped as lazy and portrayed in the media in a most unflattering way, as in the 1990s television characters Cliff Clavin of *Cheers* and Newman of *Seinfeld*.

More important than the issues of management style and job stress, however, was the concern for job security, which was especially prevalent at the post office. Despite civil service protections, many postal workers perceived—rightly or wrongly—that their jobs were on the line because of automation and reorganization, and they worried about the implications for their careers. Indeed, what opportunities were there for a fired middle-age letter carrier with skills in sorting mail, toting a leather bag, and driving a low-speed jeep with the steering wheel on the curb side? He faced the prospect of going from a relatively well-paying job with the Postal Service to taking a minimum-wage job selling cigarettes at a local convenience store or maybe sorting mail in a company mailroom.

On top of this, some postal workers felt a particularly strong sense of entitlement because of their long-term employment, civil service status, and "veterans' preference." From their perspective, they had dedicated themselves to the Postal Service, and that loyalty was not being returned.

The widespread sense of abandonment was exacerbated by efforts to downsize and streamline the Postal Service. Postal workers everywhere felt vulnerable. As one postal worker wrote in the early 1990s, "My job is my life. Thus, the U.S. Postal Service is making an attempt on my life" (Anonymous, personal communication, March 28, 1993).

Thomas Paul McIlvane couldn't have made his intentions any clearer had he express mailed a registered letter to the Postmaster General. The 31-year-old letter carrier had been a problem employee for most of his 6 years working for the post office in Royal Oak, Michigan. He had been given warning after warning concerning poor performance, for everything from taking an unauthorized lunch break and deviating from his postal route to fighting with a customer and cursing at his supervisor. On no less than four separate occasions, McIlvane was suspended from work for periods of 1 to 2 weeks at a time. He had a bad reputation for combativeness and belligerence.

McIlvane's difficulties in dealing with persons in charge actually started long before he took a job with the Postal Service. As a Marine, he was demoted in rank several times because of unwillingness to carry out the orders of his superior officers. Eventually, he was discharged on conditions that were less than honorable, which barred him from joining the Marine Corps Reserves as he had desired. Regardless of his spotty military record, however, he was still assured of "veterans' preference" points in civil service hiring by the post office.

The situation at the Royal Oak post office took a sharp turn for the worse in 1990, when a new management team was brought in from Indianapolis. Four supervisors were transferred to Royal Oak following a General Accounting Office audit, which found that employee–management relations in Indianapolis were severely strained.

It was almost inevitable that a person like McIlvane would clash with his new supervisor, Christopher Carlisle. Carlisle was a no-nonsense, in-your-face-administrator who, by many accounts, seemed to manage through fear and intimidation. According to the findings of a congressional investigation prompted by the Royal Oak shooting, "It is reported that Chris Carlisle would stand behind an employee and berate him or her hoping to provoke a response from the employee. If the employee then accosted Carlisle, he would discipline the employee" (United States House of Representatives Committee on Post Office and Civil Service, 1992, p. 55). It was also reported in the congressional hearings that Carlisle was not at all reluctant to suspend or remove an employee even if the action later would be overturned on appeal; at least the employee would suffer financially while awaiting reinstatement.

The working relationship between McIlvane and management at Royal Oak went downhill fast. Finally, on September 10, 1990, McIlvane was given his walking papers, a formal Notice of Removal from his job. Although he was afforded the right to arbitration for possible reinstatement, it took more than 12 months for the appeal to be heard. In the meantime, McIlvane, now on unpaid leave, made frequent and wide-ranging threats of violence against Carlisle and other managers. According to William Kinsley, Director of Field Operations at Royal Oak, McIlvane directed several threats at him, including a phone call in which he said, "Fuck you, faggot postmaster. I'm going to be watching you and I'm going to get you" (United States House of Representatives Committee on Post Office and Civil Service, 1992, p. 23).

Many postal employees claim to have reported McIlvane's threatening manner to the Postal Inspection Service. It receives hundreds of threat reports annually and has discretion to investigate or not investigate such situations. Apparently, McIlvane's verbal threats were never probed by postal inspectors.

The union representatives who worked with McIlvane on his appeal were also well aware of his threats to retaliate should he lose his arbitration. McIlvane told the local union head, "If I lose the arbitration it will make Edmond, Oklahoma, look like a tea party" ("Wounded gunman," 1991), referring to Pat Sherrill's massacre of 1986. The union representatives, under the erroneous assumption that they were constrained by attorney–client privilege, failed to take action on McIlvane's threats.

On November 12, 1991, the arbitrator upheld McIlvane's removal. He was informed through a message on his answering machine telling him that he had lost. That's when he really "lost it." Two days later, McIlvane made good on his promise. Armed with a Ruger .22-caliber semiautomatic rifle and hundreds of rounds of ammunition, he arrived at the Royal Oak facility at 8:45 a.m. During the next 10 minutes, he killed four employees—including his nemesis, Chris Carlisle—and wounded four others. McIlvane then pointed his weapon at his own head and pulled the trigger.

Times have changed at the post office, with a number of reforms having been implemented in response to the Royal Oak shooting spree and others before it. Although not all letter carriers may now love their job and their supervisor, morale has improved as a result of improvements in management style. The experience of the U.S. Postal Service demonstrates the value of upgrading administrative procedures rather than attempting to weed out the problem employees. The bottom line is that the derogatory term *going postal* has outlived the reality.

CHAPTER 16

Schooled in Mass Murder

As indicated in the previous chapter, at the time that he walked into the office of Standard Gravure in Louisville to open fire on his coworkers, workplace avenger Joseph Wesbecker was on long-term disability. Out of work, the middle-age Kentuckian had plenty of time to follow events in the news. Wesbecker was particularly intrigued by Patrick Purdy's January 1989 shooting rampage at the Cleveland Elementary School in Stockton, California, which claimed the lives of five Southeast Asian children. Days after reading the news about Purdy's massacre of students in Stockton, Wesbecker walked into a local gun store and paid $349 for an AK-47 very much like Purdy's.

Just before massacring his coworkers, Wesbecker left behind, in the kitchen of his home, an issue of *Time* magazine whose cover story, "Armed in America," described Patrick Purdy's shooting spree at the Stockton elementary school. Wesbecker had folded back the pages so that a photograph of Purdy's AK-47 was open and facing up. Wesbecker was every bit as angry as the drifter in Stockton, but his enemy was closer to home. Rather than pin all of his problems on Southeast Asians, Wesbecker blamed his bosses at Standard Gravure.

Patrick Purdy was a young man filled with resentment who went on a deadly rampage of his own. Although he told his half-brother that he would soon make the newspapers—and precisely 4 days later he would indeed become a headliner in the news—Purdy could not have known that his killing spree would help to inspire an act of mass murder in Louisville.

Not unlike the Kentuckian who imitated him, the 25-year-old Purdy was almost always alone, had no girlfriends, and seemed to dislike everyone. He was conspiratorial and paranoid in his thinking. In the end, he singled out a particular group—Southeast Asians—as being especially blameworthy.

For some five years, Purdy had drifted from place to place. Working as a laborer, a security guard, or a welder, he traveled to Connecticut, Nevada, Florida, Oregon, Tennessee, and Texas—to any state where his past might not come back to haunt him. Everywhere he went, Purdy challenged his bosses, and he simply couldn't hold down a job for more than a few weeks at a time.

Along the way, Purdy repeatedly got into trouble with the law. In 1980, he was arrested in Los Angeles for soliciting a sex act from an undercover police officer. In 1982, he was arrested on charges of possession of hashish, and the next year he was convicted of possessing a dangerous weapon. A few months later, he was arrested on a charge of receiving stolen property. In October 1984, he did a 30-day stint in county jail in Woodland, California, for being an accomplice to a robbery.

Three years passed, and Purdy's behavior became increasingly outrageous. In 1987, he was arrested for indiscriminately firing a 9mm pistol in the El Dorado National Forest. On top of this, he was charged with resisting arrest for kicking a deputy sheriff and shattering a window of the patrol car with his feet. While being held in advance of trial, Purdy attempted to commit suicide by hanging himself in his jail cell and slicing open his wrist with his sharpest fingernail. But like everything else he tried, Purdy even failed at taking his own life.

By January 1989, life had become completely hopeless for Purdy. He despised almost everyone, but especially people in positions of authority and especially his "enemies," the newcomers to America's shores. Purdy had a special hatred for Southeast Asians. He often bragged about his father's conquests in the Vietnam War, slaughtering all those "gooks." Purdy fantasized about following in his dad's army bootsteps, but it would have to remain a fantasy because Patrick was only 7 years old when the U.S. forces pulled out of the Vietnam conflict.

Purdy would fight his own war against Southeast Asians. He would try one more time to achieve something big, and this time, his mission would not fail. For weeks, Purdy had been living in Room 104 of the El Rancho Motel on the edge of Stockton, California, a riverfront agricultural city located some 80 miles east of San Francisco. He needed to concentrate, to plot his final assault on those who were to blame for his miserable existence. "General Purdy" spent hour after hour, day after day, in his "war room," manipulating the hundreds of toy soldiers, tanks, jeeps, and weapons that he had collected in order to simulate an attack and to develop an effective military strategy. There were toy soldiers everywhere: on the shelves, on the heating grates, even in the refrigerator.

Purdy prepared himself for battle as well. Perceiving a conspiracy involving people in charge, he displayed symbols of anti-Americanism boldly and loudly. He had carved the words *freedom* and *victory* into the butt of his AK-47 military assault rifle. On the camouflage shirt that he wore over his military jacket, he wrote "PLO," "Libya," and "Death to the great Satin." As reflected by the mistaken inscription for the name of the devil, spelling was never Purdy's strong suit . . . but then, he didn't seem to have any strong suit.

On Tuesday morning, January 17, Purdy donned his military flak jacket, picked up a handgun and his AK-47 semiautomatic assault rifle, and drove his 1977 Chevrolet station wagon a couple of miles to the Cleveland Elementary School in Stockton—the same elementary school he had attended from kindergarten to third grade. But things recently had begun to seem different to him, and it wasn't just having grown older. When he had lived there as a child, the neighborhood was White; now it was predominantly Asian.

Arriving at the Cleveland School just before noon, Purdy could see hundreds of young children—most of them refugees from Cambodia, Vietnam, China, and Mexico. Purdy preferred the term *boat people* when he spoke disparagingly of

Asian refugees. Despite the chill in the air, the children played joyfully at recess on the blacktop in front of the brown stucco building, unaware of the war that would soon be declared.

As a diversionary tactic, Purdy parked his car and then set it ablaze with a Molotov cocktail in a Budweiser bottle. Then, he eased through a gap in the fence surrounding the school building and walked onto the crowded school grounds, where he opened fire.

Over a period of several minutes, Purdy sprayed 60 rounds from his AK-47 at screaming children, firing in a sweeping motion across the blacktop. He showed no emotion; he just leaned back and calmly continued firing as automatically as his weapon. Purdy and his AK-47 were as one, and the romping, playful children, who had their whole lives ahead of them, seemed to him little more than objects, things, or targets.

Purdy didn't stop until he heard the sirens of approaching police cars. No one would take him alive. He removed the handgun from his belt. He had saved this gun for one purpose. Purdy died instantly from a single shot from the gun on which he had written the word *Victory*. Purdy's victory toll was high. Five children, ages 6 through 9, all from Southeast Asia, were dead, and 29 more, in addition to one teacher, were wounded.

Purdy's murderous rampage against innocent children was based, at least in part, on racial hatred. He had frequently made hostile racial comments to coworkers about the influx of Southeast Asians into the United States and had protested bitterly about the large number of Southeast Asian classmates in industrial arts courses he was taking at the local community college. He complained that the newcomers were taking all the jobs, and he resented having to compete with them. Just prior to his unconscionable murder spree, Purdy told another resident of the El Rancho Motel, "The damn Hindus and boat people own everything" (Green, 1989).

Purdy may have been delusional, but he was correct in noting that the demographics in his community had changed dramatically. In less than eight years, the population of Southeast Asian refugees in Stockton had gone from fewer than 1,000 to more than 30,000. In his manner of blaming others for his failures, he prepared himself to fight back against the influx of "yellow people" in his own way.

But Purdy did not choose to attack some workplace that he felt was infested with immigrants, nor did he set his sights on a restaurant or shopping mall populated by newcomers. More to the point, why did Purdy choose this particular set of targets—children in a schoolyard—to carry out his mission?

Purdy did not feel the need to leave behind a note explaining his actions; thus, we can only speculate about his reason—if he had one—for targeting a schoolyard, of all places, in which to carry out his attack. He may have wanted to avenge the difficulties he had experienced with boyhood classmates at the Cleveland School almost 20 years earlier. Perhaps he was angry that the poor education he felt he had received there had left him ill-prepared for life; he had written, in private notes to himself, about how dumb he felt. Or, if his design was to get back at society for his own misfortunes, he may have targeted its most cherished members, children. Perhaps Purdy's thinking was more tactical in deciding that a schoolyard was a fairly confined and well-populated area in which he could easily gun down dozens of victims without risk of being overtaken. Certainly, he wasn't about to pick on someone his own size or anyone equally armed. Whatever the contributing factors, Purdy definitely hated the newcomers from Vietnam and Cambodia who had taken over his old elementary school, if not the entire community. Most likely, he deliberately set his sights on a school that had a majority—more than 70%—Asian population.

Patrick Purdy was a rebel with a cause—actually, in his paranoia, he had plenty of them. Of course, Purdy's victims were total strangers to him and were not responsible for his disappointing existence. To him, they may have seemed no different from the toy soldiers, the plastic Viet Cong, he had maneuvered back in Room 104 of the El Rancho Motel. Yet, at the same time, they were symbols of everything in his life that had gone wrong.

There may be one more important reason why Purdy chose, in January 1989, to target a school to carry out his murderous intentions—the copycat factor. Beginning in May 1988, there was a string of school shootings around the country, all of which were well-publicized nationally and all of which were carried out by adults, not students.

In September 1988, James Wilson of Greenwood, South Carolina, went on a shooting spree at a local elementary school. When the police searched his home, they discovered that Wilson had pinned to his wall a photo of his hero, clipped from the cover of *People* magazine. His hero was Laurie Dann, who had committed a similar crime at a school in Winnetka, Illinois, a few months earlier. Between May 1988 and February 1989, a dozen separate episodes of shootings occurred at schools around the nation, culminating in Patrick Purdy's massacre of Southeast Asian children in Stockton. Just 2 weeks prior to Purdy's rampage, while he was holed up in a cheap Stockton motel room, national TV talk shows devoted hourly episodes to discussions of the schoolyard shootings in Winnetka, Greenwood, and elsewhere.

Patrick Purdy was not the only former student to commit a mass murder at the elementary school he had attended years earlier. In December 2012, the nation was rocked by one of the most horrific school shootings in American history. While the students at Sandy Hook elementary school in the picturesque town of Newtown, Connecticut, were seated in their classrooms, a former student, 20-year old

Photo 16.1 This undated identification photo released Wednesday, April 3, 2013, by Western Connecticut State University in Danbury, Connecticut, shows former student Adam Lanza, who authorities said opened fire inside the Sandy Hook Elementary School in Newtown, on Friday, December 14, 2012, killing 26 students and educators. (Associated Press/Western Connecticut State University)

Adam Lanza, broke through the locked front door of the school and attacked students and faculty with an AR-15 semiautomatic rifle, killing 20 first graders and six adult staffers. He then took his own life by shooting himself in the head. Before attacking at Sandy Hook, Lanza had already shot to death his mother in the Newtown home they had shared.

In the aftermath of the Newtown school massacre, one of the few reforms advocated by both the president and the National Rifle Association involves increasing the presence of resource officers in the schools. This also happens to be one of the few recommendations that has a realistic chance of improving the safety of our children—and it has little if anything to do with having a gun-toting security guard on board when a rampage killer enters the classroom.

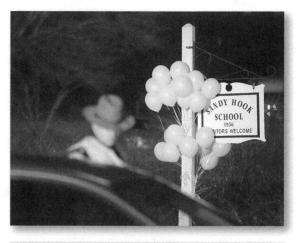

Photo 16.2 White balloons decorate the sign for the Sandy Hook Elementary School as a Connecticut State Trooper stands guard at the school's entrance, Saturday, Dec. 15, 2012, in Newtown, Connecticut. A gunman killed his mother at their home and later walked into Sandy Hook Elementary School Friday and opened fire, killing 26 people, including 20 children. (Associated Press/David Goldman)

In fact, a police presence at Columbine High School in April 1999 didn't stop two students from shooting down 34 of their schoolmates and teachers, killing 13 of them. In February 2008, having police officers on the campus of Northern Illinois University failed to prevent a former student from opening fire in a lecture hall where he killed five and injured another 19. It took 2 minutes to commit mass murder at Northern Illinois; the police arrived only 4 minutes too late but it might as well have taken an hour.

The real contribution of competent, community-minded school resource officers may be more educational than confrontational. Their role in the prevention of rampage murders may not depend so much on carrying a firearm as on carrying a life-saving message to the students and faculty.

According to a study by Eric Madfis (2012), the majority of averted school rampages were thwarted not by metal detectors or surveillance cameras, but because students informed authorities about a threatening remark made by a schoolmate. In too many cases, however, students who become aware of a threat in the hallway or over the Internet have ignored it. To inform on a peer is to "snitch" or "rat"—something that is widely regarded as uncool, even if it has the potential to save lives.

When they achieve the trust and confidence of students, school resource officers may be in an ideal position to provide programs aimed at breaking the culture of silence that has characterized many of our schools in the past. Effective resource officers typically walk the corridors, make connections with the students, and provide educational programs that provide an effective response to natural disasters as well as armed intruders.

In March, 2009, a student at Merrimack High School in New Hampshire approached Michael Murray, a resource officer who had served at the school for more than nine years and was trusted by faculty and students alike. The student informed Murray that he had heard two of his classmates planning to take hostages at the school through the barrel of a gun. Within a few minutes, the two suspects had been apprehended.

School resource officers have also contributed to the resolution of potentially violent school rampages in areas from Anchorage, Alaska, to Bedford, Massachusetts; from Tehama, California, to Lexington County, South Carolina; from Sarasota, Florida, to Laurel, Maryland.

Another function of the school resource officer is to reduce the prevalence of bullying. This is an important antiviolence role, because the overwhelming majority of school rampages have been perpetrated by students who—having being bullied or humiliated on a daily basis—target their classmates. The rampage killers feel like pariahs or outcasts and decide to get even with the entire school.

Some wait until they have graduated to seek revenge. At Virginia Tech in 2007, for example, the killer of 32 innocent college students and faculty chose to target a convenient and vulnerable set of victims on campus who acted as surrogates for his real enemies—his classmates in middle and high school who had humiliated him for his flat affect, shyness, and difficulty with the English language. The Newtown killer may have employed the same psycho-logic. He had reportedly been a student at Sandy Hook Elementary School as well as Newtown's middle and high school, where he may have been a victim of severe bullying. Apparently, his negative experiences in the classroom never left his consciousness, even as an adult.

Most states now have antibullying statutes, but many such laws and policies are less than effective. Schools should be held responsible for allowing such practices to continue unabated. Any school that fails to intervene should face tough sanctions.

Resource officers have established or supported the enactment of effective antibullying programs in their schools. The town of Boaz, Alabama, for example, recently initiated its Stand for the Silent program, an antibullying effort that seeks to teach high school students that it is socially unacceptable to harass or torment their classmates. Aside from their teaching role, resource officers in Boaz High School have also set up designated receptacles in which students can leave anonymous reports of bullying incidents.

The majority of Americans support the notion of resource officers. They now serve in half of all of our public schools. Even if every school in the United States had one, however, there would remain a limit as to how safe and secure we are able to keep our children. Keep in mind that children are everywhere, not only in schools but also on buses and playgrounds, in parks, at community centers, skating rinks, cinemas, daycare and preschool programs, teen centers, swimming pools, and so on.

Hundreds of children are shot down every year not by a semiautomatic rifle with a large capacity magazine wielded by a rampage killer, but by one of the two hundred million small-caliber handguns on the streets and in our homes. Moreover, the largest number of our youthful homicide victims is murdered not by some deranged classmate or stranger, but by their own parents. Typically, it is one shot—one vulnerable victim.

DISGRUNTLED STUDENTS

On October 1, 1997, 16-year-old Luke Woodham walked into a Pearl, Mississippi, high school just hours after having killed his mother. Pulling out a gun from under his trench coat, the chubby, bespectacled youngster immediately murdered two schoolmates and then sprayed bullets into a crowd of students, injuring seven more. His motive? To take over the school, kill all the students, and escape to Cuba.

In the aftermath of the Pearl, Mississippi, shooting spree, parents, teachers, and students around the country became extremely anxious about school safety. Their fears were more than confirmed by subsequent events wherein mass shootings at schools become an all-too-frequent nightmare (see Table 16.1).

Exactly 2 months after Woodham's shooting rampage, 14-year-old Michael Carneal, a freshman at Heath High School in West Paducah, Kentucky, opened fire on an informal prayer circle held in the school's lobby, killing three girls and wounding five other students. On March 24, 1998, two boys, 11-year-old Andrew Golden and 13-year-old Mitchell Johnson, pulled the fire alarm at their Jonesboro, Arkansas, middle school and then began shooting at students and teachers as they filed out of the building. When the gun smoke cleared, four students and a teacher were dead, and many more people were injured.

Months later, school massacres occurred twice more in the same week. On Tuesday, May 19, a Fayetteville, Tennessee, high school senior shot and killed a classmate over a romantic rivalry. Two days later, 15-year-old freshman Kip Kinkel from Springfield, Oregon, armed with a .22-caliber semiautomatic rifle, turned his high school cafeteria into a battlefield after having been suspended the day before for bringing a gun to school. At Thurston High, Kinkel killed two students and wounded 25 more. Earlier, at home, he had killed his parents.

In the aftermath of the widely publicized string of school shootings, most children identified with the pain of the victims. They grieved for slain students whom they knew only through television reports, discussed their fears with parents and classmates, and prayed that history would not repeat itself in their own school.

More than a few students, however—those who, like Kip Kinkel, felt alienated and frustrated—apparently identified instead with the power of the perpetrators. Such feelings are the foundation for the copycat phenomenon. Some of these students may have fantasized about following in their "hero's" footsteps, and a few may have acted on those fantasies. Not only was the new breed of

Table 16.1   Mass Shootings at Schools in the United States, 1996–2012

Date	School, Location	Shooter(s), Age(s)	Victim Count
February 2, 1996	Frontier Junior High Moses Lake, WA	Barry Loukaitis, 14	1 teacher and 2 students killed; 1 wounded
February 19, 1997	Bethel Regional High School Bethel, AL	Evan Ramsey, 16	1 teacher and 1 student killed; 2 wounded
October 1, 1997	Pearl High School Pearl, MS	Luke Woodham, 16	2 students killed; 7 wounded
December 1, 1997	Heath High School West Paducah, KY	Michael Carneal, 14	3 students killed; 5 wounded
March 24, 1998	Westside Middle School Jonesboro, AR	Mitchell Johnson, 13; Andrew Golden, 11	1 teacher and 4 students killed; 10 wounded
May 21, 1998	Thurston High School Springfield, OR	Kipland Kinkel, 15	2 students killed; 25 wounded
April 20, 1999	Columbine High School Littleton, CO	Eric Harris, 18; Dylan Klebold, 17	1 teacher and 12 students killed; 23 wounded (plus 2 suicides)
March 5, 2001	Santana High School Santee, CA	Charles Andrew Williams, 15	2 students killed; 13 wounded
March 21, 2005	Red Lake High School Red Lake, MN	Jeffrey James Weise, 16	7 students killed; 5 wounded (plus suicide)
October 2, 2006	Amish school Nickel Mines, PA	Charles Carl Roberts IV, 33	5 students killed; 5 wounded (plus suicide)
December 14, 2012	Sandy Hook Elementary School Newtown, CT	Adam Peter Lanza, 20	20 students and 6 teachers killed (plus suicide)

youthful mass killers featured on the covers of most national publications, but there were even websites on the Internet that served as tributes to their bold "heroism" and "martyrdom."

At the very least, the copycat phenomenon can determine the timing and form of a murderous attack. If a widely publicized killing occurs at a school, the publicity provides the idea to murder in the classroom rather than at a shopping mall or a law firm. If the publicized killers use firearms, then those who imitate are also likely to use guns rather than a knife, explosives, or a hammer. Finally, the copycat effect is short-lived, causing a number of similar attacks to be committed over a limited period.

For a few disturbed individuals, the publicity given to killers can provide a source of role models, even inspiring some of these individuals to attempt to realize their dreams of stardom and grandeur. There are fads among killers, just as there are fads among dress designers.

The copycat phenomenon tends to occur when a murder receives much media attention. Twenty years ago, a child might have been inspired by his friends down the block. Now, thanks to the pervasiveness of television, that child is just as likely to follow the lead of teenagers in Pearl or Springfield. Like their adult counterparts, teenage killers can be inspired by other real-life killers, but they also may be inspired by fictional portrayals in films and video games. Kip Kinkel had been fascinated with the popular movie version of Shakespeare's *Romeo and Juliet*.

In June 1998, after a seemingly relentless string of school shooting episodes, summer vacation mercifully arrived. Over a 2-month summer vacation, would the contagion effect dissipate? When school opened in the fall, parents were scared. In fact, a 1998 poll conducted by the Shell Oil Company found that three quarters of parents surveyed were very anxious about school shootings and violence, topping the list of school-related concerns, well ahead of worries about peer pressure, declining academic standards, the poor quality of teaching, and limited availability of educational equipment and supplies. For parents, an old adage applied: Safety first.

Despite parental concerns arising from the previous year's bloodshed, the 1998–1999 school year was relatively uneventful—that is, until April 20, 1999, when a school shooting of such immense proportions occurred that public thinking and debate about student safety and security were altered radically, perhaps permanently. After months of planning and preparation, 18-year-old Eric Harris and 17-year-old Dylan Klebold armed themselves with guns and explosives and headed off to Columbine High School in Littleton, Colorado, to celebrate Adolf Hitler's birthday in a manner befitting their hero. By the time their assault ended with self-inflicted fatal gunshots, a dozen students and one teacher lay dead. The police later found an entry in Harris's diary, in which he discussed the pair's plans to blow up Columbine High, then hijack a plane and fly it into the New York City skyline!

In understanding the horrific actions of schoolyard snipers, it is important to examine their relations with peers. At Columbine, Harris and Klebold generally were seen as geeks or nerds from the point of view of many of the large student cliques—the jocks, the punks, and so on. Though excluded from mainstream student culture, they banded together and bonded with several of their fellow outcasts in what some came to call the "Trench Coat Mafia." The image they attempted to create was clearly one of power and dominance—the goth incivility, the forces of darkness, the preoccupation with Hitler, the celebration of evil and villainy. Harris and Klebold desperately wanted to feel important; and in the preparations they made to murder their classmates, the two shooters got

Photo 16.3   Not unlike disgruntled employees, Dylan Klebold and Eric Harris, captured on video as they sought victims in the school cafeteria, turned Columbine High School into their personal battlefield. (Associated Press/ Jefferson County Sheriff's Department)

their wish. For more than a year, they plotted and planned, colluded and conspired to put one over on their schoolmates, teachers, and parents. They amassed an arsenal of weapons, strategized about logistics, and made final preparations—yet, until it was too late, not a single adult got wind of what Harris and Klebold intended to do.

Harris, the leader, likely enjoyed the respect and admiration of Klebold, who in turn probably felt uplifted by the praise he received from his revered buddy. In their relationship, the two boys got from one another what was otherwise missing from their lives: They felt special, they gained a sense of belonging, and they were united against the world. As Harris remarked, as he and his friend made last-minute preparations to commit mass murder, "This is just a two man war against everything else" (O'Driscoll, 1999).

When the scourge of school shootings emerged, some criminologists speculated that it was just the next phase of the youth violence epidemic. What had started in the inner city, according to this view, had spread to Middle America. The issue of lethal violence inside schools struck a nerve with the public. Unlike crack and gang violence, which had infested primarily minority neighborhoods in the urban core, school shootings occurred in suburbs and rural communities that had been largely immune from the urban bloodshed. Indeed, seeming invulnerability to the problems of urban areas may help explain why such extraordinary murders occurred where they did. The residents of towns such as West Paducah, Springfield, Littleton, and Pearl felt impervious to crime, violence, and poverty—what they regarded as big-city problems. As a result, they never prepared for the possibility that teenagers in their town might become so alienated and marginalized as to go on a shooting spree at school to get even with teachers and classmates. Whereas urban schools initiated programs and policies in the area of conflict resolution, peer mediation, and counseling, small-town and suburban schools tended to rest on their laurels.

The copycat effect on the string of murders can be seen in the similarity of personal characteristics of killers. Most of the perpetrators of school violence in the late 1990s were White boys in small-town schools. If the first killers had been Black youngsters from inner-city schools, it is likely that many of the later school massacres would have been committed by other Black, inner-city youth.

Political observers capitalized on the differences in public response to youth homicide in cities versus elsewhere as a clear indication of racism. Most Americans seemed apathetic when, to an increasing extent, Black kids were shooting each other, but once murder spread to the mostly White hinterlands, demands for action were heard loud and clear. Although this allegation is likely valid, there was another major change in the pattern of school violence that cried out for media and public attention—the emergence of mass murder.

During the period when the string of school massacres occurred, the total number of school homicides actually was falling, roughly in parallel to the decline in youth killings generally. Though homicides arising from a conflict between one victim and one perpetrator are newsworthy at the local level, these episodes rarely make national news, whether or not the participants are Black, White, or Latino. The events of the 1997–1998 school year got everyone's attention, all the way to the White House, which established a Presidential Advisory Committee in the wake of an episode in President Bill Clinton's home state of Arkansas. As the body counts grew larger, murder grabbed the attention of the nation.

Mass murder at school by disgruntled pupils was a scary new wrinkle in the problem of school violence. A decade earlier, schoolyards were the targets of unbalanced adults looking to attack society where it hurt the most. School snipers were likely not to be teenagers but instead middle-age adults such as Laurie Dann, the 36-year-old resident of Glencoe, Illinois, who went on a rampage with a .22-caliber handgun in a Winnetka elementary school in May 1988. Actually, there were 12 different school shootings by adults between 1988 and early 1989, the last of which was Patrick Purdy's January assault on the Cleveland Elementary School in Stockton, California.

It is not an incidental fact that the more recent spate of shootings involving student perpetrators also occurred at schools rather than at some other location. Notwithstanding research findings suggesting that most schools do not experience serious forms of violence, the school day itself can present certain issues and risks. Not only do children congregate in large numbers while at school, thereby creating occasions for conflict, but the school setting also can sometimes breed feelings of inadequacy, anxiety, fear, hostility, rejection, and boredom. For some vengeful or alienated children, school can represent an ideal place, both logistically and symbolically, for getting even or settling a score.

The episode in Littleton, Colorado, more than one decade ago, was so powerfully and deeply ingrained in the nation's collective psyche that "doing a Columbine" became a widely known code for threatening the safety and security of a school. After Columbine, schools around the nation went on red alert. Many heightened security—employing metal detectors, surveillance cameras, and even armed guards—to try to protect the school setting from the latest threat. Some schools went as far as to institute "Columbine drills" to prepare faculty and students to respond appropriately should a student open fire in a hallway or classroom. Several legislators around the country even proposed a concealed weapons law for teachers, suggesting that arming the faculty would serve as a deterrent; none of the proposals gathered much political support.

Administrators also responded with tough zero-tolerance policies against weapons or even menacing words, putting students on notice that guns, knives, or threats of violence would not be tolerated.

None of these quick fixes appears to have significantly reduced the risk of schoolyard mass murder, but many of them remain in force today. A number of administrators responded at another level by attempting to deal with the fundamental core issues such as bullying and the climate of fear that pervades many schools around the country. Their efforts have recently led most states—at least 41—to enact antibullying statutes.

A GLOBAL PERSPECTIVE

According to Madfis and Jack Levin (2013), the majority of school rampage shootings outside of the United States have involved chronic bullying as well as a longstanding desire for revenge. In January 2003, for example, Edmar Freitas went back to his former high school in Tajuva, Brazil, where he opened fire on eight students and faculty members. The 18-year-old former student, because he was overweight, had been regularly humiliated by his classmates since the age of seven. Before committing suicide, he decided to get even through the barrel of a .38 caliber pistol (Morena, 2011).

Table 16.2 displays information pertaining to a number of school massacres occurring since the year 2000 in countries outside the United States. In Emsdetten, Germany, 18-year-old Sebastian Bosse injured 27 people at his former school in November 2006 because he wanted revenge in what his suicide note called "a revolution of the rejected" against the students who had made his life miserable at school (Böckler, Seeger, & Heitmeyer, 2010, p. 281). Similarly, Pekka-Eric Auvinen shot to death the principal, a school nurse, six students, and himself at his high school in Jokela, Finland, in November 2007 after being frequently bullied by his schoolmates since the fourth grade (Kiilakoski & Oksanen, 2011). In September 2008, Matti Juhani Saari entered the Kauhajoki School of Hospitality in Kauhajoki, Finland, where he shot to death nine students and then took his own life. For years, Saari reportedly had been a victim of bullying by his classmates. His high school classmates had targeted Saari for hurtful name-calling, pranks, and physical attacks (Kiilakoski & Oksanen, 2011). In March 2009, 17-year-old Tim Kretschmer killed nine students and three teachers at his former high school in Winnenden, Germany. Kretschmer had long been mocked by other students ("German school rampage," 2009; Rayner & Bingham, 2009). In April, 2011, 23-year-old Wellington Menezes de Oliveira shot to death 12 students at his alma mater, the Tasso da Silveira School in Rio de Janeiro, Brazil. The killer was constantly being harassed by other students in part because of a physical disability. In a video recorded two days prior to his rampage, he suggested that he sought revenge for all "who have been humiliated, attacked, and disrespected for being different" ("Rio school massacre," 2011).

Bullying was not, however, the only form of long-term frustration which school rampage shooters in countries around the world had experienced.

Table 16.2   Mass Shootings in Schools Outside the United States 2000–2011

Date of Rampage	Shooter's Name, Age	Killed and Injured	If suicide	Location	If bullied	If student	Victim type
April 26, 2002	R. Steinhäuser, 19	16/6	Yes	Erfurt, Germany	No	Former	Staff and students
October 21, 2002	H.Y. Xiang, 36	2/5	No	Melbourne, Australia	No	Current	Staff and students
January 27, 2003	E.A. Freitas, 18	0/8	Yes	Taiuva, Brazil	Yes	Former	Staff and students
June 6, 2003	A. Boonkwan, 17	2/4	No	Pak Phanang, Thailand	?	Current	Students only
September 28, 2004	R. Solich, 15	3/5	No	Patagones, Argentina	?	Current	Students only
September 13, 2006	K.S. Gill, 25	1/19	Yes	Montreal, Canada	Yes	Former	Students only
November 20, 2006	S. Bosse, 18	0/5	Yes	Emsdetten, Germany	Yes	Former	Staff and students
November 7, 2007	P. Auvinen, 18	8/0	Yes	Jokela, Finland	Yes	Current	Staff and students
September 23, 2008	M. J. Saari, 22	9/0	Yes	Kauhajoki, Finland	Yes	Current	Students only
March 11, 2009	T. Kretschmer, 17	15/9	Yes	Winnenden, Germany	Yes	Former	Staff and students
April 7, 2011	W.M. Oliveira, 24	12/20	Yes	Rio de Janeiro, Brazil	Yes	Former	Students only

Unlike most of their counterparts in the United States, school shooters in other countries had been plagued with persistent academic failure. For example, Robert Steinhäuser's school shooting in Erfurt, Germany, on April 26, 2002, was less akin to those of his bullied American student counterparts and more like many workplace avengers who feel as though they have been unjustly fired or overlooked for accomplishments and promotions

(Fox & Levin, 1994). Robert Steinhäuser had a longstanding reputation as a lazy student who had been repeatedly disciplined for truancy and negligence by his teachers. Hence, his primary targets were teachers rather than peers. According to eyewitnesses, Steinhäuser aimed his weapon only at the teachers, although two students were killed by shots fired through a locked door. During a period of high unemployment, Steinhäuser believed he had been robbed by the faculty of his only opportunity to be accepted into a college and to have a successful career (Gasser, Creutzfeldt, Naher, Rainer, & Wickler, 2004).

ON TO COLLEGE

Forty-one-year-old Robert Flores Jr., a student in the nursing program at the University of Arizona, was struggling in his coursework and facing academic withdrawal. But before that could happen, he chose a different route for ending his career pursuit—murder and suicide. On October 28, 2002, he set out to execute the nursing faculty whom he apparently blamed for his academic failures. First, he hunted down one of his instructors in her second-floor office, shooting her point blank at her desk. Next, he moved to a fourth-floor classroom and fatally shot two more of his professors as a classroom of about 20 students looked on in horror and disbelief. Having accomplished his objective for the day, even though it was probably not as fulfilling as the unattainable one that brought him to the university, he ordered the students out of the classroom and then took his own life.

Prior to the campus massacre, Flores had typed a 22-page letter of explanation, titled "Greetings from the Dead," and mailed it to the local newspaper. In this portion of the letter, his view of the responsible parties—the pompous and uncaring faculty—is crystal clear. Although he denied feeling vengeful, his characterization of the faculty, not to mention his subsequent actions directed against them, suggests otherwise:

> To the sociologist, it wasn't the Maryland sniper. I have been thinking about this for a while. To the psychiatrist, it's not about unresolved childhood issues. It is not about anger because I don't feel anything right now. To Ellen Goodman, it is not about gun control. I have had guns for a long time and it was my trade in the military. I do not have gun magazines. A waiting period or owner registration would not have stopped me. I have a concealed carry permit but I have never brought a gun to the University (until now). I was a boy scout. I cross the street at the crosswalk. It is not about revenge as I have always thought that revenge was a waste of time and energy. I guess what it is about is that it is a reckoning. A settling of accounts. The University is filled with too many people who are filled with hubris. They feel untouchable. Students are not given respect nor regard. It is unfortunate that the only force that seems to get any attention from the University is economic force.

Whereas the 1990s brought focus to conduct and disciplinary issues confronting secondary schools, a radically different form of campus violence has commanded our attention in recent years—specifically, shooting rampages at colleges and universities, highlighted by massacres at Virginia Tech and Northern Illinois University less than 10 months apart. Although incidents at middle schools, high schools, and institutions of higher education all fall under the umbrella of school shootings, there are, in fact, several characteristics of mass shootings at college campuses that make them unique.

The most striking and important distinction surrounds issues that motivate campus shooters and their younger counterparts. Shootings at high schools are often precipitated when students feel bullied or persecuted by their classmates or teachers (Vossekuil, Reddy, Fein, Borum, & Modzeleski, 2002). However, the perpetrators of multiple shootings at colleges and universities are often graduate or professional students—older individuals who turn to violence in response to what they perceive to be unbearable pressure to succeed or the unacceptable reality of failure (Fox & Burstein, 2010). As shown in Table 16.3, at least half of the multiple-victim campus shooting sprees implicated a current or former graduate or professional student or a faculty member. Rather few were committed by traditional-age undergraduates.

Unlike undergraduates, students in graduate and professional programs often lack balance in their personal lives, narrowly focusing on academic work and training to the exclusion of other interests and other people in their lives. Students who had been at the top of their class in high school and college may come to find themselves struggling to get by with just passing grades. No longer supported financially by parents, they experience great pressure to juggle assistantship activities or outside employment with coursework and thesis research, with little time for attending to social networks. At some point, their entire lifestyle and sense of worth may revolve around academic achievement. Moreover, their personal investment in reaching a successful outcome can be viewed as a virtual life-or-death matter. Compounding the problem is the fact that faculty mentors, the gatekeepers to success, may be insensitive to the pressures placed upon their students. At the extreme, some faculty may even maintain an oppressive relationship with graduate students, perhaps perpetuating a power imbalance they themselves suffered in graduate school. Regrettably, not all faculty members are sensitive to the enormous and often unrestrained power they have over students.

Foreign students experience additional pressures because the academic visas allowing them to remain in this country are often dependent upon their continued student status or full-time employment. Also the stress factor related to the need to succeed, if not excel, is frequently intensified for foreign graduate students from certain cultures where failure is seen as shame on the entire family.

Cultural factors may help to explain the surprising number of college campus shootings that have occurred at the hands of Asian students, even though murder rates overall are low among Asians (both Asian immigrants to the United States as well as native populations in Asian countries). Seung-Hui Cho,

Table 16.3   Multiple Shootings at Colleges and Universities in the United States, 1991–2013

Date	School	Shooter, Age	Role at School
November 1, 1991	University of Iowa	Gang Lu, 28	Graduate student
August 24, 1992	Concordia University	Valery I. Fabrikant, 52	Faculty
December 14, 1992	Simon's Rock College	Wayne Lo, 18	Undergraduate student
January 26, 1995	University of North Carolina	Wendell Williamson, 26	Former law student
August 15, 1996	San Diego State University	Frederick Davidson, 36	Graduate student
June 28, 2000	University of Washington	Jan Chen, 42	Medical student
August 28, 2000	University of Arkansas	James Easton Kelly, 36	Former graduate student
May 17, 2001	Pacific Lutheran University	Donald Cowan, 55	None
January 16, 2002	Appalachian School of Law	Peter Odighizuwa, 42	Former law student
October 28, 2002	University of Arizona	Robert Flores, 40	Nursing student
September 2, 2006	Shepherd University	Douglas Pennington, 49	Parent of students
April 16, 2007	Virginia Tech	Seung-Hui Cho, 23	Undergraduate student
February 8, 2008	Louisiana Tech	Latina Williams, 23	Undergraduate student
February 14, 2008	Northern Illinois University	Steven Kazmierczak, 27	Former graduate student
October 26, 2008	University of Central Arkansas	Four teenagers	None
April 10, 2009	Henry Ford Community College	Anthony Powell, 28	Student
February 12, 2010	University of Alabama, Huntsville	Amy Bishop, 45	Faculty
March 9, 2010	Ohio State University	Nathaniel Brown, 51	Custodian
May 10, 2011	San Jose State University	Napoleon Lavarias Caliguiran, 54	Spouse of student
April 2, 2012	Oikos University	One L. Goh, 43	Former nursing student
January 15, 2013	Hazard Community College	Dalton Lee Stidham, 21	Ex-boyfriend of a student
June 7, 2013	Santa Monica College	John Zawahri, 23	None

the Virginia Tech gunman, struggled throughout his violence-shortened life in terms of assimilating to American culture. In addition, 7 students were killed during an April 2012 shooting rampage at Oikos University in Oakland, California, a small private college primarily for students of Korean descent. The Korean-born shooter, One L. Goh, 43, had recently been expelled. The most telling example, however, involved an accomplished graduate student from China, who felt humiliated and betrayed when not being considered the very best in his class.

By the fall of 1991, after having failed in repeated efforts to have a perceived injustice reversed, Chinese-born Gang Lu knew that his best and last resort was a firearm. For this 28-year-old grad student, things had changed dramatically. In the course of a few years, he went from being widely considered a rising star in his program to an object of shame and pity.

In 1985, Gang Lu had been chosen for a coveted doctoral fellowship in physics at the University of Iowa. But achievement never came easy for Gang Lu, as he had toiled hard in school throughout his life, painstakingly preparing for national science tests given by the Chinese government to identify the academic elite. Unfortunately for Gang Lu, within a year after entering the program at the University of Iowa, a brighter doctoral prospect arrived in the department who was also from his homeland of China—a younger, handsome, charismatic rival for whom everything—not just academics—came easily.

It didn't take long for Linhua Shan, the new arrival, to eclipse Gang Lu in his pursuit of excellence. For Gang Lu, the final straw came when Shan was nominated by the department for outstanding doctoral dissertation. Unable to think objectively, Gang Lu couldn't accept that Shan's thesis was brilliant, while his own was just competent and workmanlike—nothing that would turn the scientific community on its ear.

Gang Lu's disappointment was only part of the problem. Failure to win the D.C. Spriestersbach dissertation prize would deny him a significant advantage in seeking a tenure-track post in the tight job market. He felt his work had been judged unfairly by the department chair and other professors who had the power to nominate the prize winner. From Gang Lu's perspective, they would have to pay for destroying his chances, ruining his life, and bringing shame upon him.

After several attempts to appeal the decision up through the university's administrative hierarchy, Gang Lu saw only one way to even the score. He appointed himself judge, jury, and executioner.

On November 1, 1991, after months of anguish and detailed planning, Lu launched his all-out assault. He knew that his adversaries would be gathered at a regular Friday afternoon physics department seminar held in Room 309 of Van Allen Hall. Shortly after 3:30 p.m., Lu removed from his briefcase his doomsday device, a .38-caliber revolver that he had purchased in July during the early stages of his planning. Without saying a word—he didn't need to, as everyone was already painfully aware of his grudge—Lu started blasting away. He killed Professors Christoph Goertz and Robert Alan Smith, both members of his dissertation committee, and shot Linhua Shan, his "successful" rival for the prize.

Lu then traveled down the hall and killed the department chair, Dwight Nicholson. Next, he went across campus to "discuss" matters with T. Anne

Cleary, Associate Vice President for Academic Affairs, with whom he had filed an appeal. Lu let his gun do the talking, killing Cleary and wounding her receptionist, who was little more than an impediment along his murder route. Lu then returned to the physics department to finish off Shan, who had briefly survived his injuries. Having done what he came to do, he had only one final element to his plan—suicide.

Lu had worked out every detail of his rampage, and he was chillingly methodical in his implementation. In 12 short minutes of terror on campus, he got his revenge, having killed five members of the university community and wounded one more.

It is difficult for many people outside the academic world to appreciate the concepts of academic life and academic death. The phrases "publish or perish" and "curriculum vitae" both reflect the virtual life-and-death significance of academic achievement and failure. Gang Lu understood this and felt that his career was doomed before it had begun.

THE ROLE OF VIOLENT VIDEO GAMES

Besides imitation of notorious crimes and criminals, fictional portrayals of murder and mayhem can also potentially provide a source for modeling behavior. Certainly, concern over the negative impact of violent entertainment is hardly new. However, the realism of today's entertainment options has intensified the debate.

It can be tempting to try to blame entertainment media—especially video games—for various stunning episodes of extreme violence. A Gallup poll taken in the wake of the April 1999 Columbine massacre found that 62% of the over 1,000 adults surveyed nationwide felt that entertainment media was a major cause of school violence (Newport, 1999), and 83% supported restrictions on sales of violent media to children (see Carlson, 2002). Furthermore, a Gallup poll of approximately 1,000 adults nationwide taken immediately following the December 2012 Sandy Hook shooting found that 78% of respondents believed that reducing the depiction of gun violence in entertainment media would be effective in decreasing the risk of mass shootings (Newport, 2012).

It is not surprising that most schoolyard shooters (as well as some adult mass murderers) played violent video games in their spare time. Violent people are often attracted to violent entertainment, on TV, in film, or through game consoles. But, the ability to document a direct causal link indicating that consuming violent entertainment leads to violent behavior has eluded social science researchers for years (Brief of Social Scientists, 2010; Ferguson, 2011; Grimes, Anderson, & Bergen, 2008).

Much was written in the popular press about the fact that Sandy Hook shooter Adam Lanza spent long hours alone in the basement of his Newtown home playing violent video games and had a rich collection of titles that featured military-style warfare (see, for example, Edelman, 2013). Reportedly, his favorite was "Call to Duty," also a game frequently played by Norwegian mass murderer 32-year-old Anders Breivik and 34-year-old Aaron Alexis who in 2013 killed 12 at the Washington, DC, Navy Yard.

In Lanza's case, his obsessional game-playing may have been more a symptom of his personality and temperament than the cause. As a socially awkward youngster, reportedly with Asperger's syndrome, his social isolation may be the key to his preoccupation with gaming as well as his rampage against an unwelcoming society. Moreover, the large number of hours he devoted to his gaming may in part have just filled the void left by his withdrawal from interpersonal relationships with real people rather than virtual characters.

The entertainment industry has, at times, been used as a convenient scapegoat, and censorship as an easy solution. Lawsuits directed against various media organizations have occasionally been launched, albeit unsuccessfully, when it was discovered that some mass murderer had been obsessed with violent entertainment.

Fourteen-year-old Michael Carneal, who killed three classmates and wounded five others at the Heath High School in West Paducah, Kentucky, was a fan of *Basketball Diaries*—a 1995 film in which a high school hoops star, played by Leonardo DiCaprio, daydreams of shooting up his high school class. Carneal also enjoyed playing violent video games, including *Doom* and *Quake*. Within months of the shooting spree, the parents of the three slain children filed a $130 million lawsuit naming the producers and distributors of *Basketball Diaries*, as well as computer game companies and two Internet pornography sites, for their alleged role in causing Carneal's violent outburst. The legal long-shot fizzled in August 2002, when a Federal appeals court in Cincinnati dismissed the case, ruling that it was "simply too far a leap from shooting characters on a video screen to shooting people in a classroom" (James v. Meow Media, Inc., 2002).

Concerns about the negative effects of violent video games on impressionable children also led to the passage of a 2005 California ban on the sale of such game to minors, although the U.S. Supreme Court ultimately judged the prohibition to be unconstitutional in a 7–2 decision ruling on *Brown v. Entertainment Media Association* (2011). It has long been easy to point fingers at this profitable industry, while ignoring some of the root causes of violence that are much more difficult to resolve.

SHOOTING FOR INFAMY

The string of schoolyard mass shootings that occurred during the late 1990s and early 2000s had the American public wondering what was different about schools and the students attending them. However, the clustering of several school massacres within a few years of each other was at least to some extent, if not mostly, the result of copycatting—or contagion—than any fundamental and lasting shift in adolescent behavior patterns. In other words, exposure to massive media coverage of shootings and their aftermaths can potentially encourage imitators. Not only are children and adolescents exposed to the idea of getting even for perceived injustices through violence, but they are taught that such violence can earn them celebrity status. Indeed, more than the media coverage itself, it is the notoriety that popular culture showers on school shooters that teaches our youth—especially alienated and marginalized teenagers—a lesson about how to get attention and how to be in the spotlight.

This so-called copycat effect, while widely accepted in the popular media, has had only limited attention in scholarly research. Spencer Kostinsky, Edward O. Bixler, and Paul Kettl (2001) provided some empirical support for the imitative effect spurred by the Columbine High School shooting by analyzing reports of threats of violence against students, faculty, or the school that were submitted under state mandate to the Pennsylvania Emergency Management Association (PEMA). Examining the daily counts of all threat reports following the Columbine shooting, the researchers noted a sharp spike immediately after the April 1999 massacre and then a gradual decline thereafter. Because the state reporting requirement was implemented only after the Columbine shooting, there were no comparable data prior to the episode. However, interviews of school officials suggested that threats had previously been a much rarer occurrence.

It is not clear whether the large jump in the number of reported threats following Columbine reflected a genuine increase in threatening acts or just an increased readiness of school officials to alert state authorities to such events. Although students may have been more apt to make threats in response to the massive attention given the two Columbine shooters, it is also possible that school personnel were more inclined to interpret virtually any level of threat as a sign of danger. Similarly, as time passed, students were likely distracted by other matters from issues—from studying for finals to preparing for the prom—and school officials may have become less skittish in dealing with routine disciplinary matters. The copycat effect, therefore, can influence both the one who makes a threat and the one who receives and responds to it.

The copycat effect is not so much about the nature of a crime but the extent to which it is covered, the way in which it is portrayed, and the context in which it is described. All of these factors were seen in the extreme—and not for the best—in the aftermath of the April 16, 2007, mass shooting at Virginia Tech in which 23-year-old Seung-Hui Cho killed 32 and wounded 17 others at the normally quiet and serene campus in Blacksburg. The media approach to the crime was unrestrained and ubiquitous, increasing the potential for others to follow in the gunman's bloody footsteps.

The shooting spree started in the early morning hours. By 7:15 a.m., the campus police had received a 911 call concerning a double homicide at Ambler Johnston Hall—an incident that the authorities were quick to regard as a domestic dispute turned fatal. By this theory, the campus was no longer in danger and no further steps were needed to protect the campus community. Of course, what the campus officials did not realize at the time was that the killer was still alive and had taken a break from what would be a much more devastating rampage—a break to make a planned and important errand at the post office.

Just as the campus was settling into the normal weekday routine, gunfire erupted suddenly and ferociously at Norris Hall, which was home to the School of Engineering and also contained numerous classrooms. In a manner typical of deliberate mass murderers, Cho had entered the building, chain-locked the main entrance to secure it from intruders, and even placed a sign warning of an explosion should anyone tamper with the makeshift barricade. Over the next several minutes, Cho executed 25 students and five faculty members who were misfortunate enough to stand in his path of destruction.

Equipped with their mobile satellite trucks, the news media quickly blanketed the Blacksburg campus. The coverage on the cable channels was nonstop. As the reported death count rose, so did the intensity level of those whose job it was to relay the news to the millions of Americans who were glued to their television sets.

When the carnage reached 20 dead, reporters proclaimed this a new record for school shootings—a breaking development embellished by streaming and screaming alerts on the screen. The Virginia Tech shooting had indeed eclipsed Charles Whitman's infamous 1966 tower-top shooting at the University of Texas, a murderous mark of distinction that had survived for more than four decades despite the bloody episodes at Columbine High School and elsewhere. The TV anchors, talk-show hosts, and various talking heads all seemed to be quite impressed, if not obsessed, with the enormity of the Virginia Tech carnage.

Photo 16.4 This photo of 23-year-old Seung-Hui Cho was part of a multimedia packet he sent to NBC News during his shooting rampage at Virginia Tech where he killed 32 and wounded 17 others. (NBC/ Author)

Within hours, as the death toll climbed higher and higher, there was more "breaking news." With more than 30 victims dead at two locations on Virginia Tech's campus, the record for the largest mass shooting of any type and at any venue—previously held by George Hennard for his 1991 massacre at the Luby's Restaurant in Killeen, Texas—had been shattered. For the remainder of the day and evening, viewers were told repeatedly that this had been the biggest, the bloodiest, the absolute worst, the most devastating, or whatever other superlatives came to mind.

Notwithstanding the cruel absurdity of treating human suffering as any sort of achievement worthy of measuring in such terms, there is little positive that can be derived by keeping or highlighting such records. But there is one significant negative: Records are made to be broken.

Of course, the overwhelming majority of Americans who watched the news and listened to the videotaped sounds of semiautomatic gunfire would have identified with the pain and suffering of the victims, their families, and the entire campus community. However, a few would instead have identified with the power of the perpetrator.

Some Americans share and perhaps empathize with the frustration and alienation felt by the Virginia Tech shooter, even going so far as to view him as a hero. Imagine a narrative in which the campus shooter is revered as someone with the guts to take matters—and guns—into his own hands and strike back at some perceived injustice. An intense focus on records invites challengers to mimic and even outperform their role models.

In the weeks following the Virginia Tech massacre, there was no one—fortunately—who even came close to challenging Cho's top ranking in the mass murder list, but many were encouraged to fantasize at least about mimicking the man whose acts they perceived as bold and heroic. Dozens of threats were reported on college campuses around the country. Of course, part of this rise in threatening behavior may not just suggest a copycat effect but may reflect greater nervousness among college officials to treat any threatening words or gestures as a genuine sign of trouble.

Cho's position in mass murder lore is more than just his record victim count. His side trip to the post office was for the purpose of sending a package to NBC television—and a message to America—about his grievances. It didn't take long before executives at the network, upon receiving a videotape from Cho, decided to air the tape rather than just hand it over to the authorities. Apparently, it was too good of a ratings opportunity to pass. Thanks to NBC, and the countless media outlets that followed suit, Cho's place in history was sealed.

A CLOSE COPY

The April 2007 Virginia Tech massacre reverberated much like Columbine in terms of copycat threats of violence. Within days, threats of bloodshed, often with references to the Virginia Tech shooting, prompted lockdowns or evacuations at college and high school campuses around the country.

As if the horror wasn't newsworthy enough, NBC decided to release the menacing photographs and video that the gunman Seung-Hui Cho had mailed to the network on the very day of his shooting. It didn't take long for Seung-Hui Cho, posthumously, to become as big as the Columbine duo of Klebold and Harris in terms of undeserved celebrity. However, although Cho's image seems to have had greater exposure than did the Columbine shooters, the fact that he was Korean, rather than Caucasian like the majority of Americans, actually limited the extent to which he would challenge Klebold and Harris as an iconic role model for others.

The contagion effect is much more profound when the imitator shares characteristics with the role model, prompting copiers to identify with their hero of sorts. Not by coincidence, the mass shootings at middle and high schools in the late 1990s almost exclusively implicated White teenagers in small towns or rural areas. Of course, the incidence of school shootings in such unlikely locales as Jonesboro, Arkansas; West Paducah, Kentucky; and Pearl, Mississippi, may also have been a consequence of the lack of security preparedness in rural areas. Alternatively, Katherine S. Newman, Cybelle Fox, and David Harding (2007) argued that in rural and small towns, it can be more difficult to escape the humiliation of failure in an environment where everyone knows everything—especially the dirt. However, copycatting could also help to account for the small-town thread linking these schoolyard massacres. When some White kid from a small town is widely publicized after shooting up his high school in response to repeated bullying, some other White teenager from small-town America would tend to identify with the shooter and his predicament much more than some Black student attending an inner-city school.

ADULT COPYCATS

The late 1990s was not the only time when schools were under siege by armed assailants. A decade earlier, the fears of parents and school officials were focused on school intruders—adults, not children—who used defenseless students as surrogate targets to exact a measure of revenge against society. From the assailant's perspective, what better way to have an impact than to terrorize society's most cherished and defenseless members?

After the armed assaults by Laurie Dann and subsequently by James Wilson, several other schools were targeted, seemingly at random, by adults. Although most of the episodes did not result in any fatalities of students or faculty, it appeared to be open season on schools and schoolyards. After several months and many shootings, the string of shootings came to a horrific end when Patrick Purdy set sight—literally—on the Cleveland Elementary School in Stockton, California, to vent his anger.

The late 1980s' pattern of armed assaults at schools by adult outsiders reemerged nearly two decades later with three separate incidents shortly after the start of school in 2006. On September 27, 53-year-old Duane Roger Morrison took siege of the Platte Canyon High School in Bailey, Colorado, not very far from the site of the Columbine shootings. Armed with a revolver and a semiautomatic, Morrison held hostage six female students whom he also sexually assaulted. He eventually released most of his hostages but killed one girl when she tried to escape. The day of terror ended when Morrison turned the gun on himself.

Just one week later, in another incident having a sexual motive, 32-year-old Charles Carl Roberts IV took hostages at a one-room Amish schoolhouse in Pennsylvania. Roberts ordered the male students and adult females to leave but maintained control of 10 young Amish girls inside the small building. Roberts came prepared with a shotgun and handgun, material for tying up the girls, barricade equipment, and candles, toilet paper, and other supplies suggesting that he planned for an extended stand-off with the police. Phoning his wife from the scene, Roberts confessed that he had fantasized about molesting girls for years. As it happened, the police arrived sooner than Roberts had anticipated, giving him little opportunity to rape any of his hostages. He did, however, shoot all 10 at close range, killing five of them.

OVERSTATING THE COPYCAT EFFECT?

In his 2008 book, *School Shootings: What Every Parent and Educator Needs to Know to Protect Our Children*, Joseph A. Lieberman discusses several cult-hero icons who appear to have influenced Virginia Tech shooter Seung-Hui Cho. Of course, Cho's admiration for the two Columbine shooters, Dylan Klebold and Eric Harris, was clearly reflected in both his writings and recordings. But Lieberman also suggests some fascinating, yet questionable, connections between Cho and Kimveer Gill, a 25-year-old who opened fire at Dawson College in Montreal in September 2006, killing one and wounding 19 before taking his own life.

In explaining Cho's actions, Lieberman emphasizes the similarity between Cho's widely disseminated photographs and videos and those that Gill recorded prior to his deadly assault at Dawson College. Both Cho and Gill are shown brandishing weapons and pointing their guns straight at the camera lens. However, in the YouTube era, where young adults routinely upload video clips of themselves, is it that unusual for two young campus shooters both to chronicle their violent potential in this way? And how unique would it be for someone posing with guns for the camera to aim a weapon menacingly at the lens? Cho may not have been influenced by Gill in any way; both shooters may have been coincidently motivated by the same desire to document their murderous plans.

Attempts to prove the copycat effect through anecdotal evidence don't always lead to solid conclusions that can be generalized. Many fine scholars have been misled, for example, by a widely repeated tale about the 1996 school shooting by 14-year-old Barry Loukaitis and the influence of the novel *Rage,* published two decades earlier by Stephen King using the pseudonym Richard Bachman. In King's story, a high school student takes his algebra class hostage at gunpoint after killing two teachers. Loukaitis, who owned the book and had read it several times, similarly barged into his math class dressed in a long trench coat and armed with two pistols and a high-powered rifle. After killing a teacher and two students, Loukaitis said sardonically, "This sure beats algebra, doesn't it?"—a line reportedly lifted straight from *Rage.*

This often-repeated illustration of copycatting is quite intriguing, but also not exactly accurate. Although Loukaitis did make the remark, no such line appears in King's book. The closest is when King's assailant makes the wisecrack, "This sure beats panty raids." As rumors and legends often develop, the curious connection was first reported in a national news story published in the *New York Times.* Because of sharp criticism of the book, including allegations that it may have recklessly helped to inspire a wave of school shootings, Stephen King insisted that his publisher take *Rage* out of print. Since that time, many others have told the tale of "sure beats algebra" without checking the actual text of *Rage.* This does not mean, of course, that Loukaitis was unaffected by King's writings in a more general way, just not exactly as rumored.

CHAPTER 17

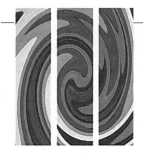

Fighting City Hall

On October 15, 1992, John T. Miller, a 50-year-old "deadbeat dad," murdered four county workers in Watkins Glen, New York, who were responsible for collecting child support money. Having been arrested several times over a span of 20 years for nonpayment of child support, Miller was on the run from a system that he felt was stacked against men like himself. He felt victimized. Even though his daughter had matured into her late 20s and was now on her own, he was still compelled to pay $6,780 in arrearages. Moreover, he had never married the woman who had filed the claim against him, and he denied that the girl was his. Still, he refused to consent to a blood test that might have proven his lack of paternity and absolved him of legal responsibility.

After years in hiding, the system caught up with Miller while he worked as a driver for New Era Trucking, Inc., of North Ridgeville, Ohio. Upset upon discovering that his paycheck suddenly had been reduced, Miller learned from his supervisor that the court in Schuyler County, New York, had begun to garnish his wages.

Frustrated and angry, Miller drove nonstop to Watkins Glen to try to resolve the dispute that he had thought was behind him. Speaking with supervisor Florence Pike at the Schuyler County Courthouse, he was told that "it was no mistake and there is nothing that we can do" (Stanley, 1992).

The next day, Miller closed his "account" for good. At 10 a.m., he returned to the courthouse, carrying a briefcase and a duffle bag filled with ammunition. He walked up the stairs and into the child support office on the second floor. It was payback time. Removing a 9mm semiautomatic pistol from his briefcase, he immediately shot 48-year-old Nancy Wheeler, a senior account clerk in the child support unit. Walking across the hall to another office, Miller shot, in quick succession, Florence Pike, age 50; investigator Phyllis Caslin, age 54; and part-time account clerk Denise Van Amburg, age 28.

Deputy Sheriff Alfred Foote was quick to arrive on the scene from his office on the first floor, but not quick enough to save the lives of Miller's four female victims. After ordering the building to be evacuated, Foote and other officers cornered the gunman in the second-floor hallway where he stood poised with his pistol pointed at his head.

Foote tried to defuse the situation by asking the gunman if he needed any assistance. But Miller was calm, notwithstanding his suicidal pose, and assured the deputy that no one else was in danger. "Nobody can help me now," said the gunman. "I have hurt everyone I was going to hurt" (Stanley, 1992).

"He told us that people didn't have to hurry," recalled Foote. "They could take their time, that he had done what he had come there to do" (Stanley, 1992).

Miller then started talking about the child support payments and became agitated. "The people here have ruined my life," he yelled. "I can't get a job or a wife because I owe so much child support" (Stanley, 1992). Miller then walked in a small circle, as though to gather courage, and pulled the trigger, ending his life.

ATTACKING THE SYSTEM

Multiple murders aimed at "the system" often appear indiscriminate or random, but these acts are more selective than they look. Miller chose his victims not because they, as individuals, were directly responsible for his financial plight—they represented the organization that he thought was unfair and that he blamed for his problems.

In today's modern, complex world, more and more people are forced to deal on a daily basis with megasystems—large and impersonal bureaucratic organizations. When things go wrong and a client or customer has a complaint, who in the megasystem should be held accountable? In Miller's case, where did the buck stop? The boss who deducted money from his paycheck was only obeying the law. The clerks in the child support office were only carrying out a court order issued elsewhere. The judge who issued the order had an obligation to impose the law. To get reparations, Miller didn't target any one of these participants in particular; he targeted the entire system.

Mass murder in the workplace, therefore, is not limited to just embittered employees or former employees. Miller's four victims were murdered at their work site, but not his work site. It isn't only workers and former workers who blame their problems on a "company," that is, a public agency or private firm. Disgruntled customers and clients sometimes seek to avenge perceived mistreatment by banks, loan offices, law firms, and courthouses through mass murder.

Rather than blame the boss, certain mass killers who cannot hold a decent job and suffer from serious personal problems might lay the responsibility for their hardships at the doorstep of some local institution and its clients. This is especially the case when the institution in question has been unsuccessful in assisting its client to assimilate into the mainstream of society.

In April, 2009, Jiverly Wong—a 42-year-old Vietnamese immigrant—was despondent about having lost his job at a Shop Vac assembly plant in Binghamton, New York. His anger was not, however, directed toward the company, but instead toward the nonprofit American Civic Association, whose mandate involved helping immigrants in the Binghamton area with counseling and resettlement. Wong's facility with the English language was extremely marginal, and he seemed to blame the immigration service center.

Wong arrived at the association in downtown Binghamton as a citizenship class was in progress on a Friday morning. Barricading the backdoor so as to trap his potential victims, Wong shot to death 13 people, critically injured another four, and then took his own life. The police arrived to find all of the bodies in a classroom and 37 terrified survivors hiding in closets and a boiler room on the premises.

LEGAL BATTLES

Many people on the losing end of a legal battle do not necessarily go after the adversaries who beat them. Instead, they go after the legal system—what they see as the unlevel playing field on which they were forced to compete and lose.

For example, 45-year-old George Lott opened fire with a concealed 9mm handgun during an appellate court proceeding in Fort Worth, Texas, on the morning of July 1, 1992. It appeared to those present in the crowded fourth-floor courtroom that Lott was shooting wildly at anything that moved. It looked as if the two attorneys who were slain, as well as a third attorney and two judges who were wounded, just happened to be at the wrong place at the wrong time.

Lott escaped through the mass confusion, only to show up 6 hours later at television station WFAA in Dallas. He wanted to tell his side of the story. Speaking with anchorman Tracey Rowlett, Lott outlined his deep-seated grudge against the judicial system that he believed had been unfair to him.

"I sat and I listened awhile," explained Lott in a taped interview (American Broadcasting Company, 1992). "I got up and I shot several of them. I was shooting at the bench—at the judges. You have to do a very horrible, horrible thing to catch people's attention."

Lott was outraged by the way his divorce had been handled. Two-and-a-half years earlier, a jury had awarded custody of his son Neal to his ex-wife. The judgment was later upheld by the Second Court of Appeals, in the same court-room in which Lott later committed the shootings.

Lott's legal problems were not just domestic. He himself was a lawyer, but hardly a successful one by any standard. After graduating from the University of Texas Law School in 1981, he opened his own law office in South Fort Worth, hoping to build a viable law practice. Four months later, he was out of clients and out of business. For the next few years, he didn't work, and he rarely left his apartment except to tend to his fishing boat. By 1988, things had gotten so bad that he allowed his state of Texas license to practice law expire.

Lott's long-standing frustration with the judicial system came to a head when he lost his visitation rights after his ex-wife accused him of having sexually molested their son on several occasions. A hearing on the sexual abuse charges was scheduled for the end of July, but Lott never faced these charges in court. Instead, he faced charges of first-degree murder, was convicted, and was sentenced to die.

"This is a horrible thing I've done," Lott admitted on the day of the shooting (American Broadcasting Company, 1992). "I do expect to be killed for it. I believe in capital punishment. And if anything deserves capital punishment, this does."

The State agreed. On the morning of September 20, 1994—just 18 months after committing mass murder—Lott was executed by the state of Texas.

FILING A GRIEVANCE

Whereas John Miller and George Lott sought revenge against public institutions, other mass killers perceive that private organizations—"money-grubbing," heartless corporations—deserve to "die" for all the wrongs that they inflict. At one time, the only option available to an irate customer was to file a complaint with the company or with the Better Business Bureau. Increasingly, however, it has become "appropriate" to file a grievance with a semiautomatic weapon.

Mark Barton's exit line dripped with evil sarcasm. "I hope this won't ruin your trading day," said the 44-year-old stock investor as he wrapped up his July 29, 1999, bloody rampage in Atlanta's financial district (Barstow, 1999). Armed with two semiautomatic pistols, a Colt .45-caliber and a Glock 9mm, the gunman had navigated deliberately through two Atlanta investment offices, All-Tech and Momentum Securities, located just across Piedmont Road from each other. The afternoon shooting spree left nine people dead and a dozen others wounded. By sundown that evening, Barton turned his gun on himself after being cornered by police at a gas station several miles northwest of the scene of the crime.

What was it that caused Mark Barton to snap? And did he, in fact, snap? Barton surely didn't just wake up on that warm July day and spontaneously decide to perpetrate a bloodbath. His crime spree was hardly sudden and episodic. Two days earlier, Barton had rammed a claw hammer into the skull of Leigh Ann, his 27-year-old second wife, then stuffed her body into a closet at their home in the Atlanta suburb of Stockbridge. The next morning, he took his two children, 12-year-old Matthew and 8-year-old Mychelle, to get haircuts. Later that night—the eve of his downtown shooting spree—Barton bludgeoned his son and daughter as they slept in their beds. He then held each child face down in the bathtub to ensure that they would not wake up in pain. Once he was certain they were dead, he tucked them both into their beds and placed a favorite toy next to each of them—a Game Boy for his son and a stuffed animal for his daughter.

Barton was so deliberate in his actions that he left a note at his home explaining his motives. "I killed Leigh Ann because she was one of the main reasons for my demise," Barton wrote. "I killed the children to exchange them for five minutes of pain for a lifetime of pain. I forced myself to do it to keep them from suffering so much later. No mother, no father, no relatives" ("I Am So Sorry," 1999). He left several other notes around the house relaying whatever sentiments came to mind. Next to his son's body, Barton placed a brief message to God: "I give you Matthew David Barton—my son, my buddy, my life. Please take care of him" ("Shootings in Atlanta," 1999).

There is considerable evidence, moreover, that Barton's murder string may have actually started 6 years earlier. He was a suspect in the untimely death of his first wife and her mother at his in-laws' home in Alabama. Not only did this clear the way for him to be with his 21-year-old girlfriend and mistress, Leigh Ann (who later became his second wife and next victim), but the life insurance proceeds also became invaluable to him to get a fresh start on his slumping career.

The popular image of a killer who shoots randomly at human targets without rhyme or reason hardly characterizes Barton's crimes or, for that matter, the actions of most mass killers. It was no accident or random choice that Barton selected two Atlanta offices as the location for his vengeful shooting spree. The two day-trading centers were the very places where he was ruined financially. He failed miserably in the high-stakes, high-pressure occupation of day trading in volatile technology stocks.

Barton lost $153,000 in a single day, forcing Momentum Securities to call in his credit. He turned next to All-Tech and pushed his losses to almost half a million dollars. He also resented those around him who had profited so handsomely on trades of shares of Internet stocks such as Amazon and Yahoo! As he wrote in his suicide letter, "I don't plan to live very much longer. Just long enough to kill as many of the people that greedily sought my destruction" ("Shootings in Atlanta," 1999).

The kind of diffuse anger, both inside and outside the home, expressed in Barton's shooting spree has been seen repeatedly when customers and clients decide to register their complaints in deadly fashion. On June 18, 1990, for example, 44-year-old laborer James Edward Pough called his boss to say that he had some things he had to do that day and wouldn't be in to work. His important errand was to pay a visit to the General Motors Acceptance Corporation (GMAC) office in Jacksonville, Florida. Six months earlier, Pough's 1988 Pontiac Grand Am had been repossessed because he had been unable to manage the monthly payments on his $9.95 hourly wage as a laborer. Even after he gave up the car voluntarily, GMAC had informed him in March that he still owed $6,394. Also during the month of January, Pough's wife, Theresa, had walked out on him, and by March, she had succeeded in obtaining a restraining order that barred him from having contact with her. With all that had gone wrong up to that point, Pough was left to contemplate his loneliness, misery, and total despair.

Pough's despair turned to anger. At 10:45 a.m., he burst through the main entrance at the GMAC facility and immediately opened fire on two customers waiting at the service counter in front. He then went behind the counter, and, for a full 2 minutes, blasted away at frightened employees as they scrambled under desks and out of back-room exits in an effort to flee. Pough was relentless in his pursuit of victims, following them from desk to desk and shooting many of them a number of times. He shot until he thought he had gotten everyone inside. He then fired a single round from his .38-caliber revolver into his head.

Pough's final homicide toll at the GMAC office reached eight, seven women and one man. Five more victims were wounded from the gunfire. It was later discovered that Pough had actually begun his killing spree on the day before his assault at GMAC, when he fatally shot two pedestrians.

Pough felt that GMAC, as a corporate entity, had put him in an economic hole. He was a poorly educated laborer who lacked the economic sophistication to comprehend the discrepancy between market value of the car and the amount remaining on the car loan. It wasn't just the money that mattered to him, however; it was the injustice. He had given back the car, but somehow still he owed them thousands of dollars. "How dare they?" he wondered.

It isn't just a laborer like Pough who is motivated to commit mass murder as payback for economic hardship. In fact, white-collar wheelers and dealers can respond violently if they feel cheated. Because of, or perhaps despite, legal representation given to clients, lawyers are particularly vulnerable to people who suffer financial catastrophe. At the August 1993 convention of the American Bar Association (ABA), in fact, one of the main topics of discussion was the rise of anti-lawyer sentiment in America. Participants expressed their outrage over jokes that ridicule attorneys, fearing that the tarnished image might provoke unhappy clients to commit violence against them. At the core of the discomfort and concern felt by the ABA members was a horrible mass killing that had occurred at a prestigious West Coast law firm barely a month earlier.

It happened on a sunny summer afternoon, July 1, 1993, in downtown San Francisco. A stocky 55-year-old man wearing a dark suit and carrying an oversized, lawyer-style briefcase rode the elevator of a glass and granite high-rise in the financial district to the offices of the law firm of Pettit and Martin on the 34th floor. The smiling workers he passed in the corridor couldn't have known what Gian Luigi Ferri carried in his briefcase or in his heart.

Ferri walked briskly toward the law firm's conference room and pulled one of his three semiautomatic pistols from his case. He immediately sprayed the room with bullets as terrified lawyers and clients headed for cover. He then turned into an attorney's office down the hall and once more opened fire. Three people were killed on the spot; three more were wounded.

Ferri took the fire stairs to the 33rd and 32nd floors, where he found even more targets for his rampage. Never stopping to reload, he shot to death five more people and wounded another three. As he attempted to escape down the stairway, two of his pistols jammed, and he was trapped between police coming in both directions. He took his third firearm from his briefcase and fired a final fatal shot under his chin into his brain.

Ferri was an Italian immigrant with a bachelor's degree in psychology who had divorced his wife in 1977. He tried his hand as a mortgage broker but was plagued by a series of bad financial deals as well as bad luck and a bad temper. His situation had deteriorated so much recently that he approached a law firm in Los Angeles to declare personal bankruptcy.

A note that police found on Ferri's body blamed his problems on "criminals, rapists, racketeers, lobbyists" (Reinhold, 1993), and on the Food and Drug Administration (FDA) because it refused to regulate the food additive monosodium glutamate, which he believed had almost killed him on three occasions. Most of all, his note blamed people associated with a failed trailer-park business venture in the early 1980s—and especially his counsel in that deal, the law firm of Pettit and Martin.

Pough, Miller, and Ferri were all middle-age men who saw financial ruin ahead of them, not because of an employer who had fired them but because of what they perceived to be an unjust and deceitful company, agency, or firm. For Pough and Miller, sums of approximately $6,000 were enough to break them psychologically, if not financially. Ferri's loss was more substantial, taking him from financial success to bankruptcy.

Economic resentment can be felt not only by vengeful employees but also by disgruntled clients and customers who seek to "win one for the little guy." In a complex, bureaucratic society, more and more citizens are feeling powerless against the red tape and unresponsiveness of the system. Most, of course, will do little more than complain loudly about the injustice of government and big business. Only a few will literally fight city hall.

INCREASING ALIENATION

Thirty years or so ago, it was virtually unheard of for a dissatisfied customer to seek murderous revenge against a firm or company. Part of the problem lies in the impersonal or ineffective responses of customer relations departments. Increasingly, consumers are frustrated by automated phone systems with endless and confusing button pushes and lengthy holding queues, notwithstanding the claim by a recorded "receptionist" that one's call is very important. Often, a frustrated caller is transferred to someone's voice mail, which announces that the right person to talk to is away on vacation—virtually a phone system dead end. On occasions when a live human being picks up, it is often some overburdened, uninspired, and poorly trained customer relations representative who would never have been hired during less prosperous times. All too frequently, the customer relations associate attempts to justify incompetence by suggesting that the computers are down or that a computer error is to blame for the inability to resolve the predicament. In many companies, customer relations personnel are the last to be hired and the first to be fired. In short, customer service has too often become customer disservice.

With virtually every company having an Internet site, getting help and satisfaction is almost impossible. The corporate web pages (absent address and phone numbers) instead offer a section on FAQs—frequently asked questions—but they often do not include the questions that angry consumers seem to have.

Unlike prescriptions for reducing employee violence, a company can rarely profile or screen its clientele or refer angry customers to an employee assistance program, yet a solution to the problem of the vengeful customer is clear. In the face of growing alienation and cynicism, large companies and agencies must upgrade and humanize their customer relations efforts. They must make easily accessible an adequate number of competent and concerned human beings rather than impersonal machines. Above all, companies must remember the adage that the customer is always right—especially when he is holding an AK-47.

CHAPTER 18

Hate Motivated Mass Murder

Lodged on the northern face of Mount Royal, overlooking the distinguished homes in one of Montreal's more affluent suburbs, the site of the École Polytechnique is as charming as the sound of its name. The University of Montreal School of Engineering, as it is known to English-speaking Canadians, is also known throughout North America as the site of one of the most devastating mass murders of all time.

On the rainy and cool afternoon of December 6, 1989, just after 5:00 p.m., 25-year-old Marc Lepine walked into the six-story, yellow-brick engineering building. He was ready for battle and bent on revenge. A man on a mission, Lepine was armed with a .223-caliber Ruger Mini-14, a semiautomatic hunting rifle that was anything but "mini" in terms of the carnage it could produce. Although weighing a mere 6.5 pounds, the Mini-14 is capable of propelling 2-inch-long cartridges at a velocity of more than 3,000 feet per second. The standard Mini-14 model ordinarily holds but five rounds in its magazine, but Lepine, planning for quick action, had equipped the rifle with a 30-round banana-clip extension. He also brought with him more than 100 rounds of ammunition. Lepine realized the enormous task that lay ahead of him, and he came prepared.

During the preceding week, Lepine had visited the engineering building on several occasions. He had designed his route as carefully as would any self-respecting engineer. On this Wednesday afternoon, however, Lepine had in his mind a single purpose—to get even with women, especially feminists, whom he held totally responsible for all of his troubles.

With his weapon concealed within a green plastic garbage bag, Lepine moved slowly and quietly through the doors of classroom C-230. Inside, he interrupted 60 undergraduates—9 of them women—who were listening to an end-of-semester presentation by one of their fellow classmates. Dressed in a blue sweater and blue jeans, Lepine looked like a student who had mistakenly entered the wrong class. Even the emblem on his back—a skull adorned with glasses—was not all that unusual for college students to wear. But when the intruder removed his weapon from the plastic bag and starting shouting orders, it was clear that the man had not just taken a wrong turn.

In a calm but forceful voice, Lepine instructed everyone to stop immediately what they were doing. Wearing a menacing grin on his face, he then directed the women to move off to one side of the classroom and commanded the men, including Professor Yvon Bouchard, to leave. Some students were too frightened to move. Others were slow to respond, some thinking that it was all a charade, just a bad joke. But Lepine showed them he wasn't kidding by firing a shot into the ceiling to hurry the students along. "I want the women," Lepine began to yell. "You're all a bunch of fucking feminists. I hate feminists" (Sussman, 1989).

Having gotten everyone's undivided attention, Lepine started blasting away at the nine terrified women, hitting all of them and killing six. But he wasn't through. Leaving room C-230, Lepine moved methodically through corridors and between floors, shooting any woman who crossed his path. He maneuvered his way to the bottom floor and into the cafeteria, which was cheerfully bedecked with red and white balloons and various holiday decorations, and once again opened fire on frightened students.

The once festive atmosphere in the cafeteria was decimated, the decorations overshadowed by blood on the tables, chairs, and floor and by bodies of the dead and wounded strewn about. The gunman returned upstairs to look for more victims.

By the time the police arrived—delayed by a miscommunication that initially had dispatched them to the women's dorm—Lepine was ready to end the assault on his own. Pressing the gun against his forehead, he muttered "Ah, shit," and then squeezed the trigger (Time-Life Books, 1992, p. 155). When the police tactical squad entered the building, they found only the aftermath of a wave of destruction. They discovered the bodies of 14 women, ages 21 to 31. The police also found Lepine's lifeless body at the front of a third-floor classroom, his head shattered from a bullet shot at close range. Searching the body of the killer, police found a revealing, three-page handwritten suicide note in his pocket explaining his hideous outburst. "I have been unhappy for the past seven years," Lepine lamented. "And, I will die on December 6, 1989. . . . Feminists have always ruined my life" (Time-Life Books, 1992, p. 144).

An addendum to Lepine's mission statement contained a list of the names of 19 "opportunistic" Canadian women, including a sportscaster, several police-women, and other public figures—the very kind of "feminists" he so thoroughly despised. "The lack of time," wrote Lepine, "has allowed those radical feminists to survive" (Time-Life Books, 1992, p. 144).

CHOICE OF VICTIMS

It appeared as though Lepine had carefully and thoughtfully assembled his *Who's Who* of women doing men's work, going as far as to research the phone numbers of many of them. But if Lepine had in mind a hit list of women whom he detested and blamed, then why did he not target them specifically for his attack on feminism? Although his anger and resentment may have been irrational, he was well aware that such a battle plan was strategically impossible. It surely would have been difficult for him to avenge his troubled life by executing one victim at a time, running through his list of upstart women in a serial fashion. Rather, he needed to kill a lot of women in a short period of time, and just about any feminists would do.

But if his desire was to achieve large-scale revenge, then why did Lepine not attack the nursing school, where far more women would be under his gun? Lepine's grudge was directed not so much toward womankind in general or against women who were performing traditional female roles such as nursing. His resentment instead was focused on ambitious feminists who were pursuing careers within the male domain, such as engineering. Not only were his student engineers symbolic of feminism, but, in a sense, these women also were literally taking his seat in classes. Lepine himself, because of his poor academic skills, had been denied admission to the very same school of engineering where he exacted his revenge.

A LIFE OF FRUSTRATION

Those who are psychoanalytically inclined might speculate that Lepine's contempt for women was a generalized form of his hatred for his mother. Perhaps she abandoned him at an early age, or perhaps he believed he was a victim of child abuse at the hands of his mother. Lepine's violent rampage at the University of Montreal could then be interpreted as a desperate final attempt to get even with his mother: His unfortunate victims were only surrogates on whom to act out his pent-up rage.

Actually, Lepine seemed to have positive feelings about his mother, Monique Lepine, even though as a teenager he was not happy that she spent so much time at her nursing career and thus too little time with him and his younger sister, Nadia. Lepine instead seemed to have detested his father, a man who had brutally assaulted both his wife and his children and who showed very little interest in his family. At their divorce proceedings in 1970, Monique testified that her husband was abusive and that he showed little control of his emotions. He had beaten her in front of the children, he had struck her in the face, and he had hit Marc so hard that the young boy bled from his nose and his ears. When Marc was only 7 years old, his father threw him, his sister, and his mother out of their apartment.

By the time he was 14 years old, the boy's resentment was so intense that he decided to take his mother's name—Lepine. It was at that time that Gamil Gharbi, son of Algerian-born Muslim Rachid Liass Gharbi, became known as Marc Lepine. Perhaps it would not be too farfetched to suggest that Marc Lepine's final assault was an extreme version of his father's behavior toward his mother. Marc Lepine may have hated his father, but ultimately he identified with the aggressor.

Changing his name from Gamil Gharbi to Marc Lepine also may have been much more than a repudiation of his father's lineage. It also represented his desire to fit in, to be like everyone else, to be French Canadian.

Life was not easy for Marc Lepine. He was not like everyone else, not even close. He was the quintessential loser. He attempted to join the army but, for reasons that were never completely clear, was rejected. Of course, he resented how women of the military were given equal recognition. After all, they were barred from the front lines; what's more, Lepine felt that they had no place in the military aside from their roles as secretaries and nurses.

Lepine's rampage was a violent act of bias against an entire group of people—in this case, women. As such, it was unquestionably a hate crime—as hateful and as criminal as one can imagine. His suicide note and his remarks to his surviving victims made it abundantly clear that Lepine blamed all women for his personal failures. He looked for feminists behind every negative experience that he had.

BLAMING WOMEN

Despite (or perhaps because of) advances in the role of women in Western societies, there are other mass murderers, aside from Lepine, who have targeted women because they fail to conform to the killers' own personal beliefs concerning gender differences. Many men, holding an old-fashioned view of women's roles, resist and resent changes in the area of gender, yet this motivation for mass murder reflects an extreme end of the backlash spectrum (Bell et al., 1997).

Mass killer George "Jo Jo" Hennard was similar to Lepine in his intense hatred of women. Hennard's crime itself would not necessarily have suggested a vendetta against any group in particular, but testimonials from his neighbors and his own written words clearly revealed that he blamed women, above all others, for everything that went wrong in his life and wanted to get even with them.

On Wednesday, October 16, 1991, the day after Hennard turned 35, the long-haired, good-looking man from Belton, Texas, celebrated his birthday with a bang. Hennard loaded up his two semiautomatic pistols—a 9mm Glock 17 and a Ruger P-89—put on his shades, and jumped into his 1987 Ford Ranger pickup truck for the 15-mile trip west to Killeen.

Lunchtime at Luby's Cafeteria was particularly crowded that day. Some 200 diners, many of them treating their supervisors for National Bosses Day, were squeezed into the popular red-brick restaurant. Only some saw what happened, but all heard the crash as a light blue pickup truck—Hennard's Ford—came smashing through a 6-foot-high plate glass window next to the front entrance and crushed a table full of customers.

Surprised but concerned, diners dropped their drinks and sandwiches and rushed to help the driver, whom they imagined had been in a traffic accident. But this was no accident. With a cigarette dangling from his lips, Hennard stepped from his vehicle, aimed his gun directly at one of the customers he had hit in the crash, and fired. Next, he gunned down a group of people, one by one, as they stood motionless clutching their trays in the serving line. Moving through the eatery, the gunman coolly and methodically targeted his victims. "Wait till those fuckin' women in Belton, Texas see this!" Hennard shouted with a smirk. "I wonder if they think it was worth it!" (Hightower, 1991).

By this time, everyone in the restaurant had been stunned into silence. They now understood exactly what was going on—there was a mass killer among them, and he was determined to shoot at anyone in his path. Some tipped over tables for cover; others played dead on the floor. A few escaped by hurling a chair at a window pane and crawling out through the broken glass. Twenty-eight-year-old Tommy Vaughn threw his own 6-foot, 6-inch, 300-pound body through a glass window. One clever employee, 19-year-old Mark Mathews, crawled inside the kitchen's oversized dishwasher, where he stayed until he was rescued the next day.

Suzanne Gratia, who had taken her parents out for lunch, painfully witnessed both of their deaths. She and her mother had ducked behind a table when Hennard shot her father, Al, in the chest from just a few feet away. Suzanne spied an escape route through a broken window, but her mother, Ursula, instead chose to creep out from behind the table to protect her critically wounded husband. She draped her body over his and stared directly into Hennard's face, inviting him to shoot her, too. He obliged.

The police arrived just a few minutes later, although it must have seemed, to the survivors, more like a lifetime. After several volleys of gunfire in which he was wounded twice, George Hennard retreated to the restroom. He realized that his killing spree was over, and he ended it by shooting himself in the head. At last, victory was his, or so he thought.

Including one victim who died a few days later, Hennard's murder toll at Luby's totaled 23. Nineteen others were wounded in the attack, some seriously.

Days before the Killeen massacre, Hennard was one of millions of Americans who were glued to their TV sets watching the highly rated broadcast, on nearly every station, of Senate confirmation hearings for soon-to-be Supreme Court Justice Clarence Thomas. These proceedings were, of course, not anything like the usual confirmation broadcast on C-Span. These particular hearings turned on the issue of whether Thomas had sexually harassed Anita Hill when she worked for him at the Equal Employment Opportunity Commission.

To some American men, the irony of seeing the man responsible for developing and enforcing policy on harassment in the workplace himself being hung out to dry was an outrage. To Hennard, it was even worse. He complained loudly and publicly that Anita Hill's allegations were ludicrous, and that the situation signaled how women were being allowed to take over territory that rightfully belonged to men. Watching the Senate hearings as he ate dinner at a small neighborhood grill, Hennard started screaming at the TV, "You dumb bitch! You bastards opened the door for all the women!" (Chin, 1991, p. 67).

Hennard blamed females generally, not just Anita Hill, for causing what he saw as the decline of American civilization. In June 1991, Hennard had walked into a local FBI office and attempted unsuccessfully to file a civil rights complaint against the women of the world.

"He said women were snakes," recalled Jamie Dunlop, a former roommate of Hennard (Chin, 1991, p. 66). Even more revealing of his deep-seated resentment, Hennard sent an angry letter to two young women, neighbors he hardly knew, complaining about the female vipers who were destroying his life:

Do you think the three of us can get together someday? Please give me the satisfaction of someday laughing in the face of all those mostly white treacherous female vipers from those two towns who tried to destroy me and my family.

It is very ironic about Belton, Texas.

I found the best and worst in women there. You and your sister are on the one side. Then the abundance of evil women that make up the worst are on the other side.

I would like to personally remind all those vipers that I have civil rights too. Just because I did not hire an attorney they do not have carte blanche to do what they want in violation of these rights.

I will no matter what prevail over the female vipers in those two rinkydink towns in Texas.

I will prevail in the bitter end. In conclusion, I ask you do not disclose the contents of this letter to anyone other than immediate family members. It is no one else's business but ours anyway. ("Mass Slayer's Letter," 1991)

Hennard's mass shooting was in large part motivated by hate, especially his hatred for women. In the heat of the moment, however, a spillover effect took hold: His anger and resentment became generalized to include just about everyone in Belton County.

The Luby's massacre, like others that have occurred over the years, reminds us painfully that no place is absolutely safe—not a restaurant or a school, not a church or a shopping mall. And, thanks to a quiet, middle-age systems analyst from Pennsylvania, the same can be said about health clubs, places that so many Americans consider their oasis for working out the stresses and frustrations of daily life.

On the evening of August 4, 2009, George Sodini, a 48-year-old systems analyst, brought more than just workout clothes to the LA Fitness Center in Collier, Pennsylvania, a suburb of Pittsburgh. Like Marc Lepine and several other mass murderers, he was hunting for women, especially the beautiful and athletically fit types who ignored him despite his own efforts to appeal to the opposite sex.

Sodini barged into a women's aerobics class, uninvited, of course. He then turned out the lights, removed his gear, which included a 9mm semiautomatic handgun and a .45-caliber revolver, and started shooting. Discharging more than four dozen rounds, Sodini killed three of the women in the class and wounded nine others. He then turned the gun on himself.

For Sodini, the health club was nothing more than another venue for feeling rejected, particularly by the young, attractive women crowding the weight rooms and exercise classes. The club became, as a result, the very spot he chose deliberately to work out his frustrations, not with weights and a treadmill, but with a loaded firearm. Sodini's victims may not have known him very well, if at all, but that is precisely part of the reason why they were targeted. He sought revenge against youthful and athletic women, the sort who never took the time or made an effort to get to know him.

There are so many features about this shooting spree that are tragically textbook. Like most mass killers, Sodini struggled through a long history of failure and rejection, from childhood, with a brother he regarded as a bully and a father he saw as distant and unconcerned. His feelings of rejection continued through middle age after decades without consummating an intimate relationship. It reached the point where life was absolutely meaningless and the future seemed to promise only more of the same.

Rather than take responsibility for his own inadequacies in relationships, Sodini—in typical mass murderer fashion—externalized the blame, projecting his problems onto all the young beautiful women he so desperately desired. Plus, he blamed Black men for stealing away all the good-looking White women he had hoped to date.

As the classic loner, Sodini wrote in his blog about being "isolated," about having no "close friends," about spending so much time by himself. The May 18, 2009, entry was representative of many of his pathetic, lonely laments:

> Women just don't like me. There are 30 million desirable women in the US (my estimate) and I cannot find one. Not one of them finds me attractive. I am looking at The List I made from my May 4th idea. I forgot about that for several days. That tells me where I stand. These problems have gotten worse over a 30 year period. I need to expect nothing from me or other people. All through the years I thought we had the ability to change ourselves—I guess that is incorrect. Looking at The List makes me realize how TOTALLY ALONE, a deeper word is ISOLATED, I am from all else.

Then on August 2, 2009, just two days before his shooting spree, Sodini wrote in his blog

> The biggest problem of all is not having relationships or friends, but not being able to achieve and acquire what I desire in those or many other areas. Everything stays the same regardless of the effert [sic] I put in. If I had control over my life then I would be happier. But for about the past 30 years, I have not.

From Sodini's viewpoint, it wasn't only women who had rebuffed him; it was all of humankind. In his extreme loneliness, he was without emotional support and comfort. There was no one there to help him deal with his demons, to encourage him to do the right thing, or at least to help him gain some perspective on his situation.

THE KILLER AS VICTIM

Mass murder inspired by hate, such as Hennard's assault at Luby's Cafeteria, derives from generalized resentment aimed not at a few individuals but at an entire group of people who are seen as responsible for the perpetrator's problems. The murderer is convinced that the country has changed for the worse, that politicians are leading the public down the garden path to total ruination, and that people like himself—the little guys—have lost all control of their destiny. From his point of view, he is losing out, he is being victimized, he resents it, and he is looking for someone to blame.

A growing number of observers have applied the term *downward mobility* to characterize the economic plight of an entire generation of Americans who are slipping and sliding their way down the socioeconomic ladder as income inequality continues to widen the gap between rich and poor. For the first time in generations, many Americans believe that children will not enjoy a better standard of living than that now being enjoyed by their parents.

Instead of believing that they should help those who are less fortunate, many Americans feel personally threatened by the growing presence of women, new-comers, and minorities, who are seen as competing for diminishing amounts of wealth, status, and power. In fact, the traditionally dominant group of White males feels as if it is being challenged, to an increasing extent, by a broad range of "outsiders." The economic pie is shrinking, and there simply aren't enough slices to go around.

Cultural diversity and increasing economic competition together have produced a pervasive sense of resentment and close-minded, twisted logic in the hearts and heads of many hateful Americans. They find many convenient scapegoats at whose feet to lay blame for their own personal failures and disenchantment:

- Jews have too much power; they are responsible for our recession and therefore my unemployment.
- Blacks and women unfairly benefit from reverse discrimination; because of affirmative action, I can't get a promotion.
- Immigrants are taking our jobs and they're not even qualified; I've busted my butt for years, and just because of the illegals I can't even feed my family.
- All Muslims are terrorists; because of them, I feel anxious about the future.
- Asians are grabbing all the college scholarship money paid for by my tax dollars; because of them, my son might not be able to attend college.

What are disgruntled and resentful Americans—fed up with unfair competition and sick and tired of feeling victimized or disadvantaged—to do? As little as 15 or 20 years ago, they might have grabbed a cold beer from the refrigerator, turned on the reruns of *All in the Family,* and let somebody else take care of the problem. But Americans are now much more likely to respond assertively or even violently—to translate their resentment into action. Some have an ax to grind, but they choose to use something far more powerful than an ax to settle their grievances.

On occasion, hate crimes go well beyond an assault on one or two individuals. A few hatemongers are ready to wage war against any and all members of a particular group of people. In the hatemonger's view, all out-group members are subhumans, either animals or demons, who are bent on destroying our culture, our economy, or the purity of our racial heritage. He is concerned, therefore, about much more than eliminating some Latinos or Blacks from his neighborhood or a handful of women from his place of work. Instead, he believes that he has a higher order purpose in carrying out his crime. The perpetrator is on a moral mission: His assignment is to make the world a better place to live, to rid the world of evil. He perversely believes that his aggressive act is, in actuality, one of self-defense: "Get them before they take over."

By the legal definition, hate-inspired crimes, including massacres, involve some protected group based on race, religion, ethnicity, national origin, disability, gender, gender identity, or sexual orientation. More generally, murderous hate-mongers have also targeted categories of individuals who fall outside the purview of state and federal hate crime legislation. In the early morning hours of March 25, 2006, 28-year-old Kyle Huff targeted ravers—young people who attend all-night dance parties where electronic and rave music are played. At a rave after-party in Seattle, Huff opened fire, killing six ravers ranging in age from 14 to 32. He then placed the gun in his mouth and pulled the trigger, taking his own life (Fox, Burgess, Levin, & Wong, 2006).

Kyle and Kane Huff were twin brothers who had lived together in Seattle for almost five years, after leaving their home in Whitefish, Montana. While they were students at Whitefish High School, the twins looked and acted differently—they wore trench coats, combat boots, and long hair and were pretty much ignored by most other students, who regarded them as outsiders. But the twins also had family members to give them the support and encouragement they needed. After graduation, Kyle was able to keep a full-time job.

After moving to Seattle, however, Kyle's employment picture became more and more sporadic. He had been working off and on as a pizza deliveryman but was out of work at the time he went on his rampage. Two months earlier, he had worked at a nearby Pizza Hut. He also briefly delivered for Pagliacci Pizza. Two years before that, he was employed for a few days at a Domino's Pizza close to his apartment but was quickly fired for his unreliability. With every lost job, he became more and more frustrated.

He then began to stalk ravers, perhaps seeing in their lifestyle everything lacking in his. They were sociable; he was not. They had sexual relationships and lots of friends; he did not. They were able to have fun; he was always deadly serious. But unlike many mainstream members of the Seattle community, the ravers were tolerant; they emphasized respect for differences and peace rather than competition and rivalry. Kyle was an outsider in the social and work scenes, but he was accepted—even if only peripherally—by the ravers.

Almost one month after the massacre occurred, the manager of an apartment complex about a mile from Huff's apartment inspected a nearby dumpster and discovered what he thought was a bomb but turned out to be only modeling clay and wires. Wrapped into the "bomb" was Huff's handwritten suicide note, dated 3 days before he committed mass murder and apparently meant to be read by his twin brother Kane.

In the following suicide letter, Huff explains that what he sees as the "hippie" preoccupation with "the world of sex" is destroying our country. "This is a revolution," he tells his brother. And he urges Kane not to kill himself but to help fight for the cause.

03/23/06

To Kane From Kyle

I hope that you will find this letter after the fact. Don't let the police or FBI keep you from haveing it, this is my last wish for you to see this. Don't kill yourself moron. That's the last thing I would want to happen, As long as your alive, so is part of me, ya know, I hate leaving you by yourself, but this is something I feel I have to do, My life would always feel incomplete otherwise. I can't let them get away with what they're doing, kids like me and you are seriously dying over this shit, I hate this world of sex that they think they are striving to make, this is a revolution brother, the most important thing to happen since Man began, to let it die out would be a crime. I will never able to "cum" with them, I will always see it as hell. The things they say "and do" they're rapeing us are just too disturbing to me to just ignore and try to live my life with. I know this is a short letter and might sound stupid, but it would take a book to properly explain this to you, I don't have the time for that, or the will. The basic jist of it is that they're fucking, next to us when we're really high to make us freak out. And trying to stop are heart by making it palpitate And they are doing it it's just a question of if were willing to be OK with it. And obviously im not. Maybe someday you'll be willing to help me kill this hippie shit. I know that its going to get worse now, but that's part of the …

Now kids Now!!!

Bye Kane. I love you.

SETTLING A GRUDGE WITH A GUN

Not every hate crime is clearly marked as such. Even when the crime is perpetrated exclusively against the members of a particular group, we cannot always be sure that it was motivated by bigotry or bias.

On July 10, 2003, Doug Williams decided to exact a measure of sweet revenge. The 48-year-old employee at a plant in Meridian, Mississippi, had long complained to his White coworkers that Black Americans were nowadays being given preferential treatment. According to Williams, this was especially true where he worked. During his 19 years with the company, he was passed over for promotions repeatedly, and he was reminded of his bad temper and forced to attend anger management classes. Then, he was carefully monitored by his bosses, as though he was some kind of a hothead.

Now, seated in a meeting with managers at his factory job, Williams once again felt angry. He felt he was being humiliated, told that he hadn't put racial issues aside; he wasn't trying to get along with his Black coworkers. Having heard quite enough, Williams bolted from his chair and ran from the room. His parting words: "Y'all can handle this."

In December 2001, Williams had verbally threatened a Black coworker. Then, in June 2003, he went to work wearing a white hood over his head that seemed reminiscent of the Ku Klux Klan. Afterwards, he stayed home for several days rather than give in to the pressure to remove it. Now, he was being reprimanded by the very managers who had refused to acknowledge his importance to the company, had previously admonished him for his bad temper, and had denied him the promotions he deserved.

On July 10, after leaving the meeting at which his insensitivity and anger were discussed, Williams returned with a rifle strapped to his back and a shotgun in his hands. He said, "I told you about fucking with me" (Levin & Rabrenovic, 2004, p. 54) and immediately sprayed the room with bullets, killing two of his coworkers. He then ran through the factory, firing at point-blank range at fellow employees. Three more were fatally shot before Williams took his own life. The final body count: four Blacks and one White. Williams had always claimed to be keeping score on those who offended him. From his viewpoint, he had just evened the score.

Williams was far from the first hate-filled American to settle a grudge with a gun. Thirty-four-year-old Richard Baumhammers, an out-of-work White immigration lawyer in suburban Pittsburgh, despised immigrants, Blacks, and Jews. He feared that White Christian Americans were being pushed out by a growing presence of Third World upstarts. He believed that American citizens would soon have to reside in isolated suburbs, surrounded by immigrants from impoverished nations.

In April 2000, Baumhammers went on a deadly shooting spree. His first victim was his Jewish next-door neighbor, a woman whom he had known since childhood. After shooting her to death, Baumhammers then set her house ablaze and drove off toward two local synagogues, where he fired bullets into their windows. He then drove from place to place over a 20-mile area, searching for anyone who might possibly be an immigrant or a person of color. An hour later, Baumhammers had killed four more people—a man of Indian descent who was exiting a local grocery store, a Vietnamese American worker, a Chinese American manager of a popular Chinese restaurant, and an African American man who was leaving a karate school.

The mass murder at a Sikh temple in suburban Milwaukee on Sunday August 5, 2012, was referred to as an act of "domestic terrorism" by the Oak Creek police chief, meaning that the attack was perpetrated by a resident of this country rather than someone from Asia or the Middle East.

According to Bureau of Alcohol, Tobacco, Firearms and Explosives (ATF) spokesman Thomas Ahern, the killer,

Photo 18.1 Wade Michael Page, the White supremacist who killed a half-dozen people at a Sikh temple in suburban Milwaukee in August 2012, acted alone. His hatred was, however, shared by members of the neo-Nazi punk rock band to which he belonged.

Wade Michael Page, who committed suicide after taking the lives of six people and wounding another four, was a White male approximately 40 years of age. Page was an army veteran who lived nearby. The Southern Poverty Law Center reports he participated in a neo-Nazi punk rock band and was a longstanding White supremacist.

Page's rampage was the first mass murder but hardly the first violent episode aimed at Sikh Indians during more than a decade after the September 11 attack

Photo 18.2 On the morning of August 5, 2012, white supremacist Wade Michael Page shot to death six people and wounded another four at a Sikh temple in Oak Creek, Wisconsin. The killer then committed suicide by shooting himself in the head. (AP Photo/Jeffrey Phelps)

on America. Hate can be quite diffuse, targeting a broad range of innocent victims—including those who are mistaken for other groups. Sikhs, for example, are often mistaken for Muslims given their turbans and beards.

Just four days after 9/11, Balbir Singh Sodhi, a 49-year-old immigrant from India who wore a turban and a beard, was shot down and killed while in front of his gas station in Mesa, Arizona. The gunman, Frank Roque, then opened fire on a man of Lebanese descent and an Afghan family nearby. He was angry about the terrorist attack on America and was looking to retaliate against anyone who might possibly have been Muslim or Middle Eastern, or who had dark skin and spoke with a foreign accent. His reward? Serving a life sentence in a maximum security prison.

Hate can remain dormant in a culture, emerging without warning from the darkness in response to some threatening episode. In the weeks after September 11, 2001, the FBI reported more than 40 anti-Arab and anti-Islamic hate crimes across the country. In addition, there were more than 300 reports of harassment and abuse filed with the Council on American-Islamic Relations. For several months after the attack on America, hate crimes directed against Muslim Americans increased by 1,600%, according to 2001 FBI statistics.

Unfortunately, the tit-for-tat mind-set has not ended even more than 12 years after the horrendous 2001 attack on New York City, rural Pennsylvania, and Washington, DC. The thinking is "you got us, now we will get you." Thus, one hate crime can inspire large scale, ongoing violence between groups. It has happened repeatedly in Northern Ireland, Israel, and India. It can, and has happened, in the United States.

If the killer in Wisconsin turns out to be like most other mass murderers, he will have suffered prolonged frustrations, blamed everybody but himself for his personal miseries, been socially isolated, and experienced some catastrophic loss—the loss of a job or an important relationship—for which he blamed foreigners in his community.

Unlike most other mass killers, however, when someone goes on a rampage based on hate against an entire group, he is not aiming to eliminate a particular set of individuals—his family members, coworkers, or classmates. Instead, his killing spree is random within the group he regards as the enemy.

Any Sikh Indian is at risk. Indeed, anyone who has dark skin, speaks with a foreign accent, or wears a turban is regarded as the enemy. The killer isn't interested in whether the victims are married or single, have children, follow a favorite baseball team, or have the same personal problems that he has. He has dehumanized his potential victims long before he arrives at his crime scene. To him, their only important characteristic is their cultural or physical difference.

The massacre in Wisconsin might not have targeted Sikh Indians in particular. It is more likely the act of an American who despises anyone who is not in the mainstream of American society. Police in Chicago and New York suggested they pay particular attention to Sikh temples, just in case another bigoted individual decides to settle a gripe through the barrel of a gun. Yet, the next set of victims could just as easily have been Muslim, Jewish, Catholic, Hindu, or Buddhist.

MINORITY AGAINST MAJORITY

White males cannot, of course, claim sole ownership of resentful attitudes. Many minority Americans are angry as well: They see a racist behind every possibility for advancement. Some even envisage a large-scale conspiracy on the part of White supremacist groups, corporations, and government to deprive them of success, if not their lives. Thus, whereas Baumhammers, Williams, Lepine, Hennard, and Purdy were all members of the dominant group beating back the threat of a minority, mass murder can also serve as the weapon of a minority to retaliate for perceived oppression.

In a suburb not far from the city of Pittsburgh, a 39-year-old Black resident of Wilkinsburg was at his wit's end. After a lifetime of racial insults and slights, Ronald Taylor felt that he could no longer tolerate what he believed to be the continuing racist neglect by his White maintenance man, John DeWitt. The front door of Taylor's apartment unit had remained broken for some period of time without being repaired, and Taylor fixated on his White maintenance man as the source of the problem.

On March 1, 2000, racial revenge was on Taylor's mind. Leaving his apartment, he remarked to a Black neighbor living nearby that he wasn't going to hurt any Black people—that he was just "out to kill white people." Taylor was true to his word. Not finding John DeWitt, he instead fatally shot a carpenter who had been working in the building. Then, he walked to a fast-food restaurant in the Wilkinsburg business district, where he shouted "White trash. Racist pig" and opened fire again, killing two and injuring two more (Levin & Rabrenovic, 2004, p. 55). All of Taylor's victims were White.

A horrific shooting that shocked New Yorkers and appeared to many as an indiscriminate shooting by a madman actually was more a carefully orchestrated hate crime. The gunman was indeed mad, but specifically because of feelings of personal slight and racial discrimination.

On any other day, it was the 5:33 local to Hicksville, but on December 7, 1993, it was the 5:33 express to hell. Hundreds of commuters, exhausted from a long workday in Manhattan, boarded the Long Island Rail Road commuter train at Penn Station, unprepared for the horror that would soon erupt in the third car. Just about 6:10 p.m., as the train raced toward Garden City in suburban Nassau County, a heavyset but gentle-looking Black man rose quietly from his seat at the rear of the car and turned the weary scene into instant chaos.

Without warning, the gunman pulled from his canvas bag a Ruger P89 9mm semiautomatic pistol, a lightweight handgun known for its high velocity and accuracy, and started filling the air with gunfire. Stunned riders struggled to find cover in a death train that offered very little. The gunman slowly walked backward down the aisle, row by row, shooting alternately to his left and then his right.

Midway through the car, the assailant paused to reload with a second 15-round clip, then promptly resumed his attack. He moved to the front of the car, disappeared momentarily into the vestibule connecting to the forward car, but soon returned to finish his sweep of the third car. Fifteen rounds later, when again he stopped to reload, three heroic commuters rushed at the gunman and pinned him against a seat. Moments later, the train pulled into the Merillon Avenue Station. As terrified commuters bolted from the train, an off-duty railroad police officer who was on the platform to pick up his wife boarded the third car and handcuffed the restrained gunman.

By the time the 3-minute barrage had ended, four victims—three men and one woman—lay dead, and another 19 were wounded. The death toll rose to six as two young women later succumbed to their severe bullet wounds. As bad as it was, the carnage could have been worse. The gunman came prepared with a bag filled with more than 100 rounds of black talons, deadly hollow-nose bullets that penetrate the body and then ricochet within.

The scene of the massacre was beyond anyone's worst nightmare. "There was blood on the train, on the platform, down the steps," reported one member of the rescue team, "40 to 50 feet of blood" ("He Wouldn't Stop Shooting," 1993). Surviving witnesses, the luckier ones, spoke frantically of a madman who went berserk and shot randomly. To them, the attack appeared totally indiscriminate. After all, no one on the train had provoked this man physically or verbally—he seemed to have just suddenly snapped.

Notwithstanding the impressions of witnesses to the horror, there was a method to this man's madness. A handwritten note found in the assailant's pocket—which may have been intended as a suicide script—later revealed that the crime was a planned act of vengeance against races and institutions that he despised with a passion. He saw racism everywhere—in the workers' compensation system that failed to assist him sufficiently after his work-related injury, and at Adelphi University, which had suspended him in June 1991 for belligerence and contentiousness. He espoused hatred of Whites, Asians, and conservative "Uncle Tom" Blacks—people who possessed the very things he did not, especially money and a job. These were his oppressors, and they would have to pay for his misery.

The gunman may not have known his victims, but he was nonetheless selective in determining when, where, how, and against what kinds of people he would avenge his deep disappointments and dark despair. With deliberation and planning, he sought out a place and time—a commuter train at the evening rush hour—that would guarantee that he could target "rich folk" who were gainfully employed. The gunman was so in control of his actions that he purposely postponed the slaughter until the train had passed the city limits of New York. Not only was he certain to attack suburbanites within suburbia, but, according to his murder plan, he also wished not to embarrass David Dinkins, an African American who at the time was the mayor of New York City.

Perhaps on account of the racially charged nature of this incident, the police and the mass media withheld for a day—until the initial shock had passed—the fact that the gunman was Black and that his motive involved racial hatred. But as more of the details surfaced about the man arrested at the scene, it appeared that 35-year-old Colin Ferguson was mass murder waiting to happen.

Ferguson was himself the product of affluence. Born January 14, 1958, the son of a successful pharmacist and executive, Ferguson was raised in Havedale, a well-to-do suburb of Kingston, Jamaica. As a youth, the intelligent and intense boy benefited from the very best education that money could buy at an elite prep school. Ferguson seemed to have a bright future ahead of him.

All this privilege and potential, however, started to unravel when Ferguson was 20. First, his father was killed in an automobile accident, then his mother died from cancer a year later. With much of the family fortune spent on medical bills, Ferguson moved to the United States seeking a new start, but it was just the beginning of the end. Over the next decade, his expectations would be shattered as his American Dream became a dreadful nightmare. Beginning as a clerk for Eddie's Liquor and Junior Market Stores in Long Beach, California, Ferguson moved from job to job, chronically feeling that his employment was beneath him. His career troubles escalated after moving to Long Island. He fell from a stool while working as a clerk for the Ademco Security Group of Syosset, Long Island, forcing him to go on workmen's compensation.

Surviving on his small weekly checks was a struggle. Eventually, Ferguson was awarded a lump-sum settlement of $26,250, but these funds didn't go very far. Soon thereafter, Ferguson was once again hounding the Workman's Compensation Board, sometimes calling several times a day, trying to reopen his claim for increased support.

For a while, Ferguson found some satisfaction by resuming his studies, but his academic success was short-lived. In the spring of 1990, he made the dean's list at Nassau County Community College. He then transferred to Adelphi University in the fall, but within a year he was suspended for his repeated arguments with faculty over issues of racism.

Even his hopes and dreams for marriage and family were frustrated. In 1986, he married Audrey M. Warren, but the relationship was brief and rocky; the couple separated after a year and were divorced shortly thereafter.

Having failed at work, school, and home, Ferguson was nearing the end of his ability to cope. One final indignity was being told by his landlord, Patrick Denis, that at the end of the month he would be kicked out of his home, an undersized, one-room refuge in Flatbush that he rented for $150 per month. Denis, himself a Black American, had overheard his tenant rant and rave on repeated occasions about the need for Blacks to kill Whites. He became increasingly alarmed about Ferguson's mental instability and wanted nothing more to do with him. For all of Ferguson's misfortunes, disappointments, and frustrations, there would be hell to pay. Ferguson was there to collect in full on the ill-fated 5:33.

CHAPTER 19

Going Berserk

The August 12, 1966, issue of *Time* magazine led with a story of national pride—the wedding of Luci Baines Johnson, daughter of President Lyndon and Mrs. Lady Bird Johnson. Americans certainly love a wedding, but apparently they are more fascinated by murder. The presidential wedding was unceremoniously upstaged by a story of national sorrow. The cover photo of *Time* highlighted another Texan, Charles Whitman. On August 1, 1966, Whitman had climbed atop the 307-foot tower on the campus of the University of Texas in Austin and had opened fire on the campus from a vantage point behind the tower's huge clock. Ninety-one bloody minutes later, 14 people were dead or dying. Thirty more lay injured in a 16-block area surrounding the tower; strewn with casualties, it looked more like a war zone than a college campus. Another victim of Whitman's rampage was the fetus of a woman 8 months pregnant that was stillborn. In addition to these casualties, Whitman had killed his mother and his wife the night before, and Whitman himself was gunned down by a team of four officers at the top of the tower.

To those who knew Charlie casually, he was the all-American boy, certainly not the popular image of a deadly killer. A committed and hardworking student, he had earned all As during his final semester at the University of Texas; over his entire college career as an architectural engineering major, his average was in the B range. He also seemed to be a friendly and caring fellow. After having been an Eagle Scout in his youth, Whitman as an adult served as a scoutmaster and impressed the scouts' parents as being good with the children. Being a bright student and a respected member of the community, he seemed to have a promising future. But his parents, his wife, and his friends knew the real Charles Whitman, a troubled man who, according to his psychiatrist, was "oozing with hostility" (Lavergne, 1997, p. 70). Whitman had in fact told the doctor that he thought about "going up on the tower with a deer rifle and shooting people" (Lavergne, 1997, p. 71), but the therapist considered this to be merely one of the many idle fantasies that depressed college students entertained about the tower. Whitman also beat his wife on occasion, as reportedly his father—whom he hated passionately—had done to the mother Charles loved.

Photo 19.1 Random massacres, such as Charles Whitman's shooting spree from the University of Texas tower, attract the most attention yet are the rarest form of mass murder. (Associated Press)

Charles Whitman was proud to have served in the Marines. However, his military career was not as honorable as some believed. He had been demoted from corporal to private for a number of transgressions, including assault, gambling, and the possession of illegal firearms. While in the Marines, he was decorated for achieving the class of sharpshooter. Whitman was well acquainted with guns even as a youngster. "Charlie could plug a squirrel in the eye by the time he was sixteen," said his father, in a dramatic example of understatement (Lavergne, 1997, p. 5). During Whitman's spree at the tower, an onlooker three blocks away remarked to a friend that they were safely out of range; then he was shot.

Whitman had the hostility to commit the crime as well as the skillful shot, needing only to amass the large arsenal of weapons that Texas law permitted him to purchase. It was only the delay of a few minutes, when Whitman stopped to shoot a receptionist and some tourists who stood between him and his gun post that prevented him from opening fire between class periods on the thousands who would have been under his gun.

PARANOID THINKING

Most mass killers target people they know—family members, friends, or coworkers—in order to settle a score, to get even with the particular individuals whom they hold accountable for their problems. Others seek revenge against a certain class or category of people who are suspected of receiving an unfair advantage. But a few revenge-motivated mass murders stem from the killers' paranoid view of society at large. They imagine a wide-ranging conspiracy in which large numbers of people, friends and strangers alike, are out to do them harm.

As we have seen, family and workplace mass murder typically is committed by a perpetrator who is clearheaded and rational, though resentful and depressed. By contrast, a random mass murder often reflects the distorted thinking of a psychotic on a suicidal mission.

Mullen (2004) has labeled this type of massacre as *autogenic*. Based on a detailed examination of five cases, he concluded that autogenic mass killers share certain social and psychological traits, including social isolation, feelings of persecution verging on delusional, an absence of remorse, and suicidal intentions. Most also exhibit an extreme sense of entitlement as well as a self-righteous view of their troubled life.

This kind of mass killer blames the world for his problems and decides to get even. The more people he kills, no matter who they are, the sweeter the revenge. To some extent, this psychotic reasoning also may be found in certain hate-motivated mass killers, such as Patrick Purdy, who targeted absolute strangers just because they were Southeast Asians. But those who carry out a random massacre believe that almost everyone is their enemy. They hate virtually all of humanity.

Mass murderer William Cruse, for example, suspected that nearly everyone was against him. He focused his anger on his noisy neighbors and gossipy grocery clerks, and on the children who played on his block, but he really hated all of the residents of the Palm Bay, Florida, community in which he lived.

On a Thursday evening, April 23, 1987, the 59-year-old retired librarian went on a bloody rampage in a local shopping center, killing six people and injuring another 12. At his trial, several psychiatrists testified that William Cruse suffered from a severe mental illness known as paranoid schizophrenia. He believed that he was the target of a wide-ranging conspiracy to destroy his life, and he often imagined seeing acts of disrespect and indignity that were designed to anger him.

As a young man, Cruse seemed happy and healthy enough. He graduated from the University of Kentucky in 1951 with a BA in history and in 1954 with a master's degree in library science. From 1955 to 1967, he worked as a librarian at the Cincinnati Public Library.

But Cruse had long-standing psychological problems that became more severe with advancing age. As a middle-age adult, he was described by neighbors in his home state of Kentucky as a weird and strangely cantankerous man who despised children. In 1980, he was charged in Lexington with public intoxication.

After Cruse moved to Palm Bay, his already considerable paranoia deepened. He was convinced that the people on his block were spreading false rumors that he was a "homosexual," "effeminate," and "queer." The clerks at the local Winn-Dixie and Publix supermarkets must have heard the gossip somehow, Cruse imagined, because they appeared to stare at his crotch whenever he went shopping. He even thought he saw one grocery store clerk stick out his tongue at him, for no good reason.

Almost every afternoon for 2 years before his rampage, the nondescript, gray-haired man would visit the Palm Bay Public Library located little more than a mile from his home. He never spoke to employees nor did he check out a book. For a few minutes daily, he sat quietly by himself at a table and read the *Wall Street Journal*.

From Cruse's paranoid perspective, the neighborhood children repeatedly harassed him and trespassed on his property. He interpreted normal juvenile behaviors as personal assaults on his privacy. If a child attempted to retrieve a wayward ball, Cruse saw it as trespassing. If the kids on the block made noise, he took it as harassment. In response, he shouted obscenities and made sexually suggestive gestures. After a while, Cruse felt so beleaguered that even a child innocently strolling past his house was enough to send him into a frenzy. He would rush out and shoot his rifle into the air.

At 6 p.m. on the fatal evening in April, Cruse heard a noise outside his house. He peeked through the blinds to find two young boys walking back and forth past his bungalow. Cruse confronted them outside, screaming vulgarities at them, but they only laughed in his face. Enraged even more, he then rushed back into his house to get his three guns—a Ruger .223 semiautomatic rifle, a .357-caliber Ruger revolver, and a Winchester 20-gauge shotgun—and a bagful of bullets.

By the time he came back out front, the boys were nowhere to be found. Having nobody else to victimize, Cruse aimed his rifle at a 14-year-old boy who was shooting hoops in his driveway across the street, striking him in the buttocks. He then jumped into his white Toyota and drove to a nearby shopping mall in which the Publix supermarket was located. First, he opened fire at point-blank range on two college students as they strolled nonchalantly in the parking lot. Then he walked over to a woman who was sitting in her car and shot her in the head.

Cruse must have been thinking of all those grocery store clerks who he thought had sneered at him and had challenged his sexuality, as he tried in vain to get into the Publix Market through an automatic exit-only door. But he was so confused that he couldn't find the entrance. Giving up in frustration, he then drove his Toyota to the Winn-Dixie supermarket in a shopping center across the road. Rushing to the grocery store, he confronted two policemen who had been dispatched in response to the shooting. Cruse quickly gunned them down as they attempted to block the entrance to the store. He then shot his way through the Winn-Dixie, firing at frightened customers and employees as they fought to get out of his way.

Cruse followed a 21-year-old woman into the ladies' restroom and, for 6 hours, kept her hostage. In the meantime, the police formed a human barricade surrounding the store. Cruse talked to his captive about killing both of them, but shortly after midnight, he released his hostage. The police apprehended him as he attempted to escape.

Cruse pleaded not guilty by reason of insanity. He claimed no memory of the tragic massacre, and defense psychiatrists confirmed that he was a paranoid schizophrenic. Despite Cruse's history of bizarre behavior and delusional thinking, the jury wouldn't buy the defense. Perhaps fearing that he might escape too easily if they were to return an insanity verdict, the jury found Cruse guilty on six counts of first-degree murder and recommended the death penalty. On November 30, 2009—more than 20 years after he committed mass murder—Cruse died in his cell on Death Row, but of natural causes.

Unlike mass killings in which specific victims are targeted because of a grudge, random massacres are not necessarily preceded by some clear-cut precipitant such as the loss of a job or a relationship. The psychotic killer can create his own catalyst in his mind, even if no major external event occurred. Thus, for example, a clerk who is perceived to stick out his tongue is enough to drive someone like William Cruse over the edge. Also, unlike family-related and workplace rampages for which the perpetrators generally engage in long-term planning, random slaughters occasionally are spontaneous, in response to objectively trivial or innocuous experiences. There is no evidence, for example, that William Cruse contemplated, for any longer than a few moments, his attack in Palm Bay.

CONFUSED STATE OF MIND

Part of the reason why random massacres occur so infrequently is that their perpetrators are typically too out of touch with reality to carry out their plan of attack in an effective, methodical manner. They may attempt mass murder, but generally they fail to complete it—perhaps succeeding in killing one or two of their many "adversaries." Indeed, it may be difficult to concentrate on killing scores of people if "the voices" keep interrupting.

The deranged mind of 26-year-old Dion Terres of Kenosha, Wisconsin, apparently prevented him from exacting as much revenge on society as he had sought. He lived by himself, had no real friends, and hated the world and everybody in it—everybody, that is, except for Ted Bundy, Jeffrey Dahmer, Aileen Wuornos, and Adolf Hitler, all of whom he admired. More than just a serial killer groupie, Terres believed that his thought processes were just like those of serial killers, except that he was smarter. In addition to his odd fascination with the champions of murder, Terres suffered from numerous delusions. He claimed to have exhumed the corpse of Abraham Lincoln and to have placed it in his bathtub. He reported hearing voices and he worshipped Satan.

For Dion Terres, 1993 was not a good year. In March, he was fired from his job assembling cellular phones at the Motorola plant in Arlington Heights, Illinois. Irate over being terminated, Terres went out and purchased an AR-15 assault rifle from a local gun dealer, though he thought twice about using it on his former boss. In August, the other shoe dropped, and Terres thought a third time about using his rifle. His girlfriend, 16-year-old Kimberly Sinkler, said she wanted nothing more to do with him after he began making veiled threats about raping and poisoning her. He even went so far as to follow Kim to her job at a local hospital.

By August 10, Terres could take no more of life. It was time to get the justice he believed he deserved. Dressed for battle in his military fatigues, he tossed two guns, including the AR-15 that he had bought in March, onto the passenger seat of his blue sedan and drove 2 miles to the McDonald's on Pershing Boulevard in Kenosha. Parking in the lot next to the drive-through, Terres grabbed his weapons and, in a panic, locked his car behind him. At this point, he realized that he had locked his keys inside the car—and, worse, his 30-round gun clip for the semiautomatic. He was getting more and more confused and disoriented. Rather than abort his mission, Terres threw the useless AR-15 onto the pavement, forgetting about the spare clip in his breast pocket, and decided to forge ahead with just his .44-caliber revolver.

There were some 20 employees and customers inside the restaurant when Terres made his entrance. Standing over two young boys who were eating their lunch, he shouted, "I want everybody out of here!" (Lisheron & Tijerina,

1993). Before anyone could move, however, Terres fired away. Fifty-year-old Bruce Bojesen was shot in the head and died instantly. Sandra Kenaga, age 39, died the next morning from back wounds. One other person received a minor injury in the arm. Terres saved the last bullet for himself. He shoved the revolver under his chin and pulled the trigger.

Those who survived the attack were lucky—lucky because Terres had locked himself out of his car, had forgotten to take the clip from inside, and had forgotten about the spare clip he was carrying. They were lucky that Terres's state of mind got in his way. He had everything it takes—the frustration, catastrophic loss, isolation, conspiratorial thinking, and access to firearms—to become a mass killer. He had everything, that is, but the ability to think clearly and act methodically.

Mass murderers who attempt to settle a grudge against a particular list of victims—such as an estranged father or husband or an embittered employee—tend to be middle-age. It is generally not until they reach their 30s or 40s that life's frustrations accumulate to the point that they seem intolerable and insurmountable. But those killers who actually go berserk and kill indiscriminately as a result of psychotic thinking can come from any age group. Schizophrenia, for example, often has its onset in late adolescence. Thus, someone as young as Terres, or even younger, can perceive that the whole world is out to get him, so he decides to get them first. Any minor incident could trigger a rampage.

LONG-STANDING MENTAL ILLNESS

In December 2007, Robert Hawkins, a 19-year-old man with a history of mental illness, carried the semiautomatic rifle he had stolen from his stepfather's home into an Omaha, Nebraska, shopping mall and took the elevator to the third floor of a department store, where he opened fire at random on customers and employees. Before killing himself with a gunshot to the head, Hawkins took the lives of eight innocent people. The killer left a suicide note in which he apologized "for everything" but then added "Now, I'll be famous."

Apparently, the appeal of infamy was a result of the gunman's immediate miseries as well as his long-standing mental illness. He had moved out of his parents' house a year earlier and, 2 weeks before his rampage, had broken up with his girlfriend and then lost his job at McDonald's. To add insult to injury, Hawkins had been arrested 11 days earlier and was due in court a couple of days after his rampage on a charge of underage drinking.

Like so many of those gunmen who go berserk, Hawkins's troubled past extended back into his early childhood. By the age of 6, he had already taken psychiatric medications, undergone psychotherapy, and been hospitalized for depression. At the age of 14, he spent time in a mental health treatment center after threatening to kill his stepmother with an axe. For a period of 4 years, Hawkins became a ward of the State of Nebraska and was hospitalized twice more for depression-related illnesses. He was diagnosed with attention deficit disorder, mood disorders, and oppositional defiant disorder. To the very end, family members and friends described him as being plagued by psychiatric problems.

The pseudocommando, Rambo-style killer isn't always a man. It was in the late afternoon of October 30, 1985, that a young woman walked hurriedly from the parking lot into a shopping mall in Springfield, Pennsylvania. Unlike other shoppers, with their bags and packages in hand, 25-year-old Sylvia Seegrist carried a .22-caliber semiautomatic rifle and was dressed in battle fatigues and black boots.

Pausing briefly at the entrance to the mall, Seegrist eyed her prospective victims and opened fire. Her first target was a 2-year-old boy who couldn't escape fast enough. Seegrist fired point-blank at the youngster; his body slumped to the ground in a heap. She then rushed into the mall, firing indiscriminately at least 15 times as she made her way along the main walkway through the crowd of shoppers. One bullet hit a 64-year-old man as he attempted to take refuge in a nearby shoe store. Seegrist continued her shooting spree until a college student managed to wrestle her to the ground and take her weapon. By that time, she had hit 10 people with gunfire, killing three of them.

At her arraignment, Seegrist told the judge, "Hurry up, man. You know I'm guilty. Kill me on the spot" (Botsford, 1990). She was charged with murder, attempted murder, aggravated assault, and possession of an unregistered firearm but was later found to be criminally insane and was committed indefinitely to a psychiatric hospital.

Only the criminal aspects of the case had been resolved. What remained was a question of civil law: Was the shopping mall in some way responsible for Sylvia Seegrist's rampage and therefore liable to the victims for the damages? Was the mall negligent in failing to provide adequate security for its customers? Should the mall have initiated commitment proceedings against Seegrist, who had been known to the security force for her belligerent and threatening manner?

In court, a security expert for the plaintiffs in the civil suit testified that a well-trained guard stationed at the main entrance to the mall could have stopped Seegrist from shooting customers. The plaintiffs' psychiatrist noted that she had visited the McDonald's restaurant in the mall shortly after a widely publicized rampage at the San Ysidro McDonald's in July 1984. At that time, she had suggested—mainly to herself but out loud nonetheless—that she might repeat Huberty's mass murder in Springfield and pointed her finger like a gun, while saying "rat-tat-tat-tat." Several more times over the course of the next year, she returned to the mall, acting in a bizarre manner and making threats or threatening gestures. The psychiatrist for the plaintiffs suggested that the mall management should have attempted to have Sylvia Seegrist committed to a mental hospital, but didn't.

The defendant's psychiatrist testified that it was extremely doubtful that Seegrist would have been committed for making threats. Pennsylvania laws had been tightened in recent years in order to prevent unjustified civil commitments. It was no longer possible to hospitalize a person against his or her will without clear-cut proof of dangerousness. Moreover, even if successfully committed, Seegrist could not have been held very long anyway. A criminologist testifying for the defense emphasized that most people who make threats never follow through with them. He argued that a reasonable person could not have foreseen the occurrence of the crime, because it is extremely rare. Even if it had been foreseeable, Sylvia Seegrist's shooting spree was still unstoppable—unless, of course, the entire mall had been turned into an armed camp (Sherman, 1990).

In February 1990, a Delaware County jury decided that the shopping mall was indeed liable for damages and awarded an undisclosed amount of money to Sylvia Seegrist's victims. Seegrist herself remains hospitalized in an institution for the criminally insane. Only after murdering three innocent strangers was there sufficient proof to ensure that Seegrist would receive the long-term psychiatric care that she had long needed for treatment of psychosis.

Sylvia Seegrist was truly an exceptional case. Not only is it rare for a woman to murder strangers, but it is equally uncommon for a woman to kill in the manner that she did. Even though females sometimes commit murder with a firearm, it is usually a handgun, not a military assault rifle. Seegrist used a .22-caliber semiautomatic and dressed in military fatigues.

Serious mental illness is apparently an important predisposing factor in the lives of rampage killers. Unlike their more prevalent counterparts who target family members, coworkers, or classmates, those who kill indiscriminately either within a category (e.g., women) or against humankind in general seem to suffer from severe psychopathology. They may be delusional and hallucinatory, killing in the course of a psychotic episode. The more random a massacre, the more likely it is that serious mental illness plays a role.

One clue that killers may be psychotic is their age at the time that they go on a rampage. Aside from school shooters who target their classmates, mass murderers generally tend to be at least in their thirties if not older. Their motivation usually comes from seeking to get even with those particular individuals whom they blame for their personal miseries, but they are typically not psychotic. Instead, they have suffered some catastrophic loss—the loss of a job or money, the loss of an important relationship, or the loss of academic standing—and seek to exact a measure of revenge against those who are regarded as responsible. Most middle-age mass killers are selective in targeting specific individuals—coworkers, family members, or classmates. Some have gone out of their way to avoid taking the lives of easy targets who are perceived to be entirely innocent of having contributed to the killer's miseries. In 1986, for example, postal worker Patrick Sherrill, the evening before he attacked fellow employees in an Edmund, Oklahoma, postal facility, made a phone call to his good friend and colleague at the post office warning him not to come to work the next morning.

By contrast, those killers who have committed a random massacre of strangers in a public place—a shopping mall, a parking lot, a cinema—are frequently in their early to mid-20s, a stage of life during which the symptoms of severe mental illness (e.g., schizophrenia) begin to take hold. Schizophrenia is a serious illness that often appears during late adolescence or early adulthood and is frequently marked by an inability to distinguish fantasy from reality or to be in touch with other people. The condition's characteristics include having delusions and hallucinations, as well as withdrawal, lack of emotion and motivation, and attention and memory problems (Mayo Clinic, 2012). People who suffer from a particular form known as paranoid schizophrenia may hear voices that aren't there, feel anxiety and anger, and believe that people are out to get them. Most schizophrenics never kill anyone, but a few lose the capacity to think clearly about themselves and others, perceiving that everybody is out to get them.

Ted Kaczynski, the so-called Unabomber who sent letter bombs through the mail for some 18 years, was still an undergraduate student when he developed the symptoms of schizophrenia. Twenty-four-year old Jared Loughner, who, following his deadly rampage at a public rally for Arizona Congresswoman Gabby Giffords in Tucson, was diagnosed as paranoid schizophrenic by more than one psychiatrist; Sylvia Seegrist was 25 years old when she killed three customers at a mall in a Springfield, Pennsylvania, shopping center. Seegrist who had been diagnosed as suffering from paranoid schizophrenia was found not guilty by reason of insanity.

Similarly, the Aurora cinema killer, James Holmes, was only 24 when, in 2012, he directed gunfire indiscriminately at total strangers in the audience of a showing for a new Batman film. After leaving his PhD program in neuroscience at the University of Colorado in June 2012, he opened fire in a crowded cinema rather than on campus where he might have taken the lives of the professors on his graduate committee. As indicated earlier, there have been other graduate students who blame professors for their loss of academic standing, but they usually aim their violence at faculty and students, not at dozens of strangers in a motion picture audience.

The Aurora killer's indiscriminate rampage provides a clue as to his mind-set. On campus, Holmes had seen a psychotherapist who specialized in schizophrenia. The schizophrenic diagnosis would explain a number of characteristics that depart from the profile of a typical mass killer.

It would explain why Holmes dyed his hair red and then informed the police "I am the Joker" when he was apprehended. If schizophrenic, he might really have believed it.

It would explain why he booby-trapped his apartment with explosives in order to take the lives of police officers but then told the police about it before they entered the building. His original intention was to rig his apartment so that attention was diverted from his cinema attack. But he seemed to be profoundly confused, suffering from a serious thought disorder that prevented even more innocent lives from being taken by the bombs in his apartment.

It would explain why he never intended to commit suicide. Most other mass murderers set out to take their own lives, even if they don't succeed. This killer went to the crime scene wearing protective body armor and then dropped his weapons and gave himself up without a struggle.

Schizophrenic or not, there is really little that can be done to deter a mass killer once he has murderous intentions. But we should attempt to intervene in the life of a troubled individual long before he becomes troublesome. The Virginia Tech mass murderer Seung-Hui Cho had been bullied and humiliated throughout middle and high school but was never helped by staff members or bystanders. It was only during his college days that an instructor who felt threatened by Cho's behavior in class attempted to get him into counseling. At that point, it was simply too late to avert disaster.

A Gallup poll taken after the Washington Navy Yard massacre in which 12 people were fatally shot by an apparently deranged gunman revealed that Americans fault the mental health system for mass murder, even more than inadequate gun laws (see Saad, 2013). Apparently, according to John Q. Public, guns don't kill, psychotic people do.

It would certainly be a fitting legacy to the tragedy of mass murder if mental health services were expanded and improved. Countless people who struggle psychologically would benefit as a result. However, greater access to treatment options may not necessarily reach the few individuals on the fringe who would seek to turn a school, a movie theater, or a military facility into their own personal war zone. With their tendency to externalize blame and consider themselves victims of injustice, mass killers demand fair treatment, not psychological treatment on demand.

The postmassacre initiative to aid the psychologically impaired is the right thing to do, but for the wrong reason. For example, during a speech in Hartford, Connecticut, delivered months after the Newtown school shooting, President Barack Obama (April 8, 2013) urged Congress to respond: "We need to help people struggling with mental health problems get the treatment they need *before it is too late*" [emphasis added]. We should endeavor to help the mentally ill out of concern for their well-being, not just because we are worried about the well-being of those they might kill.

We must resist the urge to equate mental illness with mass murder. Unfortunately, the timing of current proposals to upgrade the mental health system whose flaws have been exposed by mass murder tends to stigmatize the vast majority of people who suffer with mental illness, as if they too are mass murderers in waiting. We might not only fail to prevent mass murder but make it less likely that those most in need will seek appropriate treatment.

CIVILIAN BATTLEFIELDS

It is not possible to trace how Sylvia Seegrist developed her unusual passion for military paraphernalia, but for 41-year-old James Oliver Huberty, fascination with firearms was somewhat of a family tradition, dating back at least to his great-uncle, who had invented a machine gun used during World War I. There were guns everywhere in the Huberty home—in the bedroom, in the kitchen, on the shelves in the parlor, and, of course, in the basement, where James maintained his own makeshift firing range. He spent hours practicing his shooting, that is, when he wasn't cleaning his guns or modifying a semi-automatic into a fully automatic-fire instrument. He especially loved his dearest friend and companion—his Uzi, one of several guns he took to McDonald's on July 18, 1984.

For most of his adult life, Huberty had been slipping down a deep hole of depression and paranoia. By the time he moved his family to California and then lost his job as a security guard for a condominium complex in San Ysidro, he had reached rock bottom. On that fateful Wednesday in July, after an uncharacteristically relaxing family outing with his wife, Etna, and his two daughters, Zelia and Cassandra, Huberty was ready for Armageddon.

Huberty changed into his favorite, most comfortable clothes, military fatigues that he had purchased through an army surplus mail-order catalog.

He wrapped his favorite weapon, an Israeli-made Uzi assault rifle, in a blue-and-white-checkered blanket and said good-bye to his wife and daughter Zelia. "I'm going hunting," he told his wife of 19 years.

In the middle of San Ysidro, a working-class suburb of San Diego just north of Tijuana, Mexico, there are no hunting grounds. Etna knew that, but she also knew that her husband frequently babbled nonsense. Recently, he had been experiencing hallucinations, including imagining a 3-foot Jesus conversing with him in the living room. She urged her husband to seek professional help, and he was beginning to realize that he needed it. In fact, on July 17, he placed a call to a local mental health clinic seeking an appointment. By the time that someone from the clinic called back, however, it was too late.

And a-hunting he did go—hunting for humans at the McDonald's just a few blocks down San Ysidro Boulevard. Huberty drove the short distance to the popular family restaurant and parked his beat-up Mercury sedan in the parking lot out front. He then strode through the door, armed to the teeth and hungry for revenge.

Looking up from their Happy Meals, children sat frozen in disbelief as Huberty started shouting and shooting. "I've killed a thousand," screamed Huberty, "I'll kill a thousand more" (Time-Life Books, 1992, p. 127). People both inside and outside the restaurant were in his line of fire. One young girl died from a bullet wound in the back of her neck, despite her mother's attempt to shield her. Two teenage boys, riding bicycles past the restaurant, were struck down by stray bullets, as was a motorist on the freeway behind the McDonald's.

When the police arrived, the area resembled a battlefield. By the time a police sharpshooter from the SWAT team drew a bead on Huberty from a distance, 21 people had been killed and more than a dozen wounded in the 77-minute siege.

Huberty's trip to the San Ysidro McDonald's may have taken a matter of minutes, but his journey in effect began decades earlier, back in Ohio. It was a journey lowlighted by failure, withdrawal, and disappointment.

Shortly after marrying Etna in 1965, James took a job working for a Canton funeral home. His career as a mortician was short-lived, however. Even though he did a fine job in the embalming room, his cold and unsympathetic demeanor with grieving mourners was a significant problem. Trying his hand next at welding, Huberty spent more than a decade working for Babcock & Wilcox, an engineering firm in nearby Massillon. Things worked out quite well for James; with overtime, he earned a decent salary. But then, in 1982, hard times hit and the plant closed, leaving Huberty nowhere to turn except to the West Coast.

Throughout his years in Ohio, Huberty became increasingly reclusive, cutting himself off from all friends. Even his relationship with Etna was one of dependency rather than companionship. She cooked, cleaned, and washed for him; managed the household expenses and other matters; and even chauffeured him back and forth to work. Besides his job, the only activity that he found satisfying was working with his gun collection. Being without friends was not a problem—he could always count on his guns.

If only we had gun laws as strict as those in England, some Americans lament, James Huberty might never have become such a prolific mass killer.

Of course, they likely have not heard of Michael Ryan, a resident of Hungerford, England, who killed 15 people and wounded just as many during a 4-hour siege through town before taking his own life. His victims included his own mother, his neighbor, and his two dogs, but most of those gunned down were perfect strangers who just happened to get in Ryan's way. Ryan was able to accomplish his tour of murder, which began at his home and ended at the school that he once attended, despite the country's rather restrictive gun laws.

Ryan, a 27-year-old good-for-nothing, had long had a bad reputation for belligerence. Despite his argumentative nature, however, he never had a brush with the law or involvement in the mental health system. Indeed, neither a criminal record nor a history of profound mental illness is a requirement for mass murder, even the indiscriminate type. Although he may have tended toward paranoia, he was far from psychotic in his thinking. Thus, each time Ryan applied to have his gun permit expanded, he was able to survive the screening process—a process that included an interview with local police to verify his sporting purpose.

By 1987, Ryan was licensed legally to own semiautomatic rifles for the sake of sportsmanship, but he viewed it as a license to murder. Ryan used his large cache of weapons that he had legally purchased under English law to take target practice on humanity. In the process, he committed the crime of the century, at least by English standards. In America, it would have been the crime of the week.

It took more than a large arsenal of weapons for Ryan to carry out his assault on his hometown. He developed the gun-handling skills through membership in a variety of gun clubs, the same memberships that earned him the legal right to own his weapons. But mass murderers don't have to join hunting clubs to become expert marksmen. Many of them are trained to handle high-powered firearms in preparation for military careers. The skills they acquire in the military for going to war prepare them in civilian life for going berserk.

When it comes to pseudocommandos, Julian Knight of Melbourne, Australia, was as pseudo as they come. For as long as he could remember, and with his interest fostered by his adoption into a military family, the 19-year-old Aussie had focused nearly all his energies and thoughts toward a career in the military. In short, Knight was obsessed. He fashioned himself as a military man—better yet—a war hero. But the only war he would ever fight was a civil war. On August 7, 1987, along Hoddle Street in Melbourne, the "enemy" consisted of innocent strangers, seven of whom were killed and 19 more of whom were wounded.

Unlike other pseudocommandos, such as James Huberty and Patrick Purdy, Knight survived to become a hero in his own eyes. "I performed exactly as my Army superiors would have expected me to perform in a combat situation," reflected Knight from his jail cell. "In other circumstances I would have gotten a medal for what I did" (Time-Life Books, 1992, p. 70).

Knight was indeed well trained to kill. He received his first gun, an air rifle, as a gift for his 12th birthday. Even with this relatively "harmless" initiation into weaponry, within 2 years, Knight was being trained in the use of an M16 rifle. Within 2 more years, Knight was learning ambush tactics after joining the Melbourne High School cadet unit. By the time he reached the military academy, he was expert in the use of a variety of pistols, automatic rifles, submachine guns, grenade launchers, and hand grenades. His passion consumed all aspects of his life. In school, for example, he sought to use his favorite periodical, *Soldier of Fortune* magazine, as reference material for his school papers.

Julian Knight may have had a clear vision of his career goals and ambitions, but his intensity likely led to his downfall. He was rejected on all fronts, beginning with his birth parents when he was a 10-month-old baby. His obsession with combat played a major role in his troubles with classmates as well as in his rejection by his girlfriend just a few days before the shooting. His weird fascination with the military was disturbing, even scary, to those around him.

Most critical, however, was his failure at his lifelong ambition to graduate from the Duntroon Military College, an elite program for training military officers. Despite finishing high school with C grades, Knight was accepted into the prestigious military school in 1986. After all, he was bright, with an IQ measured as high as 132. But in the military academy, his personality got the better of him. Knight had difficulty accepting the rigid hierarchy of authority and frequently became embroiled in disputes with his superiors. His hopes for a military career all but ended in a Canberra night club when he pulled a pocketknife on a sergeant, leading to his expulsion from Duntroon.

During the 9 weeks after his arrest for assaulting his superior officer, Knight became increasingly depressed and desperate. Added to his frustration over his failing military plans, the transmission in his car blew up and his girlfriend left him. He was now ready to do what he had been trained to do—kill. He would finally get even with the world that had for so long cruelly rejected him, and he would get a chance to demonstrate his incredible power.

Just after 9:30 p.m. on the evening of August 7, Knight left his apartment on Ramsen Street in the Clifton Hill area of Melbourne, armed with a Ruger .22-caliber semiautomatic rifle, a .308-caliber M14 rifle, and a 12-gauge Mossberg pump-action shotgun. He also packed 200 rounds of ammunition—enough for an army, albeit an army of one. During the next 40 minutes, Knight exhausted his entire cache of ammunition as he walked north on Hoddle Street and doubled back along the railway tracks, shooting indiscriminately. Following a shootout in which a police helicopter was shot down from the sky, Knight was captured by "enemy forces." But he still took his parting shot at the police, later charging in the press that they were "ill-equipped and ill-prepared" (Conroy & Murdock, 1988, p. 21). As a self-styled authority on military tactics, Knight surely felt he knew better.

On the afternoon of April 15th, 2013, near the finish line of the Boston Marathon on Boylston Street, two brothers allegedly planted a couple of pressure cooker bombs among the spectators. Exploding seconds apart, the assailants' bombs killed three and injured at least another 264. Later that day and still on the loose, the suspects, who were identified as 19-year-old Dzhokhar and 26-year-old Tamerlan Tsarnaev, also shot to death an MIT police officer and, during an exchange of gunfire, wounded a transit police officer. Attempting to escape by automobile, Dzhokhar accidently ran over and killed his older brother and then fled into a nearby 20-block neighborhood, where he hid in a boat in the backyard of a resident. Thousands of police officers conducted a thorough

Photo 19.2 As they walked among spectators, the suspects in the Boston Marathon bombing were caught in a still frame by investigators who pored through hundreds of hours of surveillance video footage. (Associated Press/FBI)

manhunt, leading to the capture and arrest of the surviving brother, Dzhokhar.

The alleged Marathon bombers apparently came to identify closely with the cause of radical Islam, but that is not the whole story. These marathon terrorists were more like rampage killers who enter a school, cinema, or shopping mall and indiscriminately target anything that moves. Their motive for planting explosives near the finish line of the marathon seemed to be revenge: They apparently blamed the United States for wars in Afghanistan and Iraq, but they also seemed to blame everybody but themselves for their personal miseries.

It has been reported that Tamerlan was intensely angry—so much so that he disrupted a prayer service at his local mosque. The brothers' uncle referred to the two terrorists as "a couple of losers." And, it was true that Tamerlan had recently suffered some major losses. He had become unemployed, on welfare, and dependent on his wife's meager income. Moreover, the older brother claimed to have had no American friends and apparently did little better befriending fellow Muslims aside from his younger brother, being recently expelled from his own mosque. The final straw may have occurred when Tamerlan, who was reputedly the best boxer in New England, was declared ineligible for national competition because of his lack of U.S. citizenship. Referring to the Boston Marathon bombing, President Obama used the term *self-radicalizing* to indicate the absence of an organized network such as al Qaeda.

BRAIN ABNORMALITIES

The only combat that tower sniper Charles Whitman ever saw was his one-man attack at the University of Texas in Austin. Whitman's case did, however, spark a battle of sorts within the medical community about the connection between violence and brain abnormalities. Whitman's postmortem examination revealed a walnut-size, highly malignant tumor of the brain (a glioblastoma multiforme). Could not the presence of a profound abnormality in Whitman's brain explain what looked to be a sudden, episodic attack of violence in which 14 people died and 31 were wounded?

University of Michigan psychologist Dr. Elliot Valenstein (1976) pointed out that Whitman's violent behavior was anything but episodic or sudden. In fact, Whitman had written his detailed plan for mass killing in his diary days before the actual massacre, describing not only how he intended to protect his position on the tower and how he planned to escape, but even what he was going to wear. Moreover, Whitman's killing spree did not occur in quick succession: The night before, he killed deliberately. First, he traveled to his mother's apartment in Austin, where he stabbed her in the chest and shot her in the head. He then sat down and wrote a note, placing it on his mother's body:

Monday, 8-1-66, 12:30 AM

To Whom It May Concern
    I have just taken my mother's life. I am very upset over having done it. However, if there is a heaven she is definitely there now.... Let there be no doubt in your mind that I loved the woman with all my heart.... (Lavergne, 1997, p. 103)

Photo 19.3   Charles Whitman's massacre on the campus of the University of Texas in Austin was widely regarded as "the crime of the century," indicating the rarity of such multiple murders during the decade of the 1960s.

Returning home, Whitman then stabbed his wife three times in the chest, an event he noted in the margin of a letter explaining why he needed to kill her: "3:00 AM Both Dead" (Lavergne, 1997, p. 108). No one can say with certainty what role Whitman's tumor played, because its location in the brain was obscured by the gunshots that ended his life. Although the debate over Whitman's behavior may never be settled, the assumption that the tumor was responsible is clearly not justified. The same kind of reasoning was used to try to account for James Huberty's 1984 murder spree at a McDonald's restaurant. Hopeful that some neurological abnormality might be the cause, pathologists examined Huberty's brain tissue. They were disappointed when the autopsy failed to reveal a tumor or any other physical explanation for his rampage.

Notwithstanding the lack of conclusive evidence linking organic abnormalities to Whitman's and Huberty's murderous rampages, there is considerable research on the contribution of biochemical dysfunction to severe mental illnesses such as schizophrenia and manic depression. As noted in Chapter 5, there has been a recent upsurge in research that focuses on biological factors in the etiology of the serial killer. It may be just a matter of time before we identify a neurological factor, interacting with environmental causes, that accounts for random acts of mass murder.

DEADLY WEAPONS

Whatever the source of his grudge against society, the mass killer must also have access to a means of mass destruction, and the United States, in particular, makes it easy enough for a vengeful madman to purchase all the guns and ammunition needed to carry out his attack. Massacres can and do occasionally happen in countries such as England, Australia, Canada, and elsewhere, but nothing to match the bloodshed in the United States. Although gun proponents are correct when they argue that firearms are not to blame per se for the behavior of mass killers, guns do make their attacks far bloodier. It would have been nearly impossible for James Huberty to quickly slay 21 people with a knife or his own hands. In addition to the greater lethality of the firearm, guns also distance the attacker psychologically from his victims. It is possible that James Huberty or Sylvia Seegrist might not have been emotionally able to kill young children had they had any physical contact with their victims. But with a rifle, they could dispassionately shoot down innocent strangers as if they were moving objects in a video game or even toy soldiers on an imaginary battlefield.

Table 19.1   Deadliest Mass Murders in the United States Since 1900

Name(s)	Victims	Year	Primary location	Place	Weapon(s)
Timothy J. McVeigh	168	1995	Federal building	Oklahoma City, OK	Bomb
Julio Gonzalez	87	1990	Night club	New York, NY	Fire
Andrew Kehoe	45	1927	School	Bath, MI	Bomb
Jack Gilbert Graham	44	1955	Airplane	Denver, CO	Airplane
David Burke	43	1987	Airplane	Cayucos, CA	Airplane
Seung-Hui Cho	32	2007	College	Blacksburg, VA	Gun
Adam Peter Lanza	27(26+1)	2012	School	Newtown, CT	Gun
Humberto de la Torre	25	1982	Hotel	Los Angeles, CA	Fire
George Jo Hennard	23	1991	Restaurant	Killeen, TX	Gun
James Oliver Huberty	21	1984	Restaurant	San Ysidro, CA	Gun
Charles Whitman	16(14+2)	1966	College	Austin, TX	Gun

Name(s)	Victims	Year	Primary location	Place	Weapon(s)
Ronald Gene Simmons	16(14+2)	1987	Home	Dover, AR	Gun/Knife
Patrick Sherrill	14	1986	Post office	Edmond, OK	Gun
Eric Harris & Dylan Klebold	13	1999	School	Littleton, CO	Gun
George Banks	13	1982	Home	Wilkes-Barre, PA	Gun
Howard Unruh	13	1949	City street	Camden, NJ	Gun
Jiverly Wong	13	2009	Immigration center	Binghamton, NY	Gun
Nidal Malik Hasan	13	2009	Military base	Fort Hood, TX	Gun
Willie Mak, Benjamin Ng, & Tony Ng	13	1983	Night club	Seattle, WA	Gun
Aaron Alexis	12	2013	Navy yard	Washington, DC	Gun
James Eagan Holmes	12	2012	Movie theater	Aurora, CO	Gun
Mark O. Barton	12(9 + 3)	1999	Office building	Atlanta, GA	Gun
James Ruppert	11	1975	Home	Hamilton, OH	Gun
Michael Kenneth McLendon	10	2009	Home	Geneva, AL	Gun
James Edward Pough	10(8 + 2)	1990	Office building	Jacksonville, FL	Gun

Note: Victim counts in parentheses represent death tolls at separate locations.

For mass murderers like Huberty and Knight, the gun is like an old friend. In times of stress, they might go target shooting to ease frustrations. Some mass killers have even measured their own self-worth in terms of their marksmanship abilities. It is easy to understand, therefore, why so many have seen the firearm as the way, ultimately, to resolve their grudge against society.

The availability of high-powered, rapid-fire weapons of mass destruction, like those used by James Huberty, is surely a large part of the reason why the death tolls in mass murders have been so large in the recent past. As shown in

Photo 19.4   This photo released Tuesday, Feb. 22, 2011, by the U.S. Marshal's Service shows Jared Lee Loughner, who pleaded guilty in the Tucson, Ariz., shooting rampage that killed six people and left several others wounded, including then-U.S. Rep. Gabrielle Giffords. Hundreds of pages of police reports in the investigation of the shooting were released Wednesday, March 27, 2013, marking the public's first glimpse into documents that authorities have kept private since the attack on Jan. 8, 2011. (Associated Press/Pims County Sheriff's Department via The Arizona Republic)

Table 19.1, three quarters of the deadliest mass murders in the United States have occurred since 1980, most of which involved firearms as the exclusive or primary weapon.

In January 2011, Jared Loughner, a 22-year-old distraught and angry loner, allegedly shot to death six and injured another 14 outside a supermarket in Tucson, Arizona. Loughner's primary target was apparently Gabrielle Giffords, a Democratic congresswoman who had voted for certain liberal policies that the shooter opposed (but who also supported Second Amendment rights). It became clear in the aftermath that the shooter had planned for months to assassinate Representative Giffords, purchasing his semiautomatic 9mm Glock, equipped with an extended magazine, several weeks before and waiting for an opportunity to make contact with his intended victim when she met with constituents. In addition, inside a safe at the house where Loughner lived with his parents, investigators found the handwritten statements "I planned ahead" and "my assassination," as well as the name "Giffords" and what appeared to be Loughner's signature. Notwithstanding Loughner's bizarre behavior in the months prior to the shootings, he was able to pass a federal background check, allowing him legally to buy the weapon reportedly used to shoot his primary target along with others who happened to appear in the crosshairs of his sight.

Can any form of gun control prevent a person like Loughner from accessing powerful weaponry? Unfortunately, background checks, as prescribed by the Brady Law of 1994, do not necessarily provide effective preventive measures against the onslaught. Few mass killers have criminal or psychiatric records. Furthermore, most mass murderers would not consider buying a weapon through illegal means. After all, they see themselves as law-abiding citizens who are only looking for some justice.

CHAPTER 20

Weapons of Mass (Murder) Destruction

The Century 16 theater in Aurora, Colorado, easily sold out all its tickets for the July 12, 2012, midnight premiere of the *Dark Knight Rises*. Inconspicuous among the crowd of Batman fans, even with his bright red-colored hair, was 24-year-old James Eagan Holmes. Shortly after the film began, according to authorities, Holmes left the theater by a rear door that he propped open for his return once he gathered up his arsenal of weapons, ammunition, and military paraphernalia. Dressed head-to-toe in protective gear and wearing a gas mask, Holmes reportedly set off two tear gas grenades and then started spraying the darkened theater with bullets from an AR-15 assault rifle, a 12-gauge shotgun, and two .40-caliber handguns. In just a matter of minutes, 12 people were killed and dozens more wounded before Holmes surrendered himself to the police.

When the authorities searched Holmes' apartment, they found evidence of his long-term planning. He had purchased, over the Internet, thousands of rounds of ammunition and had set booby-traps at his apartment which were success-fully disabled by the police. As details surfaced about this deeply disturbed man who had recently failed out of graduate school, many people questioned how and why it should be so easy for someone on the fringe of sanity to acquire such deadly weapons.

Apparently, James Holmes was one of the many men who found high-powered weaponry to be the answer to all problems. The overwhelming pre-dominance of men among those implicated in mass murder goes well beyond any notions of gender differences in aggression. The particularly high percentage of male mass killers has much to do with the weapons of choice among these assailants—that is, rifles, shotguns, pistols and revolvers, as well as explosives. Men have unequal access to and training in the use of handguns and long guns, often from sport shooting and sometimes through military service. The vast majority of mass murderers employ a firearm, if not several. Indeed, it is difficult to kill a large number of people at one time using other weapons such as a knife or a club. Typically, mass killers are fascinated with guns; own large collections of rifles, including military-style assault weapons; and have the shooting skills to match. The same can be said of explosives in terms of the training and fasci-nation that is far more common among men.

Photo 20.1   James Eagan Holmes, accused of killing 12 people in a shooting rampage in an Aurora, Colorado, movie theater, appears in Arapahoe County District Court in Centennial, Colorado. The University of Colorado at Denver has released thousands of documents that may relate to the man accused in the Colorado theater shootings. More than 2,000 records were released Wednesday Dec. 5, 2012, after news organizations, including The Associated Press, requested them to learn about James Holmes's year at the school. (Associated Press/*Denver Post*, RJ Sangosti Pool)

Twenty-five-year-old Charles Whitman, for example, had grown up around firearms. His father, himself a gun aficionado, had taught Charles to hunt when he was a young boy. Charles later fine-tuned his marksmanship skills while serving in the Marines.

Charles Whitman's 1966 assault from the Tower at the University of Texas was widely termed the "Crime of the Century," reflecting the rarity of such mass murder at the time. Of course, those who saw Whitman's crime as history-making could not have imagined what new and much deadlier slaughters lay ahead in the remaining quarter of the century. Whitman's crime may have helped to define the term *mass murder* in the American consciousness, but more recent tragedies have pushed the limits of public anxiety to the breaking point. We have witnessed massacres in schoolyards and shopping malls, trains and planes, post offices, and fast food establishments. People everywhere wonder, "Is nowhere safe?"

Several factors have coalesced recently to produce a deadly mix of resentment and despair. A growing number of middle-age men are losing those aspects of their lives that give them meaning and support, particularly their families and their jobs. A shrinking and more competitive labor market has left thousands of men feeling hopeless and worthless. A high rate of divorce, greater residential mobility, and a general lack of neighborliness have left many men feeling very much alone. Though their crimes are reprehensible, a few of these desperate people feel that they have no place to turn and no means to resolve their problems other than use of their guns. The one problem they don't have is finding a high-powered weapon of mass destruction.

On November 1, 1991, Gang Lu, a 28-year-old Chinese-born graduate student at the University of Iowa, methodically shot and killed five people whom he held responsible for denying him a coveted prize given for the top science dissertation. In advance of his on-campus massacre, Gang Lu had written to his sister in China outlining his funeral wishes, sending along the contents of the bank account he shortly wouldn't need. He also wrote a letter to the media outlining his grievance against the physics department and describing how his gun would help to right the terrible wrongs that had been done to him. "Private guns make every person equal, no matter what/who he/she is," he wrote. "They also make it possible for an individual to fight against a conspired/incorporated organization such as Mafia or Dirty University officials."

In the wake of virtually any large mass shooting, significant debate surfaces about the role of firearms in facilitating a bloodbath. Of course, guns didn't make Gang Lu lose out to his rival countryman nor did they encourage his desire to kill those whom he blamed for ruining his life. However, for Gang Lu, the gun was a necessary instrument to achieve his desired outcome, and it was likely the only weapon that would do. Certainly, knives or other objects would not have made it possible to execute his entire hit list without being subdued. Explosives, on the other hand, might have provided a means of mass destruction—much like what occurred in Bath, Michigan, on May 18, 1927, when Andrew Kehoe detonated a cache of explosives hidden in the basement of a local school, killing 38 children, five adults, and himself. However, Gang Lu's plan was not to kill just anyone, but exclusively those who were his intended targets for payback. A firearm was his only logical choice.

Firearms, especially high-powered ones, are the weapons most often used in rampage-style killings. Among the two dozen mass murders in the United States involving at least 10 victims slain, three quarters involved a firearm. Handguns and rifles are, of course, far more lethal than knives or clubs for the assailant who seeks to kill large numbers of victims in a short period of time. In countries where guns are relatively inaccessible, mass killings are far less likely to occur, even if the motivation for large-scale destruction exists. For example, China's strict gun laws prevent angry would-be mass murderers from securing a firearm and going on a deadly shooting spree. At the end of April 2010, a knife-wielding man in his forties burst into the Leicheng First Primary School in the city of Leizhou and stabbed 18 children and a teacher before being subdued by the police. All of the victims were wounded, but none suffered life-threatening injuries.

MASS SHOOTINGS AND GUN LEGISLATION

One of the many predictable patterns surrounding mass murders and mass shootings is that they tend to spark heated public and political debate about gun control and gun rights. Because of their high-profile nature in terms of publicity (see Duwe, 2000), mass murders are often exploited for the sake of advancing some political agenda, and this is especially true when it comes to the role of firearms as a contributing factor to mass murder. Mass shootings have served as ammunition in the debate over gun control but used, ironically enough, by advocates on both sides of the issue to further their cause.

In the wake of particularly deadly and widely publicized shootings, gun-control proponents have argued that the carnage would not be so great were it not for the easy availability of high-powered firearms, especially

Photo 20.2   Aaron Alexis, Washington Navy Yard shooter. (Associated Press/FBI)

assault weapons. By playing on public sentiment and sympathy associated with horrific crimes, they have pushed legislation at both the state and federal levels.

At the same time, gun-control opponents argue that if more people were armed, there would be more defense against mass shooters and victim counts would be much lower. In the wake of a high-profile public mass shooting, gun sales and registrations for concealed weapons classes often increase. Apparently, few of these alarmed (and now armed) citizens fully considered how people react under such unanticipated and suddenly chaotic situations. The notion that they will whip out their loaded weapon, gun down the assailant, and save scores of innocent lives in the process is far more fantasy than realistic expectation. At the same time, a post-massacre spike in gun sales potentially creates greater peril to the extent that at least some newly armed citizens act irresponsibly out of a profound and irrational sense of concern for their personal safety.

Rather than being deterred, a dedicated gunman might even secure additional weapons from those victims who are carrying their own firearms. Aaron Alexis, the 34-year-old Washington (DC) Navy Yard shooter who killed 12 people, had attempted to obtain a semiautomatic rifle in a Lorton, Virginia, gun shop but could not meet the legal requirement that purchasers be residents of the state. As a result, Alexis entered the navy yard armed only with an 870 Remington pump-action shotgun which he carried unobtrusively in sections and then assembled in a men's room. Moving through the building, he apparently obtained a couple of semiautomatic 9mm pistols and ammunition from two of his fallen victims. Many of the navy's employees at the yard were carrying authorized firearms, but their presence in large numbers did not discourage the amassing of a large body count (National Broadcasting Company, 2013).

Whatever the value to various changes in gun policy, mass shootings certainly tend to drive public opinion and motivate politicians to act. The 1989 mass shooting at the Cleveland Elementary School in Stockton, California, in which Patrick Purdy executed five children and wounded 30 others, resonated around the country. Even President George H. W. Bush, a staunch pro-gun Texan with strong political ties to the National Rifle Association, softened his stand just a bit by signing a temporary ban on importation of foreign-made assault weapons, which did little but advance the interests of domestic firearms manufacturers.

Following the 1993 massacre at a San Francisco law firm in which eight people were killed by a disgruntled former client who was armed with a pair of 9mm semiautomatic IntraTec-9s handguns, a .45-caliber pistol, and hundreds of rounds of ammunition, the California legislature enacted a ban on particularly destructive models of firearms. However, because the legislation identified prohibited guns by name and model, rather than by type, certain gun manufacturers cleverly reissued their weapons with a slight modification in design and a new model number. In fact, the IntraTec Firearms Company renamed the IntraTec-9 as the IntraTec DC-9, with virtually no change in design or function.

Besides the San Francisco law firm incident, the early 1990s witnessed a disturbing flurry of high-profile shootings, including Gang Lu's 1991 shooting spree at the University of Iowa and the 1991 massacre of 23 lunchtime diners at Luby's Cafeteria in Killeen, Texas. The anxiety and publicity over these and other shooting rampages prompted Congress to pass and President Bill Clinton to sign the Public Safety and Recreational Firearms Use Protection Act of 1994, better known as the Assault Weapons Ban. However, this federal law included a sunset provision stipulating that the ban would expire in 10 years if not extended by Congress. By 2004, the mood in the country and on Capitol Hill had shifted to the right, and efforts by a minority of elected officials to reaffirm the prohibition failed to avert expiration.

SCHOOL SHOOTINGS AND POLITICAL WILL/WON'T

Mass shootings, especially those involving schools, have put tremendous pressure on political leaders to identify and implement legislation designed to protect children from active shooters, be they some unhappy student avenging years of bullying or a disgruntled adult seeking payback against all of society by targeting defenseless innocents. And the path of political buck passing stops at the front door of the White House.

A late-1990s cluster of school shootings, seven of which involved multiple victims, prompted a proactive response from President Bill Clinton. One week after the Columbine massacre, Clinton pushed for a series of gun-control initiatives, which were strongly criticized by gun-rights advocates. At the political fringe, a group known as Cutting Edge Ministries condemned the Clinton administration for its gun-control response. Cutting Edge released a map, displaying the major school shootings that had occurred during Clinton's presidency.

Oddly enough, the locations of the handful of school rampages fell almost exactly along two straight lines intersecting at Hope, Arkansas—Bill Clinton's birthplace. Based on this evidence, Cutting Edge claimed that the President was involved in an unholy conspiracy to disarm America. As further proof, Cutting Edge inferred from the timing of the incidents that a deliberate attempt had been made to obfuscate the plot: "[T]he plan was drawn up before the first school shooting occurred. If Edinboro had been followed by Paducah, then by Jonesboro, for example, in a straight timeline, someone would probably have spotted the connection. But, if each successive school shooting were random as to time, then the chance of discovery would be far less."

It wasn't long after the late-1990s spate of school shootings subsided that one of the more gun-friendly presidents claimed occupancy of the Oval Office, calming the fears and concerns of the "I'll give you my gun when you pry it from my cold, dead hands" crowd. During the eight years of President George W. Bush's administration, the stranglehold that the National Rifle Association (NRA) and other pro-gun groups had over the political agenda grew tighter. Moreover, facilitated by the shift in political balance produced by Bush's two appointees, the U.S. Supreme Court affirmed the validity of the Second Amendment in successful challenges of long-standing gun bans in Washington, DC, and Chicago.

President Bush had a rather different position on gun control than did his predecessor, particularly with respect to promoting school safety. In the fall of 2006, President Bush's alliance with the gun lobby was tested when a string of four school shootings occurred over a period of just two weeks. Bush hastily convened an invitation-only White House summit on school violence, excluding from the event anyone seen as a gun-control advocate. President Bush, First Lady Laura Bush, and other members of the hand-picked lineup of speakers made no mention of the common thread among the school-based rampages that had prompted the conference. No matter what the speakers believed about the role of firearms, the topic of gun control was the elephant in the room, conspicuously absent from the discussion.

The November 2008 election of President Barack Obama was expected to bring a new approach on guns. The Democratic nominee had promoted various gun-control measures during his campaign, which gave the NRA and other gun-rights advocates reason for concern. However, based on Obama's first term in the White House, the pro-gun rhetoric was hardly consistent with political reality. If anything, Obama was, from the point of view of gun-control groups, disappointingly friendly to the gun lobby, so much so that the Brady Center to Prevent Handgun Violence gave him a failing grade.

Even though Obama's first term showed no evidence of a presidential push for gun control, critics from the NRA interpreted this as just a clever ploy. At a 2012 speech to the Conservative Political Action Committee (CPAC), Wayne LaPierre, Executive Vice President of the NRA, outlined Obama's scheme to ambush the Second Amendment. "All that first-term lip service to gun owners," argued LaPierre before a decidedly receptive audience, "is just part of a massive Obama conspiracy to deceive voters and hide his true intentions to destroy the Second Amendment during his second term!"

The NRA spokesperson was explicit in his grim view of a possible second Obama term: "We see the president's strategy crystal clear: Get re-elected and, with no more elections to worry about, get busy dismantling and destroying our firearms' freedom, erase the Second Amendment from the Bill of Rights and excise it from the U.S. Constitution." LaPierre concluded his remarks with a note of urgency: "This is the most dangerous election in our lifetime. If Obama wins, we'll go to our grave mourning the freedom that will be lost."

In a hotly contested race against Republican challenger Mitt Romney, who vowed to protect the rights of gun owners, Obama appeared unwilling to pursue a gun-control platform. During a nationally televised debate that took place weeks following a stunning mass shooting at an Aurora, Colorado, movie theater, the candidates were asked by a member of the audience about the possibility of restoring the now defunct federal assault weapons ban. Obama, as well as Romney, danced around the question, presumably for fear of alienating a major block of voters who hold gun rights as a paramount issue.

Shortly after his reelection, Obama did change his tune, but not so much because of any second-term immunity from political fallout that had been predicted by LaPierre and the NRA. Rather, just a few weeks after celebrating his November victory, Obama's hand was forced when Adam Lanza walked into a Newtown, Connecticut, elementary school, massacred 20 children and six teachers over the course of a few horror-filled minutes, and swiftly increased the intensity of the debate over gun control.

In the aftermath of the Newtown school shooting—a drama that unfolded as millions watched on their televisions and computer monitors—media pundits and political leaders alike decried the expiration of the 1994 federal ban on certain military-style assault weapons. Several members of Congress, with support from the Obama administration, pushed to restore the ban on assault weapons and large-capacity magazines holding more than 10 rounds of ammunition. With solid opposition from the National Rifle Association (which instead advocated for armed guards at all school entryways), the hurriedly crafted gun-control bills failed to achieve a majority.

THE ASSAULT WEAPON DEBATE

There is some evidence that a ban on certain high-powered military-style firearms may have an impact on levels of gun crime generally, or at least cause displacement to less deadly alternatives (Kopel, Woods, & Roth, 2004). But in terms of mass shootings, the 1994 ban does not appear to have produced much in the way of the desired effect.

A comparison of the incidence of mass shootings during the 10-year window when the federal assault weapon ban was in force against the time periods before implementation and after expiration shows that the legislation had virtually no impact, at least in terms of murder in an extreme form. As shown in Table 20.1, the yearly average incidence and victimization levels during the federal prohibition were not especially different than in the years before or after the law was in force.

Notwithstanding the loud rallying cry about assault weapons that was heard in the chambers of Congress and on the public airwaves, the overwhelming majority of mass murderers actually use firearms that would not be restricted by an assault-weapons ban (see Duwe, 2007). According to the Mother Jones database of public-setting rampages, assault weapons are not as commonplace in mass shootings as some gun-control advocates believe. Specifically, only one quarter of the public mass shootings between 1982 and 2012 used assault weapons. By contrast, nearly half used semiautomatic handguns and the remaining quarter used either shotguns or revolvers (Follman, Pan, & Aronsen, 2013). Moreover, the mass murderers who killed with an assault weapon could have

Table 20.1   Comparison of Incidence and Victimization in Mass Shootings by Time Period

Time Period	Incidents		Victims	
	Total	Average	Total	Average
1976–1994	335	17.6	1,536	80.8
1995–2004	193	19.3	876	87.6
2005–2011	144	20.6	699	99.9

Source: Supplementary Homicide Reports, 1976–2011, Federal Bureau of Investigation, Washington, DC.

identified, if necessary, an alternate means of mass casualty, although that could possibly have impacted the death toll.

In an analysis of mass shootings from January 2009 through January 2013, Mayors Against Illegal Guns (2013) confirmed the limited role of military-style assault weapons in mass shootings. Only 13 of the 56 incidents examined by this gun-control group involved assault weapons or high-capacity magazines. Of course, limiting the size of ammunition clips would at least compel a gunman to pause to reload or switch weapons, potentially giving others a brief window of opportunity to escape or even intervene (see Barry, McGinty, Vernick, & Webster, 2013; Best, 2013). However, such an initiative would likely limit access to only newly produced accessories. Unfortunately, there is an ample supply of large-capacity magazines already in circulation for anyone determined enough to locate one.

EXPANDED BACKGROUND CHECKS

Unlike the fiercely debated issue of banning certain high-powered weapons, most Americans, including a majority of gun owners, support the idea of improving the process for conducting background checks on all gun purchases, including transactions at gun shows. Many public officials and private citizens alike insist that we must find a way to keep guns away from our most dangerous element (see Barry et al., 2013; Best, 2013). However, they are often blinded by passion and anger from confronting the practical limitations to achieving that desirable objective.

Most mass murderers do not have criminal records or a history of psychiatric hospitalization (Dietz, 1986). They would not be disqualified from purchasing their weapons legally. James Holmes, for example, may have given off a dangerous vibe to those who knew him and he had been seen by a psychiatrist, but neither prevented him from purchasing guns and ammo over the Internet.

A recent examination of 56 mass shootings over the 4-year time-frame from 2009 through 2012, conducted by Mayors Against Illegal Guns (2013), found no indication that any of the assailants were prohibited by federal law from possessing firearms because they had been adjudicated mentally ill or had been involuntarily committed for treatment. And in just 4 of the 56 cases, there was evidence that concerns about the mental health of the shooter had been brought to the attention of a medical practitioner or legal authority prior to the shooting spree.

People cannot be denied their Second Amendment rights just because they look strange or act in an odd manner. Moreover, would-be mass killers can usually find an alternative way of securing the needed weaponry. For example, several mass shooters have used firearms purchased, borrowed, or stolen from a family member or friend (see Follman et al., 2013). A recent example is provided by Adam Lanza's school rampage in Newtown, Connecticut. The 20-year-old killer may have suffered from serious mental health issues, but his weapons were secured from his mother's collection of firearms.

CONCEALED CARRY

Mass shootings have been exploited just as effectively by pro-gun groups to promote legislation allowing ordinary citizens to carry concealed weapons in public places—so-called right-to-carry (RTC) laws. The same Luby's Cafeteria shooting that prompted calls for the assault weapons ban inspired one Texas woman who survived the massacre to launch her own campaign to liberalize laws concerning carrying loaded weapons in public places.

On October 16, 1991, Suzanna Gratia Hupp helplessly watched her mother and father die as George Hennard Jr. methodically blasted away at a crowd of stunned and defenseless customers in Luby's Cafeteria in Killeen, Texas. In the midst of the carnage, she had a clear shot at the assailant and reached for her purse to get her gun. But Hupp soon realized she didn't have it with her, as state law prohibited citizens to carry guns concealed inside pocketbooks or clothing.

Believing to this day that she or some other customer might have been able to overtake the gunman if licensed gun owners were allowed to have guns in restaurants or other public places, she became an outspoken and forceful advocate for concealed weapons laws. Hupp suggests that gun-free zones—such as schools and day care centers—are especially attractive to mass murderers because there they can kill people "like fish in a barrel" (see Hupp, 2013).

Riding a wave of publicity following the Luby's murders, Hupp became the first Texan to be awarded a lifetime membership in the National Rifle Association. She traveled far and wide to push an anti-gun control agenda and was later elected to the Texas legislature largely based on her visibility on the gun issue. In 2010, Hupp also became an author, writing in her book, *From Luby's to the Legislature*, about her personal experiences as victim and advocate. Commenting on several multiple shootings, including the Virginia Tech rampage, she argues for liberalized right-to-carry laws based on assumptions about the perpetrator's mind-set:

Think how just the knowledge that someone—or more than one—may be legally armed and could shoot back would prevent these nut jobs from taking the final step. In the case of these guys who are going for a high body count, yes, it is likely they could kill a few people. But they sure as heck would not get thirty-two before they were taken out of action. (Hupp, 2010, p. 111)

Hupp was hardly the only gun-rights advocate to suggest a connection between mass murder and citizen disarmament. Students for Concealed Carry on Campus (SCCC), a national grassroots organization, insisted that the extent of carnage from the April 2007 Virginia Tech massacre would have been considerably less had students (and staff) other than the gunman been armed and ready to retaliate. Ironically, at the time of the Virginia Tech shooting spree, a bill was stalled in the Virginia General Assembly that would have empowered licensed gun owners to carry concealed weapons on the Blacksburg and other campuses in the state.

Notwithstanding the told-you-so attitude among some gun advocates following the Virginia Tech tragedy, law enforcement and security officials were not quite so comfortable with the notion of a heavily armed campus. Dana Schrad, executive director of the Virginia Association of Chiefs of Police told the *Christian Science Monitor*, "I have my own concerns that, had there been a number of people who had been in that classroom with guns, [there could have been] additional persons killed just as a result of poor judgment calls" (Flesher & Marks, 2007).

In August 2011, with memories of the Virginia Tech shooting spree still fresh in people's minds, the Virginia Tech police received a phone tip from three teenagers attending a summer program with information about a possible gunman. The campus police acted quickly in line with the guidelines from the U.S. Department of Education that were crafted specifically based on the school's horrific shooting 4 year earlier. A campus-wide alert was sent warning of a potentially dangerous situation: "Person with a gun reported near Dietrick. Stay inside. Secure doors. Emergency personnel responding. Call 911 for help."

As it turned out, the three young witnesses to a man carrying what seemed to be a handgun covered by some type of cloth were mistaken. Still, it was wise for campus authorities to err on the side of caution. After several hours of follow-up investigation with no indication of danger, the campus police lifted the warning. Of course, by then classes had been cancelled and everyone had gone home.

This episode points out potential problems with the campus concealed carry movement. If concealed weapons are permitted, how many times will a nervous observer report seeing a "man with a gun" (or worse, if this observer is also armed)? How should campus authorities respond to a report of what appeared to be a handgun covered with a cloth? How many times would campuses be closed down and classes interrupted by false alarms?

In genuine active-shooter situations, moreover, one must wonder how it would be possible for anyone, no matter how well trained in firearms use, to be able to distinguish the "good guys" dressed in denim and toting backpacks from the "bad guy" dressed in denim and toting a backpack. In addition, there is evidence that even trained gun owners, when suddenly immersed in a chaotic shooting scene, may not have the special skills needed to respond without making matters worse (American Broadcasting Company, 2009). Despite the potential risks of expanding gun possession on campuses, the Students for Concealed Carry network has in recent years had some success in convincing legislators that the body count in episodes like the 2007 Virginia Tech massacre would be reduced were properly licensed and trained students allowed to carry guns to class. However, in light of the low rate of serious violence on campus and the high prevalence of substance abuse and depression among college students, it would seem ill-advised to encourage gun carrying by anyone other than duly sworn public safety personnel.

Even more dubious is the possible impact of concealed weapons in a darkened cinema. Some have argued that James Holmes's body count at the premiere showing of a Batman movie would have been reduced if members of the audience had been carrying guns. Wouldn't an armed spectator have shot down the intruder before he had had a chance to spray bullets into the crowd? Maybe so, but it is also possible that the anxiety-provoking crisis in a darkened auditorium would have made the killer, who was dressed in costume just like many others in the audience, entirely indistinguishable from his innocent victims.

In the aftermath of a mass murder, even law enforcement often cannot distinguish victims from killers. Survivors are marched single file from a crime scene, forced to keep their hands over their heads—just in case they turn out to be perpetrators rather than victims. During the first few hours after a mass murder, media representatives frequently report incorrectly the presence of two or more killers operating in concert. Following Aaron Alexis's September 2013 rampage at the navy yard in Washington, DC, for example, there were unsubstantiated, yet scary, media reports of one or two additional gunmen who were still on the loose. As it happened, however, Alexis had acted alone.

Whether a well-armed citizenry—in schools, on college campuses, or in society more generally—encourages more violence or discourages concealed carry remains a hotly debated issue. Are would-be murderers deterred by the risk that their intended targets may be armed, or do they just fortify themselves for a shootout? And in the event of a confrontation between an assailant and armed citizens, do more innocent people get shot in the crossfire?

The potential for citizens to mount a counterattack while an assailant stops to reload is but one reason why many gun-rights advocates argue against gun restrictions, at least for law-abiding, licensed gun owners. Specifically, many contend that the establishment of gun-free zones (e.g., schools, churches, courthouses and other government buildings) makes citizens vulnerable to attacks by armed assailants.

Proponents for expanding concealed carry rights suggest that having more people armed in public spaces would not only serve as a deterrent, but permit citizens to overpower an armed assailant. These proponents suggest that mass murderers avoid attacking locations in which they would expect considerable armed resistance, such as a police station or gun club (Kopel, 2009). Of course, many mass murders occur in places that are not designated as gun-free zones. Generally, the choice of location is based on the nature of the grievance, and has little to do with whether resistance will be met. And while there has not been a mass shooting at a police station, several active shooters have specifically targeted cops. Over a 10-day time-frame in February 2013, for example, former LA police officer, Christopher Doerner attacked police officers and their families. The series of shootings resulted in four deaths, including three police officers, and left three police officers wounded. The subject of a massive multiagency manhunt, Doerner ended his killing spree with suicide.

Whatever the deterrent or intervention effects, detractors have voiced concerns that a sudden shootout between an assailant and citizens armed with concealed weapons could potentially catch countless innocent victims in the crossfire. As mentioned, mass killers are often described by surviving witnesses as being relaxed and calm during their rampages, owing to their level of planning. In contrast, the rest of us are taken by surprise and typically respond frantically.

Whether permitting concealed carry impacts the risk of mass murder is, of course, an empirical question, and not just a debate involving hypotheticals. John R. Lott and William M. Landes (2000) analyzed the effect of right-to-carry laws in 23 states on the incidence and magnitude of multiple-victim homicide over the time frame of 1977 through 1995, concluding that such legislation works to suppress the risk and extent of mass violence. However, Grant Duwe, Tomislav Kovandzic, and Carlisle E. Moody (2002), applying a more appropriate statistical model to a time frame expanded through 1999, concluded that the effect of right-to-carry laws was negligible, neither encouraging nor discouraging mass shootings.

ARMED FACULTY AND SCHOOL SECURITY

The debate over an armed citizenry has focused specifically on elementary and secondary schools, and the need to protect vulnerable populations of students from armed assailants. Following the December 2012 school shooting in Newtown, amidst fervent demands for stiffer gun control being heard far and wide, the NRA took a very different approach. The powerful gun-rights group proposed that we equip every school in America—schools of every size, level, and type—with an armed guard, someone who would be prepared to ward off any dangerous intruder.

In subsequent months, lawmakers in as many as six states have promoted legislation to arm school teachers and train them to shoot. For example, a South Dakota law, effective July 1, 2013, created "school sentinels"—teachers, administrators, security guards, and even volunteers from the community empowered to carry guns inside of schools to protect the student population. And, based on a nationwide poll by the Gallup organization, nearly two thirds of Americans see merit in this idea (Newport, 2012).

Supporters of firearms-for-faculty laws maintain that ever since the early 1990s, when the U.S. Congress established schools as gun-free zones, an armed assailant, be it a student–insider or a stranger–intruder, could be assured to face little or no opposition. The belief is that arming teachers and administrators might serve as a powerful deterrent to anyone contemplating a Columbine-style school shooting. It is hard to imagine, however, that a vengeful student, who is willing to die by police gunfire or by his own hand, would be dissuaded by knowing that the faculty were armed. He may even welcome the chance to shoot it out with the principal at high noon in the school cafeteria.

The truth is that thousands of schools already have sworn police officers on site. Columbine High School, in fact, had an armed school resource officer on duty the day in 1999 when two alienated adolescents turned their school into a war zone. Of course, Columbine was a fairly large campus with nearly 2,000 students enrolled, and the cop couldn't be everywhere at once. It would have taken a small army to patrol the entrances and hallways that numerous to eliminate the risk.

Arming teachers, even with a requirement for firearms training, creates the potential for tragic overresponse by anxious school personnel. Every year in the United States, thousands of students are expelled for being in possession of a gun at school (and sometimes just for fear of gangs or bullies). What would occur if these students were observed by a faculty member who was also armed and ready to respond with gun fire in order to protect the school population? In addition, what would be the result if an armed teacher were to mistake a cell phone or any shiny object for a gun, especially in a climate where concerns for school shootings are elevated? At the end of the day, school teachers are in the position to be educators, not executioners.

If using armed faculty to protect our schools and school children is the way to go, then what about the playgrounds and playing fields outside the buildings. And what about the fleet of yellow school buses transporting the kids home after school? Are we going to arm the bus drivers as well?

Notwithstanding the horror associated with school massacres, whether they implicate an angry student seeking payback or a deranged adult looking to hurt society in the most profound way, these are exceptionally rare events. Transforming our schools into armed fortresses hardly provides a comfortable and carefree learning environment with its constant reminder that children have targets on their backs.

Whatever we do to fortify schools and shield students from harm should be commensurate with the extremely low likelihood of an active shooter striking any particular school. We need to protect our children's sense of innocence as much as their physical safety.

A FINAL WORD

Gun-control advocates often point to other nations as proof that reducing the extent of private gun ownership will lessen the risk of mass murder. Although Great Britain has far tighter restrictions on guns than does the United States, mass shootings have occurred in British families, schools, and even public places. On June 2, 2010, a down-on-his-luck cabbie Derrick Bird from Cumbria, a small town north of London, used two licensed firearms, a .22 rifle and a shotgun, to kill his brother, his lawyer, and 10 others chosen largely at random. Although many Brits saw this as a failure of gun control to prevent assailants bent on destruction, and others as justification for tighter restrictions, no set of laws can guarantee that mass shootings will never occur. Were it not for its strict gun laws, England could conceivably experience more episodes than it does.

Whatever the effects of restrictions on gun purchasing, on the one hand, and right-to-carry provisions on the other, it does make logical sense that if society were purged of deadly firearms, the risk of mass murder would be minimized. Following the 1996 Port Arthur shooting rampage in which 28-year-old Martin

Bryant gunned down 35 people, the Australian government responded swiftly in an attempt to control high-powered weaponry. In the 1996 National Firearms Agreement, the Australian states and territories banned the importation, manufacture, sale, and possession of automatic and semiautomatic firearms. In addition, the government launched and funded a massive gun buy-back program that netted over 600,000 of the newly prohibited weapons. The Australian government also implemented mandatory licensing and registration of all firearms (i.e., those not covered by the ban on automatics and semiautomatics). Although there is some debate concerning the law's effect on gun crime generally, there have not been any mass shootings in the half-dozen years since the law took effect (see Chapman, Alpers, Agho, & Jones, 2006; Baker & McPhedran, 2007).

It is certainly difficult to compare Australia with the United States, given that the two nations differ in many respects—demographically, economically, and culturally. Of course, Australia does not have a constitutionally-protected right to gun ownership that would make such an initiative virtually impossible to achieve in American society, where personal freedoms are valued above virtually all else.

Part IV

Epilogue

CHAPTER 21

Remembering
the Victims

During the Christmas season of 1978, residents of West Summerdale Avenue in Des Plaines, Illinois, watched in horror as body after body was removed from the crawl space beneath the Gacy home, house number 8213. In the days to follow, as news crews focused their cameras on John Wayne Gacy's burial ground, neighbors were interviewed repeatedly about what they knew, what they saw, and how they felt.

Even after all 29 bodies were excavated from the property, interest in the murder site persisted. A steady stream of tourists invaded the block, understandably upsetting neighbors, just to get a glimpse of the infamous house of horrors. Gacy's home eventually was razed, yet curiosity seekers still came by to stare at the ground in the empty lot that once entombed so many young victims. Anonymous visitors decorated the weed-filled yard with their macabre artistry, including a replica of an electric chair and fake tombstones. Some gawkers, too lazy or too embarrassed to get out of their cars, chose instead to drive in circles around the block. "It got so you wouldn't know what you would see when you looked out the window," commented one neighbor (Kiernan, 1993).

In 1988, a decade after the gruesome discovery, the lot on which John Wayne Gacy's house once stood finally was sold, and a new building was constructed on the site. The new owners, eager to distance themselves from the tragedy of a decade earlier, were able to have their house number switched. Despite the change in appearance and address, however, the location forever remains the site of a horrible serial killing and, on occasion, still attracts sightseers to Des Plaines.

In Killeen, Texas, souvenir collectors had a field day. By answering a "For Sale" ad, they could snoop around the home once occupied by mass killer George Hennard Jr. Pretending to be serious house hunters, they walked through the house, and many took small mementos of their visit to the madman's mansion.

The Oxford Apartments in Milwaukee, site of Jeffrey Dahmer's grisly crimes, also became a tourist trap, attracting curious visitors from as far away as Japan. In November 1992, the 49-unit building was demolished. The owner had to place guards and barbed wire around the property to fend off arsonists and scavengers, some of whom offered the guards as much as $75 for a souvenir brick.

Neighbors of Ronald Gene Simmons in Dover, Arkansas, didn't wait for the bulldozers to arrive. The ramshackle house in which 14 members of the Simmons clan were shot and strangled was burned to the ground late one night, a year after the murders. The motive for this arson was clear: to remove all tangible reminders of the mass killing.

Unlike matters at the homes of Simmons, Dahmer, and Gacy, business remained as usual at the sites of many other mass killings. Luby's Cafeteria reopened for business weeks after the mass killing of 23 customers and employees, and the Edmond, Oklahoma, post office was closed for only 1 day for the purpose of cleaning up. Edmond letter carriers had to deliver the mail, even that stained by the blood of their coworkers. The residents of the town received their blood-soaked letters in plastic bags bearing the printed apology, "The contents have been damaged in handling by the Postal Service. . . . We regret any inconvenience you have experienced."

Newtown, Aurora, Littleton, Blacksburg, Dover, San Ysidro, and Edmond have one notable trait in common. They are all small communities not widely familiar on a national scale, until, that is, they became host to mass murder. When mass murder strikes a small town, it becomes forever associated in the minds of millions of Americans with the heinous act that occurred there. The goodwill and charity of its citizens are quickly overshadowed by the act of a single gunman. Residents of Edmond, for example, would like their town to be remembered for popular Olympic gymnast Shannon Miller or for the 1988 Professional Golfers' Association (PGA) Championship held there; to their chagrin, however, Edmond is far better known

Photo 21.1 Included among the 15 crosses erected to memorialize the victims of the Columbine High School massacre are two representing the shooters, who took their own lives. (Associated Press/Eric Gay)

in many circles for the 1986 post office massacre. Similarly, the Chamber of Commerce of Littleton, Colorado, would no doubt prefer that the word *columbine* bring to mind Colorado's white and lavender state flower rather than the site of the 1999 school shooting.

In addition, it is particularly difficult for members of a small town to move beyond the community stigma brought on by a mass murder. Townspeople tend to identify closely with the geographic unit in which they live. Everyone feels victimized, therefore, even those not directly hurt.

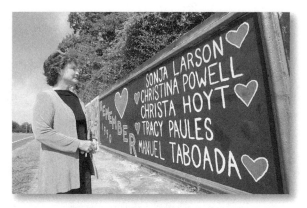

The impact of mass murder on the public image of big cities is minimal by comparison. New York may have had its Son of Sam murders, but people from Omaha or Santa Fe hardly think of this particular serial killing spree when they consider visiting the Big Apple.

Photo 21.2   The Gainesville, Florida, community maintains a special wall in memory of the five college students brutally murdered by a serial killer. (Associated Press/John Raoux)

Even the September 11 attack on the Twin Towers failed to reduce permanently New York City's attractiveness to tourists. Similarly, the Los Angeles area is more associated with Disneyland characters and Hollywood stars than with Richard Ramirez or Charles Manson; Montreal is better known for its hockey team and French food than for the massacre of 14 female engineering students.

In the aftermath of the Montreal shootings, members of the university community, the city, and the nation as a whole came together to memorialize the victims of the tragedy. Long after the slain students were eulogized and buried, their memories were sustained by a plaque bearing the names of the dead, which was placed conspicuously on the building in which the murders had occurred. Years later, a second memorial was constructed out of stone and placed near the campus arts center. This project was initiated by a local women's group and sponsored by local businesses.

Attempts to pay tribute to the victims of a mass slaughter do not always come off as smoothly as in Montreal. In San Ysidro, California, for example, a controversy raged for years over how to commemorate the victims of the McDonald's massacre, most of whom were Hispanic. Immediately after the 1984 incident in which 21 victims were murdered, the McDonald's Corporation tore down the bullet-ridden restaurant and donated the property to the community.

Following the McDonald's gift, politicians debated what to do with the land. Some argued that a large-scale memorial would be out of place in a congested commercial area or that it would only bring back painful memories. Others contended that constructing a memorial of decent proportions—a park or a chapel—would make a fitting tribute, and besides, it was simply the right thing to do. Hispanic residents were particularly outspoken as advocates for an official monument. According to an ancient custom observed in rural parts of Mexico, the site of a tragic death is sacred. It is held that the spirit of the deceased remains at that spot.

While the public debate dragged on, one concerned resident of San Ysidro took it upon himself to build, at the murder site, his own handmade shrine—a blue wooden shed containing religious paintings, candles, and figurines. On the side of the shrine were written the names and ages of all 21 people who had been slain at the McDonald's. In 1988, finally, the acre of land on which the fast-food restaurant had stood was sold to Southwestern College for $40,000, a fraction of its original market value. Two years later, the college constructed a building, only a small corner of which was devoted to a permanent memorial.

Over the past two decades, criminologists, criminal justice officials, and the general public have become more sensitive to the needs, problems, and concerns of those left behind to grieve for murdered loved ones, their suffering a victimization of another kind. Of particular importance and value have been strategies established to assist surviving victims, those who have lost a loved one to homicide. Victim–witness advocates have been assigned by the courts to help console and inform family members who suffer through heart-wrenching testimony describing the hideous circumstances of their loved ones' deaths. At the same time, families of murder victims have found empathy and understanding from support groups like Parents of Murdered Children and private agencies such as the Adam Walsh Victim Resource Center.

The problems of surviving victims of multiple murder are intensified from those associated with single murders, partly because of the peculiarities of multiple murder itself but also because of the intrusion of the mass media. In high-profile cases, members of the media often try to get close to surviving victims to obtain quotes and stories. The attention paid by reporters is often of great comfort and support to the family, particularly in vulnerable times when any willing listener is greatly appreciated. This can be a double-edged sword, however. Surviving victims can experience a tremendous sense of abandonment when their case is no longer newsworthy and their media sounding boards move on to report on newer crimes. "At first there was like a big rush," said Jill Paiva, whose mother, Nancy, had been murdered years earlier by an unidentified serial killer in New Bedford, Massachusetts. "After that it was like everybody forgot about it and nobody cares" (Coakley, 1994).

Surviving victims understandably tend to want to know everything regarding the death of their loved ones and the efforts by the criminal justice system to bring the perpetrator to justice. Because of the newsworthiness of serial murder investigations and prosecutions, however, police and prosecutors tend to be especially cautious about sharing information about the investigation with victims' families. Officials fear that confidential material will surface in the newspaper. As a consequence, law enforcement authorities become more guarded about discussing cases even with surviving victims, out of concern that the family will succumb to pressure from the media for details.

In Gainesville, Florida, for example, the task force investigating the 1990 murders of five college students had to maintain tight control over what details of the crimes could be released to the families. Aware that reporters from around the country were constantly trying to interview the grieving parents, the police were cautious not to jeopardize the investigation. The families, in a sense, were seen as a liability.

Whether or not leaks are intentional, some information pertaining to a multiple murder and its investigation is bound to reach story-hungry reporters. When such information is released or leaked to the press, the relatives often learn secondhand about developments in the case from reading the newspaper. It is a major source of discomfort and aggravation to surviving victims that they are not the first to be told of whatever information is released to the public. Judy DeSantos, for example, whose sister was murdered by the New Bedford serial killer, frequently was caught off guard by new information printed in the local newspaper. Understanding that certain facts of the case had to remain confidential, she felt, nevertheless, that she and other family members had a right to know first, before the general public did.

Serial killers have a tendency to kill in particularly gruesome ways, often involving acts of torture prior to the murder as well as postmortem mutilation. Surviving victims, therefore, are confronted with the knowledge that their loved one suffered a great deal before dying or that the corpse was defiled and desecrated. Moreover, signs of mutilation may prevent a viewing at the funeral.

For example, the parents of Gainesville victim Christa Hoyt had to deal with the fact that their daughter had been murdered, eviscerated, and decapitated. Because of the gruesome manner in which their daughter was slain, the Hoyts were not permitted to view the crime scene photos. To do so might have provided them some degree of psychological closure, but it also would have been devastating.

Although they probably are intended merely as a defense mechanism against public anxiety, false rumors and insensitive jokes often spread through a community, and communities often have insatiable appetites for details in high-profile multiple-murder cases. These rumors and jokes tend to add insult to injury for the surviving victims. Of greater insult to surviving victims, however, is the glorification, almost hero worship, surrounding the killer. The individual responsible for the crimes is too often celebrated and even attracts admirers because of his infamy, while the victims for whom the survivors mourn are quickly forgotten.

The families of Jeffrey Dahmer's victims suffered the indignity of watching Chevy Chase make light of the case on *Saturday Night Live* while millions of viewers laughed. That indignity was in addition to the hundreds of Jeffrey Dahmer jokes that circulated for years. Even worse, the families found nothing funny about seeing Dahmer's likeness on trading cards and in comic books. Some mothers of the victims were so incensed that they appeared as guests on nationally syndicated talk shows to express their outrage over the Dahmer craze.

Surviving victims of most homicides can at least make some sense of the underlying motivation for their tragedy, even if they cannot accept its legitimacy. For example, a mother whose daughter is slain by a former boyfriend can understand the motive of jealousy. Serial killers, however, tend to select strangers as victims, and for no particular reason. As a result, surviving victims must deal not only with their loss but also with more profound questions concerning "Why?"

In multiple-victim slayings, particularly serial killings, the state often will charge and prosecute the accused on fewer than all the crimes suspected. Frequently, only a few of the stronger cases are needed to guarantee a maximum penalty. For example, Atlanta child slayer Wayne Williams was charged and convicted on only two counts of murder, even though he was linked to as many as 28 deaths. Similarly, Ted Bundy was executed for three murders in Florida but likely was responsible for dozens of other murders around the country for which he was never prosecuted. As a consequence of partial prosecution, some surviving victims can feel that their loved one was neglected by the courts and did not receive justice. Furthermore, they lack closure to their tragedy. This is particularly true in killings that involve multiple states or provinces, in which many of the jurisdictions will never have the opportunity to try the case.

Because of the motiveless nature of the crimes, serial murder cases sometimes remain unsolved. The notion that the killer got away with murder retards the healing process for the surviving victims. In massacres, on the other hand, the perpetrator frequently is killed either by suicide or from a police counterattack. In such instances, the death of the offender robs the victims' families of the chance to seek retribution and full justice, as well as to vent their anger.

Frustrated families often seek alternative channels for expressing their unresolved pain. In a positive way, they may form support groups or political action groups. Following the Pettit and Martin law firm massacre in San Francisco, for example, families of the victims joined together in advocacy against assault rifles. In a negative way, however, the families of other mass murder victims identify scapegoats for their rage. In the Palm Bay massacre, for example, local police were criticized severely following William Cruse's shooting spree for failing to respond sufficiently to complaints about his disturbing and bizarre behavior prior to the crime.

The search to find plausible explanations for seemingly inexplicable crimes often leads us to examine the roles of significant others, especially family members, who should have seen the warning signs and perhaps could have intervened. As discussed earlier, the parents, spouses, and other relatives of serial killers are criticized, usually without justification, for being oblivious to the hidden dark side of a killer living within their midst. Second-guessing and scapegoating are also commonplace in cases of mass murder, especially random slaughters of innocents, whereby friends and family are publicly disparaged for having failed to recognize a ticking time bomb presumably ready to explode. The killer's intimates are often treated as negligent, if not complicit, even when they too were killed. Haunted by self-doubt and wondering what they might have done differently, many suffer profound feelings of guilt and depression, yet they typically receive more condemnation than compassion from former friends, neighbors, and even relatives.

Etna Huberty, for example, has been bitterly chastised for not preventing her husband, James, from going "hunting for humans" at the San Ysidro McDonald's when he told her that he planned to do as much. In a poignant plea on behalf of her friend, Ann Ruiz of San Ysidro wrote in a letter to the *San Diego Union*: "Mrs. Huberty needs to conquer her guilt feelings. Her life has been destroyed and she has no idea what the future will bring. . . . Doesn't anyone have any feelings for this woman's grief? It is 22 times that of the rest of the people" (Michioku, 1984). In recognition of her suffering, $1,000 was given to James Huberty's widow out of the San Ysidro Family Survivors Fund to help her move her children back to her hometown of Massillon, Ohio. This sum of money was earmarked for Huberty by former columnist Norman Cousins, who donated $2,500 in total to the fund. When some of the other contributors learned of this, they demanded that their own donations be returned and organized a protest march.

Frances Piccione, mother of one of the Los Angeles Hillside Stranglers, wasn't criticized for her failure to respond or for receiving victim compensation money, but she was held accountable in the court of public opinion for being a bad mother to Ken Bianchi. In addition to her villainous status, she has her own sense of grief. As she remarked tearfully, "My heart goes out to every one of the families who lost a child. I have lost a son, too" (personal communication, 1991).

Monday morning quarterbacks had a field day in questioning the role and responsibility of 52-year-old Nancy Lanza, whose son Adam massacred 20 students and 6 teachers at the Sandy Hook Elementary School in Newtown, Connecticut. Having been killed in bed by her son just hours before his December 14, 2012, school rampage, Nancy Lanza wasn't available to answer the many questions that folks raised about her parenting decisions. She couldn't defend her life from gunfire, and she couldn't defend her honor and memory from the slings and arrows of public hostility.

With knowledge of the tragic outcome, it is very easy—and perhaps entirely appropriate—to condemn Nancy Lanza for having encouraged her reclusive and directionless son to focus his attention on guns and marksmanship. She was not so fairly criticized in the PBS program, "Raising Adam Lanza," for having withdrawn Adam from the high school where he was constantly teased and bullied for being odd. Diagnosed with Asperger's syndrome, a mild form of autism characterized by difficulties in social interaction and interpreting nonverbal communication, Adam Lanza was uncomfortable relating to classmates. He also suffered from a sensory perception disorder that caused him to recoil from any physical contact. He was a rather easy mark for harassment in the school halls. For that reason, perhaps, Nancy Lanza saw homeschooling as a better alternative, even though it may have contributed to his social isolation.

According to a family friend, Nancy Lanza had grown increasingly concerned about her son's mental health in the weeks and months leading up to the massacre. Adam had become deeply immersed in violent themes, spending long hours playing war-oriented video games and meticulously chronicling details of notorious mass killers in a large computer spreadsheet. He was reportedly obsessed with the Columbine massacre.

Notwithstanding these worrisome behaviors, even people genuinely concerned about Adam Lanza's psychological and emotional well-being would, in all likelihood, never have anticipated the bloodshed that he perpetrated at home and at Sandy Hook Elementary School. It should be assumed that Nancy Lanza had the best of intentions in raising her son Adam, unless and until there is definitive evidence to the contrary.

Of course, many people are quick to think the worst and spread the blame when tragedies occur, particularly if, as in the Lanza case, the real culprit is not alive to answer the charges. And some of the families who lost children in the

Newtown massacre were not at all hesitant in publicly assailing the parenting skills and decision-making of Lanza's first and closest victim.

But the tendency to view Nancy Lanza as more a culprit than a victim goes well beyond those families personally touched by tragedy. When recalling the incident, many people consider there to have been 26 Newtown victims. In the weeks and months following the crime, tributes were held far and wide in memory of the victims, most of which ignored the murder of Nancy Lanza.

In April 2013, for example, the Boston Athletic Association (BAA) decided to honor the Newtown victims during the 107th running of the Boston Marathon, arguably the world's most storied footrace. According to the BAA president, the Marathon carries "special significance" in that the 26 miles of the race course would serve as a tribute to each of the 26 victims (ignoring the final one-fifth mile leg of the 26.2 mile race). Although well-intentioned, the BAA, like countless other Americans, was incorrect in saying that 26 were murdered by Adam Lanza. While there were 26 killed at the Sandy Hook Elementary School, the Newtown shooting spree actually encompassed 27 homicide victims.

Commencing with a 26-second moment of silence at the starting line, the 2013 Boston Marathon was intended as a special tribute to the Newtown shooting victims. A group of Newtown parents, calling itself "Team Newtown Strong," ran to raise money for local charities, and a banner honoring the victims hung at the end of the 26th mile. The race will, of course, long be remembered for its own tragic outcome. At the finish line, not far from a VIP section in which Newtown families were invited to watch the race, two bombs exploded, the dirty work of two mass murderers with their own mission in mind.

Finally, the children of men and women who are convicted of multiple homicide or who commit suicide following their murder spree must endure not just the hardship of growing up without their parent, but the permanent blemish on their family name. Many children in these situations have chosen to change their names in order to distance themselves from the stigma. Others like Jackie Wood have been outspoken about the way in which the innocent relatives of not-so-innocent murderers are often unfairly ostracized in their communities. Wood was only 9 years old when her mother was convicted for her part in the murders of several nursing home patients in Grand Rapids, Michigan. It was difficult enough for Jackie to confront the teasing and mistreatment at school and in the neighborhood because of her infamous mother. Additionally challenging was having her friends prohibited by their parents from playing with her anymore.

Thus, there are numerous victims of multiple murder—those who are slain, their grieving families, the killers' relatives, and even the communities that are stigmatized as a result. One participant, however, is never a victim: the person who commits the murders.

In this book, we have attempted to explain the motivations and circumstances that inspire the act of multiple murder. We have discussed the failures and frustrations that strain the coping mechanisms of the workplace killer. We have explored the loneliness and isolation of the mass murderer who lacks any form of support and encouragement. We have profiled the serial killer whose quest for power derives from an abuse-riddled childhood devoid of love and acceptance. We have examined the obedience of the cult killer to a charismatic father figure who exploits his followers' insecurities and need to feel special.

It is important that explanation never be confused with excuse. Multiple killers have raised their own variety of excuses, but we have downplayed the presumed causal connection between murder and such phenomena as pornography, child abuse, head trauma, neurological impairment, Satanism, drugs, and mental illness. Although each of these factors may contribute in some way to the making of a mass or serial murderer, none of them should be considered a determining factor, either by itself or in combination. Millions of people with similar biographies and disadvantages do not kill; many go on instead to lead productive lives. Regardless of the biological, psychological, social, and economic hardships they may suffer, multiple murderers generally are capable of making personal decisions as to how and how not to behave. They are, therefore, not victims, but instead "guilty as charged" when they make the choice to kill.

References

Abrahamsen, D. (1973). *The murdering mind*. New York, NY: Harper Colophon.

Adams, J. (1989, December 31). Joseph T. Wesbecker: The long dark slide. *Louisville Courier-Journal*.

Agnew, R. (1992). Foundation for a general strain theory of crime and delinquency. *Criminology, 30*, 47–88.

Aitken, L., Oosthuizen, P., Emsley, R., & Seedat, S. (2008). Mass murders: Implications for mental health professionals. *The International Journal of Psychiatry in Medicine, 38*, 261–269.

Akers, R. L. (2000). *Criminological theories: Introduction, evaluation, and application*. Los Angeles, CA: Roxbury.

American Broadcasting Company. (1992). Courtroom security [Television broadcast]. *20/20*. New York, NY: Author.

American Broadcasting Company. (1993, April 16). Workplace violence [Television broadcast]. *20/20*. New York, NY: Author.

American Broadcasting Company. (2009, April 10). If I only had a gun [Television broadcast]. In D. Sloan (Executive producer), *20/20*. New York, NY: Author.

American Psychiatric Association. (1994). *Diagnostic and statistical manual of mental disorders* (4th ed.). Washington, DC: Author.

Ansevics, N., & Doweiko, H. (1991). Serial murderers: Early proposed development typology. *Psychotherapy in Private Practice, 9*, 107–122.

Arluke, A., Levin, J., Luke, C., & Ascione, F. (1999). The relationship of animal abuse to violence and other forms of antisocial behavior. *Journal of Interpersonal Violence, 14*, 963–975.

Associated Press. (1992, February 17). *Dahmer tells judge he blames nobody but himself*.

Associated Press. (1993, January 28). *Cafeteria gunman's final days had hints of disaster*.

Associated Press. (2012, December 20). Poll ranks top 10 news stories of 2012. *USA Today*. Retrieved from http://www.usatoday.com/story/news/2012/12/20/year-top-news/1783303

Atchison, A. J., & Heide, K. M. (2011). Charles Manson and the family: The application of sociological theories to multiple murder. *International Journal of Offender Therapy and Comparative Criminology, 55*(5), 780–792.

Baker, J., & McPhedran, S. (2007). Gun laws and sudden death: Did the Australian firearms legislation of 1996 make a difference? *British Journal of Criminology, 47*(3), 455–469.

Bandura, A. (1977). *Social learning theory*. Englewood Cliffs, NJ: Prentice Hall.

Barber, T. X. (1969). *Hypnosis: A scientific approach*. New York, NY: Van Nostrand Reinhold.

Barnes, M. (Producer), & Rivera, G. (Director). (1984, March 19 & 26). The mind of a murderer [Television episode]. In M. Barnes (Producer), *Frontline*. Boston, MA: Public Broadcasting Service, WGBH.

Barnes, S. (1994, January 27). *Expert gives gruesome testimony in child murder case*. Reuters.

Barry, C. L., McGinty, E. E., Vernick, J. S., & Webster, D. W. (2013). After Newtown—Public opinion on gun policy and mental illness. *New England Journal of Medicine, 368*, 1077–1081.

Barstow, D. (1999, July 30). Shootings in Atlanta: The scene. *New York Times*. Available at http://www.nytimes.com/1999/07/30/us/shootings-atlanta-scene-office-building-scenes-chaos-blood-death.html

Bartels, R., & Parsons, C. (2009). The social construction of a serial killer. *Feminism and Psychology, 19*, 267–280.

Bass, A. (1991, July 7). A touch for evil. *Boston Globe Magazine*.

Beasley, J. (2004). Serial murder in America: Case studies of seven offenders. *Behavioral Sciences and the Law, 22*, 395–414.

Bell, D., Burton, M. L., Collier, J., Faron, L. C., Franklin, S. B., Jain, R. K., & Jorion, P. (1997). Defining marriage and legitimacy. *Current Anthropology, 38*, 237–253.

Best, J. (2013, June 16). *How should we classify the Sandy Hook killings?* Retrieved from http://reason.com/archives/2013/06/16/the-politics-of-gun-violence

Blakeman, K. (1989, December 30). Berdella's motive: Total control. *Kansas City Times*.

Blincow, N. (1999, May 9). Why women fall for a death row Don Juan. *Toronto Sun*.

Böckler, N., Seeger, T., & Heitmeyer, W. (2011). School shooting: A double loss of control. In W. Heitmeyer, H.-G. Haupt, A. Kirschner, & S. Malthaner (Eds.), *Control of violence: Historical and international perspectives on violence in modern societies* (pp. 261–294). New York, NY: Springer.

Bondü, R., & Scheithauer, H. (2012). School shootings in Deutschland: *Internationaler Vergleich, Warnsignale, Risikofaktoren und Entwicklungsmodelle* (Doctoral dissertation). [International comparison, warning signs, risk factors and development models]. Retrieved from http://www.diss.fuberlin.de/diss/servlets/MCRFileNodeServlet/FUDISS_derivate_000000011902/Bondue_Dissertation_SchoolShootings_volls taendig_fin.pdf;jsessionid=2E9AFB2E9AF0C2C92F91B391E2E8739C?hosts=

Botsford, K. (1990, February 3). In America: You've come a long way, Moll. *The Independent* [London].

Bowers, R. (1988, May 12). Nightmares her memory, victim says. *Arkansas Gazette*.

Brandon, K. (1993, January 12). Massacre stymies police. *Chicago Tribune*.

Brief of Social Scientists and Media Effects Scholars as Amici Curiae Supporting Respondents, Schwarzenegger & Brown v. Entertainment Merchants Association & Entertainment Software Association, 537 U.S. 418 (2010) (no. 08–1448). Available at http://www.americanbar.org/content/dam/aba/publishing/preview/publiced_preview_briefs_pdfs_09_10_08_1448_RespondentAmCuSocialScientists_MedScientists_MediaEffScholars.authcheckdam.pdf

Brooks, D. (2012, July 23). More treatment programs. *New York Times*. Retrieved from http://www.nytimes.com/2012/07/24/opinion/brooks-more-treatment-programs.html

Brown v. Entertainment Merchants Association, 537 U.S. 418 (2011).

Burne, J. (1993, June 8). Health: Murder by manipulation. *The Independent.*

Canter, D. V., & Wentink, N. (2004). An empirical test of Holmes and Holmes's serial murder typology. *Criminal Justice and Behavior, 31,* 489–515.

Carlson, D. K. (2002, January 22). *The blame game: Youth and media violence.* Gallup News Service. Retrieved from http://www.gallup.com/poll/5626/Blame-Game-Youth-Media-Violence.aspx

Castle, T. (2001). *A case study analysis of serial killers with military experience: Applying learning theory to serial murder* (Unpublished master's thesis). Morehead State University, Kentucky.

Chandler, M., & Mathews, L. (1988, December 5). Families doubt nursing home murders. *Detroit Free Press,* p. 3A.

Chapman, S., Alpers, P., Agho, K., & Jones, M. (2006). Australia's 1996 gun law reforms: Faster falls in firearm deaths, firearm suicides, and a decade without mass shootings. *Injury Prevention, 12*(6), 365–372.

Chin, P. (1991, November 4). A Texas massacre. *People,* pp. 66–67.

Coakley, T. (1994, January 24). Unsolved and unending: Slaying victims' kin still hurting in New Bedford. *Boston Globe.*

Cohen, L. E., & Felson, M. (1979). Social change and crime rate trends: A routine activity approach. *American Sociological Review, 44,* 588–608.

Conroy, P., & Murdock, L. (1988, November 11). Police weren't ready for me, he says. *Age,* p. 21.

Cutting Edge Ministries (n.d.). *School shootings have a pattern that implicate the president and his government.* Retrieved from http://www.cuttingedge.org/News/n1344.cfm

Darrach, B., & Norris, J. (1984, August). An American tragedy. *Life,* pp. 58–74.

Delisi, M., & Scherer, A. M. (2006). Multiple homicide offenders: Offense characteristics, social correlates, and criminal careers. *Criminal Justice and Behavior, 33,* 367–391.

Derber, C. (1992). *Money, murder and the American dream: Wilding from Wall Street to Main Street.* Boston, MA: Faber & Faber.

Dern, H., Frönd, R., Straub, U., Vick, J., & Witt, R. (2004). *Geografisches Verhalten fremder Taeter bei sexuellen Gewaltdelikten* [Spatial behaviour of stranger perpetrators in sexually violent delinquency]. Wiesbaden, Germany: Bundeskriminalamt.

Desire for a family draws young people. (1989, April 19). *USA Today.*

Dietz, M. L. (1996). Killing sequentially: Expanding the parameters of the conceptualization of serial and mass murder killers. In T. O'Reilly-Fleming (Ed.), *Serial and mass murder: Theory, research and policy.* Toronto: Canadian Scholars' Press.

Dietz, P. E. (1986). Mass, serial and sensational homicides. *Bulletin of the New York Academy of Medicine, 62,* 477–491.

Doerner, W. G. (1975). A regional analysis of homicide rates in the United States. *Criminology, 13,* 90–101.

Dollard, J., Doob, L. W., Miller, N. E., Mowrer, O. H., & Sears, R. R. (1939). *Frustration and aggression.* New Haven, CT: Yale University Press.

Douglas, J. E., & Munn, C. (1992). Violent crime scene analysis: Modus operandi, signature, and staging. *FBI Law Enforcement Bulletin, 61,* 1–10.

Dowden, C. (2005). Research on multiple murder: Where are we in the state of the art? *Journal of Police and Criminal Psychology, 20,* 8–18.

Duryea, B. (1993, February 2). He'd done what he came to do. *St. Petersburg Times.*

Duwe, G. (2000). Body count journalism. *Homicide Studies, 4,* 364–399.

Duwe, G. (2004). The patterns and prevalence of mass murder in twentieth-century America. *Justice Quarterly, 4*, 729–761.

Duwe, G. (2007). *Mass murder in the United States: A history.* Jefferson, NC: McFarland.

Duwe, G., Kovandzic, T., & Moody, C. E. (2002). The impact of right-to-carry concealed firearm laws on mass public shootings. *Homicide Studies, 6*, 271–296.

Edelman, A. (2013, February 17). Detectives investigating Newtown massacre find Adam Lanza's violent video games, ponder the 20-year-old mimicking a gory game scene. *New York Daily News.* Retrieved from http://www.nydailynews.com/news/national/violent-games-provide-motive-newtown-massacre-article-1.1266643

Egger, S. A. (1984). A working definition of serial murder and the reduction of linkage blindness. *Journal of Police Science and Administration, 12*, 348–357.

Egger, S. A. (Ed.). (1990). *Serial murder: An elusive phenomenon.* Westport, CT: Praeger.

Egger, S. A. (2003). *The need to kill: Inside the world of the serial killer.* Upper Saddle River, NJ: Prentice Hall.

Egginton, J. (1990). *From cradle to grave: The short lives and strange deaths of Marybeth Tinning's nine children.* New York, NY: Jove.

Eliason, S. (2009). Murder-suicide: A review of the recent literature. *Journal of the American Academy of Psychiatry and Law, 37*, 371–376.

Elkind, P. (1983, August). The death shift. *Texas Monthly.* Retrieved from http://www.texasmonthly.com/story/death-shift?fullpage=1

Elkind, P. (1989). *The death shift: The true story of nurse Genene Jones and the Texas baby murders.* New York, NY: Viking.

"The Exorcist" and "the Devil." (1991, July 29). *Milwaukee Journal.*

Federal Bureau of Investigation. (2001). *Crime in the United States.* Washington, DC: U.S. Department of Justice.

Fedora, O., Reddon, J. R., & Morrison, J. W. (1992). Sadism and other paraphilias in normal controls and aggressive and nonaggressive sex offenders. *Archives of Sexual Behavior, 21*, 1–15.

Ferguson, C. J. (2011). Video games and youth violence: A prospective analysis in adolescents. *Journal of Youth Adolescence, 40*(4), 377–391.

Ferguson, C. J., & Hartley, R. D. (2009). The pleasure is momentary . . . the expense damnable?: The influence of pornography on rape and sexual assault. *Aggression and Violent Behavior, 14*(5), 323–329.

Fisher, H. D. (1992). *Jeffery Dahmer: The unauthorized biography of a serial killer.* Champaign, IL: Boneyard Press.

Flesher, J., & Marks, A. (April 18, 2007). Should students be allowed to carry concealed weapons? *Christian Science Monitor.*

Flynn, C. P. (1999). Animal abuse in childhood and later support for interpersonal violence in families. *Society and Animals, 7*, 161–172.

Follman, M., Pan D., & Aronsen, G. (2013, February 27). A guide to mass shootings in America. *Mother Jones.* Retrieved from http://www.motherjones.com/special-reports/2012/12/guns-in-america-mass-shootings (Originally published 2012)

Fox, J. A. (2004). *Uniform crime reports (United States): Supplementary homicide reports, 1976–2002.* Ann Arbor, MI: Inter-University Consortium of Political and Social Research.

Fox, J. A. (2009). *Multiple-victim shootings and unemployment rates.* Unpublished working paper, Northeastern University, Boston, MA.

Fox, J. A. (2013, January 31). Responding to Mother Jones. *Boston. com*. Retrieved from http://boston.com/community/blogs/crime_punishment/2013/01/responding_to_mother_jones.html

Fox, J. A., Burgess, A., Levin, J., & Wong, M. (2006). *Panel report on the March 25, 2006 Capitol Hill shooting*. Seattle, WA: Seattle Police Department.

Fox, J. A., & Burstein, H. (2010). *Violence and security on campus: From preschool through college*. Santa Barbara, CA: Praeger.

Fox, J. A., & Levin, J. (1985, December 1). Serial killers: How statistics mislead us. *Boston Herald*, p. 45.

Fox, J. A., & Levin, J. (1989, July). Satanism and mass murder. *Celebrity Plus*, pp. 49–51.

Fox, J. A., & Levin, J. (1994). Firing back: The growing threat of workplace homicide. *The Annals of the American Academy of Political and Social Science*, 536(1), 16–30.

Fox, J. A., & Levin, J. (1996). *Killer on campus*. New York, NY: Avon.

Fox, J. A., & Levin, J. (1998). Multiple murder: Patterns of serial and mass murder. In M. Tonry (Ed.), *Crime and justice: A review of research*. Chicago, IL: University of Chicago Press.

Frazier, S. H. (1975). Violence and social impact. In J. C. Schoolar & C. M. Gaitz (Eds.), *Research and the psychiatric patient*. New York, NY: Brunner/Mazel.

Gabbard, G. O. (2003, October/November). *Diagnosis and treatment of antisocial personality disorder*. Paper resented at the American Psychiatric Association's Institute on Psychiatric Services, Boston, MA.

Gasser, K. H., Creutzfeldt, M., Naher, M., Rainer, R., & Wickler, P. (2004, April 19). *Bericht der Kommission Gutenberg-Gymnasium* [Report from the Commission Gutenberg-Gymnasium]. Retrieved December 28, 2011, from http://www.thueringen.de/imperia/md/content/text/justiz/bericht_der_kommission_gutenberg_gymnasium.pdf

German school rampage "happened in seconds." (2009, March 11). Retrieved December 23, 2011, from http://www.msnbc.msn.com/id/29630925/ns/world_news-europe/t/german-school-rampage-happened-seconds/#.TwPWFtTOy6U

Gibson, D. C. (2006). *Serial murder and media circuses*. Westport, CT: Praeger.

Gilligan, J. (1997). *Violence: Reflections on a national epidemic*. New York, NY: Vintage.

Gladwell, M. (2007, November 12). Dangerous minds. *The New Yorker*. Available at http://www.newyorker.com/reporting/2007/11/12/071112fa_fact_gladwell

Goffman, E. (1959). *The presentation of self in everyday life*. New York, NY: Anchor.

Goldberg, C. (1992, April 28). I was like a crazed wolf. *Los Angeles Times*.

Goldberg, C. (2000). *The evil we do: The psychoanalysis of destructive people*. Amherst, NY: Prometheus.

Goleman, D. (1993, July 2). A misfit who turns to murder. *New York Times*.

Gollmar, R. E. (1981). *Edward Gein: America's most bizarre murderer*. Delavan, WI: Charles Hallberg.

Goodney Lea, S. R. (2007). *Delinquency and animal cruelty*. New York, NY: LFB Scholarly.

Gottfredson, M. R., & Hirschi, T. (2003). A general theory of crime. In F. T. Cullen & R. Agnew (Eds.), *Criminological theory: Past to present: Essential readings*. Los Angeles, CA: Roxbury.

Gray, M. (1982, January 25). $100,000 soaked in blood. *Maclean's*, pp. 19–21.

Green, L. (1989, October 7). Stockton killer hated Asians. *San Francisco Chronicle*.

Griffiths, R. (Producer & director). (1993, January 3). *Murder by number: Wesley Allen Dodd*. CNN News. Atlanta, GA: CNN.

Grimes, T., Anderson, J. A., & Bergen, L. (2008). *Media violence and aggression: Science and ideology*. Thousand Oaks, CA: Sage.

Gross, M. D., & Wilson, W. C. (1974). *Minimal brain dysfunction*. New York, NY: Brunner/Mazel.

Haggerty, K. (2009). Modern serial killers. *Crime, Media, Culture, 52*, 168–187.

Hansen, M. (2006). How the cops caught BTK. *ABA Journal, 92*, 44–48.

Hare, R. D. (1993). *Without conscience: The disturbing world of the psychopaths among us*. New York, NY: Pocket Books.

Harrington, A. (1972). *Psychopaths*. New York, NY: Simon & Schuster.

Hazelwood, R. R., Dietz, P. E., & Warren, J. (1992). The criminal sexual sadist. *FBI Law Enforcement Bulletin, 61*, 12–20.

Hazelwood, R. R., & Douglas, J. E. (1980). The lust murderer. *FBI Law Enforcement Bulletin, 49*, 1–5.

Hazelwood, R. R., Warren, J., & Dietz, P. E. (1993). Compliant victims of the sexual sadist. *Australian Family Physician, 22*, 474–479.

Heilbrun, A. B. (1982). Cognitive models of criminal violence based upon intelligence and psychopathy levels. *Journal of Consulting and Clinical Psychology, 50*, 546–557.

Hempel, A. G., Meloy, J. R., & Richards, T. C. (1999). Offender and offense characteristics of a nonrandom sample of mass murderers. *Journal of the American Academy of Psychiatry and the Law, 27*, 213–225.

He wouldn't stop shooting. (1993, December 8). *New York Daily News*.

Hermann, M. A., & Finn, A. (2002). An ethical and legal perspective on the role of school counselors in preventing violence in schools. *Professional School Counseling, 6*(1), 46–54.

Hickey, E. W. (2010). *Serial murderers and their victims*. Belmont, CA: Wadsworth.

Hightower, S. (1991, October 17). *Killer may have had vendetta against women*. Associated Press.

Hirschi, T. (1969). *Causes of delinquency*. Berkeley: University of California Press.

Holmes, R. M., & De Burger, J. (1988). *Serial murder*. Newbury Park, CA: Sage.

Holmes, R. M., & Holmes, S. (2001). *Mass murder in the United States*. Upper Saddle River, NJ: Prentice Hall.

Holmes, S. T., Tewksbury, R., & Holmes, R. M. (1999). Fractured identity syndrome: A new theory of serial murder. *Journal of Contemporary Criminal Justice, 15*(3), 262–272.

Howlett, J. B., Haufland, K. A., & Ressler, R. K. (1986). The Violent Criminal Apprehension Program—VICAP: A progress report. *FBI Law Enforcement Bulletin, 55*, 14–22.

Hupp, S. G. (2010). *From Luby's to the legislature: One woman's fight against gun control*. San Antonio, TX: Privateer Press.

Hupp, S. G. (2013). *Proposals to reduce gun violence: Protecting our communities while respecting the Second Amendment*. Testimony before the Senate Judiciary Subcommittee on the Constitution, Civil Rights and Human Rights.

I am so sorry . . . words cannot tell the agony. (1999, July 31). *Washington Post*.

James v. Meow Media, Inc., 300 F.3d 683, 687, 6th Cir. (2002).

Jarvis, B. (2007). Monsters Inc: Serial killers and consumer culture. *Crime, Media, Culture, 3*, 326–344.

Jeffers, H. P. (1991). *Who killed Precious? How FBI special agents combine high technology and psychology to identify violent criminals.* New York, NY: St. Martin's Press.

Jenkins, P. (1988). Myth and murder: The serial killer panic of 1983–85. *Criminal Justice Research Bulletin, 3,* 1–7.

Jenkins, P. (1993). African-Americans and serial homicide. *American Journal of Criminal Justice, 17*(2), 47–60.

Jenkins, P. (1994). *Using murder: The social construction of serial homicide.* New York, NY: Aldine de Gruyter.

Kahaner, L. (1988). *Cults that kill: Probing the underworld of occult crime.* New York, NY: Warner Books.

Kailhla, P. (1992, November 9). Concordia's trials. *Maclean's,* pp. 52–55.

Kamb, L. (2003, February 22). In their own words: The twisted art of murder. *Seattle Post-Intelligencer.*

Kellert, S. R., & Felthous, A. R. (1985). Childhood cruelty toward animals among criminals and noncriminals. *Human Relations, 38,* 1113–1129.

Keppel, R. D., & Birnes, W. J. (2003). *The psychology of serial killer investigations: The grisly business unit.* Orlando, FL: Academic Press.

Kidd, L. (1992). *Becoming a successful mass murderer or serial killer: The complete handbook.* Cleveland, OH: Author.

Kiernan, L. (1993, January 17). Buildings easier to escape than the memories. *Chicago Tribune.*

Kiger, K. (1990). The darker figure of crime: The serial murder enigma. In S. A. Egger (Ed.), *Serial murder: An elusive phenomenon.* New York, NY: Praeger.

Kiilakoski, T., & Oksanen, A. (2011). Cultural and peer influences on homicidal violence: A Finnish perspective. *New Directions for Youth Development, 2011*(129), 31–42.

Kimmel, M. S., & Mahler, M. (2003). Adolescent masculinity, homophobia, and violence: Random school shootings, 1982–2001. *American Behavioral Scientist, 46*(10), 1439–1458.

Klein, L. (Director). (1992, October 13). Mind of a serial killer [Television episode]. In L. Klein (Producer), *Nova.* Boston, MA: Public Broadcasting Service, WGBH.

Kleinfield, N. R., Rivera, R., & Kovaleski, S. F. (2013, March 29). *New York Times,* A1.

Kopel, D. B. (2009, April 16). Pretend "gun-free" school zones: A deadly legal fiction. *Connecticut Law Review, 42*(2), 515–584.

Koper, C. S., Woods, D. J., & Roth, J. A. (2004). *Updated Assessment of the Federal Assault Weapons Ban: Impacts on Gun Markets and Gun Violence, 1994–2003.* Report to the National Institute of Justice, University of Pennsylvania (NCJ #204431).Washington, DC: U.S. Department of Justice.

Kostinsky, S., Bixler, E.O., & Kettl, P. A. (2001). Threats of school violence in Pennsylvania after media coverage of the Columbine High School massacre. *Archives of Pediatric and Adolescent Medicine, 155,* 994–1001.

Lagnado, L. (1990, March 27). Fire suspect's startling confession. *New York Post.*

Lambert, P. (1994, June 21). Police arrest local teens in the cultlike killing of three Arkansas boys. *Time, 39*(24), 3.

Langman, P. (2009). Rampage school shooters: A typology. *Aggression and Violent Behavior, 14*(1), 79–86.

Lankford, A. (2013, June). Mass shooters in the USA, 1966–2010: Differences between attackers who live and die. *Justice Quarterly, 30*, 1–20.

LaPierre, W. (2012). *Saving the future of freedom.* Speech before the 2012 Conference of the Conservative Political Action Committee. Retrieved from http://www.nrapublications .org/index.php/12730/saving-the-future-of-freedom

Larkin, R. W. (2009). The Columbine legacy: Rampage shootings as political acts. *American Behavioral Scientist, 52*(9), 1309–1326.

Lavergne, G. M. (1997). A *sniper in the tower: The Charles Whitman murders.* Denton: University of North Texas Press.

Leary, M. R., Kowalski, R. M., Smith, L., & Phillips, S. (2003). Teasing, rejection, and violence: Case studies of the school shootings. *Aggressive Behavior, 29*(3), 202–214.

Leslie, L. M., & Brown, C. (1999, January 9). Mother: Killing kids saves them from suffering. *Minneapolis Star Tribune,* 1A.

Lev, M. A., & McRoberts, E. (1993, January 10). Police find bodies of 2 teenagers, 5 adults in restaurant's coolers. *Chicago Tribune.* Retrieved from http://www.chicagotribune .com/news/chi-browns-930110-story,0,5825768.story

Levin, J. (2008). *Serial killers and sadistic murderers—Up close and personal.* Amherst, NY: Prometheus.

Levin, J. (2010). *The impact of unemployment on family annihilations.* Unpublished manuscript.

Levin, J., & Arluke, A. (2009). Reducing the link's false positive problem. In A. Linzey (Ed.), *The link between animal abuse and human violence* (pp. 163–172). Brighton, UK: Academic Press.

Levin, J., & Fox, J. A. (1985). *Mass murder: America's growing menace.* New York, NY: Plenum.

Levin, J., & Fox, J. A. (1991). *Mass murder: America's growing menace* (Rev. ed.). New York, NY: Berkley.

Levin, J., Fox, J., & Mazaic, J. (2002, August). *A content analysis of* People *magazine.* Paper presented at the annual meeting of the American Sociological Association, Chicago, Illinois.

Levin, J., & Madfis, E. (2009). Mass murder at school and cumulative strain: A sequential model. *American Behavioral Scientist, 52,* 1227–1245.

Levin, J., & McDevitt, J. (2002). *Hate crimes revisited.* Boulder, CO: Westview.

Levin, J., & Rabrenovic, G. (2004). *Why we hate.* New York, NY: Prometheus.

Lewis, D. O., Pincus, J. H., Feldman, M., Jackson, L., & Bard, B. (1986). Psychiatric, neurological, and psychoeducational characteristics of 15 death row inmates in the United States. *American Journal of Psychiatry, 143,* 838–845.

Leyton, E. (1986). *Compulsive killers: The story of modern multiple murderers.* New York, NY: New York University Press.

Lieberman, J. A. (2008). *School shootings: What every parent and educator needs to know to protect our children* (Rev. ed.). New York, NY: Citadel.

Liem, M., Levin, J., Holland, C., & Fox, J. A. (2013). The nature and prevalence of familicide in the United States, 2000–2009. *Journal of Family Violence,* 1–8.

Lifton, R. J. (1986). *The Nazi doctors: Medical killing and the psychology of genocide.* New York, NY: Basic Books.

Linedecker, C. L. (1991). *Night stalker.* New York: St. Martin's Press.

Lisheron, M., & Tijerina, E. (1993, August 12). Gun rampage could have been worse. *Milwaukee Journal.*

Liwerant, O. S. (2007). Mass murder: Discussing criminological perspectives. *Journal of International Criminal Justice, 5*, 917–939.

Lott, J. R. (2012, September 10). *Did Colorado shooter single out Cinemark Theater because it banned guns?* Fox News.com. Retrieved from http://www.foxnews .com/opinion/2012/09/10/did-colorado-shooter-single-out-cinemark-theater/ print#ixzz2dOIrXblT

Lott, J. R., & Landes, W. M. (2000). *Multiple victim public shootings.* Unpublished paper. Available at http://ssrn.com/abstract=272929 or http://dx.doi.org/10.2139/ ssrn.272929

Macdonald, J. (1963). The threat to kill. *American Journal of Psychiatry, 120*, 125–130.

Madfis, E. (2012). *Averting the unlikely: Fearing, assessing, and preventing threats of rampage violence in American public schools.* Northeastern University, Sociology Dissertations. Paper 17. Retrieved from http://hdl.handle.net/2047/d20002766

Madfis, E., & Levin, J. (2013). School rampage in international perspective: The salience of cumulative strain theory. In N. Bockler (Ed.), *School shootings: international research, case studies, and concepts for prevention* (pp. 79–104). New York, NY: Springer.

Magid, K., & McKelvey, C. A. (1988). *High risk: Children without a conscience.* New York, NY: Bantam.

Malamuth, N. M., & Donnerstein, E. (1984). *Pornography and sexual aggression.* Orlando, FL: Academic Press.

Malnic, E. (1987, December 12). Note of doom written by Burke, FBI says. *Los Angeles Times.*

Mass slayer's letter to two young women he admired. (1991, October 17). *Houston Chronicle.*

Masters, B. (1985). *Killing for company.* London, UK: Coronet.

Mayo Clinic. (2012). *Schizophrenia.* Available at http://www.mayoclinic.com/health/ schizophrenia/DS00196

Mayors Against Illegal Guns. (2013). *Mass shootings since January 20, 2009.* Retrieved from http://libcloud.s3.amazonaws.com/9/56/4/1242/analysis-of-recent-mass-shootings.pdf

McCleod, M. (Director). (1992, November 10). Monsters among us [Television episode]. In M. McCleod, *Frontline.* Boston, MA: Public Broadcasting Service, WGBH.

Mead, G. H. (1934). *Mind, self and society.* Chicago, IL: University of Chicago Press.

Meddis, S. (1987, March 31). FBI: Possible to spot, help serial killers early. *USA Today.*

Merton, R. K. (1957). *Social theory and social structure.* Glencoe, IL: Free Press.

Michaud, S. G., & Aynesworth, H. (1983). *The only living witness.* New York, NY: Linden.

Michioku, S. (1984, July 25). [Letter to the editor]. United Press International.

Miller, K. S., & Knutson, J. F. (1997). Reports of severe physical punishment and exposure to animal cruelty by inmates convicted of felonies and by university students. *Child Abuse and Neglect, 21*, 59–82.

Morena, M. C. (2011, April 8). *Survivors of similar case as Rio to relive trauma.* Retrieved December 17, 2011, from http://ultimosegundo.ig.com.br/brasil/sp/sobreviventes+ de+caso+semelhante+ao+do+rio+revivem+trauma/n1300036730840.html

Morton, R. J., & Hilts, M. A. (Eds.). (2008). *Serial murder: Multi-disciplinary perspectives for investigators.* Washington, DC: Federal Bureau of Investigation, Behavioral Analysis Unit-2, National Center for the Analysis of Violent Crimes.

Mullen, P. E. (2004). The autogenic (self-generated) massacre. *Behavioral Science Law, 22*(3), 311–323.

Murray, J. P. (2008). Media violence: The effects are both real and strong. *American Behavioral Scientist, 51,* 1212–1230.

National Broadcasting Company. (2013, September 17). *12 victims killed, 8 wounded in shooting at D.C. Navy Yard, suspected gunman killed.* Retrieved from http://nbcwashington.com/news/local/Confirmed-Shooter-at-Navy-Yard-One-Person-Shot-223897891.html

Newman, K. S., Fox, C., & Harding, D. (2007). *Rampage: The social roots of school shootings.* New York: Basic Books.

Newport, F. (1999, May 13). *Public continues to believe a variety of factors caused Littleton: Parents and family issues top the list.* Gallup News Service. Retrieved from http://www.gallup.com/poll/3856/Public-Continues-Believe-Variety-Factors-Caused-Littleton.aspx

Newport, F. (2012, December 19). *To stop shootings, Americans focus on police, mental health: Democrats substantially more likely to see assault gun ban as effective.* Gallup News Service. Retrieved from http://www.gallup.com/poll/159422/stop-shootings-americans-focus-police-mental-health.aspx

Nichols, P. (2009, Spring/Summer). Neurocriminologist probes the biology of crime. *Penn Arts & Sciences Magazine,* pp. 16–21.

Nordheimer, J. (1989, January 25). Bundy is put to death in Florida after admitting trail of killings. *New York Times.*

Norris, J. (1988). *Serial killers: The growing menace.* New York, NY: Doubleday.

O'Driscoll, P. (1999, December 14). Release of tapes infuriates families. *USA Today.*

Obama, B. (2013, April 8). *Remarks by the President on reducing gun violence—Hartford, CT* [Video file]. Retrieved from http://www.whitehouse.gov/photos-and-video/video/2013/04/08/president-obama-speaks-reducing-gun-violence#transcript

Offord, D. R., Boyle, M. H., & Racine, Y. A. (1991). The epidemiology of antisocial behavior in childhood and adolescence. In D. J. Pepler & K. H. Rubin (Eds.), *The development and treatment of childhood aggression.* Hillsdale, NJ: Lawrence Erlbaum.

Ottley, T. (n.d.). Dr. Harold Shipman. *Court TV's Crime Library.*

Palmer, S. H. (1960). *The psychology of murder.* New York, NY: Crowell.

Parello, C. (Director), & Johnston, S. (Writer). (2000). *Ed Gein* [Motion picture]. London, UK: Tartan Films.

Pendlebury, R. (1993, May 29). Allitt is locked away forever. *Daily Mail* [London].

Penman, A. (1988, January 3). Chronicling a massacre. *Boston Globe.*

Phillips, D. (1983). The impact of mass media violence on U.S. homicides. *American Sociological Review, 48,* 560–568.

Pittman, C. (1993, January 31). Laid to rest where he felt most at peace. *St. Petersburg Times.*

Police hunt "perfect student" as suspect death cult witch. (1989, April 14). *Toronto Star.*

Polner, R. (1993, November 8). Son of Sam killer says he had help. *Newsday.*

Quinet, K. (2011). Prostitutes as victims of serial homicide: Trends and case characteristics, 1970–2009. *Homicide Studies, 15*(1), 74–100.

Quintanilla, M. (1994, January 10). Promises to keep: Patti Tate leads a justice crusade in the name of her sister Sharon. *Los Angeles Times,* p. E1.

Rayner, G., & Bingham, J. (2009, March 12). Germany school shooting: High school gunman warned of massacre on internet chat room. *The Telegraph.* Retrieved from http://www.telegraph.co.uk/news/worldnews/europe/germany/4980192/Germany-school-shooting-High-school-gunman-warned-of-massacre-on-internet-chat-room.html

Reinhold, R. (1993, July 4). Seeking motive in the killing of 8: Insane ramblings are little help. *New York Times.*

Ressler, R. K., Burgess, A. W., et al. (Eds.). (1985). Violent crime. *FBI Law Enforcement Bulletin, 54* (Special issue).

Ressler, R. K., Burgess, A. W., D'Agostino, R. B., & Douglas, J. E. (1984, September). *Serial murder: A new phenomenon of homicide*. Paper presented at the 10th triennial meeting of the International Association of Forensic Sciences, Oxford, England.

Ressler, R. K., Burgess, A. W., & Douglas, J. E. (1988). *Sexual homicide: Patterns and motives*. Lexington, MA: Lexington Books.

Richardson, E. (2000, November 21). Nurse killed to impress: Allegedly injected vets to get a "rush." *Boston Herald*.

Riedel, M. (1993). *Stranger violence: A theoretical inquiry*. New York, NY: Garland.

Rio school massacre video shows months of planning. (2011, April 14). Retrieved December 17, 2011, from http://www.allvoices.com/contributed-news/8780882-rio-school-massacre-video-shows-months-of-planning

Roesch, R. (1979). *Anyone's son*. Kansas City, KS: Andrews & McMeel.

Rolling, D., & London, S. (1996). *The making of a serial killer: The real story of the Gainesville student murders in the killer's own words*. Portland, OR: Feral House.

Rossmo, D. K. (1996). Targeting victims: Serial killers and the urban environment. In T. O'Reilly-Fleming (Ed.), *Serial and mass murder: Theory, research and policy*. Toronto: Canadian Scholars' Press.

Saad L. (September 20, 2013). *Americans fault mental health system most for gun violence*. Gallup News Service. Retrieved from http://www.gallup.com/poll/164507/americans-fault-mental-health-system-gun-violence.aspx

Sagan, E. (1981). *Cannibalism*. New York, NY: Harper Torchbooks.

Samenow, S. E. (2004). *Inside the criminal mind*. New York, NY: Random House.

Sampson, R. J., & Laub, J. H. (1993). *Crime in the making: Pathways and turning points through life*. Cambridge, MA: Harvard University Press.

Schmidt, D. (2005). *Natural born celebrities: Serial killers in American culture*. Chicago, IL: University of Chicago Press.

Schreier, H., & Libow, J. A. (1993). *Hurting for love: Munchausen by proxy syndrome*. New York, NY: Guilford Press.

Scott, C. (1978, February 11). City's "BTK Strangler" claims he's killed 7. *Wichita Eagle*.

Scott, S. L. (n.d.). Conclusion. In S. L. Scott, *What makes serial killers tick?* (chap. 13). Retrieved September 26, 2004, from http://www.trutv.com/library/crime/serial_killers/notorious/tick/conclusion_13.html

Secret confessions of BTK. (2005, August 12). *Dateline NBC* [Television broadcast].

Sedeno, D. (1989, April 13). *International manhunt underway for cult "godfather" in satanic slayings*. Associated Press.

Shah, S. (1976). The 47, XYY chromosomal abnormality: A critical appraisal with respect to antisocial and violent behavior. In W. L. Smith & A. Kling (Eds.), *Issues in brain/behavior control*. New York, NY: Spectrum.

Sherman, L. W. (1990, April 4). Was a mall to blame for a mass murder? *Wall Street Journal*.

Shootings in Atlanta: The notes. (1999, July 31). *New York Times*. Retrieved from http://www.nytimes.com/1999/07/31/us/shootings-in-atlanta-the-notes-there-is-no-reason-for-me-to-lie-now.html

Silverman, D. (1994, January 9). Mystery in Palatine. *Chicago Tribune*. Retrieved from http://articles.chicagotribune.com/1994-01-09/news/9401090503_1_palatine-massacre-marcus-nellsen-killings

Simmons, B. (1988, January 3). *Mass murderer's relationships with wife, children not working*. Associated Press.

Snook, B., Cullen, R. M., Mokros, A., & Harbort, S. (2005). Serial murderers' spatial decisions: Factors that influence crime location choice. *Journal of Investigative Psychology and Offender Profiling, 2,* 147–164.

Stack, S. (1997). Homicide followed by suicide: An analysis of Chicago data. *Criminology, 35,* 435–453.

Stanley, A. (1992, October 16). Angry at child-support demands, gunman kills 4 in county office. *New York Times.*

Starr, M. (1984, November 26). The random killers. *Newsweek,* pp. 100–106.

State of Washington v. Gary Leon Ridgway, No. 01-1-10270-9 SEA (Superior Court of King County 2003).

Suo, S. (2002, November 16). Killer turned artist peddles his drawings online. *Oregonian,* p. E1.

Surrette, M. A., & Aamodt, M. G. (2010, September 20). *Profile differences in serial killers who kill twice versus three or more times.* Paper presented at the 36th annual meeting of the Society for Police and Criminal Psychology, Honolulu, HI.

Suspect claims he killed 8. (2004, May 2). *Sunday Advocate* [Baton Rouge, LA].

Sussman, S. (1989, December 11). *Montreal mourns victims of worst Canadian mass slaying.* Associated Press.

Sutherland, E. H., & Cressey, D. R. (1984). Differential association theory. *Deviant behavior,* 125–131.

Swickard, J. (1990, June 12). Witnesses say DeLisle didn't attempt rescue. *Detroit Free Press.*

Taylor, L. (1984). *Born to crime: The genetic causes of criminal behavior.* Westport, CT: Greenwood.

Terry, M. (1989). *The ultimate evil.* New York, NY: Bantam.

Time-Life Books. (1992). *Mass murderers.* New York, NY: Time Warner.

Travers. E. (2006, September 14). Police seeking motive in Montreal college shooting. *Time.* Retrieved from http://content.time.com/time/world/article/0,8599,1535046,00.html

United Press International. (1984, October 14). *Sheriff's remark may have helped in Joubert arrest.*

United States House of Representatives Committee on Post Office and Civil Service. (1992). *A post office tragedy: The shooting at Royal Oak.* Washington, DC: U.S. Government Printing Office.

Valenstein, E. S. (1976). Brain stimulation and the origin of violent behavior. In W. L. Smith & A. Kling (Eds.), *Issues in brain/behavior control.* New York, NY: Spectrum.

Vick, K. (1990, August 29). FBI specialists are working up profile of a serial killer. *St. Petersburg Times.*

Vossekuil, B., Reddy, M., Fein, R., Borum, R., & Modzeleski, W. (2002). *The final report and findings of the Safe School Initiative: Implications for the prevention of school attacks in the United States.* Washington, DC: U.S. Secret Service and U.S. Department of Education.

Walkup, J. T., & Rubin, D. H. (2013). Social withdrawal and violence–Newtown, Connecticut. *The New England Journal of Medicine, 368*(5), 399–401.

Walsh, A. (2005). African Americans and serial killing in the media: The myth and the reality. *Homicide Studies, 9*(4), 271–291.

Wark, J. (n.d.). *The Zodiac Killer*. Retrieved from http://www.trutv.com/library/crime/serial_ killers/notorious/zodiac/2.html

Warren, J., Hazelwood, R. R., & Dietz, P. E. (1996). The sexually sadistic serial killer. In T. O'Reilly-Fleming (Ed.), *Serial and mass murder: Theory, research and policy*. Toronto: Canadian Scholars' Press.

Westermeyer, J. (1982). Amok. In C. T. H. Friedmann & R. A. Faguet (Eds.), *Extraordinary disorders of human behavior*. New York, NY: Plenum.

Williams, J. (1989, April 12). A *"human slaughterhouse" discovered*. Associated Press.

Williams, L. A. (1992, June 18). Please listen to me . . . . *Detroit News*.

Winfield, N. (1996, February 10). *Shooter claimed firing was "economic lynching."* Associated Press.

Wounded gunman, woman die after rampage in post office. (1991, November 15). *Houston Chronicle*.

Wright, J., & Hensley, C. (2003). From animal cruelty to serial murder: Applying the graduation hypothesis. *International Journal of Offender Therapy and Comparative Criminology, 47*(1), 71–88.

Zucco, T. (1993, January 30). He lost his job, and he told everybody. *St. Petersburg Times*.

Index

About the Authors

James Alan Fox is the Lipman Family Professor of Criminology, Law, and Public Policy at Northeastern University. He has written 18 books, including his newest, *Elementary Statistics in Criminal Justice Research* (Fourth Edition). He has published dozens of journal and magazine articles, as well as hundreds of freelance columns in newspapers around the country, primarily in the areas of multiple murder, youth crime, school and campus violence, workplace violence, and capital punishment. He also writes an online column for the *Boston Globe*'s website. Fox often gives keynote talks and testimony before Congress and in court. He has briefed various leaders here and abroad, including President Clinton, Attorney General Reno, and Princess Anne of Great Britain. He has worked on criminal investigations surrounding serial and mass murder cases and served as a visiting fellow with the Bureau of Justice Statistics focusing on homicide patterns and trends. Finally, Fox was honored in 2007 by the Massachusetts Committee against the Death Penalty with the Hugo Adam Bedau Award for excellence in capital punishment scholarship and by Northeastern University with the 2008 Klein Lectureship.

Jack Levin, PhD, is the Brudnick Professor Emeritus in the Department of Sociology at Northeastern University, where he co-directs its Center on Violence and Conflict and teaches courses in the sociology of violence and hate. He has authored or co-authored more than 30 books, most recently *Blurring the Boundaries: The Declining Significance of Age*. Dr. Levin has also published more than 150 articles in professional journals and newspapers, such as *The New York Times, London Sunday Times, Boston Globe, Dallas Morning News, Philadelphia Inquirer, Christian Science Monitor, Chicago Tribune, Washington Post*, and *USA Today*. He has appeared frequently on national television programs, including *48 Hours, 20/20, Dateline NBC, The Today Show, Good Morning America, Oprah, The O'Reilly Factor, Larry King Live*, and all network newscasts. Dr. Levin was honored by the Massachusetts Council for Advancement and Support of Education as its "Professor of the Year" and by the American Sociological Association for his contributions to the public understanding of sociology. He has also received awards from the Eastern Sociological Society, Association of Clinical and Applied Sociology, and Society for the Study of Social Problems. Moreover, he has spoken to a wide variety of community, academic, and professional groups, including the White House Conference on Hate Crimes, the Department of Justice, OSCE's Office for Democratic Institutions and Human Rights (a membership of 59 countries), and the International Association of Chiefs of Police.